Finding the Movement

A book in the series

RADICAL PERSPECTIVES   *A* Radical History Review *book series*

Series editors: DANIEL J. WALKOWITZ, New York University
BARBARA WEINSTEIN, New York University

Anne Enke

Duke University Press *Durham & London 2007*

Finding the Movement

Sexuality, Contested Space,
and Feminist Activism

© 2007 Duke University Press. All rights reserved
Printed in the United States of America on acid-free paper ∞
Designed by Jennifer Hill. Typeset in Warnock Pro by Keystone Typesetting, Inc.
Library of Congress Cataloging-in-Publication Data appear
on the last printed page of this book.

For Nan

Contents

About the Series

History, as radical historians have long observed, cannot be severed from authorial subjectivity, indeed from politics. Political concerns animate the questions we ask, the subjects on which we write. For over thirty years the *Radical History Review* has led in nurturing and advancing politically engaged historical research. Radical Perspectives seeks to further the journal's mission: any author wishing to be in the series makes a self-conscious decision to associate her or his work with a radical perspective. To be sure, many of us are currently struggling with the issue of what it means to be a radical historian in the early twenty-first century, and this series is intended to provide some signposts for what we would judge to be radical history. It will offer innovative ways of telling stories from multiple perspectives; comparative, transnational, and global histories that transcend conventional boundaries of region and nation; works that elaborate on the implications of the postcolonial move to "provincialize Europe"; studies of the public in and of the past, including those that consider the commodification of the past; histories that explore the intersection of identities such as gender, race, class, and sexuality with an eye to their political implications and complications. Above all, this book series seeks to create an important intellectual space and discursive community to explore the very issue of what constitutes radical history. Within this context, some of the books published in the series may privilege alternative and oppositional political cultures, but all will be concerned with the way power is constituted, contested, used, and abused.

In *Finding the Movement*, Anne Enke re-visions and rethinks the history of "Second Wave" feminism, arguably the "largest social movement in the history of the United States," through the lens of women's spaces. Eschewing the usual emphasis on foundational texts or formative organizations, Enke focuses instead on the *places* of the women's movement—bars, coffeehouses, shelters, clinics, parks, athletic fields—in Chicago, Detroit, and the Twin Cities. The centrality of place in *Finding the Movement* produces several innovative implications. It allows Enke to include actors in the rise of feminism who typically go unacknowledged, even unimagined, in more conventional narratives. The African American and mostly lesbian women in the Motown Soul Sisters softball team may not have styled themselves feminists, but their struggle for access to public space and their assertive style of play influenced the way women in Detroit and other Midwestern cities could imagine themselves, demand playing time on athletic fields, and defy heteronormative constructions of women's bodily movement and public performance. Similarly, lesbians "claiming the nighttime marketplace" provided a crucial precedent for subsequent efforts to create feminist coffeehouses, bookstores, and other ventures in commercial spaces.

Enke cogently argues for a historical perspective on the women's movement that enables us to understand the decisive and continuous presence of lesbians, working-class women, and women of color in the construction of what it meant to be a feminist. This is a sharp departure from the standard depiction of the movement as originating within a white, middle-class cohort that then fails to accommodate demands from lesbians, separatists, and women of color. At the same time, she demonstrates how the choice of specific locations, or of particular definitions of "woman" for a women-only space, often entailed exclusions that mirrored racist and homophobic attitudes most feminists disavowed. Indeed, perhaps her most compelling argument for the centrality of space as an analytical category is her ability to show that, despite feminist groups' discourse of inclusion and of welcome to all women, the locations they selected and constructed often made women desperately trying to "find the movement" feel unwelcome. As a radical and critical history of feminism, *Finding the Movement* allows readers both to experience the heady exuberance of those creative struggles for space and place, and to ponder the limits of a movement for liberation anchored to existing commercial and hierarchical practices.

Acknowledgments

Writing this book pleasantly demolished any monkish fantasy I may have had about writing being a solitary, lonely endeavor, and instead left me humbled by how necessarily social the process has been. Individuals, families, friends, communities, colleagues, and institutions have contributed in countless ways. My debts and gratitude are thus far more extensive than I can begin to explain—much less repay—in these acknowledgments. Just as conducting oral histories, archival research, and even writing have occasioned connection across communities, generations, memories, and histories, it is my hope that this book is not simply a material effect of all that labor but also an invitation for further conversation.

My research was assisted by grants and financial support from the following sources: the Institute for Research in the Humanities, University of Wisconsin; the Minnesota Historical Society; the 2001 CLAGS Award from the Center for Lesbian and Gay Studies, City University of New York; Phil Zwickler Memorial Research Fellow Grants, Human Sexuality Collection, Cornell University Libraries; Albert J. Beveridge Grants, American Historical Association; the Virginia Horne Henry Fund for Women's Physical Education Issues, University of Wisconsin; the Women's Studies Program at the University of Wisconsin; and the Wisconsin Alumni Research Foundation. Equally important, Mariamne Whatley and Jane Collins as chairs of Women's Studies and Steve Stern as chair of History supported every opportunity I had to devote my time to research and writing. And when time inevitably seemed short, Nancy Kaiser helped me *halt die ohren steif.*

Editors affiliated with Duke University Press made the production of this book a satisfying and remarkably low-stress experience for me. Early on, the series editors Daniel Walkowitz and Barbara Weinstein made themselves available for all my queries and greatly facilitated the placement of this work. Valerie Millholland, senior editor at the press, has also been a real gem, receiving my beginner's concerns with patience and efficiently responding with reassuring clarity throughout the entire process. Outside reviewers for the press provided useful suggestions on the manuscript at an earlier stage, and Miriam Angress and Pam Morrison deserve thanks for their work on the practical management of production.

Independent and institutionally affiliated archivists have helped me access a true wealth of materials that have been critical to this project. Jean Niklaus Tretter shared his own archive before it became the Tretter Collection at University of Minnesota. Estelle Carole and Bob Simpson generously shared Chicago leftist documents temporarily archived in their home. M. Kuda assisted me with contact information in Chicago, and Jane Slaughter with contact information in Detroit. I also thank Brenda Marston, director of the Cornell University Human Sexuality Collection; William LeFevre at the Walter Reuther Library of Labor and Urban Affairs, Wayne State University; Karen Sendziak at the Gerber/Hart Library and Archives; Gina Gotta, Damron Publishing; R. Russell Maylone, Special Collections at Northwestern University; David Klaassen, Social Welfare History Archive, University of Minnesota; and Kristine Baclawski at the American Radicalism Collection, Michigan State University. Alan Urquhart and Tim Retzloff each provided research assistance related to bar locations. Heather Francisco and Richard Worthington at the University of Wisconsin Cartography Lab prepared the maps. As my project assistant, Jennifer Hull brought creativity and efficiency to the task of helping me organize documentary sources; her work allowed me to rest assured that I would not misplace necessary items in what otherwise would have been a chaos of materials. Finally, I thank Jenn Holland for her superb work on the index.

I have benefited tremendously from a highly engaged and engaging intellectual community at the University of Wisconsin. For reading and/ or listening to portions of this work in earlier stages, and for their generous feedback, I thank Tom Armbrecht, Susan Bernstein, Paul Boyer,

Claudia Card, Jane Collins, Susan Cook, July D'Acci, Betsy Draine, Myra Marx Ferree, Camille Guerin-Gonzales, Brenda Gayle Plummer, Jane Schulenberg, Louise Young, and Sue Zaeske. Nothing propelled my research and writing during my junior faculty years as much as the confidence that colleagues in history expressed in this work even in the face of some mighty rough drafts. For their consistent encouragement and practical involvement in the process, I am grateful to Jeanne Boydston, Bill Cronon, Suzanne Desan, Fran Hirsch, Steve Kantrowitz, Susan Johnson, Judith Leavitt, Florencia Mallon, Lou Roberts, Brett Sheehan, David Sorkin, and Steve Stern. Judy Houck read almost every chapter in the rough; she helped me make each story more clear while characteristically refusing to simplify the historical actors involved. I consider myself lucky to have such wise, friendly, and supportive colleagues, and this book is worlds better for their insights and input.

A wider community of scholars has also carried me forward from the earliest stages of this work, reading, encouraging, and offering sage comments along the way. I owe especially much to John D'Emilio, Sara Evans, Stephanie Foote, Cris Mayo, Jeani O'Brien, John Howard, Lisa Disch, Dave Roediger, Susan Cahn, Wendy Kozol, Nancy Hewitt, George Chauncey, Peg Strobel, Liz Kennedy, Esther Newton, Van Gosse, Richard Moser, Anne Valk, Becky Thompson, Stephanie Gilmore, Kathryn Kish Sklar, Wini Breines, Linda Gordon, Evelynn Hammonds, Leslie Feinberg, Joanna O'Connell, and Kevin Murphy.

I am foremost indebted to the people who generously granted me their time, shared memories and memorabilia, and introduced me to the four cities as they knew them during the 1960s and 1970s. I regret that I cannot name each person—over 120 in all—in these acknowledgments, as it is certainly the case that each added terrific energy and insight to this project and to my own process of understanding history. Here I would like to thank those people who granted multiple interviews and who graciously set up group interviews or invited me to reunions and other gatherings. For opening the doors that started this book, I thank Toni McNaron, Candace Margulies, Janet Dahlem, Karen Clark, Martha Boesing, Kim Hines, Jo Devlin, Linda Polley, Jeanne La Bore, Eileen Hudon, Russ Helbig, Jan DuBois, and Betty Hawes. For helping me make contacts and generously sharing memories, I thank Kathleen Thompson, Rinda West, Alix Dobkin, Elaine Wessel, Vernita Gray, Jackie Anderson, Nick Patricca, Estelle Carole, Peggy Pope, Irene Lee, and David Hernandez. For helping me find the Motown Soul Sisters, for hosting gatherings that turned into highly animated interviews, and for inviting me to parties and church services that afforded innumerable informal conversations, I thank Virginia Lawrence, Jan Chapman Sanders, Jackie Huggins, Victoria Lollar, Charlotte Howza, Barb Hardison, Rev. Darlene Franklin, and Antoenette Foster. This project could not have been completed without them and all the other narrators; they not only enhanced my respect for an era and for the myriad ways people find to move a movement, they also continually sparked my compulsion to tell this story. As indebted as I am to them, all responsibility for the way I have represented the past rests at my feet alone; any inaccuracies and incomplete perspectives are due to my own limitations despite the conscientious insights of so many thoughtful participants.

As important as the social aspects of research and writing have been, family and friends also made sure that not working was just as important. For helping me maintain perspective over the years, especially through humor, good food, delightfully mundane adventures, and the creation of live and local music, I thank Jim Oleson, John D'Emilio, Judy Houck, Lisa Saywell, Claire Wendland, Mary Moore, Steve Kantrowitz, Cris Mayo, Stephanie Foote, Kat Spring and Jenny Hanson of the indomitable Katannjen, Andy Ewen, Tani Diakite, Sandy Blocker, Mark Wagoner, Eric Charry, Mamadou Diabate, Will Ridenour, and of course Zumana Diabate.

This book bears the stamps of my family history, not only in its attachment to Detroit, Chicago, and the Twin Cities, but also in its drive to comprehend two decades of social movement. First off, Chris Enke taught me a love of questions and all the ways that a good question can lead beyond one's own imagining. He also showed me that in work and in living a life, it is never too late to try something new. Jim Enstad, Chris Enstad, Sophie Pfeiffer, Patty Enstad, Jim Mondoux, and Michael and Ryan Boevers kept a homey and sweet foothold for me in the Twin Cities. David Enke is a perpetual marvel, along with Annie, Nic, and Devon: by example, they have taught me the most important things about communities and ecosystems, and about hard work, faith, and creativity. I wrote this book also with my brother, Paul Enke (1958–87), and my mother, Mary Crane (1935–93), very much in mind and heart. It was partly through their eyes that I, as a child growing up in the midst of the Vietnam antiwar movement, first came to appreciate the hope and rage that moved the generation prior to my own.

Above all, I thank Nan Enstad. She has encouraged me from the moment I first began the small and unlikely seminar paper that, over the next many years, grew into this book; all the while, she believed in it and in me. From Minneapolis to Greensboro to Madison, she has applauded my various and often peculiar explorations in the world of sound, offered me ongoing reason to work with the written and spoken word, and understood me when language fails utterly. Whether we are dipping in the blue perfection of Lake Superior or finding ground for our grief seeds, she makes everyday life precious. It is to her that I dedicate this book about ordinary acts in ordinary places that made an extraordinary world.

Upper Midwest

Map prepared by Heather Francisco, Cartography Lab, University of Wisconsin, Madison, 2006.
For city maps, see pages 140–144.

Locating Feminist Activism

I n 1971, Eileen Hudon, an American Indian, Catholic woman, suspected there was a movement that could help her. For years, her husband had beaten her and attempted to keep every means of autonomy from her: money, transportation, shoes, even a pen and paper. Hudon repeatedly searched the "one resource available" to her. As she explained, "I remember being twenty-one, and looking in the *phonebook* in Minneapolis, and I was looking through it trying to find the *women's movement*, wondering how to find the women's movement. Because I knew the women would understand what was happening to me. And I couldn't find it in the phonebook: What do I look under? Where do I go? There's no way to find the women who understand."[1]

Hudon's narrative reveals that by 1971, "the women's movement" was widely known; even someone as isolated as she was could imagine "the women" out there who understood and had solutions to the structural conditions that contained her and other women in violent households. Though she also knew people connected to the American Indian Movement (AIM) who were protesting police brutality in Minneapolis, Indians had not yet collectively addressed women's status in Native communities or within the racist hierarchies of the United States.[2] Neither did Hudon's immediate social network know how to respond to her distress: her husband was a nice guy, after all. The women's movement, she thought, would be the obvious place to go. The phrase "women's liberation" was in the airwaves, on the streets and on the shop floors, in schools and the halls of government, in kitchens and in bedrooms throughout the United States. Everywhere, it seemed, women were resisting gender roles and their relegation to "second place" in a society structured around binary gender divisions that seemed to privilege men in virtually every arena. Throughout the South and the Midwest as well as the East and West Coasts, in rural as well as urban and suburban communities, feminism was changing institutions, landscapes, and lives. Yet many people who had heard of the women's movement did not know where, literally, to find it.

How does one locate a movement that could reach a woman in her home and at the same time seem utterly inaccessible to her? A movement that was "everywhere" and yet nowhere the same? A movement nearly infinite in its origins as well as its continued and changing expressions? Self-identified feminists formed thousands of large and small organizations throughout the United States during the 1960s and 1970s; they wrote, mimeographed, and published innumerable essays, tracts, and manifestos proclaiming feminism's goals and the best strategies for attaining them. But people also enacted feminism through a dazzling array of action that was spontaneous, unattached to named organizations, and left little record in print. As much as some feminists sought to directly change structural and institutionalized inequities, even more women found ways to build lives and generate movement against the day-to-day barriers that told them to "stay in their place." They resisted segregation, wife-beating, gay-bashing, gender and sexual harassment, and police brutality; they built alternative economies and alternative communities; they shared material and educational resources; and they provided shelter, health, and reproductive care where it had been denied. Many came to call themselves feminists, but many did not; many identified with "women" primarily, while others identified with family and community of origin; many embraced politicized identities, and many more disavowed political motivation. Some who could not even find the women's movement, and others who did not care to, actually helped produce it. It is no wonder that historians Linda Gordon, Rosalyn Baxandall, and others have considered the "second wave" of feminism to be the "largest social movement in the history of the United States."[3] But understanding it as such requires windows into broad social contexts to see the ways that ordinary women and men across race, class, and gender expression became involved in diverse activities that constituted the movement.

One night in 1974, a hospital chaplain took Eileen Hudon and her young children to Women's Advocates, a newly opened shelter for battered women. The next morning, Hudon recalled, "I overheard all these different conversations going on between [the shelter staff]. I was just mopping up the bathroom—that was my chore for being in the shelter. And I remember thinking, 'why can't I be in those conversations? I *finally* found the women's movement, and here I'm mopping the *bathroom!*'" For Hudon at that particular time, "taking part in all these conversations" and the mobility they implied, "seemed unattainable."[4] But as a location inhabited by diverse women, the shelter inspired and required new places of movement; even as a temporary resident, Hudon ultimately did take part in the conversations at Women's Advocates, and those conversations changed her as well as the shelter. The successes and limitations of existing services in fact compelled Hudon to find women where they were, and soon she began coordinating anti-violence programs throughout rural Minnesota. In 1980, she and three other American Indian women engaged in grassroots activism to form an Indian anti-violence program: the four rented a phone line from a Twin Cities church, printed matchbooks with their number and a definition of abuse, and then distributed the matchbooks to "every place that Indian people gather: so we went to Laundromats, supermarkets, bowling alleys, all the Indian organizations, and finally to the bars. We knew that through the grapevine, these thousands of matchbooks would get around the community." Soon after they opened Women of All Nations Shelter.[5] In similar ways, countless people who could not or did not find the women's movement in the phone book became critical actors in the popularization and ongoing emergence of feminist activism.

Just as Hudon and so many others initially puzzled over *where* to find the women's movement, I, too, look to space and place for new ways to apprehend the emergence, proliferation, and on-the-ground manifestations of feminist activism during the 1960s and 1970s. Oral histories first led me to puzzle over the connections between space, women's *movement*, and feminism. Undertaking what I thought would be a small research project on feminist history in the Twin Cities, I conducted interviews with an initial fifteen or so women who had started a coffeehouse in Minneapolis. As I listened to their life histories in person and again on tape, I realized that they consistently narrated their lives through references to places and movement through highly contested geographies: their life stories described pathways, and these pathways were not simply metaphors of journey but actually the product of struggle over who may occupy ostensibly public spaces. Frequently, narrators discussed their experiences of passing through public space, fighting for legitimacy within spaces closed to them, and creating new spaces of their own. In effect, they were narrating their discovery of social hierarchies embedded in built environments, as well as their confrontations with those hierarchies.[6] Through their narratives, I also began to glimpse the collective politicization of place, and I began to see *movement* as a collective, spatial process. As my project expanded, the more I listened with an ear to contested spaces, the more I heard a story of grassroots movement fueled by diverse people who did not necessarily identify themselves as political activists or feminists, but who nevertheless found and founded feminist activism.

Following this lead, I prioritized my research around contested space and place rather than around feminist ideologies or identities—although of course those also came into play in interesting ways. What would it mean for feminism and for social movement history if we took seriously the claim that the Second Wave was truly "widespread"? Surely women's movement took place *outside* and *alongside* as well as within the institutions and actors bearing the name "feminist." What would happen to the history of feminism if we looked beyond the archives of the already known and presumed feminist subject? What if, additionally, we did not privilege the social formations already identified as feminist, but instead sought to understand how those formations worked to consolidate the movement in part by brokering the signs and identities of feminism? These questions came to the fore as I shaped my project around specific sites of conflict and grassroots movement in Minneapolis and St. Paul (the Twin Cities), Detroit, and Chicago during the 1960s and 1970s. Here, I look at actual locations like bars, bookstores, parks, shelters, and coffeehouses in which activist communities came into being. Grounded in specific sites and in three urban areas of the upper Midwest, my analysis focuses on the ways in which women intervened in public landscapes and social geographies already structured around gender, race, class, and sexual exclusions and on the ways that these processes in turn shaped feminism. A focus on contested space, as opposed to a focus on feminist identity, helps explain how feminism replicated exclusions even as feminists developed powerful critiques of social hierarchy. Simultaneously, it suggests a genealogy of the movement that helps account for its breadth and reveals its diversity.

Finding the Movement extends from a twofold premise about feminist activism. First, I confirm that the movement was widespread in ways that historians have not yet explained. Increasingly, historical accounts of feminism and women's liberation show that diverse people were involved in feminism; they show the movement's reach throughout the United States and not just within coastal cities; and they show that feminism operated through grassroots as well as legislative channels. Beginning in the 1970s, feminists of color launched a critique of white middle-class hegemony within the movement, and they conceptualized feminist interventions that more adequately addressed race, class, and national hierarchies. Subsequently, historians have offered rich accounts of black, Asian, Latina, Native American, working-class, and global feminisms. While proving that feminist activism was anything but monolithic, the historiography of the movement has largely confined itself to studying feminist-identified organizations and people who embraced a feminist identity. In contrast, through a focus on sites of activism, I show how feminism exceeded feminist identification. Thus, one argument of this book is that to understand the widespread and popular nature of the movement, we must also consider relevant activism and locations that did not always—at the time —earn the label "feminist."

The second and related premise is that the archive of feminist-identified subjects in fact self-selects for the more exclusive and boundary-policing manifestations of the movement and perhaps even for those that were most directed by white, middle-class agendas. Although the historiographic inclusion of black feminist and other feminist of color organizations partially redresses this problem, I suggest we can go further. Additionally, we can seek to understand how feminist activism emerged on the ground, how feminist formation sometimes relied on exclusive identities, and how the movement nevertheless regularly exceeded its own self-definition. One way to do this is through analysis of everyday places and women's varying and contested investments in them.

Finding the Movement centrally argues that between 1960 and 1980, women in the Twin Cities, Detroit, and Chicago constituted feminist activism by intervening in established public spaces and by creating new kinds of spaces. Women took up commercial and civic spaces—bars, bookstores, cafés, and parks—in new ways, and they also created new public institutions—health clinics, shelters, and coffeehouses—oriented around women's needs and resources. At the same time, social geographies and built environments shaped activist communities as they emerged on the ground. Feminism, then, took shape as a popular movement around the limitations and possibilities of local geographies. While all women engaging public spaces during this period navigated charges of sex/gender deviance, lesbians, women in lesbian relationships, and passing women played a central role in revising the sex/gender dynamics of public space and also within feminism. Those who disavowed political motivation, as well as those who embraced a feminist identity, shared strategies if not always ideologies as they propelled the movement. But as women turned commercial, civic, domestic, and institutional spaces into sites of activism, they produced (as well as resisted) exclusionary dynamics; even feminist spaces were not "free," for as they consolidated the signs of feminism, they sowed seeds of hierarchy within the movement, particularly around race, class, sexuality, and gender expression.

Women in the 1960s and 1970s faced exclusions and hierarchies that were deeply embedded in public geographies. As historians have argued, all women in public space since the mid-1800s have been cast as sexually vulnerable at best, and often sexually suspect and punishable for their deviation from white, middle-class norms of domesticity.[7] Despite post–World War II gains in women's social and political status, everyday spaces continued to structure and naturalize racist hierarchies and gender and sexual norms. As late as the mid-1970s in many cities, it was common for bars that served white people to prohibit entrance to "unescorted women": blue laws governing public accommodations required a woman to have a man at her side, creating the appearance of a middle-class public free of prostitution and lesbianism. Urban establishments that catered to lesbians were often hidden and located in red light districts, and most prohibited homosexual dancing. Across race, class, and gender expression, a woman out at night without a man was met with suspicion and sometimes bodily harm, yet daylight did not free her of harassment on the streets, in public accommodations, and at work.

Civic spaces, too, reinforced gender/sex norms. Well into the 1970s, public parks—already embedded in racially segregated urban landscapes—denied athletic space to girls and women. Conventionally, civic athletics was an arena in which males secured masculinity through assertive use of their bodies in highly visible spaces.[8] Even when girls and women won access to civic athletic space, men regularly challenged their use of it through harassment and occasionally physical violence. The public landscape additionally buttressed the notion that women as a class were not credible economic participants. Before the mid-1970s, most banks denied women their own accounts and required a father's or husband's signature for loans of any kind; many landlords would not rent to a woman without male signatures, nor would many mortgage companies assist in purchases of property.[9] Such practices drastically limited the number of visible storefront businesses owned by women. Also into the 1970s, norms, laws, and medical practices regularly denied women sexual health care and reproductive control; most women were refused legal abortions, while some were forcibly sterilized. Many cities maintained emergency shelters for men but none for women, further announcing that women should stay ensconced within the domicile under all circumstances.

Women moved within and around these spatial conditions, and they created a massive groundswell of feminist activism by directly intervening in the built environment. During the 1960s and 1970s, they secured illicit meeting spaces on the margins of public economies, and they publicly fought to open bars to women and abolish gendered dress codes and prohibitions against lesbian congregation. They also created alternatives to bars, such as women's coffeehouses where women could socialize, dance together, and organize free of sexual harassment. Across race and class, women managed to secure quality civic space for athletic endeavors, and in the process, they grew activist communities and offered new ways for women to use their bodies in the public world. Women also built alternative means of economic exchange and support, and they set up their own lending institutions. They opened women-oriented bookstores, restaurants, cafés, and clubs, and they took it upon themselves to create shelter for women needing to get away from violent partners. They learned and taught each other medical skills and created new places in which to practice them, thereby establishing new standards of sexual health and medical practice. These kinds of interventions popularized women's movement throughout the public landscape, imprinting marketplaces, civic spaces, and public institutions with specifically feminist stamps. Feminist activism, then, was not just "everywhere" and "in the air," rather, it was known and practiced on the ground of everyday life.

People brought a variety of different interests to their movement: they were not all motivated by feminism, and many did not even consider themselves activists. Many softball players, for example, said they wanted above all to play ball; it happened that doing so required challenging the gender-, sexual-, class-, and race-based arrangements of civic space. Even as they took on this work, they did not make politicization an explicit goal. Others who did bring a specifically feminist consciousness to their work found that their interactions with everyday spaces further shaped feminist ideologies, expectations, and practices. For example, when self-identified feminists sought to provide shelter for women in violent relationships, they received opposition from neighbors, police, and other avenues of public regulation. From this evolved a now-common feminist critique of the institutions that privatized domestic issues and reinforced patriarchal control over women. Ideals of feminist health care, too, were profoundly shaped by women's ability to secure some kinds of spaces for practice and not others. In a variety of ways, then, women's interventions in conventional social geographies helped bring activist constituencies into being.

The spatial argument of this book has implications for understanding a key controversy within the historiography of feminism, namely, the place of lesbians in the movement. Although historians agree that lesbians, bisexual, and passing women have been important to feminism, movement histories—with some important exceptions—obscure their influence; in most, lesbians appear *as such* only if and when they politicized their sexual identity.[10] But a history of women's engagement with public space is necessarily also a history of sexuality, a field with which this work is in constant conversation. I employ a spatial analysis of women's movement to help explain why lesbianism (as well as sexuality and gender expression more broadly) were so formative of feminist activism. Whenever women entered—much less sought to change—the public landscape, they encountered specters of sexual deviance. All activists, regardless of sexual preferences or gender expression, met with persistent lesbian-baiting and homophobia alongside sexism, and it is thus not surprising that sex/gender liberation became central to feminism in general. But analyzing the ways that women navigated conventional public spaces and developed new feminist spaces reveals that women coped with sexism and homophobia in countless, often conflicting, and always spatially practiced ways. Lesbians—or, more accurately, butches, fems, studs, ladies, passing women, bulldaggers, gay women, women in lesbian relationships, bisexual women, and lesbians—took a leading role in many of these navigations, and thus, they are prominent in this historical study.[11]

A spatial analysis of feminist activism sheds new light on sexuality in the movement in part by reinterpreting the workings of identity politics. Most feminist histories directly resist the "good 1960s, bad 1970s" declension narrative common to studies of radicalism; after all, in the 1970s feminist activism (and gay and lesbian liberation) arose to shake the country in lasting ways.[12] Nevertheless, synthetic feminist histories share with histories of radicalism a sense that identity politics spelled ruin. Second Wave narratives beginning with Freedom Summer, and those beginning later with radical feminist organizations, portray an initial feminist unity preceding a fraying trajectory as women placed increasing emphasis on sexual identity, racial identity, class identification, gender identity, sectarian identity, ideological purity, and so on, one "group" after another "splitting off" the originary whole.[13]

I do not question that identity politics were costly, nor that we must still grapple with their legacies. I do suggest, however, that the prevailing identity politics model of social movement history distorts even as it explains. By foregrounding identity and ideology, many histories of the Second Wave create two impressions that run counter to their own findings. First, it appears as though feminist identity grew out of an originary, radical, and unified mission: in the beginning, everyone rode the wave. Second, comprehending the Second Wave according to feminist identity and ideological positions has had the effect of reifying the very identity politics most feminist historians seek to critique.[14] We still need new ways to historicize and understand conflict that do not make a small handful of identities and ideologies more primary, more stable, and more universal than they may have been. Focusing on sites of activism helps contextualize emergent identity categories by showing how diverse people generated social positions and identities in the process of inhabiting public spaces already built around exclusions and privileged access. Among feminists, certain identity categories became thinkable and operative as women created place *and* as they constantly sought to transform the terms of inclusion. To the extent that identity played a part in women's activism during the 1960s and 1970s, we might pay more attention to people's *embodied* but not static *locations* in a world of "constitutive sociality."[15] Rather than holding identities responsible for causing divisions, a spatial analysis instead sees the consolidation of identities as an *effect* of spatial practices. Furthermore, spatial practices included contestation, and thus consolidation was never complete.

Reliance on identity politics as an explanatory framework has contributed to the vexed place of lesbian existence in feminism—specifically, the tendency to ignore it unless lesbians politicized their identity has cast lesbians in the leading role of a play about divisive sexual identities. Historians have documented lively sexual invention propelling feminist organizing in this period: women demanded sexual autonomy, many questioned monogamy, scores became bisexual or lesbian, some became gender separatists or lesbian separatists, and everywhere women politicized the bounds of intimacy.[16] However, even while elucidating the dynamic complexity of sexuality among women, many narratives of the Second Wave continue to invoke "the gay-straight split" in monolithic terms and charge that "lesbianism," in particular, divided feminists.[17] A spatial lens affords a more compelling understanding of sexual emergence and the role that lesbians played in the movement. To be sure, lesbians and bisexual women disrupted the appearance of a sexually unmarked group. This became most apparent as women created explicitly feminist spaces; rather than being preexistent or static, particular sexual identity categories became imaginable and usable in relation to particular spaces and the multiple stakes that actors had in those spaces.[18]

No spatial analysis of feminist activism would be complete without consideration of women's space and separatism. In 1969, Pam Allen's concept of "free space" for women's consciousness-raising instantly became popular because movement women were already seeking just that.[19] By the early 1970s, most feminist-identified women—straight and bisexual as well as lesbians—unapologetically promoted separate space in which to organize, socialize, dance, teach, learn, and develop new skills, authority, and autonomy from men. It was common, if also radical, to seek "a space of our own."[20] But through processes discussed in this book, the meanings ascribed to "women's space" changed dramatically between 1967 and 1977: increasingly, women's space came to imply lesbian space. Much of feminism, in turn, sought to distance the movement from "separatist" spaces by representing them as lesbian, narrowly focused, renegade, and exclusionary. A deeper engagement with the trajectory of women's space offers a more satisfying history of feminism, showing that all along, *all* feminist-identified spaces constructed a culturally specific version of "woman" as the subject of feminism. From the outset, the creation of women's space was neither incidental nor ancillary but rather integral to feminist emergence and to the establishment of the movement's parameters.

Historians have widely agreed that race and class hierarchies have beset feminism from the outset, and yet the dimensions of these conflicts have been notoriously difficult to narrate. Feminism was historically tied to the civil rights movement and was often antiracist in intent, yet it often engendered race and class exclusion. How, then, do we understand the exclusions and hierarchies, and the ways that they contributed to the differential visibilities of actors and agendas within the movement? What was "white" and "middle class" about this movement when women of color and working women helped generate it from the beginning? A spatial analysis shows that conflicts within feminism gained form and name within tangible spatial contestations over environments already laid through with race, class, and sexual hierarchies. Far from being "spaces apart" or "free spaces," feminist spaces emerged in just such embedded environments; to an extent, they even appeared to substantiate social status by brokering access to them. At the same time, spatial contestation everywhere ensured that feminist activism would never be confined to but would regularly exceed the parameters suggested by self-identified feminist spaces.

This work joins a vibrant and growing body of scholarship on grassroots feminist activism indicating that the Second Wave paradigm—far from simply naming an era—has defined feminism too much according to white women and predominantly white organizations in the urban Northeast. Kimberly Springer, Benita Roth, Nancy Hewitt, Anne Valk, Sherna Berger Gluck, Wini Breines, and others have conclusively demonstrated that women of color generated feminism around a great array of issues. Equally exciting, Dorothy Sue Cobble has argued that women in the labor movement—far from being the "slow bloomers" of the Second Wave in the 1970s—built a feminist agenda from the 1930s on. Together, these works insist that the parameters of feminism bear careful reconsideration.[21] Joining this scholarship, *Finding the Movement* focuses on contested spaces in four cities of the upper Midwest to admit a broader set of actors and agendas into the history of the movement; people became part of this study not by virtue of membership in a named feminist organization or adherence to an already-identified feminist agenda, but because they participated in the politicization of particular places in which we may see the provisional coalescences of a movement.

This multi-urban framework draws attention to the ways that feminist activism took shape around the particularities of local geographies. To be sure, in all three urban contexts, bars, bookstores, and restaurants were important commercial arenas of activism; civic park spaces in all three urban areas yielded rich histories of women's efforts to desegregate athletic fields; similarly, the kinds of feminist spaces through which women institutionalized the movement bear commonalities as service-oriented or socially oriented spaces in all four cities. But people found feminist activism as it took place locally; even ties with activism elsewhere were mediated through local conditions and spaces. By the same token, *what* people found depended very much on localized environments. While a national story may be told about, for example, the emergence of feminist bookselling, examination of local contingencies reveals why women's bookstores took the shape they did and what that kind of space then meant for the local appearance of feminism as well as for the movement as a whole. Studying women's movement in three urban areas helps make those contingencies more visible than they would be if the study were defined by the borders of just one city. At the same time, pathways of activism connected these cities: for example, softball players, musicians, and entertainers as well as their fans and self-identified activists physically carried print media, insights, skills, and strategies throughout the United States and beyond. A multicity study reveals the ways that feminist activism was deeply embedded in the local even while simultaneously influenced by connections across region and nation. It should be clear, therefore, that this is not a linear, direct comparison of cities, nor of statically imagined spaces (e.g., women's health centers) across cities using any one-to-one correspondence. My analysis frames each instance of contested space in each locale to address distinct questions about the constitution of a movement.

The urban, upper Midwest is an apt region for a study that rethinks the parameters of feminism. Scholarship has thus far focused less attention on the upper Midwest than it has on the coasts, although the Midwest generated a great deal of decidedly feminist activism.[22] Without a doubt, a different and necessary story would also emerge through an in-depth exploration of rural or suburban activism, but for now I leave that to others.[23] Much that is conventionally associated with feminism hails from the four cities I study here: in Minneapolis, there is Amazon Bookstore, the country's oldest feminist bookstore; St. Paul is home to Women's Advocates, the country's oldest battered women's shelter; Chicago not only boasts the Chicago Women's Liberation Union, the country's largest grassroots feminist organization, but also *Lavender Menace*, one of the country's first and longest-lasting lesbian news periodicals; women in Detroit staged some of the first zap actions for child care and reproductive rights and later led attempts to create a nationwide feminist lending institute in conjunction with opening the country's first internationally conceived, multi-use women's building. The upper Midwest also allows consideration of the ways that less explicit, uncanonized, popular activism fueled the movement, thus affording a dramatic rethinking of the parameters of feminist activism locally, regionally, and also nationally. Finally, as the three largest urban areas in the Midwest, Chicago, Detroit, and the Twin Cities each offer their own distinct insights into the relationship between public geographies, women's movement, and feminism.

Chicago was known as "the city of neighborhoods." At midcentury, grade school children in Chicago studied maps that organized the city into discrete neighborhoods based on ethnic and racial demographics, and they lined up infant mortality rates exactly with neighborhood boundaries. The lesson taught that neighborhoods (place) were self-evidently conflated with race and class (identity), all neatly bounded and map-able.[24] Entire social movement strategies have been built around this conception of people and place. Perhaps the most utilized in the 1960s and 1970s was the "neighborhood organizing strategy" attributed to Chicago labor organizer Saul Alinsky, who proclaimed that "you do the most to organize in your own community." In the late 1960s, alongside the emergence of the Black Panther Party and the decision of the Student Non-Violent Coordinating Committee to become a black organization, neighborhood-based organizing became the modus operandi of the Black Panther Party, Young Lords, Native American Committee, Chicago Indian Village, Young Patriots, Students for a Democratic Society, Rising Up Angry, La Gente, and the Outreach group of the Chicago Women's Liberation Union: all had "their" geographic areas, and many referred to the maxim "organize among your own" to explain the race and class base of their work.[25] But of course boundaries were never so neat in practice. Just who is "your own?" According to what criteria? A single neighborhood could be a locus of both white feminist and Native American action; a predominantly white feminist neighborhood enclave might also be home to handfuls of black lesbian and Latino/a activists.[26] People's personal histories crossed criteria lines all the time, making neighborhood identity both more appealing and less monolithic. How, then, did feminism take shape within a city of neighborhoods?

In Detroit during the 1960s and 1970s, structural and social conditions posed such tangible challenges to women's movement that connections between space and organizing styles are particularly clear. Jobs had been leaving the city since the 1950s, but following the riots of 1967, Detroit lost half of its manufacturing and retail economy, and its infrastructure crumbled. White flight quickly turned Detroit into the city with the smallest concentration of whites (22 percent) out of all of the United States' most populous cities.[27] Minimal public transportation ensured that neighborhoods segregated by race and class would not be casually traversed, nor would the line between Detroit and its rapidly growing suburbs. Earlier in the century, excluded from mainstream white institutions in Detroit, African Americans in black neighborhoods built institutions for health care, financial assistance, business, and even an autonomous, highly localized government. Most African American women I interviewed called Detroit a "black city": all of them had grown up during the 1950s in "all-black" neighborhoods that were demolished to make way for freeways, housing projects, and urban renewal; most had little contact with white people. At the same time, the white women I interviewed regularly referred to Detroit not as a black city but as a "working-class city." This was a claim to a proud class identity, a reminder of Detroit's bygone industrial jobs, and also a claim to whiteness in a city that most whites had abandoned by the early 1970s. The title "working-class city" also recalled a history of white ethnic diversity and Catholic influence and marked the resilience of Detroit's remaining white inhabitants: by the end of the period under study here, more whites in Detroit occupied census tracts where the poverty rate exceeded 40 percent than in New York City, Chicago, Los Angeles, or any of the other ten largest cities in the United States.[28] Meanwhile, suburban zoning refused anything associated not only with blackness but also with sexual immorality: feminist bookstores were all right, lesbian bars were not. Social and geographic barriers contributed to relatively isolated activist communities. Yet women *did* organize, moving within, around, and because of larger structural changes. How did these contingencies affect what feminism looked like in Detroit and beyond?[29]

At a time when many Midwestern cities were rusting under deindustrialization and globalization, the Twin Cities gained tens of thousands of jobs, benefiting from an exceptionally diversified economy.[30] Many women I interviewed in the Twin Cities attributed their ability to spend time and energy on unpaid activism to the fact that the cost of living even by the mid-1970s was still relatively low; young women without children often lived on one part-time job, and—at least for educated white women —jobs were available. Many women expected the Twin Cities and state governments to extend their historic commitment to social welfare funding beyond education and health care to address feminist concerns; many also questioned the prevailing view of the Twin Cities as "white and middle-class," a view that depended on the segregation of poor people and people of color from many avenues of civic life.[31] Yet more than a river separated the two cities even as they grew more intertwined by the latter part of the twentieth century. Through the first half of the twentieth century St. Paul developed a working-class, Catholic identity, whereas Minneapolis strengthened its middle-class, Protestant public face.[32] In the 1960s and 1970s, social activism, freeways, and new jobs helped bridge the river and the cities, but zoning and activist cultures continued to reinforce distinctions between them. For example, in the early 1970s, every bar that lesbians—feminist and otherwise—worked to make "our own" was located in St. Paul, and most feminist-identified institutions such as bookstores, resource centers, and coffeehouses settled in Minneapolis (Women's Advocates was a major exception). How did feminism take shape around actual resources, dominant messages of well-being, and ongoing class distinctions between the cities?

The particular spaces examined in *Finding the Movement* emerged organically through my research. I found the many spaces that I analyze here through something similar to the "snowball method" that researchers use to find research subjects: just as one participant might tell a researcher about several more potential contacts, one space inhered pathways to others—some similar and some surprisingly different. Oral histories have been critical to this discovery. Archived sources, such as the minutes of a Detroit Feminist Health Project meeting, might (on a good day) include an address. But they virtually never include a discussion of why the meeting was there and not in some other neighborhood or of how women came to the meeting and what social and cultural boundaries they had to traverse to arrive there. In contrast, women's narratives of their lives were "travel stories," to use de Certeau's term.[33] And the ways that narrators arranged time, place, and activity in their memories provided important clues about the meanings they made of their activity.[34]

Early in my research, I looked for deliberately feminist spaces like A Woman's Coffee House. Perhaps the most celebrated and notorious of feminist institutions in Minneapolis, the Coffee House operated out of a downtown church basement and served as a hub of feminist and lesbian organizing beginning in 1974. Though predominantly white and middle class, hundreds of women across sexual identity, race, and class populated the Coffee House on weekend nights; many remember it as "the pulse of the feminist community."[35] There, one might say, one could find "the women's movement": women came from near and far to A Woman's Coffee House, and they grew a feminist and lesbian grapevine that contributed to a coffeehouse network spanning the country. Indeed, through traveling performers, fans, and newsletters, participants in the Minneapolis Coffee House learned of Mountain Moving Womyn's Coffeehouse in Chicago when it opened a year later. Mountain Moving had its roots in a women's self-help, antiviolence, crisis phone line, emerging to provide a *place* in a way that a phone line could not. Although the link between antiviolence work and a women-only coffeehouse seemed natural in Chicago, in the Twin Cities it was far less so. A Woman's Coffee House opened only months after the Women's Advocates battered women's shelter opened in St. Paul, but these two very different kinds of women-only spaces only peripherally overlapped as overt feminist institutions. Women's Advocates' founders, always dealing with emergencies, knew about the Coffee House but felt they rarely had time to participate in what they perceived to be an entertainment-oriented venue, and some, moreover, felt they should not "intrude on" an important space "for lesbians."[36] As I explored avenues such as these, it became clear that even the most obvious feminist institutions consisted of shifting layers of accessibility and contested boundaries.

Equally important were the pathways between these kinds of institutions and other, less distinctly feminist spaces. More than I could have anticipated, people who participated in A Woman's Coffee House *and* Women's Advocates directed me to a prior and concurrent marketplace of gay bars in the Twin Cities. The "chem.-free" Coffee House began in part as an alternative to bars, and yet many Coffee House participants helped create and defend bars for women. Few women sheltered at Women's Advocates cared foremost about lesbian activism at bars, but many did frequent a gay bar within walking distance of the shelter because they figured that there, they would not be hit on. As historians have shown, bars were key sites of GLBT activism from the 1940s through the 1960s.[37] But just how were gay bars and feminist activism related? That they were positively connected in the Twin Cities intrigued me, especially because the prevailing queer studies narrative suggested that feminist institutions of the 1970s had arisen from prudish middle-class sensibilities to supplant a stable, visibly erotic, and working-class butch/femme subculture earlier developed around bars.[38] When I looked chronologically and synchronically at the development of gay bars and feminist and lesbian institutional spaces, I saw cultural interdependence and interpersonal negotiation rather than the eclipse of one class by another. To be sure, all spaces fostered communities and exclusions around perceptions of class, race, generation, gender, and sexual expression: different kinds of places helped produce, for example, "bar dykes" and "feminist lesbians." But people did not stay in their place, and neither were spaces unrelated. Feminism found itself (in part) in bars and along pathways to them, and those processes directly shaped the movement.

The snowball method of finding spaces led to a diversity of feminist sites, but opening up feminism to a broader set of agendas required following some less clear leads. For example, several white women at the Coffee House—including the founders—had earlier developed "out" feminist lesbian sociality as they bodily asserted their presence on public softball fields. Their role models included the Avantis, a working-class team of white athletes who would have nothing of feminism but who aggressively occupied civic athletic space and expanded opportunities for girls and women to play on quality diamonds. The Avantis had learned that in part through their relationship with the Motown Soul Sisters of Detroit, a black softball team who had resisted segregation, demolition of black neighborhoods, and sexual scrutiny of black women in public in order to play ball in civic parks. Women who frequented A Woman's Coffee House knew nothing of the Motown Soul Sisters: those among them who had played on an "out lesbian" softball team regularly challenged the harassment they received for occupying civic space in Minneapolis, but they did not know that their style of struggle (and indeed, feminism itself) owed something to Detroit, a city where the story of softball was a story of segregation, community organizing, and challenges to gender- and race-laden stigmatization of women in public. Like many feminist-identified women, when I began to learn about the Coffee House, I was not looking for Detroit or for civic space, much less softball, and yet those were historic arenas toward which the Coffee House led.[39] From each site of activism, pathways led in many directions chronologically and culturally as well as spatially; in historical perspective, these pathways are the clues toward understanding the distances that women traveled—sometimes by relay—as they built the movement.

Altogether, *Finding the Movement* closely analyzes movement in and through three different kinds of spaces: commercial spaces such as bars, bookstores, and cafés; civic spaces, such as public parks and softball diamonds; and self-proclaimed feminist institutions, such as shelters, health clinics, and coffeehouses that women built to deliberately politicize what had been commonly regarded as merely personal and private issues. I was drawn to commercial spaces in part because "the marketplace" has long been recognized as a central arena of public order and also of social movement formation, yet women's utilization of it has not always been clear. Some scholars have suggested that women have been unable to create a discernible presence in the marketplace; others have charged that the marketplace "sold out" the movement.[40] The feminist record, too, reveals ambivalence on women's involvement in a marketplace that necessarily reproduces social hierarchies of all kinds. Deeper engagement with the ways that women won access to commercial leisure spaces and also built feminist commercial spaces, shows that women simultaneously used and sought to alter marketplace relations; indeed, these processes both constituted and popularized feminist activism.

In principle, civic spaces—especially city parks—epitomize the functions of public space: as arenas that make possible the activities of leisure, community-building, and political participation, they affirm and compose a public, a citizenry. Although few historians have analyzed women's use of civic athletic space in this light, women who fought for and utilized park diamonds in the 1960s and 1970s encountered these ideals and their contradictory applications. As with commercial space, civic athletic space lent itself to both avowedly *apolitical* activism (it's just about leisure) and avowedly feminist and lesbian liberationist activism (it's all about politics). In contrast, distinctly feminist institutional spaces maintained a consistently explicit political mission. They aimed to make services, resources, and social space newly available to women while also radically altering conventional social institutions and the hierarchies meted out by them. In the process, feminism itself ambivalently became part of the contested public landscape. Commercial, civic, and institutional spaces were key arenas of movement-building, and all provided the terms by which actors and emergent communities asserted varying investments in the spaces themselves.

Above all in my analyses, I was drawn to ordinary yet extraordinary sites of sociality and cultural formation. The specific places I study here were certainly not the only locations of feminist activism, and all intersected with many others that would be worthy places for close analysis (universities, women's theaters, and women's prisons, to name just a few). I do not propose to exhaustively represent the spaces of feminism within any urban area. Instead, I consider a handful of particularly productive cultural sites in each urban area as windows into the processes through which activist communities constituted themselves and constituted feminism as a mass movement. Exploring contested spaces as sites of sociality admits dynamic assemblages of actors to the story of feminist activism; it also helps explain the multiple manifestations of feminism and people's variable relationships to the movement. In the everyday spaces analyzed here, people talked, banded together, raised consciousness, played, loved, and fought; through them, people dismantled existing social hierarchies and built new ones. Taken together, the spatial stories throughout this work show that women built cultures of activism across sometimes surprising social and regional contexts; equally, they show that local barriers to such exchange profoundly influenced the ideals and parameters of feminism.

Just as people's narratives led me to consider space, so particular sites of activism led me to locate the people who occupied them. I conducted interviews with over 120 people, all of whom became part of this study because of their involvement in contested spaces. One could roughly characterize narrators according to established demographic terms: 8 percent identified as American Indian; 6 percent as Latina (with one Latino); 24 percent as African American; 62 percent as white (a full third of whom emphasized Jewish or other ethnic identity). Six percent identified as men, 92 percent as women, and 2 percent as trans. By background, occupation, or current social status, narrators spanned class: the majority (over 70 percent) who identified as middle-class actually included white-collar professionals, people who earned a wage, and people who owned small businesses; narrators included teachers at all levels, people who worked in health care or social services, people who worked in prisons, cab drivers, writers, welfare or Social Security recipients, and civil service employees. They included people who identified as lesbian or gay, heterosexual or bisexual, and people who resisted sexual identity categories.[41] Although these kinds of characteristics might be delineated with more or less precision, narrators themselves made more or less of them in their life histories and stories of spatial engagement. What became clear above all is that

demographic characteristics and social identities were constituted inconsistently—with varying qualities and relevance—throughout narrators'
lives. In the everyday spaces considered here, actors could forget some
aspects of their social identities while developing and performing others.
Thus, while demographic characteristics were related to broader social
hierarchies, only in the context of specific locations did some of them
demand particular investment. Rather than relying on them as static features, then, I prefer to show their constitution as part of the process of
spatial creation and social movement.

I have organized this work into three parts to provide analytical clarity
to women's interventions in various kinds of public spaces. Part I focuses
on commercial spaces. Specifically, chapter 1 analyzes women's navigation
of and impact on the nighttime marketplaces of house parties and bars,
and chapter 2 investigates the dynamics of alternative marketplaces, such
as feminist bookstores and cafés. While many activists associated with bar
spaces disavowed political motivations, many associated with bookstores
and cafés embraced political motivation and feminist identity. Scholars of
grassroots activism have shown that people developed social movements
in the twentieth century by laying claim to market-driven space: actors
created purchasable styles, built neighborhood enclaves, and formed businesses to serve specific communities, and in those ways, they publicized
their political interests. These scholars have also assumed that because
women historically have not had the capital that white, middle-class men
have had, women have been unable to make public assertions through
claims to public space.[42] Without dismissing the power of capital, my
research instead shows women's creative negotiations with the marketplace. Women did not escape capitalism, but they did intervene in conventional commercial terrain by creating alternative commerce and community in bars, bookstores, restaurants, and cafés; in fact they *used* the
marketplace even as they critiqued the ideological and economic forces
that restricted women's movement and constructed class, race, gender,
and sexual exclusions.

Part II, on civic space, concentrates on women's efforts to secure softball diamonds in public parks for their own use. Chapter 3 analyzes the
politicization of civic space by women who disclaimed feminist motivation, and chapter 4 considers explicitly feminist and "out-lesbian" organizing in these same spaces. Public parks, in some senses, were conceived as
the most purportedly civic of all urban public spaces: theoretically in-

tended to be "places where people could meet, relax, and mix," public parks might strengthen "urban civility" and even democratic participation in community life.[43] In Detroit, the Twin Cities, and Chicago during the 1960s and 1970s, parks were simultaneously sites of community-building and contestation, as people both relied on and challenged the race and gender segregation of the larger urban landscape. Moreover, in all three urban areas, parks directed the movement and activities of the public within, signifying uses and users of different park spaces according to gender as well as class and race; athletic spaces, in particular, secured male masculinity in large part by prohibiting women's use of them. During the 1960s and 1970s, women newly occupied softball diamonds to overturn their systematic exclusion from public athletic spaces. In the process, they challenged racial segregation and sexism, built visible feminist and lesbian cultures, and asserted new ways for women to move through the public world.

Part III on institutional spaces analyzes named feminist spaces such as shelters, health clinics, coffeehouses, and clubs. Such spaces institutionalized feminism in several respects. All directly interfaced with more mainstream social institutions, changing them even as they also altered the public landscape. Shelters, for example, had to establish arrangements with local police and many social service agencies; most of those arrangements required changing existing laws and interpretations of laws about property. Creating sexual health clinics also required negotiation with neighbors, and with city, state, and federal officials around zoning and the legality of feminist health practice in buildings other than conventional medical establishments. Women's coffeehouses, more often than not, sought to provide a noncommercial meeting ground in which lesbians could develop a positive and public culture; more often than not, they found regular meeting space in churches. Many service-oriented feminist institutions sought and received government and/or corporate funding, and some sought to become profit-making corporations unto themselves. Most of these negotiations began with an interest in formalizing a "women's" or "feminist" space in the public world. All of them involved compromise: feminists left a deep and lasting imprint on mainstream institutions, but many felt that the process scarred the very soul of the movement. As this book shows, however, the movement nowhere began pure and not-yet-scathed. Feminist institutions might be the places where it is easiest to see not only the growing pains of the movement but also the ways in which issues of property directly shaped the goals and public face of feminist activism.

Considered together, the mobile constellation of spaces and institutions that constituted and were constituted by feminist activism over the years should not obscure the fact that most grassroots feminism developed not by master plan but out of the opportunities and contingencies of daily life and women's hopes for change. *Finding the Movement* highlights a grassroots movement that, if coherent, was certainly not unified: it was a movement made of coalition and conflict, exuberant experimentation and reactionary doctrine, contradiction and transformation; a movement both visionary in its impulse toward democratic participation, and unwitting— and at times intentional—in its practices of exclusion; a movement that could be life-giving and devastating to its participants; a movement that changed the world and yet fell short; a movement that despite backlash, continues to emerge in ever new forms. It was and is also a movement inextricably intertwined with gay, lesbian, bi, trans, intersex, queer, and other movements toward sex/gender liberation. Turn first, then, to some unlikely commercial spaces that became a staging ground for women's movement: the bars.

Part I

*Community
Organizing
and
Commercial
Space*

One

"Someone or Something Made That a Women's Bar"

Claiming the Nighttime Marketplace

One January night in 1972, the historically straight, predominantly white Poodle Club bar on East Lake Street in Minneapolis refused entrance to two white women. Within two days, gay men and lesbians formed an action group, Gay Political Activists, specifically to take over the bar in protest. They entered in heterosexual pairs, but once inside, regrouped as gay and lesbian couples to occupy the dance floor. Bar management allowed them to stay, later explaining, "business was slow that night anyway." Less than a week later, the bar again denied entrance to two white women. In response, *Goldflower Feminist Newsletter* organized a mass picket that drew over 100 protestors on February 4. The women who had created *Goldflower* a mere month earlier were well practiced at this: Shirley Heyer, a self-identified "old bar dyke" tapped faithful connections she had made over years at gay bars, and younger women brought countercultural resources to what was advertised as a feminist demonstration. Far from enlightening bar managers, the feminist picket drew a hostile response: male bouncers and managers yelled, shook their fists in women's faces, and physically tore the picket signs away from women's backs and hands. The picketers left, never to return. It was worth making a statement at the bar, but the bar itself was not worth fighting for.[1] The event was significant, however, in that straight women, lesbians, and gay men collectively sought to challenge the sexism and homophobia that organized public, commercial space.

The bar's discrimination policies made plain some of the ways that all women were excluded from conventional commercial social spaces. Poodle Club managers defensively avowed that women were always welcome there; indeed, women's patronage was critical to a business that literally capitalized on heterosexuality. At the same time, the managers openly discriminated against homosexuals, claiming that gays and lesbians disrupted the normal functioning of the bar. Though men who arrived in all-male pairs or groups were rarely denied entrance, women without male "escorts" were often turned away at the door—usually on the grounds that they were "unable to prove their age," even when they presented legal ID cards. What legal ID cards actually could not prove was a woman's heterosexuality: only a man could produce that appearance. Bouncers and bar owners thus turned "unescorted" women away for failing to abide by heteronormative restrictions on women's autonomy and mobility. The protest action at the Poodle Club offers a snapshot of the influence of "bar dyke" activism on emerging feminist activism, their interdependence, and their combined impact.

Feminism found itself in part through struggles such as these. Bars acted as mainstays of public space; whether conventionally heterosexual or queer, bars organized sociality, social status, and social norms. As such, they became key sites of women's activism around public space itself, and they therefore provide windows into the emergence of publicized feminist challenge. Through the 1960s, lesbians—butches, fems, studs, ladies, gay women, and women seeking women—provided the driving force behind demands for leisure spaces in which women could openly congregate, particularly at night. Though bars were the most public meeting places that non-normative women could call "home," that space had to be won, too. Rules prohibiting "unescorted women" mandated against the visibility of lesbianism and prostitution; and virtually all bars, including gay bars, prohibited lesbian dancing and other obvious homosocial intimacy. In response, women protested straight-appearing bars for requiring escorts, and they protested gay bars for not welcoming women enough. Inadequately served by conventional venues, women also built alternative spaces for nonsexist, queer-friendly, and racially affirming commerce that supported their own emergent communities. As they did so, they became a constituency capable of making collective political demands on the public landscape.

By the early 1970s, much of this activism became explicitly associated with feminism. Some women who had long fought for bar space began to consider themselves feminists, and—as a glance through just about any feminist periodical of the early 1970s will show—many feminist-identified women began to protest women's exclusion not only from gay bars but also from straight bars, lunch grills, and other normative public accommodations. Taking inspiration not only from civil rights efforts to desegregate public space but equally from queer demands for a nonhomophobic landscape, feminist activism emerged partly in a nighttime marketplace structured around gender and race hierarchies. Feminist-identified women increasingly politicized their demands on commercial spaces: they fought to maintain and create presence in gay bars, they attempted to racially desegregate gay bars, they published feminist evaluations of bars, and they organized women's economic influence on bars. This aspect of feminist emergence is too easily overlooked, and it is altogether lost when historical analyses separate "gay liberation" from "women's liberation" or assume that feminists dismissed gay bars as vital social spaces. Feminism was not disconnected from other struggles over queer public space, but grew in part from them.[2] It should not be surprising, then, that while some of these actors claimed the label "feminist" for their actions, others did not. This chapter takes bars and bar-like commercial spaces as a starting point. Through such spaces, women across race, class, gender expression, and sexuality changed the public landscape even as, in the process, they formed distinct homosocial communities.

Because queer bars were such contested spaces, they provide a lens to bring into view the centrality of lesbians in women's struggles for expanded access to public space during this era. My focus on bars does not romanticize historical queer bars as spaces apart, nor does my analysis describe a now-lost moment of utopian possibility. Rather, as commercial sites of sociability, queer bars provide insight into the ways that feminism inherited, transformed, and sometimes accepted the structuring systems of the built environment. For over a century, queers have claimed a presence in bars and speakeasies despite gay bashing, police raids, and arrests. Queer bars were virtually alone among licensed commercial venues to affirm women's sex/gender self-determination; as such, they fueled increasingly visible lesbian and transgender cultures.[3] Accordingly, queer theory and gay/lesbian historiography have celebrated bars and the bold women who fought for them during the 1930s, 1940s, 1950s, and 1960s. Many of these narratives rightly charge 1970s feminism with stigmatization of butch/fem expression and "role-playing." Some further suggest that feminism drove lesbian bar life underground during the 1970s. According to queer theorist Arlene Stein, the "lesbian past" consisted of a working-class sexuality that "for all intents and purposes, had disappeared from public view by the 1970s, in the face of a feminism that was middle-class and 'ladylike.' "[4] In this popular rubric, the 1950s represents an era of accessible bars, visible lesbian erotics, and expansive gender transgression, whereas lesbian life in the 1970s seems conditioned by interiority, invisibility, and sex/gender repression. A focus on the nighttime marketplace during the 1970s, however, shows that bars proliferated rather than shrank in number, that they were an ongoing site of struggle, and that lesbian life still took place in bars and house parties peopled by self-identified butches, studs, fems, gay and passing women, lesbians, and feminists. The movement of more women into a greater variety of spaces including new lesbian bars, simultaneously expanded and decentralized bar life as a site of visible lesbian sexuality.

Bars were contested spaces precisely because they were deeply embedded in the exigencies of capital and material structures. One of the ways that women resisted the limitations of nighttime commercial spaces during the 1960s was through the creation of quasi-commercial alternatives such as dollar parties and warehouse parties. On the margins of—but not outside—the economy, such spaces partially circumvented normative race and gender hierarchies. These other spaces relied on and fed the clientele of commercial spaces; they often entailed their own systems of resource exchange; and they fostered communities with the agency necessary to alter marketplace relations. Seizing alternative venues, white women and women of color became producers of marketplaces in resistance to heteronormative control. Furthermore, these marketplaces belied the binary separation of domestic and commercial spaces and of formal and informal economies. The ways in which women intervened in the public landscape of bars during the 1960s and 1970s thus laid the groundwork for the conception of feminist spaces and feminist critiques of the social hierarchies embedded in the built environment.

In turn, analysis of contestations within the nighttime marketplace yields a historical story about the materiality of the emergence of feminist activism. Far from declining, the number of women's bars proliferated dramatically beginning in the late 1960s in all three areas under study; white and black lesbians began to own their own bars, and these bars were more publicly visible than the bars that women patronized in the 1950s and early 1960s. The activism of studs, ladies, butches, fems, and gay and passing women—including some self-identified feminists—made it far more possible, common, and less deviant for women in general to inhabit and create the nighttime marketplace independently of men. Here we see the ways that women across race, class, and gender expression productively used the marketplace to make collective claims on public space and how, in the process, they suggested the contours of feminist subjectivity.

This chapter uses select cases in each urban area to highlight different dynamics and dimensions of women's expansion of nighttime marketplaces. These cases do not provide a comprehensive history, but instead illuminate the variety of actions that took place and the race and class dynamics they produced. I begin with African American dollar parties and bars in Detroit during the 1960s. Black working women used bars and dollar parties together to build an alternative economy and elaborate a visible, black, queer community. Due to extreme segregation, few had any direct contact with white bars or with sites of white feminist organizing, and few identified with women's liberation. Yet they believed that the community-building work they did as black lesbians constituted "the first feminism." This sets up a framework for understanding white women's use and creation of queer commercial space in the Twin Cities. In the Twin Cities during the 1960s, the gender restrictions that bars imposed on women made bars into locations for enactments of whiteness, and they also pushed white women to illegally occupy warehouses for gender-liberating gatherings. These dual foundations led to concerted feminist claims on commercial leisure space between 1970 and 1975, as I show through a focus on the Town House bar in St. Paul.[5] The Detroit and Twin Cities stories together lend themselves to comprehension of Chicago's multiracial Monday Night Meetings and feminist-identified organizing around gay bars between 1969 and 1975. There, as women publicized and protested bars, they contributed to the consolidation of "lesbian" and "feminist" as a white, North Side subject, despite the involvement of African American and South Side women in the expansion of the nighttime marketplace. Although localized conditions contributed to the particular feminist sensibilities developed within and around bars, some common structural conditions shaped queer commercial spaces in all three urban areas. Bars became primary locations for newly politicized enactments of social segregation; the assertion of gender, race, and class hierarchies among women; and the publication of a newly defined feminist subject.

Dollar Parties in Detroit

As scholars have noted, public spaces are structured by exclusions, and it is easy to see the ways that Detroit during the 1960s bears that out.[6] Liquor licenses and property ownership were prohibitively expensive for most people, and women faced added economic and social barriers to opening licensed gay clubs. By law, all licensed clubs prohibited homosexual dancing, and the high cost of drinks at most gay clubs largely paid white landlords and police. Those factors contributed to the complete absence of licensed queer venues owned by African American gay women, studs, fems, bulldaggers, and sooners (local parlance for women whose gender expression confounded binary categorization).[7] Even the most queer-friendly clubs were owned by ostensibly straight men, and their clientele consisted mostly of drag queens, gay men, and men seeking sex with men; though studs and fems patronized them in small numbers, "ladies' nights" were rare to nonexistent.[8] However, lacking nearby queer bars, black women and men seeking gender/sex non-normative communities were far more apt to make use of ostensibly straight bars in black neighborhoods than they were to cross color lines to congregate in gay and lesbian bars in white neighborhoods. As historian Roey Thorpe has shown, racism and segregation posed significant barriers to black women's patronage of the twenty-some white lesbian bars that operated from the mid-1930s to the mid-1960s.[9] Most black women who had grown up in the inner city during the 1950s stayed away from white neighborhoods into the 1970s.[10] Queer commercial spaces maintained segregation even when white flight created massive demographic changes between 1967 and 1973: while most suburbs refused (white) lesbian bars, white women opened new (white) urban bars ever farther from Detroit's black neighborhoods.[11] Through the 1970s, no lesbian bar in Detroit served a racially mixed clientele. In many ways, then, public and commercial spaces formally excluded black studs and fems.

Although segregation, economic limitation, sexism, and homophobia surely shaped black women's mobility in Detroit, even the most structurally marginalized groups made use of and transformed the marketplace. Studs, fems, and sooners often connected domestic and commercial arenas to build community space: they used domestic spaces as avenues into queer commercial spaces, and they used commercial spaces as avenues into queer domestic spaces. Elaborating the long-standing and highly adaptable African American practice known as house parties, black women created dollar parties—so called because that's what women paid to get in—in resistance to economic marginalization. Though they were not licensed venues, dollar parties composed a queer marketplace; they were locations through which women redistributed resources and built a queer-affirming world that did not wholly depend on access to commercial space. Doing so, studs, fems, and sooners developed community autonomy, constituted themselves as a viable market, and became a public constituency.

Dollar parties functioned in relation to bars rather than displacing them, and bars—as more public venues—often served as imperfect pathways into lesbian community. Although women's families were a source of potential homophobic rejection, some African American women who grew up in Detroit's inner city first learned of queer commercial spaces from male relatives who helped mediate gendered landscapes.[12] Even by 1971, when bars like the Barbary Coast catered directly to black women, many women were introduced to such places by men. As Yvonne Roundtree recalled,

> So one night [my son's father] called me up and said, "Get dressed, I'm going to take you somewhere." Heck he want?! . . . So we get in the car and I don't know where I'm going. He drives us to this club and he says, "You go on in there and I'll come and get you when it's over." Dropped me off, came back. . . . I partied all night. When it was over, he came in the bar and got me, he said, "Okay, did you have a good time?" . . . My son's father is an Apache. Indians accept their gay children. . . . After that he said, "Yeah, I saw it in you, [but] I wasn't going to tell you before you understood it." So that's how I winded up coming out. It was hard back then. . . . The community was hostile.[13]

Thus, while public landscapes restricted women's knowledge of queer public venues and even queer life, women drew on familial contexts to navigate those restrictions.

To a limited extent, women expected the interior space of queer clubs to permit their deviation from gender/sex norms, but the bars were not a space apart from the larger landscape.[14] For that reason, they contributed to the desirability of alternative, less visible community spaces like dollar parties. Antoenette Foster recalled the risks of occupying the streets near bars: "coming out [of the bar] was dangerous, they would get gay bashed coming out of the bar. The studs got abused a lot."[15] The violent policing of the civic streetscapes outside bars constructed as deviant the women who made their way through the streets to the bars' hidden doorways, but it did not keep them away. In fact, as much as contested streets functioned as sites for the construction of gender and sexual norms, they also compelled defense of queer gender and sexual expression both in those public places and also in the less policed spaces of dollar parties.

Within bars, women developed sociability and community mores.[16] Most used the public and commercial aspects of bar spaces to enhance courting and the elaboration of highly gendered styles, marking themselves as studs or fems. Peggy, a fem-identified woman, explained one dimension of bar etiquette expected of studs: "There were unwritten laws: if I was your woman, your buddy treated me, when you weren't there, just like you were there." Another fem, Antoenette, recalled, "And if studs was in the restroom smoking, and I walked in, they'd be: 'excuse me, excuse me,' and all be coming out the bathroom to give *me* that space. . . . You were dated. They [studs] dated. You were wined and dined and dated. It might have been three or four months before you ever went to bed. The women were good to us."[17] Commercialized leisure spaces allowed women to build community ideals of friendship and lover conduct in part through public performance: gendered purchase of drinks, tipping, seating arrangements at public tables, the gendered use of public bathrooms, and etiquette about courting; implicitly, etiquette extended from the bar to the bedroom.[18] Idealized relations thus took shape in part within the structures of commercial meeting spaces.

Alongside relatively covert queer bars, Detroit in the 1960s offered regionally distinctive, highly visible commercial contexts in which women also constructed public queer style. Peggy relished the display possible at Motown shows: "That was the time of the Motown Revue. I can remember standing in line to get into the Motown Revue. It was the time of the 1960s . . . the time of the glamorous life." National recognition of the commercially successful Motown Records and its music groups put representations of black glamour into national popular culture; even those who barely earned a living wage positioned themselves firmly within that moment as they waited outside the Fox Theater on Woodward Avenue or patronized 20 Grand Club with its music, motel, and bowling alley to boot. As Yvonne explained, "Everything was glamorous. Wigs, lashes, nails, shoes, we thought we were fine. Oh, we thought we were gorgeous." On sidewalks outside shows during the "glamorous" 1960s, studs and fems produced high style in spectacular suits, gowns, and diamonds, not only for their lovers but for a multiracial public world.[19]

But not all public life was glamorous in Detroit, and women maneuvered around as well as within commercial spaces. Many black women who asserted the glamour of the 1960s also asserted, "the sixties was terrible for us," and economic studies bear that out.[20] When Yvonne recalled being gorgeous at the Motown Revue, she quickly added, "And then the riot came, and ain't nothing never been the same. That was in '67. Then, the glamour in the city and the people with money moved [away]." Motown Records was one of the "people with money" who left the riot-torn city in 1973, underscoring its place in a longer history of capitalism and race relations.[21] While black women publicly staked a claim to glamour in streets and bars both before and after the riots of 1967, they also developed alternative social spaces that were not dependent on the vicissitudes of "people with money."

Indeed, one of the most important functions of bars was that they were public places in which women circulated information about alternative venues, such as dollar parties.[22] Dollar parties were part of a long-standing, unlicensed marketplace, and queer dollar parties above all developed under the entrepreneurship of women.[23] Compared to bars, they offered such distinct advantages to women that, as Antoenette explained, "You would go to a bar, and you actually looked for the *after* party, you *actually* looked for the after party."[24] The social world of dollar parties exceeded that of bars, drawing women from as far away as Grand Rapids and Lansing, Toledo and Cleveland, Windsor and Indianapolis, and also drawing Detroit women who dared not go to a queer bar. At dollar parties, women could freely dance together as they could in no other public place, and people literally lined the sidewalks waiting to get in. In Peggy's description, "We just heard you had a party going, and we came. Okay, they usually had them in basements, the basements would be full of people. The basement would be, the floors be sweating we partied so hard."[25] Dollar parties surpassed bars in their community- and family-building function, creating networks that extended beyond the segregated confines of Detroit's black neighborhoods.

Circumventing the restrictions of the normative marketplace, women used the apartment buildings in which they lived as the foundation for dollar parties. Until the late 1970s, it was difficult for any woman to take out a loan, buy a house, or even rent an apartment without a male signature, much less could two women do so as an admitted couple. As Peggy recalled, "Back then we had to pretend like we were sisters. You know, I had to say you were my sister to get apartments. You couldn't say, 'this is my partner.' And when we would find an apartment building that would take us, we were in there by the droves: [if an] apartment got empty, you told somebody, so apartment buildings would just fill up with lesbians, basically." Women thereby settled a queer enclave within the mixed-class Linwood Avenue neighborhood that was a center of black organizing during the 1960s. Peggy further described one illustrious apartment on Dexter Avenue and Chicago Boulevard: "It wasn't just filled up with gay people. It was filled up with—we were considered—what's that word? Not low-lifes, but social *outcasts*. Outcasts. So in that building you had a bunch of *other* social outcasts, along with the lesbians." Apartment buildings thus became a locus for an alternative community comprised of studs, fems, sooners, drag queens, transvestites, and other deviants.

Many black women, excluded from much of the formal economy, worked a variety of informal economies to bolster their incomes. As Antoenette emphasized of the 1960s, "We didn't have anything. We had little babies, and we had nothing. We had minimum-wage jobs, whatever: we were dancers, we were hookers, we were whatever we were."[26] Jobs in the inner city were ever fewer and farther between as auto plants downsized, outsourced, or shut down, and other jobs followed white flight to the suburbs. Furthermore, the Motor City failed to develop adequate public transportation to those jobs, and few women had cars at their disposal.[27] Women therefore worked around a formal job market that excluded or exploited people on the basis of race, location, gender, and gender expression. Yvonne recalled,

> There wasn't a lot of money in the community that we knew of. If you were a stud and you wore all stud clothes, it limited where you worked. You worked in factories, gas stations, car wash, anything. I mean, you know, they called them "diesel dykes." They didn't have professional jobs. Neither did the fems. But that was all part of being in the black community: neither did the fems. A lot of my girlfriends were prostitutes. A lot of my girlfriends were boosters. A lot of my girlfriends were street girls. And they had these women [studs] at home who couldn't get jobs.

Some studs were pimps and accorded a certain respect for their public savvy. Indeed, Antoenette explained, "They were glamorized. The only people during that time who really had any money were pimps, and there were stud pimps." While gender norms and racist hierarchies excluded many black women from formal employment, studs and fems created alternative livelihoods, and dollar parties helped support their efforts.

Women created dollar parties in part to redistribute resources and affirm community among a population with restricted earning power. As spaces that were at once domestic and social, dollar parties were part of an economy in which women supported themselves and their families. Many women attributed the community ethos of dollar parties to "the black culture," and asserted that queer parties especially excelled at the values rooted in that culture. Provision of food was essential: the host supplied "fish, and beef and chicken, ham," while "everybody else bring the rest." When studs and fems built house parties, they often conceived of their activities as deriving from an "ancestral" economy as a "communal people," when "to have a lot of food was a rare blessing"; during the 1960s, they considered this to be practical and politically important.[28] As Antoenette explained, "Remember when nobody had a job? Then you'd get food stamps, and you had your two dollars in food stamps, my two dollars in food stamps, your two dollars—then you've got it made: a good time! And all of us that had kids brought all the kids over, and we done fed all them kids." Yvonne concurred, "You all hunted, and then you put your food together. And the whole village ate." Dollar parties provided food, drink, and shelter for large numbers of people; they provided financial support for the host's domestic space; and they provided social space for an otherwise marginalized community. Thus, dollar parties should be understood not simply as venues on the margins of the commercial world but also as an intentional alternative marketplace that built and sustained the critical resource of community.

Dollar parties cohered an alternative community in part in response to homophobic families, churches, and activist organizations and went farther than bars could to provide shelter and comfort. As Antoenette explained, "We are social outcasts. Everything that is supposed to be holy and up above board is against this, every religion. . . . So, where are you going to go?"[29] One place she went was the Shrine of the Black Madonna, led by the radical theologian and activist Reverend Albert Cleage, within walking distance of the apartment buildings in which she and other queers lived. She recalled, "I was a nationalist during that period. Homosexuality was such a conflict because it was considered genocide. Genocide: 'homosexuality is part of the plot to get rid of blacks.' " The Shrine, the Temple of Islam Number One, New Bethel Baptist Church, the League of Revolutionary Black Workers, and the Black Panther Party all offered vital black nationalist and civil rights organizing and community to Detroit's inner city.[30] Same-sex-loving black women drew on the vital politics offered at these nearby congregations, but homophobia erected a prominent barrier to their full welcome in those places. Though dollar parties did not resolve the conflict between homosexuality and black nationalism, they supported queer congregation by taking on some of the community-building, welfare, and organizing functions that black churches offered to straight-appearing members. Dollar parties could even continue into the next day, especially on holidays. By offering a place day and night, they made it more possible for black nationalists to be lesbians and for lesbians to be black nationalists, even when women kept those identities separate in other public arenas.

As black lesbians constituted a community-minded culture in part through dollar parties, so they also asserted an increasing presence in black queer bars, such as George's Inca Room and the Birdcage. In the late 1960s, they claimed the Casbah, formerly a white women's bar abandoned by white flight. In the early 1970s, women took over weekend management of the Barbary Coast, formerly one of the most popular bars for black gay men; they turned it into a women's bar Fridays through Sundays and even began to hold special events such as weddings there.[31] The Barbary Coast was the first bar where many women remember partying "all night." However, women did not party there all night; rather, they stayed until closing, and then they piled into cars to go to Antoenette's or elsewhere for the after party. The proliferation of bars catering to black lesbians in the early 1970s depended in part on the informal community organizing that took place around dollar parties. Black women skillfully utilized the threshold between domestic space and commercial space to assert a collective presence capable of sustaining new public leisure spaces.

Despite this proliferation of lesbian bars, geographic and cultural barriers discouraged women from imagining a shared, multiracial movement growing out of bar spaces, even when civil rights and feminist activism finally increased job opportunities and geographic mobility for black studs and fems.[32] The absence of interracial queer space meant that many white lesbians doubted the existence of black lesbian communities altogether.[33] White lesbian bars—unwelcome in the suburbs—behaved as white enclaves within the city. Some African American women ventured to white bars like the Palais, Fred's, and Todd's, but, as Peggy explained,

We didn't have crossover bars: you had black bars for women, white bars for women, black bars for men, white bars for men. Music was a lot different then. You had white music, you had black music. So if you were a black girl and you went to the white bars, a lot of times they wouldn't even speak to you. Because they were nasty to us. And when you went there, the music was white music so you really couldn't dance. You went to the black bar, to be amidst your own.

It was more than a music's origins that made music "white" or "black." Though white bars played Motown music, black bars kept steps ahead of white appropriation, popularizing newer dance styles with newer songs before they reached the purview of white bars. Music, dancing, etiquette, gender expression, and location all composed queer space and also provided the markers by which women constituted race and class as well as sexuality. A history of segregation also composed queer commercial spaces. Between the 1930s and the 1960s, many bars scattered throughout Detroit catered to white lesbians; when lesbian and feminist organizing and reduced property values newly encouraged white lesbians to purchase their own bars, they had decades of public commercial space behind them. In contrast, black lesbian bars first emerged in the early 1970s on a decades-old cultural foundation of dollar parties; black women accustomed to floor-sweating basement dances "really couldn't dance" to the "white music" at white bars like Fred's, even if they were allowed in the door.

Similarly, many women who had created venues for black queer socializing intersected little (if at all) with white women who identified themselves as feminists. Segregation combined with selective media attention led to initial impressions among black studs, fems, and lesbians that women's liberation was propelled by "white women who stayed at home, took care of the babies and raised the children and kept the house clean." As Antoenette expressed it, "I remember at first I thought it was just 'burn the bra, let us work.'"[34] Where they saw common ground—around equal pay, child care, and reproductive rights—black women who built queer-friendly worlds asserted, "We might have been the first feminists. The lesbian women. 'Cause *we* stepped out there." If they saw white women "stepping out there"—and they did—they argued that "the feminist movement rode on the coattails of black activism."[35] Simultaneously, they linked their own queer activism to older community organizing traditions presented as more authentic and locally meaningful.

Despite economic marginalization, black studs, fems, and lesbians demanded harassment-free social space; they worked at whatever jobs they could get, and at those jobs they chipped away at the homophobia and harassment that they encountered in the bathrooms, break rooms, and on the line. They formed alternative community spaces in which women supported each other and each others' children and families, spaces in which sexism and homophobia were not tolerated. In mobilizing a network of domestic and commercial spaces, they elaborated what historians commonly see as a politicized "bar culture," and a politicized "community organizing tradition." Segregated from a dominant white bar culture and women's liberation, this geographic and cultural terrain provided a compelling foundation of activism similar in form and effect to that typically earning the name lesbian and feminist.

The Women's Bar in the Twin Cities

In the same years that black women in Detroit created queer spaces and political sensibility around the constraints of poverty and segregation, whiteness afforded different sorts of opportunities for creating a politicized community in the Twin Cities. Licensed bars in the area serving a predominantly white clientele discouraged women's presence throughout the 1960s. They also exerted a constricting force on women's public gender expression, and this was as true of gay bars as of ostensibly straight bars. White women circumvented these restrictions by poaching the industrial cityscape, illicitly turning urban warehouses into huge community spaces that invited non-normative gender expression and brought queer women together as a constituency. By the late 1960s, white gay women began to open their own bars, and women across class and gender expression demanded more respected space within existent bars, particularly in St. Paul. On these foundations, diverse women turned the Town House bar in St. Paul into "*the* women's bar" by 1975. Normative regulations on public space, along with underground warehouse parties, inspired white women to make collective demands on commercialized leisure spaces; these dynamics, among others, fueled feminist activism in the Twin Cities.

Most palpable to white women in the 1960s were the gender restrictions that most bars serving a white clientele imposed: the requirement to arrive with male escorts and to wear skirts or dresses rather than pants, and the studied refusal of many bartenders to serve women. These same rules also underscored racial distinction: they demanded that women approximate certain aspects of white middle-class respectability, including its attendant gender relations and hierarchies. Many bars and restaurants that catered to male homoerotic interests actually depended on white women's heteronormative appearance to affirm the racialized respectability of (white) queer male space. The conditions creating the "gay scene" at bars in the Twin Cities pushed women to resistant acts. But queer women, like queer men, drew on the social capital of whiteness to bolster their standing in public spaces; thus, they disrupted some—but not all—aspects of heteronormative performance as they paved the way for lesbian and feminist publicity.

During the 1960s, licensed gay bars were few. In Minneapolis, zoning laws strictly fixed the number of liquor licenses, and statewide blue laws required bars to close by midnight on Saturdays. Such laws contributed to the development of "3.2 joints" (licensed to sell drinks with a maximum 3.2 percent alcohol content) and unlicensed after-hours clubs that people often operated out of their own homes. The relatively small operation of 3.2 joints and after-hours clubs allowed gay men and women to own them and cater to a queer clientele with less risk of public or police attack: most were transient and depended on word-of-mouth advertising. A few licensed gay bars enjoyed greater longevity thanks in part to ownership by what locals fondly refer to as the "Jewish Mafia" who paid off police to curtail raids, violence, and shut-downs. St. Paul was a "free city"—that is, Mafia-free—and its police force was long considered to be "more homophobic and dangerous than their Minneapolis brethren"; there, gay bars were virtually nonexistent during the 1960s.[36]

Women-friendly bars were even harder to find. Lingering blue laws prohibited women from entering any bar if they were not with men and from sitting at the bar proper even when escorted. Restrictions against women actually assisted the development of queer male cruising spaces: straight-appearing establishments that upheld blue laws, such as the Viking Room of the Radisson Hotel and the Persian Palms, "were known as kind of gay bars" because there men could watch, meet, and pick up one another in a legitimized homosocial space.[37] The Viking Room, widely acknowledged as a "high-class" place, was kind of *gay*, but it was also *only kind of* gay, because it depended on blue laws that, by regulating women's appearance, explicitly conferred heteronormative status to the space.[38] If sexist blue laws helped gay men create publicly acceptable queer male space, they simultaneously hindered queer women's presence in these same places. Meanwhile, Minneapolis's licensed gay bars actively discouraged women's presence: the Happy Hour (upstairs from the erstwhile straight Gay 90s) turned women away or refused them service, and Sutton's enforced a "dress or skirt" code for women and required them to arrive with male escorts. These policies were directly tied to stereotypes of women as people who don't buy enough drinks, tip enough, or pay their way. In economic as well as sexual terms, women were bad business for gay bars, but if their presence could be regulated and limited, they could enhance the class status of queer male spaces.

In part due to the location of queer bars, many gay women did not resist the escort requirement. Between World War II and the late 1960s, most queer bars in Minneapolis existed in a poorly lit area that locals referred to as the Gateway or "patrol limits" near the river on the near north side of town, an area perceived to be unsafe for women walking alone or in couples.[39] As Dorothy F. explained, "We all stuck together in those days anyway, because we had to. We protected each other. You wouldn't even want to only socialize with women, because it seemed like there weren't enough of us to split off like that."[40] Women's linkage of men and bars went beyond safety in numbers, as many white queer women in the Twin Cities before 1965 first learned about gay bars through male friends. Nighttime commercial venues and passage to them were almost entirely mediated by men.

Through most of the 1960s in Minneapolis, many white women across class developed public gender styles within gay male commercial spaces that staged class by imposing normative appearances on women. The original Sutton's bar, on the border of Minneapolis's business district, distinguished itself from queer "dives" through its location and spacious interior indicating that its operation was "above ground."[41] Additionally, the bar required that women wear feminine attire and arrive with male escorts. This code did not put off all women; even many butch-identified women—used to wearing skirts for their jobs—were willing to don a skirt to go to a gay bar with "a bunch of fellas and friends."[42] For some, doing so enhanced the feeling that the bar was a "nice place," comparable to the straight-appearing bars like the Viking Room. It also put the bar several cuts above the "underground queer bars" like Kirmser's in St. Paul that had allowed women to wear pants when it operated during the 1950s. Putting on a skirt and an escort supported a claim to respectability in a predominantly white commercial space that otherwise signaled gender and sexual deviance—indeed, it made that space a "nice place." The conflation of "nice places" with places where white women wore skirts and were accompanied by white men linked class constructions, gender/sexual expression, racial affirmation, and location. Straight and gay bars alike actively participated in those constructions; the working- and middle-class women who went to gay bars, especially, created shared sex/gender sensibilities within the limits of that localized commercial milieu.

The continued enforcement of gendered dress codes and blue laws successfully discouraged the elaborated butch/fem styles that historians have described for cities like New York, Buffalo, and San Francisco. Not surprisingly, Sutton's and most other bars had limited appeal for women who strictly avoided women's clothing, and they certainly made no room for high fem and butch expression. Some women who passed as men gained entrance to bars like Sutton's, but most women who patronized the bar appeared to uphold public gender codes.[43] By prohibiting women's "cross-dressing," the bars encouraged the emergence of a white subculture of women who—across class—developed subtle markers of sexualized gender distinctions, and articulated correspondent public identities as simply "gay." Commercial venues thus influenced gender expression and sexual subjectivity, as women constructed localized signifiers and identities through the places in which they socialized.

Historians have argued that, through much of the twentieth century, binary gender expression (such as butch/fem) among lesbians characterized particularly working-class lesbian subjectivities in distinction from middle-class subjectivities.[44] But both class identities and lesbian subcultures took shape within public commercial venues and local conditions. In the Twin Cities, because dress and escort codes definitively muted public butch/fem appearance, narrators did not conflate gender expression with the class status of the wearer as people may have in other cities. Self-identified "butch bar dyke" Shirley Heyer asserted that in bars, "class background was not very detectable."[45] Jo Devlin claimed that "women of *all* classes had been in the bars all along," and it was not butch/fem expression that marked white working-class lesbian culture.[46] Of course, going to Sutton's did not render skirted, escorted women "middle class." But Sutton's exclusion of women who refused escorts and skirts rendered the queer bar a "nice" place. When such venues—and also most workplaces—refused butch gender expression, those exclusions at least temporarily rendered butch women outsiders: regardless of class background or occupation, butch and passing women socialized in more "underground" spaces, spaces that were not "nice," and certainly not "middle class." Arguably then, the postwar association of butch/fem and white working-class identities—at least in Minneapolis—was based in part on heteronormative associations of "nice" with "middle-class" publicity.

In Minneapolis, the bar options for white women traveling in mixed gender groups as well as for those who were "unescorted" diminished in the mid-1960s. By 1964, a "clean-up" mission prompted the demolition of entire city blocks near Hennepin and Washington Avenues, where most queer bars were located, and they were largely replaced by a new, still predominantly white business and commercial district.[47] In 1965, the "upscale" Sutton's bar moved to a neighborhood desolate but for the adjacent all-male Locker Room Baths. Sutton's let go its escort requirement but did not lift its skirt code until the early 1970s. The new location and the continuance of the dress code without the escort rule contributed to a precipitous decline in female patrons: while escort rules at the previous Sutton's had inhibited butch/fem sociability by imposing a "real man" on lesbians, male escorts also protected skirted women's presence at the bar and in the neighborhood. Women were so marginal at the new Sutton's that one small group of white women hypothesized that they were "among the first to integrate" the bar in the late 1960s. Others were quick to describe its discrimination against women along with the Happy Hour, leading to the ahistorical conclusion, "Minneapolis bars had *always* been very unreceptive to women."[48] The new "gay scene" required uninterrupted queer male performance; creating such spaces entailed newly denying women the ability to negotiate race, class, and heteronormative privileges to win entrance in cooperation with white males.

Because gay bars in Minneapolis maintained class- and gender-based exclusions, some white queer women created alternative, unlicensed venues that celebrated lesbian deviance from middle-class gender and sexual norms even while relying on racial privilege. Foremost among these were warehouse parties drawing hundreds of gay, butch, fem, and passing women on occasional weekend evenings during the 1960s. Never quite public, warehouse parties were possible partly because they were kept secret from authorities and gay bashers: there was no licensing, and "there was really nothing legal about it." With the exception of holiday parties, "you never knew where or if it was going to be until it happened."[49] Most took place in warehouse districts on the north side of Minneapolis, often within blocks of existing gay spots for white men. Women kept their operation vague: "Someone would find a space, a warehouse we could get into, and then you would find out about it through the grapevine, and the women would haul coolers of beer, and you'd have music on a portable record player with speakers. Maybe it cost a few dollars or a dollar to get in. And there would be a lot of people."[50] They resembled pre-1970s underground gay bars and after-hours clubs in that they were visible only to people with connections. But they departed from bars in that they created an economy in which money circulated among the women present; women paid themselves, they paid *for* themselves, and they were very good business in their own sexual marketplace.

Unlike bars, warehouse parties offered huge spaces in which hundreds of queer women could freely dance together or engage in other sexualized activity prohibited elsewhere. Equally important, passing women and butch women could dress up without the classed dress codes prevalent in bars and restaurants. Holiday parties inspired even more attention to dress than usual, with contests for the best-dressed butch. Connie Harlan fondly recalled, "Everyone dressed in drag. We'd go to shops where you rented suits, tuxedos, fancy men's clothes. . . . We'd look forward to it for weeks. It was fun to dress up, and some people spent hundreds. I always went as a gambler: I was a gambler, real sharp with the hat you know, and everything."[51] Warehouse parties were spaces where women could dress "in drag," some even putting on an explicitly criminal persona. Many women thus enacted a white lesbian sexuality that was especially butch— precisely that sexuality and gender expression forbidden in more public commercial spaces.

Warehouse parties offered new terms by which social legitimacy and outlaw status were measured. True, the temporarily stolen spaces of the warehouses dramatized queer women's circumscription within a larger capitalist, sexist, and homophobic public landscape. But within that space, women valorized white lesbian sexuality through styles that flagrantly denied white middle-class gender norms. Further, by seizing the space itself, women refuted normative ownership of public space and marketplace relations. Built by and welcoming to large numbers of women, the parties registered a critique of the class- and gender-laden dynamics present in so many gay and straight-appearing bars. At the same time, in a larger urban terrain dominated by whiteness, it was partly racial privilege that made this expansive work possible. Even at their least legal, warehouse parties did not simply deny middle-class norms, they also embodied them; they attested to white women's ability to seize the margins of a capitalist economy to build huge nondomestic spaces for the enactment of new sexual subcultures. On those foundations, white queer women became a constituency prepared to make concerted demands on the public landscape.

Building on the hospitality and freedom of gender expression at warehouse parties, women collectively began to seek new commercial spaces. The year 1967 marked a new era for gay bars in St. Paul, and women were at its forefront. Decades later, women affirmed their lasting impact by claiming, "The women's bars have *always* been in St. Paul," and "*all* the St. Paul (gay) bars have been owned by women."[52] Coinciding with women's growing critique of Minneapolis bars, Honey Harrold opened her first urban bar—Honey's—in St. Paul.[53] White gay women from the region arrived there in droves to play poker, darts, and pool, specifically distinguishing it from Minneapolis bars: it was small and casual, in contrast to the multisectioned Minneapolis bars; it was informal, in contrast to pretentious Minneapolis bars that promoted a middle-class atmosphere; it was a place to "just *sit at the bar* and have a drink," which virtually no Minneapolis bar permitted; and above all, it was "just for women." Women could arrive at Honey's from work or a softball game. Its corner location in a well-lit neighborhood felt relatively safe to most. When Honey's burned down in 1969, rumors circulated that "upset neighbors" had committed arson. Though unconfirmed, the rumors fueled women's determination to regain a bar of their own, and they continued to coalesce until they did.

From 1970 to 1978, while Minneapolis ordinances strictly limited the number of bars in the city, a number of new bars in St. Paul came to figure prominently in women's landscape.[54] Most women, however, proclaim the Town House bar on University Avenue to be "*the* women's bar" of the 1970s. Many women also incorrectly claim that it dates back to the early or mid-1960s. This chronological excess is due in part to the prized place of the Town House as the first and longest-lasting bar whose patrons included women across gender expression, generation, class, and political identity. But the bar was not an autochthonous women's bar; rather, it owed its status to a constant campaign to make it women-friendly beginning in the early 1970s. That campaign increased the public visibility of gay bars, gay and lesbian civil rights, and diverse lesbian cohorts—many of whom embraced the label "feminist"—in the Twin Cities.

Emmet Jewell opened the Town House as a straight bar in 1969, expecting it to be a step up from his previous bar located in a largely African
American neighborhood.[55] But in less than a year, the Town House went
bankrupt, and Jewell converted it into a gay bar. It was "almost a desperate
move" for Jewell, but "the rest is history, and it was huge," as his daughter,
Kelly, explained.[56] Bar-goers were thrilled: the Town House was proof and
prophecy that more queer persons were transforming the world around
them in part by gaining a public foothold even in St. Paul.

Men outnumbered women during the first few years of the Town
House's operation as a gay bar, but women showed up there in numbers
unseen at any previous bar with the exception of Honey's. They were
butches, fems, gay, and passing women who had danced the floors of
warehouse parties for years, and they were lesbians newly coming out in
the context of student groups and feminists groups. They included women
who believed the Town House would be a better bar than the Minneapolis
bars, and also gay women and lesbians who had never entered any Minneapolis bar. Jewell and the bar manager Greg Weiss presumed and advertised to a gay male clientele, but women found out about the bar nevertheless and, having lost Honey's bar within the previous year, they quickly
asserted their presence.

The Town House offered women many spatial advantages over other
bars. On University Avenue, the bar shared an open parking lot with
Montgomery Ward's across the street. Lower-middle-class residential
housing on the north side of the street and shopping centers on the south
side kept the neighborhood well lit. The area was not heavily patrolled,
and many believed it did not need to be; narrators report feeling safe going
there alone, even though some had their car tires slashed while they were
inside the bar. It was also accessible, on a major bus line. Inside the Town
House, high-backed booths appealed to women who wanted to scan the
action on the dance floor and at the bar.[57] Though the bar proper integrated men and some butch women, most patrons loosely segregated the
rest of the bar into women's and men's "sides."

Among the first women to assume their presence at the Town House
were Honey's loyal customers and women who had enjoyed the warehouse
parties. One narrative establishing the Town House as "theirs" revolved
not around winning it over from gay men but rather from straight ladies
who knew the space as the White House restaurant. As Connie Harlan
told it, "I remember when the Town House first opened. Before it was a

gay bar, a lot of ladies who had been shopping at Ward's would come over—it was a nice little restaurant and they'd come over for lunch or in the late afternoon. Oh! and when it switched to a gay bar ha ha ha! Oh that was a riot! We'd watch them come in, watch them take it all in!"[58] Representing ladies as awkward outsiders, this cohort of white gay, butch, and fem women asserted that they won a battle against middle-class morality in what thereby became *their own* commercial space.[59]

Ladies weren't the only ones who were initially awkward in overtly queer space. Jeanne LaBore first visited the Town House in early 1970, having recently left her novitiate at Sisters of St. Joseph. "I remember noticing someone at the bar, with slicked-back hair, and sleeves rolled up, boots . . . and I realized it was a woman, and my heart *sank*. There were only a few women there, and I thought that's all there was to choose from."[60] Barb H. similarly feared the gender of "lesbian" her first time at the Town House. "The first time I walked in the door [I saw] about three or four huge, tough-looking women—and I thought, 'whoa! Is *this* what I am?' That was my first experience in a women's bar."[61] Testifying to the strength of white, middle-class norms, some narrators feared that lesbian community depended on deviant gender and class status, and that participation would therefore entail a crushing loss of social and self-respect. Despite some women's initial intimidation and internalized homophobia, the Town House supported a surprisingly diverse (albeit almost entirely white) clientele. LaBore chose to go there "night after night, once nine nights in a row!" even though she soon discovered additional lesbian social worlds from which to choose.[62]

The Town House was a location in which otherwise divergent subcultures overlapped, sussed each other out, and constructed complex class distinctions. Sara Henderson, a "far left" activist then involved in the Women's Counseling Service (a feminist health and reproductive rights service), met "women who weren't into feminist politics" at the Town House. She admitted, "They'd look at me sort of funny when I started talking about things like that," but having different lives outside the bar did not prevent engagement within the bar. As she explained,

> There was this butch woman who really appealed to me. I couldn't even talk to her on a head level, but on another level, on a body level, that woman did things for my chemistry that no other woman, no time, nowhere, ever did. . . . She was old school, working class, not a lot of education, and a very different set of

values than what I had lived with. I would start talking and she didn't understand what I was saying, and she would start talking and I didn't understand what she was saying.[63]

Henderson's narrative associated butch gender expression with working-class and "old school" political identity to paint a stark class distinction between herself and a butch woman. Meanwhile, an assortment of wage-earning gay women considered "feminists" to be "too serious and have too many issues to go to bars"; it was thus hard for them to recognize bar dykes like Shirley Heyer as feminists even if they identified themselves that way. According to Hollis Monnett, feminists didn't "drink big or tip big"; from a bartender's perspective, feminist teachers were "the most dreaded group" of all.[64] Women thus construed subcultures around occupation, gender expression, speech, tipping, and so on, using that shared space to play out the social tropes, inconsistencies, and also the allures of gender and class distinction in their own Town House bar.[65]

As diverse women steadily built their presence at the Town House, they also noted that they were not entirely welcome. By early 1974, the hints culminated in a physical turf war. Over a period of months, the number of chairs and tables on the women's side had dwindled until one night women arrived to find "their" furniture missing altogether, replaced by a cigarette machine and an expanded dance area. In protest, they sat on the floor. Within an hour, fifty-one women and twelve men sitting on the floor around the cigarette machine agreed that the manager had systematically diminished the women's side of the bar and had generally made women feel unwelcome. When they demanded the furniture be returned, the bar manager ordered police to bodily remove every woman (but none of the men) from the bar with the charge that they were being "highly disruptive."[66]

Following the melee, Shirley Heyer led women of the Town House in a weekly picket on the busy strip outside the bar. They also filed and won a human rights suit against the bar, taking advantage of St. Paul's newly passed gay-rights ordinance; if the *city* had outlawed discrimination against gays, they reasoned, how could a gay bar discriminate against lesbians?[67] Many of these women had practiced the art of public protest in earlier battles over sexist, homophobic commercial establishments such as the Poodle Club and men's lunchroom grills. But to draw such attention to a gay bar was unprecedented; lesbian patrons and their male supporters had never demanded rights from a gay bar—and from the city—in so public a fashion. Their efforts catalyzed a thorough reversal in bar policy and effectively announced to women of the Twin Cities that "the Town House is *our* bar." For possibly related reasons, Emmet Jewell handed bar management over to his daughter, Kelly, and hired Honey Harrold as co-manager. Together, Honey and Kelly began promotions geared toward women: they started women's pool tournaments and weekend softball tournaments complete with chili parties. Pool tournaments even drew straight-identified women who loved to play with women without getting hassled by men as they did at straight bars.

By 1976, the number of women patronizing the Town House far exceeded the number of women going to gay bars during the 1960s. Narratives of the gender ratio at the Town House indicate how notable that was. Jo Devlin, for example, thought it "pretty gender-equal." Jeanne LaBore reflected a common view among women stating, "It was obvious that [other bars] were men's bars that maybe a couple women visited. At the Town House, it was the opposite." Though Jean Niklaus Tretter called it "*the* women's bar," he was among the men who enjoyed the Town House in those years, and he believed that women were rarely a true majority there.[68] Bartenders at the time, including Kelly Jewell, agreed that women were a majority *only* on Wednesdays—"cheapy night" also known as "ladies' night."[69] The fact that the Town House could be considered by men and women alike as "the women's bar" even if it lacked a female majority attests to the relative absence of women in gay bars in general prior to 1970 and to the constantly growing presence of women in the Town House after that time. Equally important, as a commercial site of activism on behalf of queer women, the Town House functioned as a meeting ground for diverse women across class, gender expression, political identity, and generation.

During the 1960s in Minneapolis, queer women did not constitute themselves as a market. Venues like Sutton's used white women to uphold (white) gay male respectability through escort and gender codes that constricted women's sexual autonomy and gender expression. Warehouse parties, on the other hand, welcomed and brought together large numbers of predominantly white women drawn from a variety of social circles and networks. That alternative space helped cohere queer women as a diverse community in the interest of nonsexist, lesbian-friendly, gender-affirming, commercialized leisure space. Then, through public protest, civil disobedience, and even enlisting the city of St. Paul in human rights claims, women bolstered the identity of the Town House as *the* women's bar. In the process, they further constituted themselves as activists—women who did not identify as feminists and women who did—collectively schooled in some useful arts of citizenship within the public landscape.

Monday Night Meetings in Chicago

While women in Detroit, Minneapolis, and St. Paul claimed nighttime leisure space through actions that seemed feminist at the time or in retrospect, some women in Chicago turned bars into feminist organizing spaces. At the close of the 1960s, diverse women converged around Monday Night Meetings in which feminist-leaning lesbian liberation efforts emerged. Meetings consisted in fact of two parts: the first part, consisting of rapping and organizing, was always held at the apartment of a participant, and people took turns hosting; the gathering then adjourned to a gay bar to finish the evening dancing and partying in a larger public context. Among other things, the multiracial meetings inspired women to organize as feminist consumer activists to change commercial venues. But—as in Detroit and the Twin Cities—bars were places that constructed race and class status. By 1973, women's efforts to influence bars and bar patronage had helped constitute the "feminist" and "liberated lesbian" as a white, North Side subject even though women of color were equally involved in expanding and making claims on the public landscape. Those constructions had a lasting impact on the appearance and definition of feminism in Chicago.

Monday Night Meetings originated with lesbian and feminist hopes of changing a homophobic landscape that prevailed throughout the 1960s. In that decade, when white women had patronized Chicago gay bars serving a predominantly white clientele, they resisted police raids, bailed each other out in the event of arrests, and defended themselves and "their" bars against extralegal attacks.[70] As Ra explained, "Cars would come in from the suburbs and all these people would get out and slam into the place. . . . You had to be prepared for that. . . . You were there maybe five nights a week, and you weren't going to give that up. That was *our* place, it was *ours*, and the harassment was not the owner's problem."[71] Meanwhile, on the legal terrain, Section 192-8 of the Municipal Code of Chicago stated, "Any person who shall appear in a public place in a dress not belonging to his or her sex, with intent to conceal his or her sex, shall be fined."[72] As one former bar owner put it, "They got you on impersonation, the oldest law in the books. You carry a badge, you're impersonating a cop. You wear fly-front pants, you're impersonating a boy."[73] However, the code was hardly the oldest law in the books: Chicago passed this ordinance first in 1964 to give police a legal basis for arresting patrons of gay bars.[74] In 1978, the city reasserted that the ordinance protected public interest by "maintaining the integrity of the two sexes" and by prohibiting "displays of offensive homosexual conduct."[75]

In practice, the enforcement of Code 192-8 cast women as gender and sexual outlaws. As Lori, a butch woman born in 1927, recalled, "Oh, you could wear pants, but only if the zipper was in the back, because those were women's pants."[76] Although gay bars were not illegal, zipper placement became the obsessive basis on which police arrested women for homosocially occupying commercial space at night. Marge Summit frequented many gay bars during the 1960s and explained, "That was a real strict thing in Chicago: fly fronts. At the [bars], when somebody yelled 'Raid!' and they had like eight paddy wagons lined up, you went in the back and you changed your shoes and turned your pants around because they'd check: they'd stand there with the flashlight *on* your crotch, fly-fronts, fly-fronts, fly-fronts. And then they'd take you downtown and put you with the prostitutes."[77] Ritualized exposure of women's crotches, combined with arrests, construed women who went to bars at night as sex/gender criminals. It was also profitable for the police who balanced raids with lucrative payoffs: according to a federal grand jury investigation of police corruption in Chicago, forty-seven police from the eighteenth police district were found guilty of extortion from fifty-three gay bars—virtually every gay bar on the near North Side—between 1966 and 1970.[78]

In search of queer leisure spaces, white women from all over the Chicago area drove past the South Side to "wide open" Calumet City on the state line. Long referred to as "sin city," Cal City was born as a watering hole when Indiana—pre-Prohibition—was dry.[79] Al Capone had a house there, and queers had nightclubs. There, lesbian bars thrived in the 1960s, especially during election seasons, when police raids on Chicago bars increased.[80] Home to small bars such as the quiet Club 307 and to dance clubs such as the Music Box and the enormous Velvet Heart, Cal City allowed women to wear fly-front pants without fear of the zipper check.[81] But even with its relaxed vice laws, Cal City posed other barriers. Between 1960 and 1980, the residential population ranged from 25,000 to 33,000 people, but never included more than 72 nonwhite residents, and never more than 35 African American residents.[82] Thus, the city's "wide open" status was greatly compromised by the extent to which citizenship depended on whiteness, and that held true in the spaces of gay bars as well.[83]

As in Detroit, black women in Chicago had long creatively shaped house parties to build cultural priorities apart from the racist and homophobic exclusions of other spaces.[84] In the late 1960s, two new black lesbian clubs on the South Side appealed to women's desire for public commercial venues. These bars, too, posed gender expectations. Vernita Gray explained, "[They] were heavy duty role bars. There was a bar on Cottage Grove called the Mark IV . . . that was like studs and ladies. Studs and ladies was the thing. So you had to be in either role. . . . We used to walk to the Mark. But you had to be into your roles at the Mark: you couldn't be out of your role. If you were there with your lady, if you were a stud, I couldn't come over and talk to your lady. . . . Okay! *These* are the *rules!*"[85] These clubs protected themselves from homophobic intrusion by keeping doors closed. The Ebony Room required patrons to knock at the door, and the doorkeeper admitted only women who marked themselves as lesbians by wearing "a stud outfit" or being a lady with a stud. While women had to look like studs and ladies to get into clubs, they also braved public censure for that same appearance. As Vernita Gray recalled, "We would be harassed sometimes on the streets by men calling us dykes, bulldaggers, he-shes, and stuff like that."[86] Gray and her friends abided by the gender codes required at these bars, but they also sought commercial spaces where "roles" did not hold sway.

Differential geographic police harassment and publicity of gay bars contributed to the racialization of women's homosocial occupation of the nighttime marketplace. Police practiced the zipper check at predominantly white bars on the near North Side but ignored South Side black clubs. South-Side aldermen saw to it that police minimized harassment of queer black social clubs.[87] In fact, police stayed away even when assistance was sought. Black and white media similarly avoided coverage of black queer events and homophobic violence.[88] At the same time, the *Chicago Tribune, Sun Times*, and *Daily News* regularly solicited the near North eighteenth police ward for information about raids and arrests of patrons at white gay bars on the North and West Sides and turned them into front-page news.[89] By ignoring homosexual congregation in black neighborhoods, and by making a spectacle of discipline in white neighborhoods,

Chicago police and media constructed gays and lesbians as white and punishable for their deviance.[90]

At the close of the 1960s, many women's desires for lesbian community and increased access to nighttime commercial venues coalesced in the form of Monday Night Meetings. Born in Hyde Park, initially Monday Night Meetings were simply a multiracial gathering of ten or so women rapping about lesbian liberation and feminism. Within a few months, meetings grew to thirty, then sixty, and soon a hundred women had joined in. Though many of these women frequently expressed the wish for "an alternative to the bars," most also wanted to go out to dance and, as cofounder Michelle (aka Michal) Brody explained, "Lesbian bars were still the closest thing to a cultural home base that we had."[91] The popularity of Monday Night Meetings was very much due to the fact that meetings began the evening in someone's apartment and continued as meetings at bars. As exciting as it was for lesbians to rap and organize in private, it was equally exciting to collectively renovate the "cultural home" of bars and stake new claims on the nighttime world of commercialized leisure.

Half of the founders of Monday Night Meetings were African American women who lived in Hyde Park or South Side neighborhoods and who were increasingly involved in gay/lesbian liberation and black feminist activism. Vernita Gray was nineteen and living in Hyde Park in the summer of 1969. She had just returned from the Woodstock festival, where she first heard of gay and lesbian liberation, when her white friends Michelle Brody and Henry Weimhoff became apartment-mates and founded Chicago's first direct action gay liberation group, Chicago Gay Liberation (which soon became the Chicago Gay Alliance, CGA).[92] Almost immediately, Gray— along with Brody, E. Kitch Childs, Margaret E. Sloan, and other women— formed the multiracial Women's Caucus of the CGA.[93] Before long, the Women's Caucus declared itself independent of the CGA, feeling that the larger organization was uncommitted to issues of gender and race within gay liberation; eventually, the Caucus became Chicago Lesbian Liberation (CLL).[94] During its first year, the Women's Caucus drew an ever new pool of women from the North and South Sides. Over time (and for reasons discussed shortly), meetings drew an increasing percentage of white new-comers and a decreasing percentage of women of color. In this first year, however, it retained its multiracial quality. Few thought of the Caucus as an organization, but instead as a more enthusiastic, sometimes spontaneous "set of events": women raised consciousness, set goals and agendas, founded and produced *Lavender Woman* newspaper, and engaged in actions. Significantly, most knew the "group" not by an organizational name but rather by the name "Monday Night Meetings."

Predicated on the desire to more collectively and more explicitly demand women's rights in the world, Monday Night Meetings continued to build on the importance of claiming nighttime commercial space, initially focusing on King's Ransom bar. King's Ransom was "small" and "dank," and yet women chose it over at least twenty other gay bars. It was centrally located in an area that maintained less rigid racial boundaries than many North or South Side neighborhoods. Though the bar served a predominantly white clientele, it contrasted with North Side bars that routinely harassed women of color. As Gray recalled of King's Ransom, "We girls would go there and dance our little hearts out on Monday night."[95] By virtue of their organized presence, women in Monday Night Meetings turned Monday nights at King's Ransom into ladies' night. Indeed, because Monday was formerly known as "slow night," women had the owner's blessings when they packed it wall to wall; there, they were even allowed to dance together.[96] Monday Night Meetings with their King's Ransom component promised new community and also a new lesbian landscape to women of color and white women alike.

Because King's Ransom was relatively comfortable for the diverse women who comprised Monday Night Meetings, the bar spared them the necessity of discussing other possible bars for postmeeting socializing. But embedded in the choice of King's Ransom was the unspoken rejection of established "dyke bars." As Brody explained, "We made occasional trips as a group to local dyke bars, but we weren't real welcome there, either. We were a mixed race group, we were hippies, we were young. None of these things went over too well in the white lesbian bars."[97] The Other You (Jo-Jo's), on West 21st and Washtenaw not far from the county jail, was one such bar. However, some women who participated in Monday Night Meetings did find Jo-Jo's to be welcoming and politically relevant. Ra, an underage South Sider, recalled, "You'd be sitting at [Jo-Jo's], and there might be a college professor, and an insurance agent, and a manager, and a prostitute, and me snuck in from the South Side, and you'd be having conversations. These were very much conversations among peers, about the issues of the day. Gay rights was one of them."[98] She granted that the bar seemed part of "an underworld," and she surmised, "I never heard of even the North Side liberated lesbians knowing anything about it."[99] Although women came from a variety of cultural locations to Monday Night Meetings, not all cultural locations suited the Women's Caucus and its emerging white lesbian political persuasion. By their own admission, many women did not know how to integrate themselves into dyke bars that maintained a strong insider culture and racial exclusivity.[100]

If many white women in Monday Night Meetings found (white) dyke bars to be inscrutable, neither did they consider going to South Side black clubs. Even in the first year or two when feminist and lesbian activism centered in the South Side and many caucus members still lived there, Monday Night Meetings never adjourned to nearby black bars. As one member confessed, "We never tried to go to the black lesbian bars, even though those were the closest to our neighborhood. As a group of mostly white women, we may have been motivated some by respect for black separatism . . . but I suspect we were mostly motivated by fear. We didn't talk about it."[101] While participants considered but chose against "dyke bars" like Jo-Jo's and the Lost and Found, black bars—like the Ebony Room and Mark IV—never made it onto the map at all. Despite its South Side birthplace and its diverse membership that included African American and white, working-class and South Side–identified women, Monday Night Meetings increasingly came to look like a white, "North Side liberated lesbian" organization in part through its consideration of bars.

In truth, the barriers were not limited to white women's fear of black bars, but included numerous factors in a rapidly changing social landscape. Movement-building interests took African American women like Gray, Childs, Sloan, Pat McCombs, and other black women to new venues where "roles" did not hold sway: as Gray put it, "As gay libbers, we stepped outside that, because we weren't as much role-oriented. We were just like happy gay lesbians." Many continued to visit black lesbian bars apart from Monday Night Meetings, but did so adhering to required cultural codes. Most white women in the Caucus were unfamiliar with the gender and sexual etiquette expected in black lesbian bars; at least one of Gray's white friends found herself literally chased out of the Mark IV when she began flirting with a stud's lady.[102] Moreover, many white lesbians were collectively building a movement in part through the formation of gender/sex subjectivities that explicitly rejected the very styles that many African American women wore proudly. And yet they chose not to talk to each other about it. Instead, they chose a bar for Monday Night Meetings that allowed women to skirt the distinctions between dyke, lady, stud, and emerging feminist lesbian subcultures. Meetings thereby represented a negotiation of the ways in which *place* contributed to race, class, gender, and sexuality, even as they attempted to forge a more unified lesbian presence in the public world.

The nighttime marketplace and movements proliferated together, and as they did, it became increasingly clear that the politics of place and gender expression contributed to the racial stratifications within feminism and lesbian liberation. Jackie Anderson, a black activist and philosopher, recalled her experience in Chicago, noting, "You couldn't be a white feminist and be *fem*. Feminists were so concerned with their looks, to cut their hair, to not wear feminine clothing, to not dress up, and to create styles against the sexism that *they* experienced as *white* women." That particular concern with looks and the conflation of sexist objectification with femininity was rooted in whiteness. In contrast, according to Anderson, "For a black woman to dress up was not a betrayal of our movement. It's about feeling good. To get dressed up to go out on a Saturday night was good, and empowering. Because Monday morning she was going to have to get up, go to work, and go back to being black trash. Dirt. That's how she would be objectified by white people."[103] Public geographies were organized a great deal around "looks": people's mobility in the marketplace had much to do with gender expression and racial appearance. As white feminists sought to increase their mobility in the public world, they did so in part by politicizing gender expression in ways that made it difficult for them to recognize studs and ladies in black bars (or butches and fems in "dyke bars") as feminists. They responded to but did not challenge the ways that gender and sexuality inhered class and race in the constitution of public space. They thus stood on whiteness as a privileged vantage point from which to evaluate the politics of gender expression and place. Simultaneously, they defined feminist sensibility.

Though meetings at the centrally located King's Ransom offered a minimally compromising option for the bar part of Monday Night Meetings, unequal access to the privatized neighborhood spaces of women's homes where meetings began created conflict. Initially, meetings at women's homes alternated between the North Side and the South Side. This was short-lived, however, because, according to Brody, "It was assumed that dark women were expected to travel to meetings in hostile white neighborhoods, while many white women objected to attending meetings at homes in black neighborhoods where they felt unsafe."[104] Conflict over meeting space roiled for months until, in late 1971, Margaret E. Sloan decisively secured the Lincoln Park Presbyterian Church on West Fullerton for Meetings. That North Side area was then still home to poor Appalachians, Puerto Ricans, Chicano/as, Asians, and blacks as well as middle-class whites and was a central hub of activity for both the Wobblies and the Young Lords. Moreover, Hyde Park had become expensive and many feminist and lesbian activists—Vernita Gray among them— were moving to the more affordable North Side neighborhoods. The new meeting location was not hostile to women of color, but neither did it ask white women to change, and the number of new members coming from the South Side decreased sharply.[105] Coinciding with the move, the formerly loosely membered Monday Night Meetings came to be known by the organizational name Chicago Lesbian Liberation (CLL). With a fixed location and increasing bar options, Monday Night Meetings began to turn into a "North Side liberated lesbian" organization.

CLL participated in a larger cultural expansion that exacerbated conflicts over space and the racial identity of Monday Night Meetings. As gay- and lesbian-owned bars sprang up on the North Side around a new lesbian clientele, King's Ransom lost its edge with many participants in CLL. In September 1972, CLL News declared, "The bar scene is pretty well settled on Monday nights with most of our women going to the UP NORTH bar, 6244 N. Western; however, some of the women can be found at the King's Ransom, at Chicago and State, so take your pick."[106] In an all-white neighborhood on the very far North Side, the Up North wasn't a "pick" for all. North-side bars notoriously required women of color to show "fifty IDs" at the door. According to Gray, "If I went to a north-side bar, I had this: my driver's license. But that's not enough: 'You need your Social Security card, you need your communion card—ha ha ha—you have a passport?' "[107] Despite the concerns of women of color, CLL News promoted the Up North as the most hospitable bar in town and the place for Monday night socializing.[108] Between 1969 and 1972, Monday Night Meetings had helped make bars a particular "cultural home" for emerging feminist lesbians, encouraging diverse women to stake a claim in the nighttime marketplace and extend it to all nights of the week. Simultaneously, they contributed to the development of a new lesbian bar culture shaped around racial segregation and gender hierarchy.

By 1972, with more bar choices on the North Side, women began to use feminist lesbian publishing to influence women's patronage of bars and to overtly pressure bars to serve women better. As they did so, they advertised a nexus of sentiments about gender, place, and liberation. For example, Loretta Mears, an African American woman who at the time was a graduate student at Northwestern University, railed against Chez Ron's bar and the gender expression she saw within. Her letter published in *Lavender Woman* declared, "I am hurting because I stood in an oppressive, rip-off bar and watched as my sisters came in wearing men's suits and shoes and men's haircuts and with what they hope is a man's identity. I stood there helpless, screaming inside with frustration and anger because I couldn't offer them a better alternative than Chez Ron and a 'fem' on Saturday night."[109] Liberation, it seemed, required establishing new places that invited women to shed their "drag." Claiming new influence in the marketplace, many women mapped gender expression and social status onto a time/space trajectory: they contrasted "old-world dykes" and "old-school lesbians" with "young political lesbians." Worlds, schools, and youth played themselves out in the places of bars: Chez Ron's and the long-standing dyke bar, the Lost and Found, were "old school"; "young political lesbians" belonged elsewhere and publicly demanded alternatives.[110] In the growing North Side marketplace, women charted their progress toward liberation in part through acts of spatial distinction and social segregation.

Monday Night Meetings—now as CLL—generated a sense of political purpose in part through a well-circulated survey of sixteen north-side bars in November of 1972. The survey solicited bar-goers to rank bars according to a variety of factors ("music," "prices," "space," "friendliness of owners," etc.). CLL published the results in *Lavender Woman* with great intent: "Hopefully these surveys do serve . . . the Chicago lesbian community in helping to end our oppression in the only institutionalized gathering places now available to us. Hopefully, also, the gay bar owners will pay attention to these surveys and make the changes that seem appropriate."[111] Such scrutiny helped bury Chez Ron's, a lesbian bar that opened in 1971 on Lincoln Avenue. For months, women had referred to it as "raunchy" and publicized the "macho, rude, and oppressive manner" of the male bartenders; they complained of being hassled when dancing together, and they called for boycotts. With satisfaction, they published Chez Ron's Obituary in January, 1973: "It *can* be said that this bar rated lowest in almost every area on the now infamous CLL Bar Survey . . . thanks to lesbian power—the bar was forced 'under' by the addition of new and better social gathering spots."[112] In many respects, the survey offered the first public articulation of lesbians as politicized consumers in the night-time marketplace.

As more women went out to more bars all nights of the week, Monday Night Meetings became less important in their function as bar outings, and attendance dwindled. Monday Night Meetings increasingly focused on CLL planning and producing CLL News and *Lavender Woman*, and they began to lose touch with the full range of Chicago's bar-going constituents.[113] Some who had been there at the vibrant, South Side birth of *Lavender Woman* felt that Monday Night Meetings and the paper "died" on the North Side.[114] In this more insular context, when women publicized their rejection of sexist or "old-style" venues and created "new and better gathering spots," they articulated—in print and action—the gender, race, and class hierarchies shaping the spaces of bars.

This became particularly apparent when two lesbian bars opened within months of each other. In August 1973, Marge Summit opened the MS Lounge, the first lesbian-owned lesbian disco in Chicago, on the north end of downtown. With a white DJ and a black DJ (together named Salt 'n' Pepper), word of MS "spread like wildfire" through the North and South Sides.[115] Vernita Gray "used to party like a champ there"; she loved the "very large bar with an even larger dance floor!" Unique among Chicago lesbian bars, MS initially drew white and African American women in roughly equal numbers. The first mention of MS in CLL *Newsletter*, however, criticized the bar for falsely advertising drink prices and requiring multiple IDs. Erroneously charging that MS "is femininely named, but not owned by women," the article continued, "We as gay women are harassed by men in the world, and after work might want to go to a women's bar to relax. But where to go?"[116] At that moment, Carol Kappa opened CK's on the North Side, and Marge Summit watched as MS's white clientele went there in droves.[117] Summit assumed that her black clientele lived on the South Side and patronized MS because "they didn't have nothing except maybe one bar, and what happens in *those* neighborhoods, guys would come in and hassle the shit out of 'em."[118] In fact, many black women who patronized MS lived on the *North* Side, and what happened in *those* neighborhoods is that racist hostility excluded black and antiracist women from commercialized lesbian space. For months, both CLL *Newsletter* and *Lavender Woman* remained silent on the issue.

Troubled by racist discrimination at bars in the summer of 1974, a handful of black lesbians and white lesbians formed a group to "integrate the bars."[119] More truly a testing mission of North Side bars, the group found that racist exclusion at CK's was among the worst.[120] When mixed-race and all-black groups stood their ground, bouncers produced spectacles of racism that outraged many patrons.[121] Witnesses demonstrated outside CK's, and attorney Renee Hanover sought a license suspension against the bar.[122] Some white women refused to patronize CK's unless the racist policies changed, but six months went by before the lesbian presses reported the ongoing issue, and none suggested an activist response. Loretta Mears broke the print silence. Her commentary, published in *Lavender Woman*, charged, "This issue was a meaningless one for most of the lesbian community.... Many women in the community who knew of the discrimination against their sisters saw fit to patronize CKs.... Several women even stated, implicitly acknowledging their racism (theirs and CKs), 'I guarantee you'll get in if you go with me.'" Mears leveled an equal complaint against *Lavender Woman*: the newspaper, she felt, had become "representative of the white lesbian community."[123] Just as many white feminists did not recognize women in South Side black bars as feminists, "the white lesbian community" began to seem commensurate with racist exclusions at North Side bars. Simultaneously, it became harder to recognize black and white antiracist activists as part of that community. The newspapers that sprung from Monday Night Meetings used differential coverage of Chicago bars ostensibly to increase women's access to the nighttime marketplace, but in the process, they participated in publicizing lesbian bars and liberated lesbians as North Side, middle-class, and white.[124]

Once Monday Night Meetings ceased to revolve around expansive, multiracial gatherings of women, the centers of lesbian publishing lost access to all the various ways that liberation-oriented African American women had "started creating some of our own things" in the early 1970s. Alongside bar-related activism, for example, Pat McCombs hosted womanist house parties, called "sets" by those who participated in them. According to Gray, sets established "the party scene for African American lesbians that we know to this day."[125] During the same years, what started as a lesbian Gay Pride picnic turned into the Belmont Rocks party associated with Chicago's annual Gay Pride celebration. In 1972, rather than going to the downtown Gay Pride march, Gray explained, "We *lesbians* said we're going to the Belmont rocks [on Lake Michigan] and have a barbecue, barbecue and potluck, that's what we lesbians are going to do—

surprise, surprise! We're going to cook, bring our boom boxes out, and just lay out and have our Gay Pride right here at the lake." Having begun with a feminist inclination, the picnic grew over the next several years to include men and even family members of African American queers. Gray is thus quick to remind anyone who considers Gay Pride a "white" event that people of color have been in Gay Pride all along; furthermore, black queers now have the second largest black gathering in Chicago.[126] "This," she says, "is the thing I love about life and living life: what started as a lesbian potluck is now 18–20,000 African Americans."[127] The womanist nighttime sets and the more public daytime picnics side-stepped the "heavy-duty roles" of black bars *and* the racist exclusions of most north-side bars. They had their roots in part in the early years of Monday Night Meetings predicated on the drive of black and white women to stake an ever-larger, community-based claim on the public landscape.

Detroit, Minneapolis, St. Paul, and Chicago all have different histories of bars and women's attempts to expand their options in the nighttime marketplace. However, by looking at these different processes, two things become clear. First, lesbians—studs, fems, butches, ladies, gay and passing women, and emerging feminist lesbians—created both alternative *and* public options in their quest for expansion of community space. Far from abandoning bars, they sought to change them and by the 1970s began to create new ones; in all three urban areas, nighttime commercialized leisure spaces for lesbians across race, class, gender expression, and political inclination proliferated. Second, some of these actions and actors carried the label feminist, and others did not. But by the 1970s, all took place within a context in which collective activism—through consciousness raising, feminism, gay liberation, and direct action demands on bars and on governments—seemed a reasonable way to intervene in the public landscape. Moreover, in the context of feminism, intervening in the public landscape seemed necessary. In many cases—within CLL, for example—women's needs for space as lesbians and their needs for space as feminists could not be separated. Seen in aggregate, these actions are part of feminism's story, its emergence, contours, and parameters.

This chapter's focus on bars contributes a missing historical analysis to feminist and queer theories of public space and sexuality. Queer theorists, including Lauren Berlant and Michael Warner, have argued that queer practices do not just theoretically or occasionally interrupt the normative public sphere; instead, they create within that sphere a long-term critique of it. Feminist theorists, too, have argued for new ways to see women's interventions in a public sphere otherwise liberally defined by white, middle-class, male subjects. Historical analysis of on-the-ground contestations shows the ways that women learned to act as an interested, non-normative group and thereby reshape the possibilities of the public landscape. Feminist activism, and even prevailing definitions of feminism, were constituted precisely through such processes, including the privileged ability of white women to announce their desires through the property of public spaces. In the same years, some feminist-identified women also set out to make a less capitalist public world. They created an overtly feminist-identified marketplace of bookstores and cafés to provide "for people, not for profit." Those alternative venues are the subject of the next chapter.

Two

"Don't Steal It, Read It Here"

Building Community in the Marketplace

Amazon Bookstore: A Feminist Bookstore. Come In and Browse. Books, Journals, Literature, Posters, Buttons, Newspapers. Hours: Monday 3–9pm Tuesday 3–6pm Wednesday 11am–4pm. 2418 26th Ave So. Tel. 729-6564. New Books and New Issues of Newspapers and Journals Arrive Periodically.—*Female Liberation*, no. 25 (March 1971), Minneapolis

The Women's Center [Pride and Prejudice Books] at 3322 N. Halsted has a large selection of feminist books, arts and crafts by women, posters, etc. They also do pregnancy testing, abortion counseling, and birth control information. If you are interested in helping in any way, call 935-4270 or drop in.—*Lavender Woman*, March 1973, Chicago

[Susan B's is] an easy-going, homey restaurant with a feminist orientation. Brief, inexpensive menu concentrating on soups (one vegetarian) are offered each evening. Coupled with a loaf of homemade bread, the meal goes for $2. . . . Tiny, comfortable, and casual.—*Chicago Magazine*, July 1975

[Poor Woman's Paradise] coffee house features entertainment by women artists in an atmosphere where women's talent and culture is cultivated and appreciated; serving coffee and herbal teas, and healthful snacks and desserts. Cover Charge is $2.00 (or $1.50 if you become a sustaining member by paying a yearly membership of 10.00).—*Moving Out* 4.2 (1974), Detroit

A glance at most feminist-identified businesses in the early 1970s— bookstores and cafés most prominent among them—reveals that their founders' primary motivation was a desire to build and foster community through provision of a new community space. Many also put into practice their deeply held belief that books, ideas, and food should be for people, not for profit. Few of these founders wanted to be businesspersons above all, but most did think that the existence of feminist commercial venues would benefit women, improve their status in the public world, and even change the marketplace itself. What happened when activists created commercial spaces with intentional (even if vague) political purpose? How did activists use the marketplace and market relations even as they critiqued commercialism? Often, the spaces they created intervened in the economy of conventional commercial terrain by providing alternative commerce and community that exceeded their founders' initial political visions. Far from simply spelling the commercialization of social movements, the marketplace sometimes fostered social action and expanded the scope of movement ideals. Overtly feminist commercial spaces interacted with surrounding neighborhoods and participated in changing urban demographics. They also influenced the movement of people across social and geographic landscapes. Analysis of these dynamics between 1969 and 1975 reveals that some kinds of commercial spaces played a dramatic role in building a culture of activism, constituting a movement, and defining its parameters.

This chapter explores the ways that four commercial venues took shape and shaped feminist community and the marketplace. The two earliest that I look at here, Amazon Bookstore in Minneapolis and Pride and Prejudice Books in Chicago, began in communes rather than in purely market-driven spaces. Amazon Bookstore opened on the porch of a commune near the University of Minnesota in 1970, first moved to a storefront in 1974, began turning sustaining profits by 1975, and exists today as the oldest feminist bookstore in North America. Pride and Prejudice opened as a living collective and feminist and used bookstore in a predominantly Latino neighborhood in 1969. While not profitably run as a bookstore, it organically morphed into the Women's Center, a port for coalitional activism. In 1973, as its original founders moved on, a group of women moved the Women's Center sign to a storefront two blocks north—a space that they more covertly called the Lesbian Feminist Center.

In the very years that Amazon became solvent and Pride and Prejudice dissolved, both Susan B's restaurant in Chicago and the Poor Woman's Paradise coffeehouse in Detroit opened as definitively commercial venues. Susan B's opened in late 1973 with little money and much volunteer labor. Wildly popular, local critics reviewed Susan B's until she had lines around the block and could no longer serve an intended community. The restaurant closed in June 1975, fully flush. In Detroit, a collective of eight women spent $1,900 to open Poor Woman's Paradise in March 1974, a café modeled on "the 1960s, early '70s kind of folk coffeehouse" but with a feminist bent. Unable to earn enough rent to pay for its three storefronts, the coffeehouse closed in June 1975, $3,900 in debt.

Alternative community spaces sprang up everywhere in the United States during the 1960s and early 1970s. Whether urban or "back to the land," they proposed alternatives to capitalist economies and social structures through communal living and collective decision making, barter systems, and more equitable distribution of resources. Most individual communes and cooperatives were short-lived, but together they played a central role in a groundswell of do-it-yourself activism manifesting in theater and radio collectives, open universities and schools, food co-ops, service-oriented collectives, and feminist bookstores, among other things.[1] As the activist Cheri Register explained, even those not living in communes valued open doors and rejected the privatization of the capitalist nuclear family: "It was the way people were living. There were more communes, and even the way I was living with my husband . . . we bought a house and people moved in and out of it. . . . There was this flux of people through our house and this sense of privacy was a lot different."[2] Challenging the dominant ideology that domestic space should be private and separate from the marketplace, communal spaces nurtured alternative social organization and commerce. Indeed, for many people, an emphasis on alternative, nonprofit exchanges—of ideas, news, a place to crash for a night or a month, and services as disparate as pregnancy testing and silk screening—helped legitimate commercial exchanges of products.

The chapter begins with Amazon to show how women created places to support the early distribution of feminist print media. While print media disseminated feminist ideas widely, it was the localized places of their dissemination that produced movement communities. On that foundation, the story of Pride and Prejudice is at once more intimate and deeply rooted in larger social geographies. Both Amazon and Pride and Prejudice used and radicalized conventional market relations as they became centers of sociality and brought a movement into being. From these early community-commercial spaces, the chapter turns to two commercial spaces predicated on the perceived existence of an already-established feminist market. But a movement-identified population did not in itself constitute a reliable consumer base. As Susan B's indicates, commercial spaces lent themselves to complex dynamics around ownership and the boundaries of the movement. In turn, Poor Woman's Paradise highlights the relationship between feminist commercial spaces and the layers of social and structural geographies upon which they were built to show how such embedded contexts often took women's movement in unanticipated directions. Together, they show that feminism coalesced in spaces shaped by local geographies, spaces that "were like a port, for everything that was going on."[3]

The core of the chapter, Pride and Prejudice Books, was a space emblematic of its time, and yet it tells a story rarely told about how unplanned and ephemeral action influenced feminist formations. As a market venture, Pride and Prejudice failed; only a handful of people remember it as Chicago's first feminist bookstore.[4] As an activist community space, it refused static identity; it lasted altogether less than four years and posted just a scattering of notices in alternative newspapers. Although almost lost to feminist archives, Pride and Prejudice did leave other traces. If you ask: where did women on the North Side go for pregnancy testing? Where did this feminist painting come from? What about this flyer advertising Chicago's first lesbian band and all-women dance? Who ran the mimeographs of *Roscoe Street Blues,* the newsletter of La Gente (a coalition of former street gangs turned community organizers)? Where did the boys in the Latin Eagles gang earn the change they needed to go swimming at the Hull House pool? If you ask these questions, you will find Pride and Prejudice. Some call it the Women's Center, and many say, "I don't think I ever bought a book, but there was always a lot going on there."[5] Forgotten in business histories, Pride and Prejudice was just the sort of store that constituted feminism as a spatial practice and mass social movement.

This chapter's narrative form highlights the relationships between people's personal decisions and larger social geographies; it simultaneously shows how politicized commercial spaces popularized feminist activism. By focusing more intimately on the particularities that shaped four spaces in three cities, it is possible to see the texture and the broad patterns of a widespread culture of women's movement. Each of these spaces helped build the movement while also revealing that the definition and parameters of "the movement" have always been contested.

Amazon Bookstore

Amazon Bookstore, opening in Minneapolis in October 1970, is now the oldest feminist bookstore in the country and one of the most successful by any measure.[6] It provided the model for countless feminist bookstores across the nation and even for the bookstore in Alison Bechdel's nationally syndicated comic strip *Dykes to Watch Out For*.[7] Proudly known by its patrons (since the mid-1990s) as "Amazon *NOT* com," it did not begin in or as a market-driven venue. Initially no more than a small collection of cardboard boxes containing books about women, Amazon Bookstore emerged from the confluence of commune-centered, leftist activist networks and two women's desire to centralize information for a burgeoning women's movement. With $200 and supportive housemates, Julie Morse and Rosina Richter started Amazon operations from the front porch of the well-known Brown House commune in which they lived, less than a mile south of the University of Minnesota in the Seward neighborhood. As Cheri Register recalled, "The Brown House was this commune on 26th Ave. and 2400. I still remember the phone number thirty years later. [Two women] started the Amazon Bookstore in the Brown House, but the Brown House was this commune of people mainly involved with draft resistance, and that was the headquarters for everything. If you wanted to find out what was going on, you called 729-6564."[8] A housemate, Don Olson, whose primary attention went to draft resistance and the budding food co-op movement, greeted Amazon's first customer, ushered her to the cardboard boxes, and helped her leave money for a book because the bookstore owners weren't home.[9] Amazon thus entered the marketplace via radical politics shaped by the birth of feminist publishing and a politically diverse commune space; it took four years for it to become a profitable business. Though the bookstore became more conventional from a business perspective and over time grew to serve an increasingly broad clientele, its owners, workers, and customers continued to use it for the distribution and support of feminist and lesbian activism locally, nationally, and internationally.

Amazon's beginnings are part of a national story of the early publication, distribution, and selling of new feminist books and newsletters. From 1967 to 1974, most book exchange happened out of cardboard boxes and backpacks that women hauled and traded around the country, forming new feminist networks in the process. Amazon's initial stock included feminist newspapers and pamphlets from Minot, North Dakota, as well as Los Angeles, from Iowa City as well as Washington, and from Denver as well as San Francisco. Women's demand for feminist conversation and print media in fact far outpaced the rapid growth of feminist bookstores in the early 1970s; commonly, boxes in porches or garages served as the places from which women distributed the materials and activist knowledge that they passed from city to city.[10] Lacking cash capital, women published and distributed print media through what scholar Jaime Grant called "genius capital"; they also depended on volunteer and unpaid labor.[11] As materials traveled from place to place via interstate freeways and regional highways, often they landed in domestic, communally occupied places that—because they traded in movement resources—functioned as centers that brought fluid communities into being.

Richter and Morse had contradictory hopes for Amazon and the movement: on one hand, they wanted to offer women-centered media that would invite masses of women, "including suburban women," to women's liberation; on the other hand, they wanted to direct the movement away from the New Left and away from socialist ideology.[12] As part of the Twin Cities' Female Liberation Group (FLG), Richter and Morse were among the founders of the local *Female Liberation Newsletter*, which began publication in 1969, just as other women were forming the decidedly socialist Twin Cities Women's Union (TCWU).[13] Richter's first *Female Liberation* article argued that the proliferation of women's liberation organizations in the Twin Cities, though exciting, created communication gaps. She hoped *Female Liberation* would bridge those gaps by centralizing information. Richter thus desired to shape the movement into a more singular entity, even while she proposed to speak to a mass base of women. The founding of Amazon Bookstore in 1970 grew out of that same desire.

Unlike the newsletter, however, Amazon was a *place*—and a nearly public one through which a great variety of people passed. While Richter and Morse increasingly envisioned a purely woman-centered movement, the Brown House confounded their efforts toward centralized control. Housemate Nancy Lehman had helped found the socialist TCWU, and she and Don Olson and other antidraft activists served as occasional proprietors of Amazon. Register described the critical dynamics of location: "There was a strong lesbian component [to Amazon] but it was much more inclusive than that. In the beginning it was just broadly feminist and

I think [that was] because it stayed in the commune. Even though it was in a house, it wasn't privatized, due to the public nature of Brown House and similar communes at the time—that functioned as community centers and activist centers. So it was accessible." Situated in a predominantly white student and New Left enclave, Amazon drew people beyond those who read feminist newsletters, but not so much the masses of "ordinary suburban" or urban women; most patrons were women and men already involved in counterculture, leftist, and social justice work. As Register explained, "You couldn't necessarily find [Amazon] in the phone book; you had to be somewhat connected. You could find it in the alternative presses."[14] For Morse and Richter, the clientele and the operation were too random. Disenchanted, in 1972 they moved out of the Brown House, sold the entire collection of Amazon books to Cindy Hanson and Karen Browne for $400, and went on to found the separatist and highly disciplined living collective Meechee Dojo.[15]

In fall 1972, Hanson and Browne reopened the box of books that was Amazon in a less illustrious house a mile south.[16] The house was unremarkable but for the large sign out front: "Amazon Bookstore Feminist Literature." In less than six months, Hanson and Browne moved the books to Minneapolis's new Lesbian Resource Center (LRC) off Lyndale Avenue in Minneapolis.[17] For almost a year, the "few piles of books" that constituted Amazon resided in LRC's downstairs storage space, accessible only to those visiting the center. As Diane Como, who helped Browne and Hanson sell books, recalled, "If anybody wanted to go downstairs and look at something, they just had to let someone know what they were doing."[18] Finding LRC in the first place was another matter. The Wedge neighborhood—mixing predominantly white homeowners, students and youth in apartments and crash pads, and small local businesses—was familiar to people across race and class coming from most parts of the Twin Cities. LRC, however, hid on a side street behind Hum's Liquor; the hand-painted Lesbian Resource Center sign—by all accounts "beautiful"—hung on an *inside* wall to reduce intrusion by a potentially hostile public.[19] As the first gay or lesbian center to occupy a storefront in the Twin Cities, LRC did not draw civic attention. Although many of LRC's clientele soaked up feminist books as life blood, most went to the center for community and other resources. Rap groups, coffeehouse evenings, practical advice, and practical actions overshadowed Amazon's existence in the Twin Cities' vital first lesbian center.[20]

In late 1973, Hanson, Browne, Como, and Karol Carlson rented Amazon's first storefront in what they considered a "shady" neighborhood on West Lake, where customers included women seeking community and men assuming that Amazon was a front for a pornography business. Amazon moved twice in the next year, finally landing on Hennepin Avenue near Uptown, a comfortable neighborhood for the predominantly white lesbian- and feminist-identified women that Amazon owners envisioned as their core clientele.[21] In addition to Amazon's name and successive locations, the interior space at each location suggested something other than an upstanding business: there was too little room for books; the pipes dripped and the ceilings leaked; the heating was poor. As Como recalled, "You were never warm. We used space heaters and fans and whatever just to keep working and keep it open so people could come in and be with us in that ice."[22] To some potential patrons, the location and the unglamorous interior space, combined with its focus on women, spelled opportunities for purchasing illicit sex. But to many women, those same features signaled a grassroots commitment to revolutionizing women's collective participation in the public world.

At both the Lake Street and Hennepin Avenue locations, FBI surveillance was insidious, as one arm of intelligence searched the women's movement for activists who had gone underground, and the other did its best to destroy what it called "revolutionary movements."[23] At the store on Hennepin, especially, although the space was uncomfortable and the business shaky, FBI surveillance validated Amazon as a coherent activist location. Feminist groups in the Twin Cities feared destructive infiltration, but FBI surveillance of Amazon was innocuous compared to the violence that COINTELPRO waged against black nationalists and the American Indian Movement. The same women unnerved by FBI visits to their homes smirked at "the FBI guys in their trench coats and wing-tips" when in the space of Amazon.[24] There they felt themselves collectively hailed as women who could "harbor revolutionary criminals," or who might themselves resist a patriarchal, capitalist machine and fight on behalf of minorities and women; it was radical, if not ultimately revolutionary, to maintain a storefront that served women first, especially women growing a feminist- and lesbian-identified movement.

Lack of capital and spatial hardship encouraged the formation of a politicized social community—an activist niche—in Amazon. Working there was a labor of love, as collective members could not expect to earn a steady wage (or a wage at all) until 1975.[25] Sometimes Amazon had no money, and collective members used their own personal funds to order new books. Carlson and Como put the store above all else: as Como put it, "the store was important to keep going. . . . We arranged our schedules around the store. We worked night janitorial jobs so that we could keep the store open and do the things that had to be done. . . . We scrimped by."[26] With its new storefront in 1974, Amazon Bookstore became "the meeting place" for local and visiting feminist lesbians in search of others like themselves, even when it meant huddling around book boxes in sub-freezing temperatures. Women bought books and exchanged newsletters from all over the country to learn what women in other places were doing to challenge sexism and homophobia, capitalism and racism. Simultaneously, through informal communication networks, activism in the Twin Cities quickly gained a national reputation. Amazon, by virtue of its existence as a meeting place for exchange of ideas and news, supported and was supported by the concurrent emergence of local feminist theater groups, a film collective, service collectives ranging from crisis and resource centers to women's construction and music production companies, and feminist natural foods restaurants and herbalists. An equally symbiotic relationship with the University of Minnesota's budding women's studies program also extended Amazon's reach to a new clientele across town.[27]

By 1975, a market niche had developed alongside the activist niche: Amazon Bookstore began to turn profits, pay some of its employee/owners, and widely advertise merchandise as did conventional merchants. Selling books only written by women, it was a space that articulated feminist, lesbian, and separatist sensibilities. Over the next five years, through wrenching turnover and turmoil in the collective that ran Amazon, the business came to resemble a viable, capitalist venture serving a broader (but still predominantly white) customer base that included local politicians, students, teachers, and some men.[28] Yet it was different from conventional business ventures in that it had become a place that used—and still uses—conventional market relations toward the radical end of providing space for a feminist movement that it had helped define.[29]

Pride and Prejudice Books

Pride and Prejudice used-book and feminist bookstore began with only two certainties: Nick Patricca and Lucina Kathmann wanted to move out of the South Side up to the North Side, and Kathleen Thompson wanted a bookstore. That these desires took the form of a "collective or commune or whatever it was," and that this turned into a community center, seemed accidental to its inhabitants.[30] Initially, two white women and two white men bent toward philosophy and human liberation, were in on the deal.[31] Patricca put down the first month's $250 rent for a building with a storefront at street level and living space above. He described Pride and Prejudice as "a tight collective," but added, "it was never really thought out: it was happenstance." Jim Schulz built two bedrooms and a kitchen behind the bookstore, and a good bit of the store itself. He explained, "The bookstore was the focus for the public face of the thing. But it wasn't a collective in the usual sense of the term. It didn't start with a plan or project or ideology. It was a very ad hoc venture, and we stumbled on things as we went along."[32]

Accident, ad hoc, or happenstance, Pride and Prejudice grew out of a counterculture that valued communal living, exchange of ideas, self-sufficiency, and open doors. As Thompson recalled, "We had, to start with, only four of us living in the building. And I opened up the bookstore. Very quickly we started accumulating other people, and it became a feminist collective. A feminist collective that had as many men in it as women."[33] Without a detailed plan, Pride and Prejudice was open to influx and input, exchange and change. Above all, participants were willing to "stumble" as they went along, allowing Pride and Prejudice to become a place of coalescence and movement. David Hernandez, cofounder of La Gente, put it thus: "Like how Chicago has always been: Halsted Street has always been like a port for a lot of ethnic groups . . . and so forth. That was the way that Pride and Prejudice bookstore was, almost like a port, for everything that was going on. But women-run, always women. It was strong that way."[34]

Aspects of the "happenstance" that led Thompson to create Pride and Prejudice were familiar to many white, middle-class women coming of age in the late 1960s. Growing up in Oklahoma the daughter of a Methodist minister, Thompson married young and, at age twenty-one, moved to the South Side of Chicago with her husband and many misgivings about the institution of marriage. In time, one of her male co-workers at Northwestern University Press introduced her to *Notes from the Second Year*, published by New York Radical Women.[35] Thompson recalled, "And my life, of course, was transformed. So that was 1969." The feeling of sudden transformation on discovering the women's movement in print was common in those years, but also common was a subsequent period of dire searching for the movement in everyday life. Thompson continued, "I was tremendously excited, but didn't know where to go from there. I wanted to make contact with other women who were a part of this movement." Even after divorcing and moving out on her own, she was "still trying to find it and not knowing where to look."[36] She first tried a feminist-oriented party at the University of Chicago, but found herself immediately out of place, awkward with her Southern accent and big hair. Eventually she "looked in the phone book or something" and found the Chicago Women's Liberation Union. Taking the El north,

> I went to the [CWLU] place on Belmont and climbed up these stairs to the second floor and walked in. And the walls were papered with anti-imperialist posters. And I was just, what's this all about? I'm trying to find women who are part of this movement. And I'm sure I still looked a lot like a country singer. It's not that people were unfriendly. But all I could think was, "I'm pretty fearless, and I'm having a little trouble." And there are a lot of women in the world who are not fearless who are trying to connect. So I left. Again.

Wanting a more open ground, Thompson decided to start a feminist and used bookstore so that "women who were afraid of more political, more leftist, more—whatever you want to call it—would have a place to come."[37] Yet she could not foresee the ways that Pride and Prejudice bookstore would become a community center shaped by diverse people.

Within a few months, 3322 North Halsted housed Thompson's bookstore and eight to ten core men and women, along with another handful of less permanent members who "shared the rent accordingly."[38] Most members were white-identified, though at one time or another they included two African American women, two Latinas, and one Latino. The collective soon grew "the annex"—a coach house down the back alley—to house additional members, and by some accounts, "there were four or five houses in that neighborhood that were *us*."[39] The core members opposed the Vietnam War, cared little about money, and leaned toward anarchic practice to discover the parameters of women's and human liberation.[40] The project of living together in a building that was at once commune and commercial space in fact produced feminist activists.

Economic processes helped shape the community activism of the bookstore. While Thompson believed that "everyone should get to read," she was, as Schulz put it, "a terrible businessperson." The store rarely had enough capital to buy new feminist books, but thanks to neighbors, it never lacked for used books. Schulz recalled, "People would leave books for us at night. It was weird: we'd open the door in the morning and there'd be a box of books there."[41] There was little formal separation between the various functions of the space, as commune dwellers, customers, and neighbors moved in and out and at times even played interchangeable roles. Some who used the space even redesignated it by hanging a sign out front declaring, "Women's Center." However marginal the business, Thompson still asserted that it was at root a bookstore: "We didn't call it the Women's Center: it was just a bookstore. But the women who started meeting there called themselves the Women's Center."[42] That uncertain bond allowed the "women's center" to be a community center in a broader sense: although little money exchanged hands, Pride and Prejudice powerfully functioned as a public market.

Pride and Prejudice offered features that would draw activist communities together. It had a public meeting space: though technically it was a store, everyone who walked in was greeted with a cup of coffee and invited to sit in the stuffed chairs while they read or discussed the news of the day. Indeed, the only effort Thompson made to control clientele was to put up a sign that read, "Don't steal it, read it here." It also offered domestic space for people who needed a couch or a floor to crash on when in town for a demonstration. More covertly, the space offered temporary shelter for women in violent relationships. Rap groups at the store spawned long-lasting theater, dance, and writing collectives, zap actions, antirape activism, and the publication of a resource directory. Pregnancy testing there fed into referral to the underground abortion service known as "Jane." Thompson, an artist and emerging author, also used Pride and Prejudice as a gallery for local women's art. The silk-screen operation that Schulz built in the basement was available to anyone involved in movement activity, as was the mimeograph machine that David Hernandez brought in. Ideologically, it was anti-orthodox: members resisted popular leftist rhetoric, even making a tongue-in-cheek rule requiring themselves to put a quarter in the kitty whenever they uttered the word *revolution*. Thus, Pride and Prejudice became a lithe intersection, a space constituted not by a movement but by movement itself.

Pride and Prejudice developed through interaction with a rapidly changing neighborhood. Before moving from the South Side, Thompson and her friends each projected their own imagined communities onto the

North Side neighborhood. Patricca, philosopher and playwright, believed he intuited the future of the Halsted-Belmont area as a center of artistic production when he found the Pride and Prejudice building: "I had a good nose. . . . The Belmont El, it just struck me as the place to be. . . . It was well positioned and I liked it. I walked around, I felt comfortable, I didn't feel intimidated. Whatever gangs were there didn't seem to bother me. . . . I said, this is where it's going to happen. I picked the building, that's how we all got there."[43] In contrast, Schulz had his mind on leftist intellectual activism, and saw the neighborhood as a near tabula rasa before they moved in. In his words, "We were the life of the neighborhood at that time. . . . Farther down Halsted Street closer to De Paul there was more activity: the Wobblies were down there and various other labor things. . . . Up where we were, we were about all there was, and when Organic [Theater] moved in up the block, that was about all there was. . . . There were gangs, there was some trouble in the neighborhood, and that police station on the corner is famous for corruption."[44] Following Pride and Prejudice, new artistic collectives and feminist and lesbian activists settled in the neighborhood as well. With sardonic truth, Schulz explained, "We were in a colonial phase, moving in all over."[45] But in fact, whether or not the newcomers arrived with a colonial mentality, the neighborhood was anything but quiet when they arrived. In 1969, all along Halsted from Fullerton up to Roscoe and beyond, poor people and people of color were already actively organizing against racism, housing discrimination, and gentrification.[46] That activism, too, shaped Pride and Prejudice.

From the point of view of those already living in the neighborhood, the arrival of Pride and Prejudice was not merely the result of autonomous individuals' decisions, but rather a product of ongoing social trends. David Hernandez, a Puerto Rican street poet and community organizer, had seen this pattern before: since the mid-1950s when the first groups of Puerto Ricans came directly to Chicago, white artists identified Puerto Rican neighborhoods as artistically rich and financially affordable. Himself an emerging artist, Hernandez's "main influence was artists moving in [to my neighborhoods]," beginning with the beat poets who opened cafés in Old Town when Hernandez was just nine years old. "For me it was always a positive experience, because the artists that came in, they didn't isolate: they would just come and blend in. Like this painter, he would sell a piece for $1,500 and just open up the kitchen and cook for all the kids, just open it up to the whole neighborhood. It was that kind of spirit. So that was my influence into the art world. And it was the same thing in Lakeview where Pride and Prejudice bookstore moved and a lot of artists coming in." That positive experience of mobile artists was not the only force that influenced Hernandez's life, however. As a member of a community that was red-lined and discriminated against in housing and jobs, Hernandez also experienced the gentrification that time and again pushed him and his community out of the neighborhoods that they themselves had helped make vibrant.[47] The Pride and Prejudice bookstore and living collective, even as it opened its doors to Latino and Latina activists, was part of that trend as well.

Hernandez was working at the Hull House Spanish Outpost—a tiny Latino resource center—at Halsted and Roscoe, a few blocks north of Pride and Prejudice, when he met Kathleen Thompson and began to incorporate the store into the neighborhood as he knew it.[48] Among the many students of Saul Alinsky, Hernandez had become a grassroots community organizer after the police murder of a Puerto Rican youth sparked the Division Street Uprising.[49] Against discriminatory real estate practices, neighborhood coalitions engaged in actions to put pressure on local landlords and city officials. A few blocks south, the Young Lords took over Lakeview Methodist Church to start the People's Church. As Hernandez explained, "It was taken over as a statement. And we needed the space for organizing." Activists used the People's Church as a space for breakfast programs, legal aid and people's rights clinics, and growing tenants' unions. Such takeovers thus served multiple purposes, according to Hernandez. "People couldn't afford to buy. We were being red-lined, had no access to *that* bank. So we had to try other means. We also took over McCormick Theological Seminary—that's De Paul University—demanding housing because De Paul was buying a lot of land around there."[50] Against large-scale gentrification projects, Hernandez and others cultivated Pride and Prejudice as a place that would be for "the people."

To Hernandez, as to many others working from a community organizing model, "the people" depended on coalition across neighborhoods, even as neighborhood-based activism was sweeping Chicago. As Hernandez put it, "We really had the whole city: Uptown we had poor whites, Southern Appalachians, and American Indians and poor blacks. Lakeview was La Gente. Lincoln Park you had the Young Lords, and then west and south was the Black Panther Party. Also you had Rising Up Angry [in Rogers Park]. So there was a lot of organizing." Between Belmont and

Addison, Hernandez, Sally Contreras, Barbara Carrillo, and others helped ethnically based youth gangs form a coalitional community organizing group called La Gente (The People) to resist police brutality and the structural and psychological effects of government-sanctioned segregation. To keep people involved and inspired, La Gente started the *Roscoe Street Blues* newsletter. They asked Thompson if the group could meet at Pride and Prejudice, run their mimeograph machine in the basement, and use the silk-screen table. "So that's how we connected with Pride and Prejudice. We were basically kind of neighbors. . . . It was truly a rich place at that time. I want to say like it was a cusp where everything just came together."[51] By virtue of its spatial and technical resources, as well as its open-door attitude, Pride and Prejudice would get "connected" with the neighborhood and beyond.

Being neighbors went beyond physical proximity and business relations, and all parties were changed in the process. Latina and white women actively brought La Gente to feminism and to Pride and Prejudice. Though one image of the *Roscoe Street Blues* newsletter was largely male, women wrote for it and pushed La Gente to confront gender as well as race hierarchies. Jude Vesely had become a VISTA volunteer in 1967 to work at the Spanish Outpost with Latinas in street gangs. She married Hernandez the next year, and when Pride and Prejudice opened in 1969, she joined rap groups at the store.[52] Living space, community space, and political space all came together when Vesely brought home *Sisterhood Is Powerful* for Hernandez to read. Days later, Hernandez stormed into the bookstore and threw the book in the wastebasket. As he complained to Thompson, "I've been fighting all these years against the oppressor, and now I have to deal with the fact that I am the oppressor, and I hate it."[53] "The fact" was much closer to home than a collection of feminist essays, and it rang true because Hernandez had heard it before from the women in La Gente. Beyond supplying a book, Pride and Prejudice functioned as a meeting ground, a place where multiple avenues of social change could and did intersect.

Tensions at those intersections were productive. The Young Lords and La Gente moved forward on the energy of women like Sally Contreras, Barbara Carrillo, Senora Mendoza, and many others. As Hernandez recalled, "The women that were in these groups started to really come up, so that was a lot of how the guys at least had their consciousnesses raised: the women would kick their asses. That's how you learned. . . . We were the boyfriends or whatever." Embarrassed to be auxiliaries, five men from La Gente and five from the living collective formed a men's rap group at Pride and Prejudice to "try to deal with women's oppression."[54] In the process, they discovered that they did not know how to talk about feminism or human liberation without fighting about racism and gentrification. Like women's rap groups that developed "process" and ground rules for communication, the men's group early established its own rule: to prevent physical fights, no one was allowed to stand up during meetings. Many considered the group a failure; in Schulz's words, "We had no idea what we were doing and we weren't doing it very well."[55] But the propinquity of Pride and Prejudice and La Gente offered these men the opportunity to grapple with what women everywhere discovered whenever they attempted to work together: coalition and coexistence—to say nothing of women's liberation and human liberation—required reaching beyond the confines of domesticity (however communally organized) and beyond one's own imagined community and neighborhood. If the men didn't know what they were doing, they thereby managed to keep the door open and help Pride and Prejudice become a location in which people coalesced in unpredictable, often stormy, and always provisional formations.

As a marketplace, Pride and Prejudice carried its founders into unanticipated community activism. Latino boys hung around Pride and Prejudice doing odd jobs, and those living in the house participated in spontaneous neighborhood actions.[56] Collective members were on call to nearby Arroyo's Liquor to serve as witnesses against repeated police attempts to frame the store owners and force the store to close. Developers had their eyes on the area, but the neighborhood—many of its inhabitants in their third wave of resistance to rising prices—did not take gentrification lying down. When La Gente sent the word out, "C'mon down to Arroyo's, we need witnesses," the inhabitants of Pride and Prejudice poured down the street.[57] Now a Starbucks Coffee Shop, Arroyo's was once a focus for small acts of resistance that built neighborhood solidarity even if activists could not prevent the sweep of corporate development.

The fact that Pride and Prejudice was a home, a market, and a political organizing/social service space contributed to the complexity of feminism in the neighborhood in other ways as well. Initially unbeknownst to Thompson, the new Chicago Women's Liberation Union office was right around the corner from her store.[58] Pride and Prejudice's work and CWLU's work intersected on many fronts, but their styles diverged to serve people in different ways. Living collective member Lucina Kathmann learned pregnancy testing from the CWLU and then opened a service at Pride and Prejudice. Although the bookstore regularly referred women to CWLU's Jane underground abortion service, the anarchy of Pride and Prejudice and the "random" nature of its pregnancy testing irked many in CWLU. As Kathmann explained, "They [CWLU members] didn't *live* where their office was, like we did. They were always setting guidelines and rules. They did pregnancy testing, but maybe on Tuesdays 2 to 4 and maybe with other restrictions. We just did anything we could at any time with whoever was at hand. This threatened them."[59] Running an illegal abortion service, the CWLU had developed elaborate screening measures as protection against police raids.[60] But given the absence of affordable pregnancy testing, feminist counseling, and legal abortions within conventional medical systems, countless women sought alternative places for testing and referral. At Pride and Prejudice, as long as someone was home, any woman could come in, leave a urine sample, and be sure that it would be properly stored and tested. The space itself thus supported efforts to serve Latina and American Indian women through informal neighborhood connections.[61] Additionally, though much of the budding women's health movement assumed that reproductive issues primarily concerned straight-identified women, Pride and Prejudice advertised in *Chicago Lesbian Liberation* and *Lavender Woman*. As a space that combined domestic, service, and commercial functions, the living collective prompted neighbors and inhabitants to play almost interchangeable roles as clients, customers, and movement builders.

The public pregnancy testing service directly intersected with the living space of the commune; tensions over these intersections revealed that the use and constitution of space—on every scale—was inherently political. As a component of women's self-sufficiency and sexual autonomy, pregnancy testing made intellectual sense to everyone living at Pride and Prejudice. But sexual autonomy could not be held in principle alone; rather, it was a *practice* that shaped commune members' everyday existence. Schulz later laughed about the pregnancy testing: "That was a problem: we just had this one fridge, and they kept putting the piss anywhere, and we kept asking to have one shelf for piss and one shelf for food, to have a little segregation in the fridge!" With honesty, Patricca avowed, "The things that get to a person are so small, so small and petty."[62] If conflicts over refrigerator space revealed deeper tensions over the boundary between public and private, between political and domestic realms, and between commercial-community space and a gentrifying neighborhood, Pride and Prejudice itself invited feminist methods for approaching the personal and political stakes involved in sharing what was, after all, contested ground.

The bookstore's public nature expanded neighbors' access to the living collective, ensuring that the living collective would be equally embedded in the movement of the neighborhood. Hernandez and Vesely were not the only "locals" who ended up living at Pride and Prejudice, nor the only ones who might have thought that other inhabitants would hardly notice when the long hours they spent at the store melded into an ongoing domestic arrangement. It was thus with some truth that Lucina Kathmann recalled, "We certainly connected with everybody [in the neighborhood], in fact it seemed like half of them moved in with us."[63] In a space that was at once store, activist center, commune, and crash pad, often little distinguished those who lived there literally and those who lived there figuratively. Pride and Prejudice was so deeply imbricated in neighborhood organizing that many remember it more as an aura of activity than as a distinct space. Vesely, for example, worked at the Spanish Outpost four city blocks away for a year before she participated in rap groups at Pride and Prejudice. But they are so connected in her mind that she conflated the two spaces, asserting, "Pride and Prejudice opened in the space that was the Spanish Outpost when the Outpost closed in 1969. It was the same place." According to calendars and paper maps, Vesely's memory is inaccurate, but this very inaccuracy speaks to the significance of the bookstore's place in the neighborhood and its deep connections with other neighborhood goals and hubs of social movement. It further reflects the fluidity of activist boundaries and intersections on the ground; identity politics notwithstanding, people did not work within static definitions of community.[64]

Pride and Prejudice was part of regional and national movement activity as well, and thus exceeded itself in almost every way. Though Hernandez felt himself in the racial minority in a predominantly white-identified commune, he added,

> But there was always a lot of stuff going on so that people were always staying there. It was that kind of crash pad: people and groups coming to town for a march or to do this or whatever would crash there. So you had all kinds of people there all the time. You had the blacks, you had Latinos, you had everybody, all the men in their berets. The gays, too, would stay there, they had their

purple and lavender crocheted berets. It was pretty interesting. . . . So everyone was here coming through.[65]

The simple project of living together went beyond the domestic and beyond the neighborhood; it went from the contents of the refrigerator to black and gay activism at the national level.

The bookstore drew the attention of named groups in town and throughout the United States.[66] As Schulz recalled, "There were lots of other places around at the time, and people would float in and want us to be Trotskyites or whatever they wanted us to be, and we weren't having any of that."[67] After opening communication with New York Radical Women whose *Notes* had catalyzed a life change for Thompson, Pride and Prejudice received a letter back requesting, "please send us a copy of your mission statement." Anti-authoritarian to the core, Thompson explained, "We were just too adverse for that. We never wrote a mission statement. We were all seriously mistrustful of dogma and of the written code. We always said if you couldn't tell what our politics were from what we were doing, then we must be doing something wrong."[68] Pride and Prejudice, that is, was not a political organization but a site for political enactment.

While collective members and neighbors at times took the rockiness of their endeavors as signs of failure, they unanimously recall the women's rap groups as Pride and Prejudice's greatest success. The rap groups—often spontaneously becoming zap groups—connected the store to activists involved in the Socialist Worker's Party and other leftist organizations; they nurtured the emergence of feminist theater, philosophy, and psychology—many of their proponents now nationally well-known; they produced women's art and helped popularize women's self-defense and women's health. Through their neighborhood members, Pride and Prejudice rap and zap groups connected with Latino/a and Indian activist efforts around housing and land reclamation.[69] Together with Chicago Lesbian Liberation, Pride and Prejudice co-produced Chicago's first all-women's dance in 1972. Chicago's first "lesbian feminist band," Family of Woman, was born at the living collective to provide music for the dance and went on to tour regional feminist venues for several years. Writing collectives spawned at Pride and Prejudice continued for well over a decade supporting the publication of diverse feminist books. Unconvinced by the "free love" of the mid- to late 1960s, women who came together through rap groups fought for reproductive control and sexual autonomy; they rejected monogamy and embraced the right to intimacy with men and women alike; and, led by Thompson and Andra Medea, they dove into the politics of rape. To those who measure the success of feminist formations according to long-term feminist identification, these are the commonly recognized seeds: the rap groups, that is, generated manifestations of "feminism" that made a narratively coherent and lasting difference. But as the larger discussion of Pride and Prejudice indicates, this apparent historical narrative coherence imposes perhaps too much teleology on places of movement that were fundamentally unruly, and too much order on spaces that were elastic crossroads for unpredictable gatherings and outcomes.

Pride and Prejudice was by no means a utopia for anyone. In the living collective, the "things so small and so petty" substantiated infinite expressions of race, gender, sexuality, class, and culture and enlisted multiple hierarchies attached to them; the quotidian was endlessly linked to larger factors, such as capitalist development, health care, and neighborhood and national movement. Changing economic conditions, daily challenges, and new opportunities and visions took collective members in new directions, and Pride and Prejudice began to dissolve. In 1972, some lesbian feminists—including some who lived in the collective—had begun to demand a "women's center" that would serve them more exclusively. Meanwhile, Thompson and Medea were deeply immersed in researching, co-writing, and touring *Against Rape*, a project that proved wholly draining.[70] By May 1973, collective members let go the lease and moved on.

Those who wanted an exclusive lesbian resource center took the Women's Center sign—originally hung at Pride and Prejudice—to launch a storefront space several blocks north. Gradually, the new Women's Center grew explicit about its separatist mission, declaring by 1974, "the former Women's Center has now become the Lesbian Feminist Center." The founding collective stated, "We know that a lesbian-feminist center has been needed in this city because there is no other place that is strictly our own." Establishing the new center helped produce lesbian feminism in Chicago: the space itself asserted the existence of "lesbian feminists" as a constituency making its mark on the landscape. Attesting to the fragility of this property, however, the center hung only the original Women's Center sign out front "for security reasons" until 1975.[71]

In contrast to Pride and Prejudice, women built the new Women's (Lesbian Feminist) Center with a defined political mission: to challenge homophobia and male supremacy by offering a place solely for lesbian-identified feminists. The Lesbian Feminist Center was a place from which to unapologetically assert lesbian existence and the necessity of separatism for feminist liberation. This was no mere gay-straight split as so many historians have called the establishment of separate spaces. The new center in fact helped construct the category "political lesbian" and credentialed "political lesbians" against all others. Women who had long been "simply lesbians" without living separatist lives, and women who maintained intimacy with men, found the door to the Lesbian Feminist Center to be less than open. As Thompson commented, "It was a bad time to be bisexual."[72] In fact, the new center was not the *place* to be bisexual or to be "simply lesbian."

Operating under the "Women's Center" sign, the Lesbian Feminist Center instrumentally imposed highly charged meanings onto the terms *feminist* and *lesbian*. Many leaders of lesbian liberation asserted their presence at the new center, but some—like Vernita Gray, E. Kitch Childs, and Shawn Reynolds—would have preferred "just a Lesbian Center: a place just for all lesbians." In Gray's interpretation, *lesbian* was not the problem. Rather, "by tacking on the word 'feminist,'" the center announced the expectation that users of the space would separate from men.[73] Setting out to create and serve a particular constituency, the Lesbian Feminist Center classified "feminist" as "political lesbian" and as separatist. The ramifications were powerful: the new Women's Center stripped the credentials for entrance from women like Thompson. In truth, neither "lesbian" nor "feminist" alone accomplished that: the separatist message depended completely on their combined attachment to a concrete place. *Place* constructed the appearance of static differences between political lesbians and others. Always experienced through place, those differences could even seem to define feminism itself. Exclusion was not new, however. Rather, the drive for separatist space made it clear that feminism had always constituted itself, in part, through places in which one did or did not belong.

Pride and Prejudice had begun as a commercial space with vague political purposes. Soon a diversity of influences organically gave it shape as the Women's Center, but—however marginal its financial transactions—it nevertheless continued to function as a true public marketplace and tangible community crossroads. Specializing in books, it also traded in ideas that came from and fostered rap and zap groups, community involvement, and other staples of social movement. It was a market that resisted the narrower aims of capitalism as it opened itself to the provision of a variety of services such as pregnancy testing, silk screening, and shelter. As a living space, it offered all of it on an ad hoc, community-generated basis, with no single group defining the communities thus served. As Medea asserted, "One of the things I learned in the whole fertile ground that Kathleen started at Pride and Prejudice was how to cross boundaries and jump, and explode things, and find the things that everyone knew and no one talked about. That's a pretty powerful thing to learn."[74] Sharing living, commercial, and neighborhood space made it impossible to develop a politics apart from the quotidian: taking women's sexual autonomy seriously meant putting up with urine samples in the refrigerator. Taking human liberation seriously meant figuring out how to get along in a gentrifying neighborhood. In that place, feminism looked like a culturally embedded and constantly changing set of practices in hopes of women's liberation, anarchy, and human liberation.

Scratching a Niche: Tea and Geography

Susan B's

"Susan B's was a great place. That was post-Women's Center, and it was just a feminist restaurant. It was a soup restaurant. . . . And feminists hung out there. Other people did too, because they liked the soup."[75] Like many women's spaces at the time, Susan B's started with an idea, very little capital, and a lot of volunteer labor. In 1973, Eunice Hundseth, a medical photographer at Evanston Hospital, found herself leaving her husband in a hurry. At one of the feminist meetings she participated in—probably one about starting a rape crisis center—she made a new friend, Kathleen Thompson, who helped her move. Like many women, Hundseth wanted a new community space. She was tired of the bar scene. Maybe she even wanted a new job. Maybe she'd open a restaurant, something small with a simple menu—soup, Thompson suggested—a place where people could eat even if they didn't have much money, a place where women would feel at home.

At that time, all kinds of people involved in feminist activism sought new kinds of community places. Chicago Lesbian Liberation, the *Lavender Woman* collective, and the Chicago Women's Liberation Union were constantly on the lookout for new spaces. Several new women's bars had opened on the North Side, but bars simply weren't everything for everyone. Many women, then, were "looking for places to hang out, looking for places to go where they felt safe and comfortable and so forth." A simple restaurant might be such a place.

Hundseth found a defunct and tiny greasy spoon in the Lincoln Park–Lakeview neighborhood that was attracting feminists, lesbians, and gay men—most of them white—in droves. The neighborhood itself seemed to bring a "scene" into being, in part due to the prior work of places like Pride and Prejudice, the CWLU office, and the Women's Center (at that moment morphing into the Lesbian Feminist Center). Despite the concurrent work of developers intent on gentrification, rent in the area was still affordable. Hundseth knew she could count on local residents—as well as those who visited from the South Side or Evanston—to act as an appreciative clientele. Just a block north of the Addison El stop, the tiny diner sat next to a popular gourmet restaurant, the Genesee Depot, run by two of Hundseth's gay male friends. Long before *Chicago Magazine* reviewed Susan B's, Genesee Depot helped advertise the soup restaurant to Chicago's restaurant connoisseurs—a crowd composed of predominantly white, middle-class heterosexual and gay couples. Around the corner on Halsted, a new lesbian bar, Augie's, fast became a favorite of women who identified themselves as socialist feminist organizers as well as longtime lesbians and those just coming out. Thus, Susan B's "just became part of the scene: it was location, location, location."[76] Location fostered clientele and community at Susan B's, all of which contributed to the public appearance and particular image of feminism.

Creating the space created community. Hundseth used savings to put down a security deposit and the first month's rent with enough left over to buy dishes. She called everyone she knew from her various women's groups to help gut the place, build a new structure, find chairs, and paint it all in bright colors. Though unpaid, many women were happy to put their muscle capital and proudly worn tool belts toward fixing up a new space, and the work ensured that the restaurant would open with a clientele who had a personal investment in its well-being. Thompson described it well: "Susan B's grew out of a community. It wasn't someplace that somebody opened and then hoped strangers would come in there: there were enough people involved in the building of it, that were very much part of the community and the communities, that people knew what it was before they ever walked into it." The construction work constituted community as much as it drew on an already-defined community: women whose paths otherwise did not cross worked together and came to feel collective ownership of the place.

As for so many women who rejected commercialism, building community and a community space came first for Hundseth. Indeed, the process of putting it together so satisfied that desire that she almost forgot what came next. As Thompson proudly narrated it, Hundseth prioritized being a businessperson no more than she herself had.

> We'd been working on Susan B's for a couple of months, cleaning, and painting and getting everything ready, and . . . finally the day of the grand opening, we're there at the restaurant getting the last stuff painted, and the last things in order, and, Eunice says, "Oh my gosh, I don't know how to make soup." Now this really happened. It sounds like a story, right? But it actually happened.

It was as though "restaurant" to Hundseth meant gathering place, and the sale of food was nearly an afterthought. She created a place, complete with women's art on the walls, where anyone could just drop in 11:30 am to midnight. Only at the last minute did she remember to provide "food for people," as the alternative ethic put it. With help from the people, she created a $2 meal.

Community literally built Susan B's product. Coming to the rescue on opening day, Mimi, who cooked for the activist-oriented Blue Gargoyle coffeehouse in Hyde Park, made the vegetarian soup, and Thompson made the meat soup. Barbara Carrillo of La Gente taught Hundseth how to bake bread, and according to *Chicago Magazine*, "the delicious, perfectly formed bread would hold its own at any county fair." In addition to critically acclaimed, homemade soups and bread, "you could have tea: you could have your tea iced or you could have it hot."[77] The product that customers then purchased was deceptively simple. Beyond the edibles, customers affirmed that the do-it-yourself ethic built community and sustained commercial space simultaneously.

Together, Susan B's location, regular clientele, and product gave the restaurant a countercultural, feminist, "small planet" feel. Even though customers spanned race and class as well as political orientation, its recognizable cultural style grew out of a feminism that itself was shaped by "naturalness" and a "politics of authenticity" most commonly associated with a young, white middle-class cohort.[78] Vernita Gray allowed that "Susan B's was a funky little restaurant that served soup and homemade bread, and was a gathering spot for women," but she linked location with cultural style when she added, "It was a North Side spot for the flannel shirt, earth shoe–wearing lesbian." Those linked characteristics of location and style did not keep Gray and other African American feminists away altogether, but they did suggest that the place would not become deeply racially integrated. Driving home her point, Gray followed her description of Susan B's with a contrasting but spatially parallel description of the MS Lounge bar: "MS was near downtown, which made it accessible from either North or South Side. It was a real diverse place with lots of beautiful women."[79] Gray's characterization of Susan B's was not simply about a restaurant; additionally, it referenced racial conflicts among feminists about North and South Side meeting spaces and bar choices that had begun in 1971 and was in full force during Susan B's lifetime.[80] In all its earthiness, the soup restaurant had landed on—and helped create—the small planet of the North Side and thereby extended the racialized valences of a north-south divide.

As a public commercial venue, Susan B's atmosphere was open enough, and the meal cheap enough, to provide "food for people" across class (homeless people and businesspeople enjoyed the place as well as those who intentionally distanced from commercialism) and across gender (men as well as women). Susan B's nonetheless existed by virtue of women's drive for an alternative space that *they* defined *in* the marketplace. A large cross-section of women loved it because it was theirs, and they loved making it theirs in the presence of men. According to Thompson,

> It was a place where being a *woman*, being a feminist, was the best thing. Other people were okay, and could come in there: a woman could bring her boyfriend in, that wouldn't be a problem. It was just that there, he wasn't going to be *as* accepted and *as* "at home" as *she* was. And if he behaved like an idiot for some reason, then there would be a lot of women to take care of the situation. You just didn't get by with any kind of sexist behavior in Susan B's, and so that made it a nice place to hang out.[81]

Able to teach and enforce the rules, Hundseth and customers alike created a commercial space in which women experienced not removal from but victory over sexist and homophobic harassment in the public world.

But it was not to last. The public world of Susan B's quickly outgrew its ten tables, particularly after *Chicago Magazine* reviewed the restaurant. No longer a place where one could drop in for a quick bite, nor a place where feminists could hang out at leisure, Susan B's drew long lines of impatient customers waiting to get in the door. The venture no longer felt "tiny, comfortable, and casual," but cramped, chaotic, and lacking in purpose. Hundseth and her partner, Linda, were overworked and underpaid and, as Hundseth told her friends, she "simply didn't feel like running a restaurant anymore." One night she quietly closed the door.[82]

While the closing disappointed countless patrons from all walks of life, some women painted it as a betrayal and sign of disunity among feminists. For example, the short-lived *off our backs* collective in Chicago published an article on the closing of Susan B's (appropriately titled, "Rumor Has It") in the "Chicago News" section of the Washington, D.C., publication, *Off Our Backs*.[83] The article boldly asserted, "Factually, the lack of matronage has plagued [Susan B's] more or less constantly, and [it] has suffered hassles from the feminist and lesbian communities for allowing males in. . . . The Lesbian Feminist Center boycotted Susan B's restaurant sporadically last year for the same reason." The author rhetorically concluded, "How is the Chicago area movement ever going to mature into a strong, self-supporting force for revolution if it continues to reject real support for feminist businesses in favor of 'political correctness,' whatever that is, and petty jealousy? Is sisterhood a joke?"[84] A meeting between angry Chicago activists, representatives of *off our backs*, and a *Lavender Woman* interview with Hundseth herself, led the Chicago *off our backs* collective to admit to irresponsible journalism: the Lesbian Feminist Center as an organization never boycotted the restaurant, and Susan B's had more than enough business.[85] But the *off our backs* article was neither the first nor last instance in which feminists linked movement "maturity" to the commercial longevity of feminist businesses. Ironically, proclamations of failed sisterhood in this context did not place blame on capitalism, structural and social geographies, or personal life choices; instead, they implied that sisterhood and revolution depended on activists uniting as committed entrepreneurs and consumers. Increasingly, the closing of commercial spaces became the focus for distress over the exclusions inherent to all feminist spaces.

The conflation of commercial longevity and movement maturity was particularly myopic in the case of Susan B's. Surely there were some women who did not "matronize" Susan B's because they resented the presence of men there. But the restaurant never lacked for customers. Combining a commitment to good "food for people" and to women's demand for public meeting space, Susan B's served a predominantly white clientele of lesbians, feminists, and others who wanted an inexpensive meal in a cheerful, friendly space. To continue operations, Hundseth could have raised prices, taken out a loan, and expanded. But the idea of getting fancy was unthinkable: there was nothing in it for her if she lost her community base and the small planet feel. Divisive rumors among feminists were thus all the more irksome; as Hundseth insisted, she wanted out of "the restaurant business" because it had become just that.

Poor Woman's Paradise

For a brief time, Poor Woman's Paradise coffeehouse in Detroit functioned just as founders had hoped it would. As the *Detroit Free Press* reported when the coffeehouse closed in 1975, "It was a place where women could go evenings without being hassled the way they might be in bars, where they could enjoy the company of other women and of nonsexist men, where there was poetry, art and music produced by their sisters."[86] Though women all over the country were energetically creating feminist venues with what appeared to be similar goals, the fourteen months of operation of Poor Woman's Paradise revealed that those goals were subject to incidental and local conditions to a far greater extent than has been acknowledged. In contrast to bookstores that composed a feminist consumer base through a distinctive product line (feminist books), feminist restaurants and coffeehouses had no distinctively feminist food to sell. Thus, they could become "feminist" only by constituting feminist customers through the less profit-generating element of atmosphere—music, decor, location, and activities.[87] Simultaneously elusive and substantive, the creation of atmosphere made crystal clear the extent to which localized social geographies directed women's movement and shaped feminism itself.

In 1971, a group of young white women—most of whom had male partners and children—created cooperative housing for their families in an eighteen-unit apartment building near Woodward Avenue at the north end of Highland Park in Detroit. Under feminist demands for egalitarian and sexually open relationships, the apartment co-op undertook a dramatic transformation: as Poor Woman's Paradise cofounder Denise Dorsz tells it, "Eventually, as things happened so often then, everybody got separated, and so then, the men ended up on the first floor, had their apartments on the first floor, the kids had apartments on the second floor, and the women had apartments on the third floor. Really!"[88] Lacking other feminist and lesbian community centers in Detroit, but with a floor of their own, women drew other women to the apartment building. They created consciousness-raising groups and formed the Women's Health Project to offer "self-help" workshops, pregnancy and venereal disease testing, and abortion and gynecological referral. As the Health Project took shape, Dorsz, then eighteen years old, moved to the neighborhood and began hanging out there. She recalled,

> Poor Woman's Paradise coffeehouse started in a very funny way. Which was, in the basement of that apartment building was a soda fountain, literally. So, we would just talk about, "Oh, wouldn't this be fun!" And then a group of us found a building on Seven Mile and Woodward and rented it [to start a coffeehouse]. Tracy Nelson had a song called "Poor Man's Paradise," and so we kind of played on that. The basement [of] the apartment building where we found the soda fountain, that was mostly what got us to think about [opening a coffee house].[89]

As happened so often then, the creation of feminist projects led to a growing demand for more public gathering spaces. Poor Woman's Paradise sought to fill that demand.

Between 1968 and 1971, Detroit women had excelled at taking to the streets, but the city had not lent itself to the creation of more stable meeting grounds. The Women's Liberation Coalition of Michigan, for example, put Detroit on the national map of feminism by sending a massive contingent of protestors to the Miss America pageant in Atlanta in 1969, but they did not put a meeting place on Detroit's map. Before the passage of *Roe v. Wade*, women staged highly visible zap actions in the streets of downtown Detroit and at the capitol in Lansing. They modeled an exceptional array of legislative and grassroots activist strategies around reproductive rights and child care; they argued—along with the Kerner Commission following the Detroit riots—that these were essential for economic justice and the survival of the city. They connected with women in Lansing, Mt. Pleasant, Flint, Grand Rapids, Ann Arbor, and Toledo. But most meetings took place in women's homes and in churches away from the inner city. WOMAN (Women's Organization to Mash Alcoholism and Narcotics), a grassroots creation, served hundreds of homeless and addicted women in the impoverished Cass Corridor neighborhood, but it operated literally on the streets for years, lacking funding to open a resource center. Women at Wayne State had created an active feminist group in 1969 and in 1971 began publishing *Moving Out*, a feminist literary magazine that included contributions by women far beyond Wayne State. But they did not gain a women's center at the university until 1976. Thus, despite its wealth of committed activism, Detroit contrasted with Chicago and the Twin Cities in that, by 1972, the city and its suburbs still had no women's bookstore, no lesbian resource center, no women's center, no feminist health center, and no women's addiction treatment center.[90] Detroit also contrasted with smaller Michigan cities such as Ann Arbor, East Lansing, and Kalamazoo, each of which maintained lesbian, feminist, and separatist newspapers and periodicals, bookstores, and coffeehouses.[91] Perhaps fitting for a city in which segregation, white flight, economic crisis, and lack of public transportation all limited women's mobility, it was Detroit's alternative radio that provided a sense of concerted movement, cohering activists through the airwaves rather than through a place on the ground.[92] But projects wanted place, and some thought a stable, commercial coffeehouse could serve that desire.

The initial vision for Poor Woman's Paradise developed from a combination of existent physical space (the apartment cooperative), local concerns, and a growing national culture of feminist-identified activism. If the old soda fountain provided an initial spark for the coffeehouse, the Health Project had revealed women's desire for politicized social space: women gathered at the apartment not only to build women's health resources but also simply to be in the company of women changing the public world. Seeking a more public venue, in 1973 white women involved in the Health Project started the nation's first Feminist Federal Credit Union to help finance the establishment of a Women's Resource Center in a storefront building on Woodward Avenue near Seven Mile Road. The new space, with a reading library, medical and legal referrals, a monthly newsletter and calendar, and a community bulletin board, facilitated the formation and meetings of thirteen various women's groups.[93] But beyond services and meetings, many still yearned for a place that would provide "a new social atmosphere wherein women can come together to talk, listen to music, drink and share their culture and varied talents," a place like a coffeehouse "owned and operated by women, for women."[94] They assumed that a thirsty women's movement would easily support an unprecedented feminist commercial venue. Thus, in the spring of 1974, eight women pooled money to open Poor Woman's Paradise coffeehouse in three adjoining storefronts on Seven Mile Road just off Woodward Avenue.

When it came to envisioning a commercial social space for women, the founders of Poor Woman's Paradise both drew on and pushed off bars. Some white women found bars to be a viable social space, and the number of bars serving white lesbians as well as the number of women bar owners had grown in the first half of the decade. Others found bars in general to be unpleasant. Gloria Dyc, a cofounder of the coffeehouse (and an editor of *Moving Out*), articulated a theme then common all over the country when she juxtaposed Poor Woman's Paradise with bars: at the coffeehouse, she explained, "you didn't have to deal with the sexual games that go on in Detroit bars. Sometimes, you know, you just want to go someplace and be alone without having to deal with that."[95] Part of creating a harassment-free space, as the founders envisioned it, depended on not serving alcohol—hence, they only served herbal tea and coffee. Acknowledging that this policy would turn many potential customers away, collective members hoped it would attract at least as many. As Dorsz explained, "We were hoping that having a nonsexist atmosphere for men and women would compensate for not being able to drink."[96] Thus, the politicized mission of Poor Woman's Paradise articulated rejection of behavior they associated with bars, the only other kind of commercial leisure space then available.

Poor Woman's Paradise instead claimed roots in an explicitly political version of social space: open evenings and Sunday afternoons, "it was really totally modeled much more on the 1960s, early '70s kind of folk coffeehouse," Dorsz recalled. More than a simple alternative to bars, the founding collective envisioned an informal, inexpensive milieu for showcasing women's theater, poetry, music, and art. In 1974, such a space—feminist or not—did not exist in Detroit. But while Poor Woman's Paradise founders imagined a countercultural form of coffeehouse with a new feminist bent, the space they actually created departed from that earlier model in one drastic way: Poor Woman's Paradise coffeehouse depended on commercial exchange every day of the week. With some exceptions, the kind of folk coffeehouses that Dorsz, Gloria Dyc, and others recalled were not strictly commercial; most operated only occasionally and usually in borrowed spaces like church basement social halls, university halls, and union halls. *Commercial* countercultural cafés, meanwhile, built their success by also functioning as meeting places for "free university" classes and coffeehouse events that sprang up during the antiwar and student movements.[97] But 1974 was a new political moment: the Vietnam War was over, and students at local universities and colleges were building as much within the institution as outside of it (for example, building women's studies and African American studies programs). Furthermore, while folk coffeehouses of the late 1960s typically developed within student or countercultural enclaves, Poor Woman's Paradise settled far from "that kind of neighborhood," hoping to cohere a women's movement still at large.[98]

The founders of Poor Woman's Paradise easily imagined that the groundswell of women's activism could sustain an autonomous economic venture, but collective members shared a primary interest in community space and relative disinterest in being businesspersons. By Dorsz's own admission, "We didn't know jack about business. We were trying to do this as a business, and no one had a clue. We were all young, lots of us were young lesbians too, so we were busy with other stuff."[99] But if these women did not have a lot of business drive, in other ways their desire for a commercial space seemed self-explanatory: they wanted a space of their own, a place where women set the terms.

As a feminist commercial venture, the coffeehouse's distinguishing product was its nonsexist space. When Poor Woman's Paradise closed, cofounder Gloria Dyc asserted success, explaining, "The men who went to the coffeehouse had a certain sensibility about the whole thing. They left their sexual prowess at home because this just wasn't the place for it."[100] Additionally, Poor Woman's Paradise relied on local culture. A handful of folk musicians performed at the coffeehouse, but—as was perhaps fitting in the erstwhile jazz capital of the world—jazz musicians provided the most regular entertainment. Jazz events, particularly "Sunday Jazz Afternoons," drew a sizable audience. They could hear pianist Eileen Orr, who had learned boogie-woogie while serving jail time for setting the General Motors building on fire in an antiwar action, or well-known jazz pianist Marian Devore, or Dee Merrick of 1940s and 1950s big band fame. Uniquely, it served as a gathering place for poets, artisans, painters, weavers, and others who shared their work through art showings and poetry readings cosponsored by *Moving Out*. While part of a growing national women's movement, the coffeehouse took shape around distinct local traditions, geographies, and politics.

Perhaps nothing so affected the ambivalent development of Poor Woman's Paradise as a feminist commercial space as its Seven Mile and Woodward location. A mile north of Highland Park and a mile south of the Ferndale suburb, Poor Woman's Paradise contributed to a growing cluster of feminist venues in a working-class, white neighborhood struggling to maintain demographic coherence against the erosion of jobs, schools, and infrastructure.[101] Highland Park itself straddled Woodward Avenue between Webb (roughly Four and a Half Mile) and Six Mile (McNichols) Road. Once a manufacturing village surrounded by the city of Detroit and inhabited by a virtually all-white population, Highland Park had grown increasingly poor since the 1950s, when manufacturers closed or moved out of the urban area.[102] As white flight accelerated following the Detroit riots of 1967, Highland Park became home to many black leftist activists who formed groups such as the Dodge Revolutionary Union Movement and the League of Black Revolutionary Workers. Drawn in part to low rents, small groups of white leftists also began to move into Highland Park's working-class and poor white and black neighborhoods.[103] In the early 1970s, young white feminists and lesbians settled in the Woodward–Six Mile neighborhood just north of Highland Park's boundaries because they were attracted to a culture of activism as well as to low rents and the activities going on in the third floor of the unnamed apartment co-op. By the mid-1970s, however, while Mayor Coleman Young blamed the suburbs for draining Detroit, it was clear to local black activists that "Highland Park's urban blight had begun to surpass Detroit's."[104] Meanwhile, the white lesbian enclave that had initially formed in relation to Highland Park began a northward drift that would ultimately settle in Ferndale and Royal Oak by the end of the decade. By 1974, with the Women's Resource Center at Six and a Half Mile, Poor Woman's Paradise at Seven Mile, and the new Feminist Women's Health Center and Feminist Federal Credit Union opening at Eight Mile, a significant collection of feminist-identified spaces settled in a neighborhood where very few African Americans lived.

Settling beyond Highland Park reinforced the racial segregation of feminist efforts in Detroit, despite interest in a multiracial meeting ground. With its excess of space, Poor Woman's Paradise turned one of its three storefronts into the Women's Cultural Center and offered that multi-use space to interested groups, but most feminist projects stayed within racialized geographic boundaries. For example, Faye Roberts and Pam Carter, the women who formed and sustained WOMAN and also founded the Detroit chapter of the National Black Feminist Organization (NBFO), used the Cultural Center as the NBFO's mailing address, having earlier built connections with some of the white women who had worked closer to the Cass Corridor area. On a foundation of Detroit community organizing and feminist politics, the NBFO chapter formed "in attempt to bring together black women in the Detroit area who are interested in organizing around and acting on those aspects of sexism and racism that affect and oppress black women as a class." The NBFO specifically called for "a separate organizational framework" built by and for black women, and the Cultural Center offered them a public address without expecting integration in return.[105] Despite sharing the large storefront space, neither did Poor Women's Paradise consider Detroit's NBFO, much less the Cass Corridor–based WOMAN project, to be integral to the coffeehouse. "I mean," Dorsz later explained, "Detroit ranks *way* up there in terms of being racially segregated."[106]

Even in a city that had erected foot-thick concrete walls during the 1940s to separate white and black neighborhoods, segregation did not depend on physical enactments alone, but also on community circumstances and interests. Although the NBFO was happy to use the Cultural Center as an address, its members put more into direct activism than into stabilizing an organizational presence. Black feminism in Detroit took shape around the immediate concerns of a community under siege: during the latter half of the 1960s and into the 1970s, police and the FBI exerted intensive surveillance and intimidation tactics against men in black nationalist and labor groups in Detroit, while women at the core of those groups struggled to gain enough power within them to keep the movement together and protect the community from further violence.[107] These factors also contributed to the development of activists who were more oriented around future generations than were most young white radicals, men and women alike. Detroit NBFO founders specifically put their energy into establishing a resource center for WOMAN in Cass Corridor and into developing the skills and connections that they hoped would allow them to open an inner city feminist health clinic.[108] Thus, while the Cultural Center as a whole undeniably spoke to a deep desire for coalitional space spanning race and class, cultural and political factors explain why, when some black feminists maintained proximity with feminist centers at Seven and Eight Mile Roads, the coffeehouse served a predominantly white clientele.[109]

At the same time, the coffeehouse claimed its roots in an array of social formations that often coded whiteness: folk coffeehouses, antiwar and feminist activism, and the collective (white) identity of being working-class people who *stayed* in Detroit. Poor Woman's Paradise drew a diverse and politicized customer base that reflected its purpose. As founders had imagined, white feminists and lesbians who "did not want to be hassled" constituted the core on any given evening. Feminist-identified lesbians "who weren't going to bars" particularly appreciated the new social venue. More surprising to the founders was that groups of white women from suburban chapters of the National Organization of Women occasionally came to the coffeehouse.[110] Additionally, the former big band singers attracted a cohort of friends who had socialized in the club-based music scene of mid-century. The most influential core, however, was "women on the left" who were involved in labor activism and—as Jane Slaughter, editor of *Labor Notes*, called it—"the working women's movement."[111] The shop floors at most remaining auto plants had only opened to women between 1970 and 1972, and many participants in the first wave of women in that workforce felt, "We owed our jobs to the women's movement."[112] Galvanized by a few successes, workers were busy establishing women's committees in United Auto Workers locals to prepare against the impending lay-offs of women in the face of outsourcing.[113] Some of those trade union activists came to Poor Woman's Paradise at the end of the day or on Sundays to relax in the company of other active women.

Diverse constituencies had contributed to labor activism in Detroit, from staunchly white-identified conventional unionists to radical Marxist organizers, from the League of Revolutionary Black Workers to the relatively integrated, nascent working women's movement. This diversity notwithstanding, one way that progressive white women normalized white identity in a city in which whites had become a minority was through the assertion of Detroit as a working-class city. The phrase "women on the left" named an almost uniformly white constituency who, in contrast to (white) "suburban women," had not abandoned the city but rather identified with the labor that had once made Detroit the "arsenal of Democracy." "Working class" thus claimed urban location and white racial identity simultaneously, distinct from both suburban whites and the urban black majority, even when black and white working women made common cause. Like the larger labor movement, Poor Woman's Paradise did not turn itself over to the agendas of black women as working women, but instead privileged the place of "women on the left."

The presence of "women on the left," along with the choice of music offered, ensured that Poor Woman's Paradise would not become a women-*only* or predominantly lesbian-identified space. Their influence on the coffeehouse had less to do with absolute numbers than it did with the sense that on one hand, their work was current in so many people's daily lives in Detroit, and on the other, they did not constitute themselves as champions of nor detractors from lesbian-identified women's activism. As Dorsz explained, "This is a working-class community. They [the labor activists] weren't lesbian identified. But women on the left were much more *open* to lesbians than the women from NOW." The founders of Poor Woman's Paradise had experienced homophobia within feminist groups and had sought to create a space that was nonhomophobic as well as nonsexist. But at a time when lesbians all over the country built coffee-houses to serve women exclusively, in Detroit, working-class identities and labor politics took Poor Woman's Paradise in another direction. Though "clearly a women's space," it was not to become a separatist space. Dorsz asserted, "In the politics at the time, a lot of the women who came from the left and from labor were pretty wedded to being inclusive of men."[114] This held true for most feminist- and lesbian-identified venues in Detroit through the 1970s; large-scale women-only events were all but unheard of.

Selling jazz events situated Poor Woman's Paradise *alongside* rather than firmly *within* the parts of the nationwide women's movement that manifested in women-only space and "women's music." As early as 1971, nearly all over the country, feminist and lesbian performers began billing themselves specifically as *feminists* and/or as *lesbians*. No longer to be marginalized or controlled by sexist and homophobic industries, "wom-en's music" or "feminist-identified music" inspired women to create new coffeehouses, concert venues, and production and recording companies. The Midwest was home to the country's first two national women's music festivals—the Women's National Music Festival in Champaign, Illinois (1974), and the Michigan Womyn's Music Festival outside of Mt. Pleasant (1976).[115] By the mid-1970s, lesbian-generated women's coffeehouses had become a staple of feminist activism and, though they took many different forms, most were as energetically fueled by the burgeoning new "women's music" as antiwar gatherings had been by folk music. Women's music production also encouraged veritable coffeehouse tours as fans and musi-cians built activist networks spanning the United States. This was not the music that built Poor Woman's Paradise, however. Instead, the coffee-house chose to sell jazz performed by entertainers deeply embedded in older Detroit traditions. Though played by women, the music "wasn't like what eventually became known as feminist-identified music."[116] Poor

Woman's Paradise, as much as it intentionally showcased female musicians, did not align itself with "women's music."

That Poor Woman's Paradise offered jazz, rock, and folk music played by women but did not consider it "women's music" indicates the deep extent to which genre had as much to do with space and place as it did with the music itself. The Chicago-based Family of Woman band enthusiastically offered its services to Detroit in the same issue of *Moving Out* that ran Poor Woman's Paradise's very first announcement.[117] Poor Woman's Paradise however, did not take them up on their offer only partly because the coffeehouse had no money to pay them. Family of Woman insisted on being billed as "Lesbian Feminist Musicians" and preferred women-only audiences, and Poor Woman's Paradise offered little of *that* kind of women's music. When the founders of the coffeehouse chose to create a space open to the public, they exposed the extent to which women's music was a *spatial* creation: women's music, that is, depended more on ensuring that audiences and musicians would constitute a bounded, exclusive community than it did on music that offered explicit lesbian or feminist perspectives.[118]

Neither Poor Woman's Paradise nor any other venue in Detroit catered to women seeking women-only space and women's music; those who sought women's music instead found it in other cities. In 1977, for example, the owners of Detroit's brand-new feminist and lesbian bookstore (Her Shelf) announced a meeting on the local viability of women's music: "Tired of going to Ann Arbor for concerts? This will be a meeting to see if there is enough woman power in Detroit to produce some concerts here."[119] Three years later in 1980, an audience of 175 turned out for Detroit's first lesbian concert, featuring Robin Flowers. Soon after, they invited the radical lesbian separatist Alix Dobkin to town. While Detroit lesbians marveled at the unprecedented event, Dobkin was not wowed. She regularly toured women's spaces from Cleveland, Ann Arbor, and East Lansing to Chicago, Madison, and Minneapolis, but skipped over Detroit: "I don't remember anything going on there. I was there once, but never went back."[120] Women-only space never became a defining feature of women's activism in the city, even when Her Shelf bookstore worked to organize lesbian separatist interests in Detroit in the late 1970s. In contrast to nearby Ann Arbor and East Lansing, women's activism and feminist venues in Detroit developed through political interests and demographic changes that inhibited gender-separatist formations, but not for lack of diverse lesbian and feminist initiatives.

Structural, geographic, and socioeconomic particularities of Detroit inhibited a steady evening clientele at Poor Woman's Paradise. Nightlife in general withered as half of Detroit's population had fled by the mid-1970s. Distances in Detroit were vast and—unlike Chicago—the city lacked efficient public transportation. Despite Detroit's reputation as the Motor City, one third of residents did not own cars. At its peak in 1974, the energy crisis further restricted movement across the urban miles that separated one part of town from another. Yet those with means and transportation often found it easier to go to Ann Arbor or East Lansing for an event than to travel across Detroit, as exclusionary housing practices and concrete walls exaggerated the geographic and cultural distance between one neighborhood and another. Commercial spaces like Poor Woman's Paradise required a population that had time, mobility, and disposable income, but Detroit was a poor city. Dorsz, not knowing "jack" about business when she cofounded the coffeehouse, came to appreciate these factors as she later devoted her work to combating poverty and racism in Detroit.

Despite successfully attracting a broad clientele, customers came to Poor Woman's Paradise in numbers too few to support the large space. Rent far exceeded income as the coffeehouse needed at least forty customers a day just to break even.[121] Toward financial stability, the coffeehouse charged a $2 cover or, alternatively, customers could invest in Poor Woman's Paradise by purchasing a yearly membership for $10 and reduce the cover to $1.50. This measure gave the coffeehouse an aura of club-like privacy and discouraged potential customers who simply did not have the cash on hand. To keep the coffeehouse running, Dorsz turned it into her own domestic space. As she recalled, "I'm trying to remember how the hell we paid for it. I know that I ended up living in the coffeehouse, and paying part of the rent myself, as rent for living there."[122] In the face of increasing debt, it was hard to glorify the situation as a commitment to alternative economies.

Ultimately, the coffeehouse could not bridge the tension between needing a bounded community—a market niche—that would provide ongoing support, and the founders' own resistance to defining patronage too narrowly. When the coffeehouse closed, Dorsz spoke to the press in dire terms about the inability of the collective to project a truly open image to potential clientele: "Like, since we were appealing to women who were in the feminist movement, we alienated women who weren't. We alienated men, who were afraid they wouldn't be welcome; we alienated straight women who thought just gay women were there; we alienated gay women who thought just the opposite."[123] It seemed that the creation of a nonsexist, public commercial venue was a feminist act so radical that it came to look like a private, ideologically closed venture. Observers took the unprecedented intervention in Detroit's commercial landscape as a statement of political persuasion, sexual identity, and separation: "men" assumed it was for women, "women" assumed it was for feminists, and "feminists" assumed it was for lesbians. "Lesbians," meanwhile, wondered if, other than bars, fully welcoming, lesbian-friendly commercial venues would ever survive in Detroit. Customers, that is, expected Poor Woman's Paradise to serve a group defined by exclusion as much as they hoped for a place that would generate community.

Although many contributed to the venture, Poor Woman's Paradise did not live up to its founders' growing political commitments: it did not overcome segregation, but participated in an already segregated landscape; it did not foster a rich constellation of feminist activists, but lent itself to the perception that "feminist women in the city just aren't as together as we would like them to be."[124] Creating a nonsexist, nonhomophobic, public, commercial venue required more than complex negotiations with communities who might or might not behave as markets; it required more than teaching men to "leave their sexual prowess at home"; and it required more than an invitation to women of color. It required an even more profound intervention in Detroit's segregated economy.

Navigating these local contingencies, women attempted to build other commercial feminist meeting grounds after Poor Woman's Paradise closed. One of the longest lasting, Her Shelf bookstore, opening in Highland Park in 1976, eventually followed the flight of white gay men and lesbians to the suburbs.[125] In 1978, the Mohawk author Beth Brant (then Dorsz's partner), opened Turtle Grandmother Books, specializing in "women of color books" (presaging the creation of Kitchen Table Press in 1980).[126] As a node for the distribution of a newly named, politicized constituency and aesthetic extending far beyond Detroit, Turtle Grandmother intervened in an otherwise narrowly defined geography of movement. And as a mail-order-only venture without floor space for customers, Turtle Grandmother also clearly bespoke the complex intersection of personal interests, community interests, racial segregation, and structural economies in Detroit.

Building Community in the Marketplace

From the early 1960s through the mid-1970s, women increasingly critiqued commercial venues that marginalized women, while at the same time intervening in racist and heteronormative public landscapes by building alternative, queer-friendly, and/or feminist commercial spaces. When women claimed spaces, opened new places, and decided which spaces were worth fighting for or fighting over and which weren't, they defined the parameters of communities and places simultaneously. By the early 1970s as women politicized feminist and lesbian venues, positive self-definition and disappointing exclusion ran side by side with the tantalizing horror of becoming a market niche. Many then read the financial success or failure of feminist businesses as a reflection of the coherence and relevance of the movement. As Gloria Dyc commented at the closure of Poor Woman's Paradise, "If it wasn't supported, then maybe it wasn't needed."[127] Feminist activism was not a commercial venture, however. Nor should the longest-lasting, most explicitly feminist commercial ventures define the historic parameters of the movement.

Women, some of them feminists, intervened in and changed the established nighttime marketplace of bars, simultaneously making queer leisure space an important site of women's movement. Women also sought to create explicitly feminist commercial spaces such as bookstores and cafés. Considered together, they reveal that the desire for particular kinds of women-friendly, queer-friendly commercial space was an integral and constitutive component of feminist emergence: commercial places like bars, Amazon Bookstore, Pride and Prejudice, Susan B's, and Poor Woman's Paradise did not simply serve an already defined constituency of self-identified feminists; rather, such places constituted feminist activism and popularized a movement.

The explicitly feminist businesses analyzed in this section spanned a time (1969–76) during which community spaces came into being alongside activists' intense efforts to define themselves and their politics. In 2004, Chicagoan Irene Lee echoed Dorsz's comment of 1975: "Back then, you could go to a *women's* space and get kicked out for being a *lesbian*." Penny Pope finished the sentence: "or you could go to a *lesbian* space and be kicked out because you weren't a *socialist*, or you weren't a *separatist*."[128] Women's spaces, by definition, invoked separation of many kinds, even in Detroit where gender separatism only minimally shaped feminist activism.[129] Apparent separatist conflicts varied greatly from city to city, both in their political and personal underpinnings and in the mode of their enactments. To the extent that struggles over politicized community were about generating and achieving feminist goals, they were equally about defining space. All activists took on that project, many by collectively intervening in the commercial world of the marketplace and constituting themselves as entrepreneurs and customers.

As the examples of commercial space in part I show, local spaces helped build the movement. But the definition and parameters of the movement have always been contested, in part because people negotiated belonging in geographically embedded spaces that could function more or less as crossroads. Even feminist-identified spaces fostered unanticipated social formations that spanned organizational and identity-based boundaries that might otherwise seem fixed and inevitable. These associations— many of them unnamed and ad hoc—are critical to understanding feminism as movement peopled by women and men across race and class. All the while, women with very different concerns were busily constituting visible feminism in the very different arena of civic spaces such as public parks, and that is the subject of part II.

Part II

*Public
Assertion
and
Civic
Space*

Three

"Kind of Like Mecca"

Playgrounds, Players, and Women's Movement

The sun was just coming up over Detroit on a July day in 1968 as players on the Motown Soul Sisters softball team arrived at Jayne Field, sleepily joking about staying out too late the night before. Jackie "Stix" or "Slim" Huggins tried to rouse the team into their favorite game-time taunts, while Jan "Rubber Arms" Chapman hummed familiar spirituals. It was going to be a hot day, and the team had a lot to do to prepare for a weekend-long invitational tournament. But they carried no bats, balls, or gloves with them that morning. Instead, they carried loads of lumber. Before hosting some of the best teams in the Midwest, the Soul Sisters wanted to improve the field that sat between the Polish neighborhood of Hamtramck and the expanding black neighborhood of Conant Gardens. As the top-ranked women's team—and only top-caliber, all-black team—in Detroit, the Soul Sisters regularly drew mixed-race crowds in the hundreds; an invitational would bring hundreds more. They wanted a concession stand and a broadcast tower. And they wanted, at least for one weekend, to claim the field as their own; they wanted, that is, to more fully desegregate one of Detroit's most popular softball parks, which for decades had served white men's teams first and foremost.

Ask any of the women who played on Detroit's best softball teams during the 1960s about how they got into softball, and you will likely hear an answer as filled with highways, demolition of homes, and segregation, as with public parks, inspirational leaders, and community athletics. Many, like Virginia Lawrence of the Brewster Jets, mark the chronology of their softball careers in relation to parks shaped both by African American entrepreneurship and the city's ill-fated urban renewal projects of the 1950s. There are athletes who, like Barbara "Bubbles" Hardison of the Motown Soul Sisters, can recall virtually every winning play of tournaments that took place thirty years ago, but she'll tell you about those plays alongside stories about the parks in towns and cities of the upper Midwest at which crowds shouted, "Niggers, go home." Stories that revolve around a lifelong love of softball and the community spirit that a team generated also hint at persistent efforts to contain gender deviance, sexuality, and interracial relationships. For the women who played on the top teams, softball entailed firsthand knowledge of where one could and could not go in a field of rapidly shifting boundaries. In a deindustrializing city known during the early 1960s as Motor Town, in the mid to late 1960s as Motown, and by the early 1970s as Murder Town, women who played softball engaged in public assertion, desegregation, and resistance to dominant norms.

This chapter offers a close analysis of women's activism in civic space through the lens of one Detroit team—the Motown Soul Sisters—and their efforts to play softball. As a noncommercial pastime that took place in ostensibly the most public of places, softball was an everyday activity in every sense of the term. The Soul Sisters themselves promoted it as such; they were not motivated by politics when they organized around practices, game schedules, fields, travel, and building sports opportunities for girls. Softball was usable, in fact, because so many people regarded it as "just a game": there was nothing inherently political in the written rules of the game, and in some contexts, playing the game carried no obvious political stakes. Furthermore, few players or spectators consciously linked women's civic softball to larger structural conditions or newsworthy matters: even the Soul Sisters, arguably Detroit's most famous team from the late 1960s to the mid-1970s, received almost no mention in print media; even though the Gordy family of Motown Records sponsored and loved the team, this relationship has been lost to posterity, entirely absent in every historic archive and museum focused on Motown. Neither have histories of feminism considered this ubiquitous pastime to be significant to the development of the movement, in part because softball was rarely embraced or promoted as a political activity.

Yet the Soul Sisters' narratives make clear that sexism, class hierarchies, racism, and homophobia—and resistance to them—fundamentally shaped the game and the civic spaces in which they played it. In fact, when they played softball, they entered a much larger cultural and political matrix of activity. Public park spaces and softball diamonds were deeply imbricated in larger structural conditions. When considered in their embedded spatial contexts, civic softball diamonds become rich sources from which to illuminate the actual mechanisms by which women constructed gender and sexual identities that were a little-noted but critical aspect of black culture and politics in the 1960s. They also provide a location for analysis of the ways in which avowedly *a*political actors directly engaged political processes. This in turn lays a foundation on which to better understand why it was that self-identified feminists saw fit to take up these same civic arenas and strategies of activism under a specifically feminist label, as discussed in chapter 4.

In 1957, antiracist activists in Detroit won suits against Detroit's explicit policy of race discrimination in housing. Two years later, the city's only African American YMCA was destroyed to make way for the new Chrysler freeway. Over the next two decades, freeway construction and urban renewal demolished black and poor white neighborhoods; federal programs and deindustrialization expedited the decimation of inner-city jobs and schools while suburban development boomed. The flight during the 1960s and 1970s of hundreds of thousands of whites opened up neighborhoods previously inaccessible to blacks, but many among the white minority that remained in the city often fiercely guarded white neighborhood enclaves. National civil rights legislation targeted at voting, education, and integration of public facilities did little to keep Detroit from becoming the most segregated city in the United States.

African Americans in Detroit continued to challenge segregation and assert political agendas in part by creating and occupying civic spaces for leisure, education, work, and the arts.[1] Little noted until now, women's softball was among the activities that shaped Detroit's politicized landscape in the 1960s. African American women used civic spaces as sites for community-building; for mobility across urban, rural, regional, and national geographies; and for the public emergence of constituencies newly organizing around race, gender, and sexuality. Those who developed high-caliber, black softball teams such as the Motown Soul Sisters especially elaborated the politics of civic space. In the early to mid-1960s, there were few serious softball leagues and teams for girls and young women in Detroit.[2] But a local African American culture of playground athletics had helped a significant number of girls develop athletic talent, and some—as women—still wanted to play hard and win. These women came together from increasingly dispersed neighborhoods with an innovative vision; as they built community sponsorship and made new claims on civic space, they not only developed women's athletics in the public landscape but also challenged multiple forms of oppression.

Soul Sister Charlotte "Stump" Howza described the team's action at Jayne Field as part of Coach Lonsdale Stokes's ongoing struggles with the city:

> You have to understand what he was up against. For a black man, the only black coach, with the only black team, in an all-white league, and in a city that is racially segregated, to ask for a concession stand—the field *needed* that—but because he was the one who asked, and because *he* asked, the city wasn't going to do it. So he bought the wood himself and took us all out there very early Saturday morning and we built it all. The broadcast tower too, we built it all. And I think that embarrassed the city.[3]

It was a gutsy thing to do, but the Soul Sisters were a gutsy team; they were more than willing to go to bat against any of the many men's teams that challenged them to a game, and they were equally willing to turn a park into a temporary construction site to challenge long-standing regulations about the uses and users of civic space.

The Soul Sisters attracted spectators in part by bringing recognizable African American cultural practices to the ball field. Playing in shiny royal blue and white uniforms, recalled Rubber Arms Chapman, "We had some real show-offs, doing antics all the time. And we always sang, sang songs all through the game, and chants and cheers. Sometimes we tried to sing the songs of the time, if someone knew how, but we *always* sang spirituals because that was something that everybody had. That was just something that's kind of inborn, you know. And we'd get *all* the fans singing and cheering. We had a lot of spirit."[4] They also had a lot of fans. As rival Virginia Lawrence recalled, "The Soul Sisters were fantastic players: if you saw them play, you'd stick around."[5] Like the music groups associated with the Motown Records label, their dazzling performance appealed to a cross-over audience. But the team, the sport they played, and the public spaces in which they played it also provided a focal point for expressions of racism, sexism, and homophobia. In the context of a city ridden with race and class conflict, it was with pride that Slim Huggins declared, "We were not well liked: we were arrogant and intimidating."[6]

Critically, these dynamics played out in highly visible places: what spaces are more ordinary than the parks that so often served as the foundation of urban neighborhoods? As civic spaces, public parks promised civility. At the same time, they often produced the illusion of civility through structured exclusions; as built environments, they took shape around larger race, class, gender, sexual, and other social hierarchies.[7] Despite the limitations of built environments, however, parks offered some distinct advantages: while commercial venues that cohered community—such as record shops, salons, and the buildings that harbored a vibrant nightlife— might be (and were) demolished to make way for freeways, there were always some parks or empty lots in which to play a game and pull people together. And while structural and economic conditions in Detroit hampered the establishment of meeting grounds to support coalitional feminist organizing, public parks could be effectively utilized to build coherence within a neighborhood and also to bring women together across neighborhoods, regions, and even race.[8] From dirt lots, playgrounds, and city parks, the Soul Sisters promoted themselves as a black team, thereby challenging structured exclusions and helping to create a black politics that demanded economic and political integration in late-1960s Detroit.

Civic athletic parks typically organized gender as well as race: historically created as male preserves, they served as locations for teaching masculinity and heterosexuality by encouraging demonstrative and highly gendered uses of public space.[9] In the 1940s and 1950s, assumptions about the gendered use of public, athletic space came to the fore when debates focused on whether it was safe for women to slide into base.[10] While such debates prescribed femininity and heteronormativity in principle, in practice, they regulated women's use of their own bodies in civic space. During the 1960s, when the Motown Soul Sisters occupied public softball diamonds, they took on highly public roles as visible transgressors and trespassers of gender, sexual, and racist norms and boundaries.

Without manifestos or a named feminist agenda, the Soul Sisters publicized a particular non-normative gender performance through aggressive occupation of civic athletic space unusual for women's teams at the time, and they worked to make public athletics more accessible to young girls and women. In those ways, they were pathbreaking; as the next chapter elaborates, their groundwork helped make possible a veritable explosion of women's athletics and visible feminist and lesbian organizing beginning in the early 1970s. Simultaneously, they confronted racist constructions of black women's sexual deviance and challenged the segregation of public spaces based on those constructions. Perhaps less intentionally, the Soul Sisters' performance helped forge a public, black queer subculture in Detroit and beyond. Tournament travel fostered interaction with teams and observers all over the country, and as the Soul Sisters crossed state lines, they mentored teams—such as the white, predominantly working-class Avantis of Minneapolis—in the complexities of race and sexuality in public space during an era in which the rules of segregation appeared to be in flux.

The efforts of a black women's softball team to desegregate civic space, build community through leisure activities, and promote new possibilities for gender and sexual expression within public space brought together several critical aspects of black culture and politics in the late 1960s. They also provide a window into the spatial politics and gender transgressions that were a critical aspect of the emergence of feminism during the same era.

"On the Playground Playing"

In 1964, one year after Dr. Martin Luther King Jr.'s Great March to Freedom in Detroit, the people who would become the Motown Soul Sisters began to get together. At fifteen years old, Jackie Huggins was bursting with what many called raw talent. She was determined to become a great ball player, but she lacked a great team. Lonsdale Stokes, who had moved from Mississippi to Detroit's West Grand Boulevard neighborhood not far from the parks where Jackie played, thought he could help bring up a team. He had played baseball in men's barnstorming leagues of the South, and, as Charlotte Howza speculated, "He must have seen a good women's team there. He *believed*, 'women are going to be big!' He arrived in Detroit and started from zero, he brought the team up, he taught us to play it and think it. He had a vision, and he always wanted to practice."[11] Several young players—like Huggins, Howza, and Victoria and Beatrice Lollar—had caught his attention playing in neighborhood games. They were not afraid to slide into base, or throw a fastball, or play hard in ways that—as adolescents—they were supposed to be outgrowing. Two years later, in 1966, Jan Chapman was eighteen years old and home from Fisk University for the summer. She was driving her ice cream truck around the familiar parks when she found a group of women engaged in an intense practice. She hadn't played softball in years, but she dared to join them for a few plays. They told her they were a new team, and they played in the top league. They laughed as she threw some balls, calling her "rubber arms," while she thought they had "arms like rifles." She recalled, "I had to *work* to play with them," but she ultimately became a star pitcher. Thus came together one of the first nationally ranked teams in the upper Midwest.

The Soul Sisters saw themselves, and others saw them, as a black team. Tryouts were open to any woman, and over the thirteen-year life of the team, at least three white women and two Chicana women played for them. The team picked up Barbara "Bubbles" Hardison ("our blue-eyed sister," in the words of Jan Chapman Sanders) after they saw her play at a national tournament late in 1967, and she stayed on as a core member for ten years. Nonetheless, observers, like the Soul Sisters themselves, participated in constructing the team as black, calling into question the racial identity of players like Hardison. Hardison's father was initially displeased at her decision to join a black team: "He says, 'well, I think you're making a mistake.' I said, 'what kind of mistake?' He goes, 'well I don't know. I just think you're making a mistake.' And I go, 'well I guess I'm old enough to make my own mistakes then for a while.' And he says, 'well, okay.' "[12] Over the years, recreation supervisors regularly told the Soul Sisters, "If you get some white players on the team, you will go far. As long as you are a black team, you will have problems at the tournaments."[13] Hardison's talent undeniably helped the team "go far," but her white presence, and that of other occasional white players, did not relieve the team of racist problems at tournaments and on the road. Indeed, sometimes "that white girl" provided a focal point for explicit expressions of racism against a team perceived as black.

In addition to the challenge of being the only black team in an otherwise white, working-class Detroit league, the team regularly faced gay-baiting. "Because not many women played," according to Victoria Lollar, "some parents were afraid. People also gave the team hassles because they said we were gay."[14] And some players were. Some of the older players came to the team from the Pink Ladies, a team sponsored by a night club called The Pink Lady. The club featured strip shows for a heterosexual-appearing audience, but it was also known as a gay women's hot spot where studs picked up the women who worked there. The Pink Ladies team sported some of the hardest hitters in Detroit, earning a reputation as a team of studs. When the team was on the wane, those who joined the Soul Sisters brought their assertive style with them.

Creating a top-caliber team required embracing an assertive gender style adapted from black men's and women's barnstorming leagues of the South, and from black women's urban "stud" athleticism. It also required the recruitment of young players who had "raw talent" but whose guardians were wary of gender and sexual deviance. To pull these people together, Stokes had to convince more than one set of parents that he would watch out for the younger players. Slim Huggins recalled, "My mom wanted me to do 'lady things,' but she gave in when she saw I was so serious about [playing softball]. But she made Mr. Stokes responsible for me, and she also told him, 'No games on Sunday. Sunday is for church.' "[15] Several concerned parents made going to church a condition for playing on that particular team. Beatrice "Rabbit" Lollar was not allowed on the team unless her sister, Li'l Vic, joined, too. Vic recalled, "*That's* why my mom made me play." Not everyone was so lucky. Thirty years later, Soul Sisters still enjoyed this story: "One girl's parents wouldn't let her join the Soul Sisters because they were afraid the team would make her gay. They made her join another team, then—ha ha ha!—she came out [as gay] on that *other* team!"[16] The Soul Sisters thus emerged as a team that reflected both black concerns about sexual respectability and also elements of a black queer subculture. Far from separable, these elements were fused together every time the Soul Sisters asserted their right to occupy the public spaces of ballparks; their very winning style was born of this fusion, and so was their contribution to desegregation and feminism.

Some sports historians and sociologists have suggested that African American gender norms made more room for female athletes than did white middle-class norms: it was not automatically "unladylike" to run fast and hit a ball hard or use one's body in an assertive manner.[17] My research, too, indicates that in urban contexts such as Detroit and Chicago, African American communities often made sporting opportunities for girls as well as for boys: as civic spaces, recreational facilities were for the community, and so were the activities available there. Many members of inner-city African American communities explicitly viewed playgrounds and recreation as critical to combating the effects of racist oppressions. Recreation leaders were often also community builders, publicizing activities and drawing adults as well as children into creative uses of park space. In these ways, they convinced even reluctant parents that rec centers kept girls (as well as boys) "out of trouble."

Nonetheless, African American gender and class norms did not provide an automatic haven for maturing tomboys. Parents or guardians often *were* reluctant about young women's participation in athletics, and community expectations were policed through use of gendered epithets and heterosexual performance. Attention to these dynamics shows gender norms within urban African American communities to be complex and inextricably tied to class and race considerations. Virginia Lawrence of the Brewster Jets noted that her interest in athletics marked her difference from other girls. "We were deemed tomboys. Okay, you're a tomboy, always playing with the boys. . . . I didn't get a lot of flack about it. I mean, except from the girls, of course. And I think basically it was jealousy because *they* wanted to be with the guys and *I* was with the guys." Her parents, on the other hand, encouraged Lawrence's athleticism as part of a legitimate therapy program earlier undertaken to treat infantile paralysis. "So," she recalled, "I didn't have anybody [saying] 'don't, stop, that's not ladylike.'"[18]

More commonly, girls did hear the message that playing ball was "not ladylike." Gender and class norms presented obstacles to most girls, and few had the opportunity to delve seriously into playground sports. Soul Sister Howza grew up frustrated with the lack of competitive girls' teams, explaining, "I couldn't stand to play with girls who couldn't play." Teammate Huggins agreed, "We went to play with the boys. I was a little bit crazy, probably because I liked to play, I loved to win." Though unapologetic, Huggins was aware that many people thought it "crazy" for a girl to be so competitive. Dominant norms suggested that being a tomboy was incompatible with being a lady. As Jan Chapman Sanders recalled,

> It just seemed natural to me to just be on the playground playing. And my mother didn't like it too much. She thought young girls should be on the porch reading books. So sometimes I would have to sneak out to play. I remember sneaking out once, because we had a championship and my mother just didn't want me to play. So I snuck out for the championship. And I had to slide into a base, and I just tore up my thigh. Yeah. And I had to go home and face it, you know. She wasn't too pleased, but then she began to see that, you know, well maybe it's not all bad. She just didn't want me to be a tomboy. And I was.[19]

It stretched local gender and class norms to suggest that playing in the park was as appropriate and uplifting as reading on the porch; most girls who wanted to play a top-notch game had to circumvent the ways that spatial arrangements perpetuated those norms.

Even girls who were encouraged to become part of an athletic tradition that included girls and women found that the gender and class transgression of participating in sports had everything to do with uses of public space. That is, it wasn't just about what a girl did, but where she did it. Playing ball in the parks earned the ambivalent status of tomboy. Some young women who refused to stay quietly near home, like Slim Huggins, could still maintain a claim to "lady things" by going to church. Enough "reading on the porch" might even keep a girl from being a tomboy: not only was it a polite activity, it could lead a young woman to college rather than to the ball field. In Detroit, some young women increased their mobility by negotiating these gender/class constructions: they could do lady things (like going to church) *and* earn tomboy status (by sneaking out for a game). Doing so paid off because, within public park culture, the status of tomboy granted girls proud and protected access to playing fields that otherwise appeared to belong to boys. Thus, in addition to engaging the politics of race and racist segregation, softball also provided one arena of challenge to constricting gender/class norms.

Playgrounds themselves were vital in that they were among the only places where girls who "loved to win" found recreation leaders and adults who were role models for competitive community sports. During the 1950s and 1960s, primary and secondary schools offered virtually no athletic opportunities for girls. During the 1960s and 1970s, the *Michigan Chronicle*, the Detroit African American weekly, projected its version of upstanding gender and athletics by routinely valorizing a variety of organized men's and boy's team sports; at the same time, women's appearance in the sports pages was rare and almost entirely limited to their activities in ladies' bowling leagues. If a girl really stayed on the porch reading the mainstream news, she'd have little idea that there was a playground of people encouraging girls to *want* to win smack in the middle of the most visible of community spaces.[20]

Fortunately, parks occupied more prominent social space than newspapers: they existed in every neighborhood, usually as the literal hub around which apartments or housing developments clustered. They often provided the central meeting grounds for a neighborhood, and multiple people used them in multiple ways simultaneously: adults and youth played softball, hoops, jacks, and jump rope; mothers watched over toddlers; people met to exchange news and simply to relax. On summer nights when it was too hot to sleep, parks became a highly social respite.

Even the aspiring porch was never far removed from the playground, beckoning girls to earn a place on the diamond.

Though the Soul Sisters came from a variety of class backgrounds and neighborhoods, they shared a common map of segregation in Detroit. Most had grown up within the small radius of mixed-class and poor black neighborhoods around Paradise Valley and Black Bottom (marked by Hastings Street, 12th Street, Gratiot, and Linwood), the working-class and middle-class "black west side" (between Grand, Grand River, and Tireman), the more uniformly middle-class Conant Gardens to the north, and Inkster, a western suburb built in the 1920s to house black River Rouge factory workers who were barred from living in the white suburb of Dearborn nearest the factory.[21] Chapman Sanders described how the boundaries of the color line shifted rapidly with suburbanization and urban renewal between the late 1940s and the mid-1960s. Though her family was relatively well-to-do (her ministerially inclined father worked for Ford, and her mother worked briefly for Chrysler), she recalled growing up within geographies drawn by racial segregation:

That neighborhood that we came from was . . . where the blacks lived in the fifties and the forties. Then we were dispersed (because of the highway) to move out, you know. To get to Fenkell Avenue—which was Five Mile—that was country to Detroit. And only the whites lived there. And when those expressways and things came out . . . the white started moving further out. It was mostly black where I grew up. . . . It was in this little pocket. Conant Gardens wasn't far. So most of the blacks were back over this way. . . . Most of the white were towards the Five Mile, Six Mile, Seven Mile. And then if you got to Eight Mile [where there was an island-like, small black neighborhood], you just knew you were in a whole other country.[22]

Growing up in Inkster, Conant Gardens, the "black west side," or on Hastings Street, whatever their class, the women who joined the Soul Sisters shared a map in which the whiteness beyond Five Mile Road rendered it "country," and suburban development orchestrated mobilities to constitute a Detroit popularly imagined as black. The suburbs beyond Eight Mile Road so dramatically disassociated themselves from Detroit and so explicitly excluded blacks from them, that they constituted a "country" that was positioned as more "other" even than Canada across the river.

Playgrounds and parks became still more important in the context of the infamous Detroit Plan of urban renewal.[23] Prior to that time, as Virginia Lawrence explained, "Most of the blacks in the city lived in Black Bottom; Black Bottom and Paradise Valley was like a town of its own within the city of Detroit." These were the neighborhoods of the thriving nightlife that made Detroit known at one time as the jazz capital of the world and later gave birth to Motown music. A product of segregation and black creative determination, Paradise Valley/Black Bottom was home not only to black hospitals, churches, recreation facilities, and other black-initiated social services and economic ventures but also to a black government that elected mayors and other officials, virtually making the area a "city of its own." Responding to the poverty and overcrowding that characterized the area, some of the country's most active black social uplift organizations and protest groups worked in their respective ways for the livelihood of the neighborhood.[24]

Under the Detroit Plan beginning in 1947, the city undertook the demolition of property in Black Bottom and Paradise Valley; by 1953, 700 buildings had been demolished and over 2,000 black families displaced.[25] The neighborhoods maintained cohesion around Hastings Street venues for public culture centering on small businesses, music, dance, preaching, and athletics. But in the late 1950s, Detroit city planners delivered yet another blow in the form of highway development. Sold as necessary replacement of inner-city slums, urban renewal consisted in large part of freeways to the suburbs. The Chrysler freeway demolished hundreds of black-owned homes and businesses, leaving untouched only much-criticized public housing high-rises, a few treeless dirt lots, and a park or two. By March 1963, the city had destroyed more than 10,000 structures and displaced over 43,000 people —70 percent of them black.[26] As the Housing Commission stridently maintained its policy of segregation, the majority of blacks ended up in increasingly crowded developments. In Virginia Lawrence's neighborhood, 12,000 people packed into one square mile of mostly substandard housing. There, she recalled, the playgrounds were "kind of like mecca."[27]

As did so many women, Lawrence punctuated the narration of her early athletic years with reference to the urban renewal and segregation that shaped her community recreation center. In her narrative, when the city was tearing up people's homes to build highways, the playground and rec center were virtually the only places providing community continuity on a daily, public basis. Her reference to an "athletic tradition" that predated the demolition furthers her claim not only to a source of black pride in prize fighter Joe Louis, but also to a cultural continuity in which it made sense for girls to be part of that same athletic space:

> I started right here at the [Brewster] Rec Center . . . I grew up right in this area. I didn't stay in the projects, I lived across the bridge, which is the freeway. As a matter of fact, the freeway runs through where my house was. . . . So I kind of grew up in the area, around Brewster Place. And the Brewster Jets, *they* could play! As a matter of fact . . . I was playing with the adult team when I was eleven years old. . . . Mattie Tilson Glover worked here at the rec center and encouraged it. When we were at the rec center we did a myriad of things: tap dancing, pitched horseshoes, basketball, I swam on the swimming team, any number of things. . . . It's been an athletic tradition for years. You know Joe Louis fought here. He *trained here*. Okay, so it's like, when you're coming up in the neighborhood, *everybody* did *everything*. When they put the highway through, they didn't take out any of this [park]. They just took out all the *homes* that were on the other side. Because right where you came across, at Wilkins Street, that's where my house sat. The street that is now the highway was Hastings. . . . At one time this was the *only* recreation center in the city that blacks *could* come to. Because, I mean, you didn't go anyplace else, not past Warren Avenue. . . . So when they tore those [houses] down, they built the housing *projects*. And there were more housing projects where the Brewster Homes are now. See, they tore those down. So, all this was government housing projects. . . . I lived across the bridge, across Hastings Street. I remember when they were digging it and everything. . . . The highway wiped out the area.[28]

With homes and businesses wiped out, park space became the means through which people constituted community and asserted tradition.

In this context of upheaval, playgrounds were uniquely stable locations, many surviving the city's razing of domestic and community space. Young women and men of the area turned dirt lots into playing fields and formed recreational softball leagues for boys and girls, men and women. Many players credit this league proliferation for maintaining a community and important role models in the midst of extreme economic and geographic dislocation. Through the leagues, young girls and women developed community-building and hard-work ethics as well as finely honed physical strength, agility, and perception. Jan Chapman Sanders, whose mother thought she "should be on the porch reading," grew up near a different park but also found role models who encouraged her to develop her own career that combines athletics with community activism:

When I was a girl, there was a playground that was about a block and a half from my home. Which was like the center of our world, you know, that's where. I mean, back in the fifties before the freeways, families were closer. The neighborhood was closer. And you had concern one for the other. And so the playground was the center of activity that kept people out of trouble. . . . And older people, that's where I learned, really, the competitive nature. Our older men and women, they played softball. And they were good. And so I got interested. . . . The neighborhood was like, you would have to call it now—it's now the expressway. But that playground is still there. They took the houses in that area, but they didn't take the playground. They went as far as that and they put that expressway through that neighborhood.[29]

Young women with athletic drive took usable space to build neighborhood and community solidarity through activities that were accessible, fun, and satisfying. Playgrounds were thus the sites in which young women developed public identities as athletes and as leaders keeping kids "out of trouble" and in the community.

Civic Parks, Civic Politics

Leisure activities like softball intentionally intersected with other civic arenas and activities more commonly considered political. In spring 1967, Charlotte Howza solicited WCHB radio station for sponsorship of Stokes's team. It was an obvious but carefully considered choice. The station, known as "the voice of progress," was the country's first radio station built, owned, and operated by African Americans. It went on the air in November 1956 to provide a public forum for black community issues, religious programming, and jazz and blues music.[30] WCHB was one of the first among several independent media sources that proliferated through the 1960s to rebuild cohesion among Detroit's otherwise displaced blacks. Radio, the presses, and new recording ventures reached out broadly and worked together to build movement. For example, in 1963, activists planned the Great March to Freedom. The *Michigan Chronicle* and the *Illustrated News* ran articles on nonviolent demonstration and civil rights and exhorted readers to participate.[31] WCHB broadcast the entire proceedings live. Dr. Martin Luther King Jr. delivered an early version of his "I Have a Dream" speech at Cobo Hall, and announced that the march up Woodward Avenue constituted the largest civil rights demonstration in

U.S. history. Motown Records, just a fledgling company in 1963, recorded *The Great March to Freedom* album to preserve the event. As others have argued, culture and politics were inextricable.[32] In 1967, WCHB said "yes" to sponsoring Detroit's premier women's softball team, aptly naming the team the "Soul Sisters." The radio station's sponsorship reinforced the importance of the overtly political endeavor of community broadcasting, and radio announcements of the team's games reinforced the importance of leisure activities by enticing listeners to the team's games.

WCHB helped provide local and national perspective on the riots that interrupted the Soul Sisters' winning season during the summer of 1967. That summer, riots broke out across the country, and the Detroit riots were then the biggest in U.S. history. On July 23, 1967, some members of the Soul Sisters were preparing to play a game at Jayne Field, adjacent to Detroit's predominantly Polish neighborhood of Hamtramck. Recalled Bubbles Hardison, "Suddenly we could see smoke in the city . . . and we found out later the riots had started."[33] Some members of the team, including Jackie Huggins and Coach Stokes, lived in the neighborhoods of the riots. Others drove in to pick them up, only to discover the source of the fires as they found themselves in the thick of it. After a day and a half, Detroit Mayor Cavanagh requested federal troops to quell the storm. The National Guard and U.S. Army arrived on July 25 and stayed until August 2. By the time they left, 7,231 people had been arrested, 43 people were dead (33 blacks and 10 whites), and countless—including one Soul Sister —were injured; at least 5,000 were homeless; and in an area covering 14 square miles, 1,300 buildings had burned to the ground.[34] For two weeks, the Soul Sisters waited for the smoke to clear and the National Guard to leave. The riots and military efforts to bring the city "back to order" meant torn-up streets and curfews that, among other things, restricted the team's mobility and playing time. WCHB kept them apprised of local conditions and more distant perspectives on Detroit.

The Soul Sisters were cramped by the impact that the riots had on softball season, but they also saw the riots in a national context of unrest. For Chapman Sanders, softball in the summer of 1967 includes an image of "Detroit going up in flames."

> In fact, I came from college [at Fisk] after being involved in the protest movement in college, you know, and half of our campus being jailed. And the dogs and the water hoses and so forth. And then I'm at home and we were imposed

with a dusk-to-dawn curfew. I'm saying, I just left this! You know. But, yeah: I remember we were heading towards [downtown]—you know, because we had a game. And we were going to the game. And they canceled the game, so we had to turn around. One of our players, Charlotte—she was from Inkster—she got out of her car to see where they were looting or something. And someone threw a bottle and the bottle hit her and it opened her mouth up. Yeah, and it lasted a long time, and we were on dusk-to-dawn curfews and things like that. Only thing, we were just so happy when it was over so we could get back to playing.[35]

The Soul Sisters' particular experience with the repercussions of the riots reveal the workings of race, sexuality, and gender in a context of highly politicized public geographies.

Though they just wanted to play good ball, the Soul Sisters entered into a history of struggles over city and suburban space that had consistently invoked gender alongside race.[36] In the five months following the riots, 67,000 white residents fled the city to move beyond Eight Mile Road (only 22,000 had left in the previous twelve months); in 1968, 80,000 fled the city. In all-white suburbs, rumors circulated that "black militants" were planning to invade the suburbs to kill white children. When the Ku Klux Klan marched in Taylor (a white suburb) in September 1967, they emphasized the need to protect white women and children from black invaders. At the same time, white segregationists included and enlisted "housewives" to serve in vigilante groups. Eleanor Josaitis, now an antiracist activist who cofounded Focus Hope, vividly recalled her preawakening, housewife days in Taylor: "I would take my turn standing over the expressway, because they were certain that the black people were going to be coming. And I would go and take my turn and stand there to stop them from coming."[37] Between August 1967 and May 1968, roughly half of white suburbanites purchased firearms, and many suburbs established gun clinics specifically to train "housewives and others" in the use of guns.[38] The Soul Sisters, however, did not fit the media-produced profile of black male "militants" and "invaders," nor that of domestic workers. The team simply wanted public park space that formerly belonged to white men, and thus they introduced new gender and race politics and strategies into a struggle that had long been narrated as one centered on black men and white women.

Within the rapidly shifting demographics of Detroit, public parks became sites of symbolic holdings: they could be "won" by blacks through desegregation laws or through white abandonment, or they could be held by beleaguered working-class whites who remained south of Eight Mile Road. Far from lying low in that climate of acute racial tension, the Soul Sisters sought alliances and sponsorship that would allow them to even more powerfully assert their right to desegregate public space. Before the 1968 season began, Charlotte "Stump" Howza solicited Motown Records for sponsorship. Her solicitation began with a letter to the company: "You are a growing company, and we are a growing team." Berry Gordy Jr., the founder of Motown Records, was not himself greatly interested, but members of his family, including his father and sister, fell in love with the team and believed their assertive public style was in keeping with the mission of the Motown Records label.[39] Motown Records had just created its Black Forum label to preserve black history and culture. Producing recordings by authors and activists as diverse as Langston Hughes, Margaret Danner, Amiri Baraka, Elaine Brown, Stokely Carmichael, and Dr. King, the company suggested that there were many ways to build a movement, and that all were important. But as historian Suzanne E. Smith has discussed, Gordy carefully avoided aligning the company with any oppositional political position that could have jeopardized Motown's profits and marketability.[40] In the wake of the riots, both Motown music and softball engaged all the politics of the moment, but without explicitly seeming to do so. Chapman Sanders speculated that Motown sponsored the team "because we sang songs and chants through our games, that's probably why they thought we could sing."[41] A team that evoked black history and culture while it entertained was irresistible.

In 1968, their first summer as the *Motown* Soul Sisters, the team claimed a consistent presence on Jayne Field, a field bounded on three sides by white neighborhoods. They and the Pink Ladies before them had played the field since 1965, thanks to the efforts of Park Board Supervisor Faye Melton, who successfully demanded that the top women's league receive playing time on the city's better fields. Her argument for gender equity did not directly address race, but in the context of public athletics, gender equity could not be divorced from racial desegregation. As in other cities in the upper Midwest, field schedules persistently privileged white men's teams, and any women's team—white or black—was "lucky" to get one game a week on a good field. In Detroit, though a handful of black teams had already gained minimal access to Jayne Field, some believed that the city would not consider Coach Stokes's requests for field improvements because Stokes was black and represented a black women's team. Thus it was that the team defiantly made the improvements themselves.

As the Motown Soul Sisters told the story of their action, they located the field within a long history of demographic changes and civil rights activism. Jayne Field sat outside the northern edge of the all-white ethnic (predominantly Polish) and working-class village of Hamtramck. The western corner of the park touched Conant Gardens, once the wealthiest black neighborhood in Detroit despite the antiblack segregation campaigns begun there in the 1940s.[42] By the late 1960s, African American mobility in the wake of white flight expanded the black neighborhood to the west of Jayne Field in both population and landmass, while racist segregation efforts focused on keeping blacks out of the small area between Jayne Field and Hamtramck to the south. When Huggins described the field by its southeast intersection at Fenelon/Charles, she implied that it belonged to Hamtramck and that the Soul Sisters had successfully staked a claim to that formerly solidly white neighborhood. When Chapman Sanders referred to the field by its northwest intersection at Davidson/Conant, she situated it within a much longer history of highly contested development practices. Either way, the field had been home turf to white men's teams for decades. Far more than a symbolic act, the Soul Sisters built what they needed, moved in, and in the process transformed one of Detroit's key sites of leisure and culture into one enjoyed by black and white men and women. As Huggins hyperbolically bragged, "We drove 'em out. It was all Polish 'til we came."[43] The Soul Sisters did not truly "drive out" Polish people: indeed, Hamtramck itself remained a white enclave surrounded by Detroit, and the neighborhood between Jayne Field and Hamtramck kept blacks out well into the 1980s. But Soul Sisters' story of their takeover of Jayne Field replaced a common declension narrative in which Detroit "gave way" to blackness, poverty, and corruption with a decidedly positive account of change and integration in civic space.

Motown Records' sponsorship of the team tangibly assisted the Jayne Field action by partially relieving the team of year-round fundraising labor and by helping the team project a popular, albeit edgy image. Though softball was a relatively inexpensive sport, players needed money for uniforms, travel, motels, and food if they were to build a Class A team that could claim regular playing time on good fields. Motown sponsorship granted them enough economic stability to imagine their future longevity as a team, and thus also imagine the action that signaled their ongoing stake in and right to noncommercial, civic space.[44]

Motown sponsorship also enhanced the Soul Sisters' unique style: like Motown's musical "girl groups," the team had stage presence to spare, but unlike the singing groups, it was presence constructed in large part through assertive—what some would read as masculine—gender performance that allowed them to take over entire parks. Mixing up signifiers of gender, race, and space made critical differences. In an era of civil rights and black nationalist challenge to the status quo, the literally on-stage blackness and hetero-sex-appeal of Motown's musical girl groups undeniably enhanced their national appeal to cross-over audiences in sometimes contradictory, market-driven ways. Similarly, the softball team, literally outside, could count blackness and gender nonconformity as part of its appeal. But their visible, unmarketable refusal of segregation and racist sexism in civic, noncommercial parks accentuated the ways that even spectatorship involved complicated participation in race and gender politics. For the team, whose primary goal was to play the best possible game in the best parks and tournaments in the country, Motown Records's sponsorship was perfect. Just as WCHB sponsorship signaled the team's identification with black cultural politics without putting the team under siege, so their choice of Motown sponsorship garnered even more popularity in a multiracial city, state, and country.

Although Motown Records was careful not to explicitly articulate an oppositional politics, the Soul Sisters were nonetheless able to use their sponsorship to position themselves as civic actors in a city that had long denied black political participation, and where the citywide high school dropout rate stood at 50 percent. Radical and black nationalist activists distributed proposals to all levels of government demanding recreational opportunities to instill "positive racial pride" for black youth. Meanwhile and with less overt political rhetoric, the Soul Sisters were busy building girls' softball and basketball leagues throughout the city.[45] Slim Huggins explained, "We really took the information we learned early in life, we took it right back into our community. We worked with little kids, we worked with teenagers, and we worked with women. And made a difference."[46] Black nationalist groups insisted that without educational and recreational facilities, youth were lost to the streets and incarceration. Meanwhile, the Soul Sisters began to coach the city's Police Athletic League program that served, as Hardison put it, "little rough boys."[47] Softball was the vehicle for the Soul Sisters' contribution to a black politics that responded to urban crisis by asserting black presence in the so-called democratic public sphere. When Detroit Mayor Roman Gribbs—himself Polish Catholic—made a city proclamation declaring one day a year to be Soul Sisters' Day, he explicitly acknowledged the civic importance of girls' and women's softball and the Soul Sisters' leadership in developing the sport in Detroit. But it mattered equally that women's desegregation of softball generated highly accessible forms of black political participation in Detroit and nationally.

It is important not to overestimate the extent and meanings of desegregation and integration in this story, however. The Soul Sisters drew white and black fans to cheer together for the same team in the same space by taking advantage of both an absence of *complete* segregation and an ironic confluence of cultural and market forces that encouraged limited change. As Suzanne E. Smith has argued of the success of Motown music, the civil rights movement in some senses created a "market" for black culture; the Civil Rights Act of 1964 nationally mandated public integration and thereby "increased the need for positive images of Black Americans." Diana Ross and the Supremes, for example, "held a unique power in a country eager for cultural symbols that racial integration was not only possible but non-threatening."[48] Similarly, black sports teams such as the Harlem Globetrotters and specific black athletes could be celebrated for performing blackness constructed in part through the invocation of an "authentic" athletic aesthetic. At the same time, both blackness and integration could be contained within a physical athletic arena. But if Motown's highly packaged music groups provided a vision of amicable racial integration, the Motown Soul Sisters softball team—always on the edge of sex/gender transgression—exposed the precariousness of that vision.[49]

Public Parks, Public Sexuality

Just as playing top-caliber softball newly asserted black women's public presence, doing so also furthered the emergence of several overlapping sexual subcultures. Analysis of this emergence in the context of softball suggests a history of sexuality that departs from those based primarily on bar life by emphasizing civic space as a visible site of female desire. In this book, chapter 1 argued the significance of bars and dollar parties for queer and feminist political formation during the 1960s and 1970s. Urban histories of GLBT emergence have suggested that before 1970, bars were the central (and sometimes the *only*) public locations of queer community. Bar life itself was designed to avoid public scrutiny, with hidden doors to protect the bar from hostile law enforcers and a homophobic public. Some histories—including this one—acknowledge that in conditions of racist segregation, house parties offered black women further protection from racist and sexist attacks as they built gender–non-normative communities. The weight of historiography centered on bars and the elusive house party thus suggests that the social world of black studs and fems took place far from public view, in dark places, hidden sometimes even from black women themselves. These histories focused on the bar/house party nexus may in fact contribute to the "invisibility" of black women's sexuality—that is, "invisibility" itself may be in part a reified product of these historical paradigms.[50] Alternatively, softball clearly provided a visible arena of queer culture for black as well as white women. A focus on black softball thus disrupts the standard queer history of sexuality paradigms and offers a new lens for recognizing public manifestations of black women's desire.

Black lesbian sexuality and stud/fem gender expression was affirmed not only in places closed to the public and to historical inquiry, it was also affirmed in wide-open spaces. The parks were in full view to everyone who happened to pass by; there were no hidden doors. The worlds of softball and the worlds of bars and house parties overlapped a great deal, but softball took place outdoors, in broad daylight. Though "not all softball players were *that way,*" as Slim Huggins put it, the Soul Sisters cohered a many-layered black queer culture in the midst of civic, noncommercial space: they were models of assertive black female athleticism, and taking over visible public space was as intentional as winning the attention of straight and queer passers-by. Park space did not function as a democratic public sphere, and yet a broader cross-section of people regularly passed through that space than would through any space that operated behind closed doors. Those people brought a heterogeneous set of interests to their spectatorship; whether observers were seeking public signs of sub-cultural and/or activist communities or simply passing the time, the Soul Sisters rewarded them with a show that wove together familiar social codes in extraordinarily original ways.

Designated the toughest team in Detroit largely because of their gen-der, sexual, and racial deviance from white middle-class norms, the Soul Sisters' style could stigmatize or advertise, depending on the audience.

Many nonathletic women who were involved in Detroit's active African American queer subculture during the 1960s went to bars and house parties, but they were equally thrilled to watch the Motown Soul Sisters and considered the team "theirs." In 2001, six of these women gathered after services at Full Truth Fellowship of Christ African American Gay and Lesbian church.[51] Decades after the civil rights movement, Stonewall, and the beginning of the HIV/AIDS epidemic, this openly GLBT church provides community, and these are some of the people who helped bring that about. When asked, "What was there, before this church, even before Stonewall?" their conversation, like the standard histories of sexuality, began with bars, but it did not stay long in that space:

> "We went to bars, those bars, but . . . But, what was the name of that *team*?!"
> "Yes, that *team*!"
> "The Motown—"
> "We had the Motown *Soul* Sisters!"
> "Yes! We did!"
> "We were *all* out watching them play—"
> "—Watching the *studs* play!"
> "Ohh yes! We'd go to watch the *studs* play, I mean, we'd be out there in the stands just *screaming*!"
> "And if you had a girlfriend that played ball, you was *in*—"
> "Uh-*huh*!"
> "*You* had a jock!"
> "Mm *hmm*, you had a *jock*!"[52]

Within that culture, women took on positive identities as fems or studs, developed through a long history of African American socializing. For many women, spectatorship of the Soul Sisters was an important arena for their self-construction as fem fans. Not all jocks were studs, but some fems claimed they "could tell, by watching 'em play, who was," and many insisted that the Soul Sisters were mostly studs. Antoenette, who frequented bars, dollar parties, and church in the 1960s, recalled, "The Soul Sisters: that's where you went if you were looking for studs." Women "went to" the team—or, more literally, they went to the team's civic games. The team and its fans thus constituted a civic space for expressing black women's non-normative gender sensibility and desire, and for thereby building a politicized, public community.

Having gained visibility through Motown sponsorship and through their endless occupation of public parks, the Soul Sisters drew together fans from black sexual subcultures that had previously appeared separate. While the Pink Ladies team had drawn fans who frequented black queer clubs, the Soul Sisters picked up that crowd and also the crowd that one fan, E. Marie, called "the gay church people." (As she explained, "that's where a lot of us found each other, in church, in the choir.") Bars were important, but not all-encompassing. E. Marie acknowledged that an entire gay sub-culture grew up in and identified *primarily* with black churches and church choirs.[53] These subcultures in fact had never been entirely separate. In Black Bottom and Paradise Valley, for example, the churches and bars shared geographical territory along and near Linwood Avenue. Though increasingly poverty-stricken, the area was one wellspring of black political and cultural production during the 1960s: on Linwood Avenue alone, people went to the Shrine of the Black Madonna (Central Congregational), or to the Temple of Islam Number One, or to the New Bethel Baptist Church, and they went to the Bird Cage and the Pink Lady. Just as, in the first half of the twentieth century, poor, middle-, and working-class black women shared more ground through community activism than is often acknowledged, so too did community-building efforts in the 1960s depend on contributions from diverse sources. But as long as communities were constituted indoors, especially in places that seemed as distinct as churches and bars, they would appear to be segregated from each other. On the ball field, in contrast, they visibly shared a new manifestation of black women's defiance and culture: Stump Howza secured the team's place in the political arena of WCHB, Motown, and black media production generally; the team's winning skills drew straight black and white fans who enjoyed watching a good game; the team's gender style attracted fem fans looking for jocks and studs; and Slim Huggins's mother and Rubber Arms Chapman's father made sure that softball would coexist and not interfere with church. As the Soul Sisters drew fans to their games in outdoor gathering places, the team itself became a shared, publicly visible focal point for people from multiple constituencies; the civic space of their games thus provided a location in which diverse people recognized themselves as a larger community within a context of black activism and women's activism more broadly.

Not all observers were fans, however, nor did they share a common interpretation of what they were seeing. Rather, they projected racialized, gendered, and sexualized meanings onto the team relative to their own constructed identities and perceived locations. Many black parents of potential team members feared that their daughters would "become gay" if they played for the Soul Sisters, not because all the players *were* gay but, as Slim put it, "probably because we put winning ahead of everything." Bubbles Hardison had played on white teams before joining the Soul Sisters, and she was used to accusations of lesbian sexuality; she nonchalantly explained, "That's just part of the game." She also acknowledged that there was some truth to the suspicions, stating, "Actually, in reality, there wasn't a team that wasn't partly gay."[54] Yet the Soul Sisters bore the "gay team" reputation more than most other teams at their level. They were the most aggressive and, by the late 1960s, the only black team in the top division leagues, and they were also the favorite team of a boisterous black fem subculture. But if from one perspective, the team was too "gay," many white parents—including Bubble's parents before they got to know the team—feared the blackness of the team, and they associated their competitive style with race, if not also with sexuality. As much as the Soul Sisters tried not to fuel their reputation as a gay team, some people's responses to their competitive style and identity as a black team linked and pathologized blackness, black women's sexuality, and queerness.

Attention to dynamics within the team reveals that they did not project a singular nor coherent image, as members coped with the inextricability of race, gender, sexuality, and class constituted in very slippery spaces. Coach Stokes went to some effort to manage the image of the team, and these efforts focused on the arenas around which respectability hinged. Defying gender and sexual norms, the team sometimes asserted the still greater deviance of the Pink Ladies—"those lesbians"—who were known to be associated with a queer bar. As the Soul Sisters told it, the Pink Ladies "used to do a little bit of everything," including "kissing in the parking lot and all that kind of stuff." Slim was quick to point out,

> That was one of the things Coach definitely didn't want his team to be involved in. Like that was his thing: "You're not going to do that." You know, he told you even though you were old enough to do it. He told you, "Don't do it when you're with me. When you're on your own, that's your business. But when you're with us, you don't do those kind of things." And occasionally he'd run across one trying to challenge him and trying to do something to contradict what he said. And he'd get rid of 'em.[55]

On a team already negotiating race and sexual stigma, definitive signs of lesbian sex would not be permitted—indeed, they would be negated in part by projecting them outside of the team itself.

Stokes's efforts nevertheless accentuated gender and sexual differences within the team itself, as he sought to "protect" the youngest players who were, after all, his first recruits. Several players who had formed the first core of the team when they were fifteen and sixteen recalled that he would not let them braid their hair in cornrows. By the time he made that rule, those players were approaching twenty, but they were still among the youngest on the team. Bubbles explained, "It wasn't *lady-like* looking. It wasn't whatever. . . . That was just him. He didn't like it. It didn't look right."[56] Cornrows, that is, could not just be a marker of racial identity; rather, they signified gender and sexual deviance in women who were supposed to approximate a middle-class (lady-like) image. Slim's interpretation of the hair rule also conflated style with sexuality and age, as she tried to make sense of the fact that *some* players *did* braid their hair:

> It was about, there were some gay females on the team. [Vic interrupts: "For sure, us being younger, he was not going to let us be involved in that same lifestyle."] With the four of us, he took ownership of us. If there were women drinking or gambling, or if the gays were together, they'd chase us away. And if he heard we were near them, or around them, he'd . . . try to talk to us, tell us, "You don't need to do that, you can just play ball." So it was always about protecting the image. Like I said, *my* family was dead set against: "you *know* that's a *boy's* game!" They didn't want me playing with . . . [trails off]. And when he came to my house, he gave that perfect gentleman speech, "I'm going to look out for her and I'm going to take care of her."[57]

Taking care and protecting the image meant prohibiting younger players from interacting with older gay players and adopting hairstyles that defied black middle-class gender norms. Playing a "boy's" game, young women's lady-ness could only be protected by a gentleman, even if the gentleman could not prevent the gender and sexual transgression of cornrows and the gay associations that accompanied the team as a whole.

Rules about socializing and hairstyle were also attempts to protect the team from racist attacks: if hairstyle marked deviant sexuality, it also marked race. At the time the cornrow rule emerged, there were two white players on the team, Bubbles and Kathleen "Kip" Relente. As Bubbles recalled, "Stokes said *they* [the black women] couldn't braid their hair. So the *white* girls got their hair braided and went to the ball field. He didn't say nothing to *us* about *we* couldn't do it. So Jan [Chapman] did it all up in cornrows—ha ha ha!" Stokes did not greatly influence the hairstyles of older team members in their thirties, nor did he think to tell the white players not to adopt a distinctly black (and in his view, deviant) hairstyle. Younger players' response had the potential to deconstruct the conflation of hairstyle with race and sexuality. However, rules about hair were not entirely of Stokes's own making. The newspaper printed Bubbles's picture —with cornrows—in part because she broke a larger social rule of racial distinction and boundaries. If, within a black context, cornrows on a woman signaled one kind of queerness, to a white audience, cornrows on a white woman on an otherwise black team marked another. White audiences might not have read cornrows as a lesbian style, but Kip's and Bubbles's presence on the team and their hairstyle transgressed racial boundaries already overdetermined by the allure and fear of racial mixing.

For a team that defied gender, race, and sexual norms, family became important in complex ways. Though Coach Stokes appealed to Slim's birth family to secure her place on the team, Slim herself was busy creating her own family. "It was hard [playing on the team] because of the reputation against us. The family thing was key, but more so, it was part of being a unit. *These* were my sisters, my family. My birth family didn't like me doing the things I liked, but these people did."[58] It was always in the context of difficult incidents that team members asserted the family nature of the team. Rubber Arms began, "We'd go to towns and experience the racism, the 'niggers go home' things. It happened so much you don't count individual incidents. You have to go ahead with your life. Because all we could do was keep playing softball. But as far as family, that's what we were. You'd sacrifice all for each other. We loved it."[59] Virginia West attested to the ongoing vitality of family in this context: "We raised our kids, cousins, nieces, the kids grew up that way with the team, callin' us all auntie—those kids had so many aunties!" As was true for other full-time ball players in the upper Midwest, for the Soul Sisters "the team really became a family"[60] in several respects.

While creating the team as family offered solidarity in the face of racism, doing so also ran counter to dominant gender expectations. Stump Howza, who was featured on a 1974 *Detroit News* story about "married women who play softball," explained, "It took a lot outta me. Because I had three families: my sisters and brothers, and *my* family, and the team."[61] Normative family commitments revolved around extended and adopted kin; though they did not always require a husband-wife-children unit, neither did they revolve around a cohort of women who initially shared little more than an obsession with softball. Normative gender/sex pressure came in the form of gay baiting, among other things. As Vic explained, "You had to be strong. People gave the team hassles because they said we were gay. Some members were, but some had families. And if you weren't messin' with a guy, you were [assumed to be] gay. But if you had a family, you couldn't play unless your family, your boyfriend or husband was into it." Howza concurred, "I had a boyfriend who didn't want me to play, and I dropped him just like that. That was *easy*. Lots of husbands and boyfriends put pressures on us: 'Why you wanna go out with her, why you wanna play that game, why you wanna sleep with her,' and all that. We were just together playing softball, all the time."[62] Many also acknowledged that there was something sensual about their intense passion for the game: teammates self-consciously described the pleasure they felt when the ball slapped into the pocket of a good-smelling glove, and they chided each other about sleeping with their favorite gloves. Not only was the lifestyle of the committed athlete a bit queer, the game itself held an aesthetic and sensual attraction that, for some, constituted athletic identity.

Despite marital, familial, class, and neighborhood differences within the team, players reacted to a singular reputation. The reputation of being sexually deviant accrued to the whole team, notwithstanding the age segregation that was intended to protect the younger players. Vic explained, "People assumed *we're* gay automatically because the four of us were always together. The *gay* people on our team knew that we weren't that way. But the reputation was, '*all* of them are gay, and that's the older ones and that's the younger ones.'" Slim concurred,

It was hard for me to convince them that everybody on the team was not that way. . . . It was just rumors to try to break up the connection between us, more than anything. That's the basis of it, trying to break up the team. And it was us four staying together, and another five staying together, but when we came to the field, we played. This five hung out in bars. This five hung out playing a sport somewhere, we played it 365 days a year.[63]

Off the field, team members separated into distinct sexual communities marked by distinct spaces. Huggins's narrative, for example, distinguished the culture of bars (gay women) from the culture of ball fields and basketball courts (full-time athletes). The ball field itself thereby became a space that was as queer as it was athletic, and in this way, forged a new, public subculture.

Spectators, too, had to negotiate whether and how they would project stigma or heroics onto the Soul Sisters. Observers interested in non-normative gender performance celebrated and amplified the team's public queerness. The pleasure of spectatorship for them came in part from being among a diverse crowd that cheered the team both despite and because of its deviance from local gender and race norms. Many other observers, however, gave the team the opportunity to demonstrate that upstanding, heterosexual black women could play ball. Televised media liked to make stories of "married women playing softball," and a few Soul Sisters regularly stepped up to the plate.[64] The team, and perhaps especially Coach Stokes, put at least one heterosexual-appearing foot forward. In that way, they offered an expanded range of possible and acceptable female gender performance within heterosexual structures. This allowed many spectators to overlook the deviant sexuality of individual members, even though the team as a whole pushed the bounds of heteronormativity within both African American and white cultural contexts. Fans were willing to project queerness or straightness onto the team, and the team supplied all the cues necessary for either reading. Though the Soul Sisters' assertions of blackness, queerness, and desegregation were too threatening to many, these exact qualities drew a fan base with many-layered desires for change. They celebrated the athleticism and seriousness and blackness of the team because those attributes had led to success by any measure, both on the field and off.

Crossing State Lines

When the Soul Sisters traveled to out-of-town tournaments, they took their politicized black cultural style and their distinctly queer publicity across state lines, extending their impact beyond Detroit. Interstate travel and tournament games engaged whole new dimensions of civic life and civic space. Though their style was forged in Detroit, its cultural connection to Black Power and queerness was apparent and offensive to many they encountered on the road, in public parks, restaurants, and hotels across the country. At the same time, many children and adult fans in other cities took the team as a positive role model of athleticism, blackness, and non-normative gender possibilities. The Soul Sisters also positively influenced other teams around the country, such as the Avantis of Minneapolis, showing them in so many ways "how to play the game." Tournament travel allowed extended contact and cultural exchange between the Soul Sisters and others especially throughout the Midwest and South, providing one avenue along which women's activism took shape nationally as well as locally.

In Detroit, the Soul Sisters made some decisions about where and when to challenge local norms shaping civic space. Playing softball nationally, the team had somewhat less control over their encounters with white supremacy. When the Soul Sisters played white teams at national championship games in Pennsylvania, Georgia, Florida, Tennessee, and other states, game officiating often turned against them. Umpires would declare a Soul Sister safe on base, only to change their minds. Or they would declare the team's bats illegal, or accuse the team of breaking codes of conduct on the field. The team traveled by bus, and interstate travel was often rough going. Incidents like the following, at a Georgia truck stop after a national tournament, were common. As Bubbles described it,

> They go in there, and they says, "I'd like to order a hamburger, a chocolate shake, and some soup." "We don't have any shakes. We're out of ice cream. We don't have any soup. We're all out of such and such and such." And then a truck driver came in and got a shake and a soup, got what *we* wanted but *we* couldn't have it. We ended up leaving there and having to get back on the bus. And it was very little of us actually getting our food.[65]

While laws regulating interracial interstate travel in Southern states had recently been abolished, civility was often meted out (or not) to sustain racist civic norms. Also in the North, the team had trouble getting food and even using public bathrooms. Jan Chapman and Charlotte Howza each told about the team stopping at a Kalamazoo rest stop to fix a flat tire and being ordered by the rest stop personnel not to get off the bus.[66]

In restaurants and on the fields, racist hostility against the team was sometimes directed toward Bubbles. Chapman Sanders recalled, "They [the waitpeople] were always throwing food at Bubbles. At one Illinois truck stop, a waitress slid her plate at her so hard it crashed to the floor, then she just scooped it up and put it down in front of her again. But she served *us* our food."[67] On the fields, spectators taunted Bubbles in ways that even more obviously targeted the blackness of the team. Several Soul

Sisters recounted that white crowds shouted about "that white nigger" on the team, yelling, "Look at that: Poor white girl's got them braids."[68] Bubbles "wore black" not only with her hairstyle but also by being on the team at all, suggesting that racial boundaries were far more slippery than segregationists wanted to allow. Her recounting of a national tournament in York, Pennsylvania, placed her experience in the context of racism against the whole team, when she commented, "York, Pennsylvania, was not a good place to be. At the time, Harrisburg was the home of the imperial wizard of the Ku Klux Klan. That was not really good. They chanted from the stands about 'those darkies, and that white girl's been with them so long, she's just like one of them.' "[69] In the upper Midwest, as in the South, white supremacy created a place for everyone; in an era of massive social movement, Bubbles did not stay in hers.

Many Soul Sisters experienced the North as "worse than" the South well into the 1970s. In the upper Midwest, the Soul Sisters were known as a show team as well as one of the best teams in the region, and even when other teams invited the competition and the show, officials and crowds were not always equally welcoming. In 1971, a team in Sheboygan, Wisconsin, invited the Soul Sisters to a regional tournament. In Bubbles's description, "They begged us to come. When we played ball, we played good ball, but we also cheered and sang songs from the bench. We'd give this whole package kind of thing, kind of like entertainment, you know. We'd get rallies going, we'd start playing. And things would happen. It would be like that. When we went to Sheboygan, [the crowds] just plain said, 'Send the niggers home!' " If white women's teams challenged normative gender constructions (and they did, as the next chapter shows), white spectators possibly recuperated their protected status by disassociating them from black teams. A show team like the Soul Sisters especially needed to be contained and their "rallies" prevented.

Alongside racist attacks, the team won the admiration and respect of many African American communities throughout the country, attesting to the impact of their challenge to racist and sexist norms. Players emphasized ways that their presence in Southern black neighborhoods created an immediate fan base. Stump Howza, after talking about the Kalamazoo rest stop, recalled, "When we'd go barnstorming—that's what Stokes called it— in the South, they'd treat us like it was the *parade* coming to town: they'd roll out the red carpet for us, follow us around and treat us like we were kings, we were *the* thing."[70] Slim Huggins also hinted at ways that the Soul

Sisters' style was particularly meaningful within some cultural contexts: "We used to chant, we used to sing. When we'd go down South, all the little kids would run up. They'd be standing around and they'd just be dancing, and they'd want to sing. We'd sign balls and give 'em to 'em. So we developed a little crew that would hang out with us whenever we were around in their community. Whenever we played, every time, they'd be right there."[71] They inspired youth and adults alike, not only by being a winning team, but by their very showy style of moving about the world. Soul Sister Rujeania Vance recalled, "The Soul Sisters were *unbelievable* players: We'd drive up in the bus humming (we couldn't really sing, but, we were *Motown*, so we *had* to play the part!), and people would just go crazy welcoming us, feeding us, inviting us in."[72] To fans, the Soul Sisters projected black pride and success—black is beautiful—by transforming older cultural forms such as barnstorming and singing into new ways of taking up public space: they were soul sisters, and they were kings.

In the upper Midwest, the Soul Sisters were more than good competition for a few other top-caliber teams. Tournament travel provided contexts for education and exchange, as teams built relationships with each other on and off the ball field. Jan Chapman, who explained that the Soul Sisters *had* to travel to find competition, especially admired the Avantis, a white, predominantly working-class team from Minneapolis: "They wore black jackets—they were tough, very tough. I think they beat us a couple times, they were very strong hitters. They were a team that reminded us we had to get our stuff together."[73] The Avantis themselves were keen to build a relationship with the Soul Sisters in the late 1960s to learn to play the game, as Avanti Linda Joseph put it, "the way it's *supposed* to be played."[74] For the Avantis, playing the game the right way meant, in part, patterning their style after predominantly black teams such as the Dana Gardens and the Rebels of Cincinnati, as well as the Motown Soul Sisters of Detroit. Doing so, the Avantis had become one of the upper Midwest's hardest-hitting teams by 1967. By that time, they were also developing a reputation as a show team—a team with the talent not only to win games but to woo the crowd with fancy routines and plays. They found a perfect, crowd-pleasing match in the Motown Soul Sisters. The two teams forged a relationship around some shared goals—especially around the desire to play a great game—and also through shared defiance of white, middle-class gender norms. This relationship introduced the Avantis to the ways that racism and white privilege affected their own softball-centered lives.

While the Soul Sisters all remember games in which officials questioned their bats, Howza specifically remembered the tournament in one Minnesota town: "The umpire disqualified all the Soul Sisters' bats, because of a rumor that they were all lead-filled, but the Avantis offered theirs to us. We all hit with that same one bat, but at least we could play. No other team would share their bats." Through invitational tournaments, the two teams built a supportive rivalry with each other that went beyond the ball field. Howza continued, "The Avantis were so nice to us, they made us feel so much at home. We tried to return it when they were here."[75] For Avanti Betty Hawes, building relationships with black teams was an important part of playing nationally ranked softball, and the Soul Sisters were her fondest team, for the competition, friendship, and education. She recalled, "When we went to Detroit, they took us to their places. And they told us, 'don't go anywhere without us.' "[76] Hospitality required attending to the differentially distributed meanings of "home" across racially segregated geographies.

Avanti Linda Joseph emphasized that tournament travel presented many kinds of unforeseen opportunities that would have been unavailable to most white working-class women in Minnesota. She explained, "We had our eyes opened about race" traveling in the South and experiencing Southern-style segregation: "We didn't know about how racial everything was. Like, going to nationals in Durham, North Carolina, it really opened our eyes about another way of life there. They were having a KKK rally and had the whole street closed. There was a restaurant with a sign that said 'no niggers allowed.' It was a real eye-opener, and I never would have been there if it weren't for softball."[77] But racism was not always so apparent to the Avantis. Joseph described York, Pennsylvania, as "a quaint little town"; the Avantis did not notice Klan influence, nor did they suspect that for some people, as Bubbles put it, "that was not a good place to be." While the Soul Sisters consciously navigated racial hostility, the Avantis experienced a world organized around white mobility.

Above all, the Avantis' relationship with the Motown Soul Sisters in their own home state introduced the Avantis to the ways that racism surrounded the game of softball. Joseph, Betty Hawes, and teammate Sandy recalled the mutual hospitality between the teams, but it was also clear that the Avantis could address only some and not all attacks against the teams. At an invitational tournament in Austin, Minnesota, for example, the Avantis initiated a walk-out boycott of a sponsoring bar (the Eagles Club) that refused to serve the Soul Sisters. The Avantis, having invited the Soul Sisters to join them at the bar, were shocked to discover such blatant racism in a venue that they had comfortably patronized for years. As Sandy explained, "We all got up and walked out. That was toward the mid-1970s. Well, that's *small* town. But the whole place was packed with teams, and everybody left, everybody got up and left. And then it was empty." Such incidents could become activist moments for players who were otherwise unaware of racism surrounding the game. Hawes summed up their encounters with racist exclusions: "Anyhow, we ran into those sorts of things. We never had *any* problems with *players*. We played a lot of black teams, but *never* had any problems on the field or anything, nothing, not even close to any problems."[78] The Avantis thus used their own good playing relationship with the Soul Sisters to distinguish themselves from a harsher public culture surrounding softball.

As teams that got to the top by defying white, middle-class gender norms, the Avantis and the Soul Sisters had much in common. Each team was considered the toughest in its respective city, and "tough" referred to a similar set of characteristics, all of which earned the reputation of sexual deviance in both contexts. Of the Soul Sisters, one Detroit woman recalled, "Most of them were big women, and their *arms*! They could throw and hit like that, even the men took note!"[79] Of the Avantis, Hollis Monnett recalled that the team "was almost feared, because they recruited the bigger and better athletes. I mean, those women could really put it over the fence!"[80] Both teams were the first in their area to introduce below-the-knee baseball pants to women's games. Spectators and Avantis alike acknowledge that "the Avantis had some rough-looking characters" who "were very intimidating."[81] Hawes surmised that "we intimidated people because we were *so* together. We were together socially, too: if it happened to one of us, it happened to all of us. We were together *all* the time."[82] And yet all returned to Joseph's explanation of the team's gay reputation: "The Avantis were the dykes, yeah. All we did to get that reputation, was, we played the game the way it should be played. The other teams didn't understand coming hard into a base, or sliding."[83] Both the Soul Sisters and the Avantis developed high-caliber women's softball within and against cultural contexts that associated size, aggression, and primary intimacy with sexual deviance. Both teams embraced as well as countered those associations, simultaneously occupying public space in new ways and carving resistant spaces out of deviant reputations.

In the absence of other queer-positive public contexts, the Motown Soul Sisters fostered an oppositional subculture around occupation of civic space, and teams like the Avantis explicitly drew on just that model. While other teams in the Midwest were also learning a more aggressive style of play, the Avantis had formed in 1961 around an additional mission: as a rule, they would not discriminate against lesbians or against women who did not conform to prevailing gender norms.[84] The team's strategy for creating a positive image included inviting the best women's teams— especially the Soul Sisters—to provide models of aggressive, hard-hitting play and an unapologetic, showy style that defied white middle-class gender norms. In this way, too, the Soul Sisters and softball brought people into diffuse politicized actions that cohered in the civil rights, feminist, and gay and lesbian liberation movements of the era.

Without proclaiming an overt political agenda, the Motown Soul Sisters transgressed the norms regulating the uses and users of public softball diamonds and in so doing, exposed the inherently political and contested nature of civic space. Softball was one of few contexts in which women during the 1960s publicly expressed assertive physicality and desire; tournament travel further allowed working-class black and white women to enact not only a local but also a national culture of women's activism. Each time the Soul Sisters occupied athletic fields, they offered models for racial desegregation, suggested new ways for women to take up public space, and asserted the positive value of non-normative gender/sexual expression. Even as freeways demolished their homes, they increased girls' and women's access to civic athletic space, and in the process they changed the significance of those very spaces and their occupants.

Just as struggles over the diamond required the Soul Sisters to develop a sense of themselves as public actors, so too did those struggles give form to social movement consciousness. The Soul Sisters took an avowedly apolitical stance even when they resisted segregation, racism, and homophobia to occupy the field. Yet these became critical dimensions of feminist activism, and many women who developed overtly feminist politics did so through very similar spatial contestations. As civic spaces, softball diamonds could not be extracted from larger structural conditions. Teams like the Soul Sisters and the Avantis together helped make obvious the ways that women entered a cultural and political matrix rich with possibility when they occupied civic athletic space. It was thus not surprising that emerging, self-identified feminists at the turn of the decade were drawn to such locations and strategies to build regional sexual subcultures and political consciousness, and that they called their work "feminist." Those feminists, and the ways they took up civic athletic spaces, are the subject of the next chapter.

COMMERCIAL SPACES
1 Augie's
2 King's Ransom
3 In Between
4 Lost and Found
5 MS
6 Other You
7 Sue and Nan's
8 Up North
9 Chez Ron
10 Ebony Room
11 Mark IV

**FEMINIST
INSTITUTIONAL SPACES**
12 Pride and Prejudice
13 Susan B's
14 Mama Peaches

INSTITUTIONAL SPACES
15 Lesbian Feminist Center
16 CWLU
17 Women in Crisis Can Ask/
    Mountain Moving (1976)
18 Mountain Moving in
    Mama Peaches (1977)
19 Mountain Moving
    (in Methodist Church)
20 Jane Addams Hull House Center
21 Hull House "Spanish Outpost"
22 Liberty Hall (aka Wobbly Hall)
23 Lincoln Park Presbyterian Church
    (Gay Women's caucus, Lavender
    Woman, Chicago Lesbian Liberation)

CIVIC SPACES
24 Horner Park
25 Koskiusko Park
26 Lincoln Park

Chicago

Map prepared by Heather Francisco, Cartography Lab, University of Wisconsin, Madison, 2006.

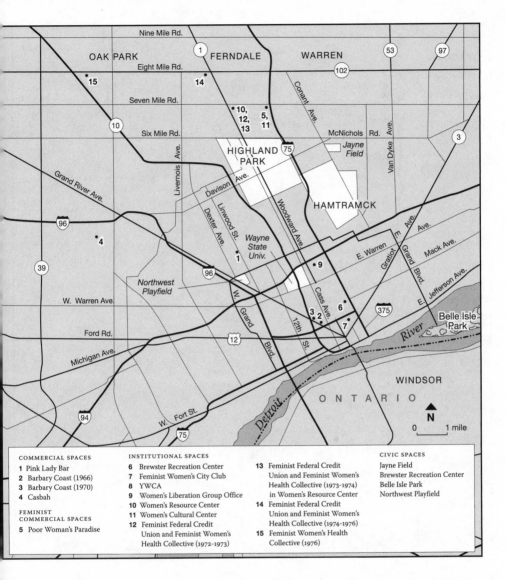

COMMERCIAL SPACES
1 Pink Lady Bar
2 Barbary Coast (1966)
3 Barbary Coast (1970)
4 Casbah

FEMINIST COMMERCIAL SPACES
5 Poor Woman's Paradise

INSTITUTIONAL SPACES
6 Brewster Recreation Center
7 Feminist Women's City Club
8 YWCA
9 Women's Liberation Group Office
10 Women's Resource Center
11 Women's Cultural Center
12 Feminist Federal Credit Union and Feminist Women's Health Collective (1972-1973)
13 Feminist Federal Credit Union and Feminist Women's Health Collective (1973-1974) in Women's Resource Center
14 Feminist Federal Credit Union and Feminist Women's Health Collective (1974-1976)
15 Feminist Women's Health Collective (1976)

CIVIC SPACES
Jayne Field
Brewster Recreation Center
Belle Isle Park
Northwest Playfield

Detroit

Map prepared by Heather Francisco, Cartography Lab, University of Wisconsin, Madison, 2006.

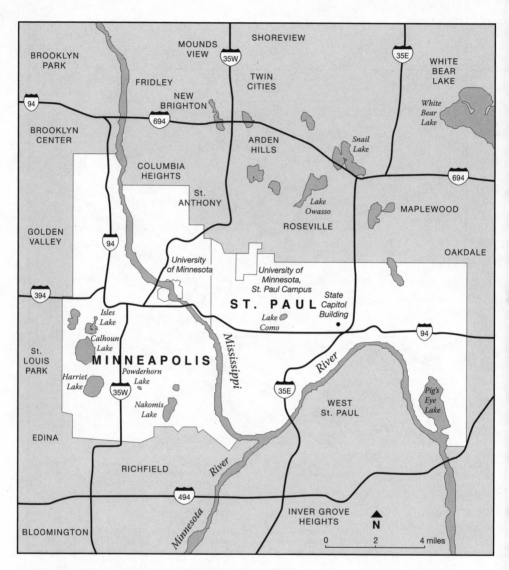

Minneapolis-St. Paul Metropolitan Area

Map prepared by Richard Worthington, Cartography Lab, University of Wisconsin, Madison, 2007.

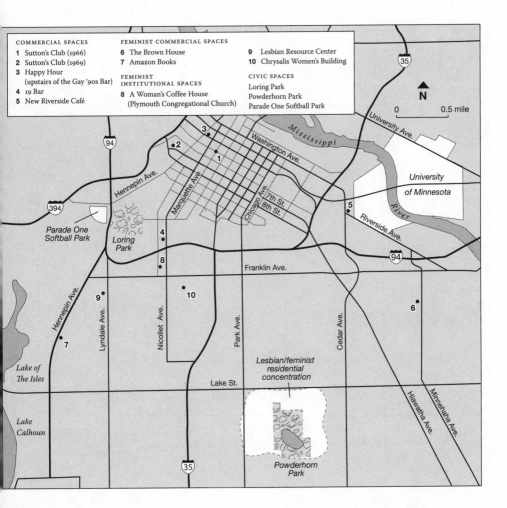

COMMERCIAL SPACES
1 Sutton's Club (1966)
2 Sutton's Club (1969)
3 Happy Hour
  (upstairs of the Gay '90s Bar)
4 19 Bar
5 New Riverside Café

FEMINIST COMMERCIAL SPACES
6 The Brown House
7 Amazon Books

FEMINIST
INSTITUTIONAL SPACES
8 A Woman's Coffee House
  (Plymouth Congregational Church)

9 Lesbian Resource Center
10 Chrysalis Women's Building

CIVIC SPACES
Loring Park
Powderhorn Park
Parade One Softball Park

N
0   0.5 mile

Mississippi
University Ave.
University
of Minnesota
River
Washington Ave.
Hennepin Ave.
Marquette Ave.
Chicago Ave.
7th St.
8th St.
Riverside Ave.
94
394
Parade One
Softball Park
Loring
Park
Franklin Ave.
94
Hennepin Ave.
Lyndale Ave.
Nicollet Ave.
Park Ave.
Cedar Ave.
Hiawatha Ave.
Minnehaha Ave.
Lake of
The Isles
Lesbian/feminist
residential
concentration
Lake St.
Lake
Calhoun
35
Powderhorn
Park

Minneapolis

Map prepared by Heather Francisco, Cartography Lab, University of Wisconsin, Madison, 2006.

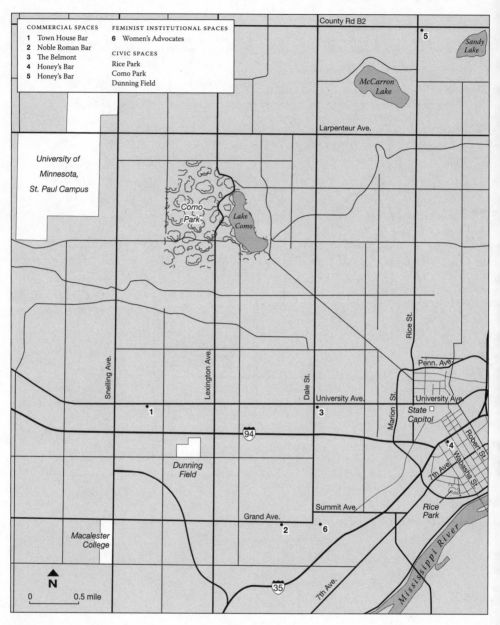

County Rd B2

Sandy Lake

McCarron Lake

Larpenteur Ave.

University of
Minnesota,
St. Paul Campus

Como Park

Lake Como

Rice St.

Penn. Ave.

Snelling Ave.

Lexington Ave.

Dale St.

University Ave.

Marion St.

University Ave.

State Capitol

94

Dunning Field

Summit Ave.

Rice Park

7th Ave.

Wabasha St.

Robert St.

Grand Ave.

Macalester College

N

0   0.5 mile

35

7th Ave.

Mississippi River

St. Paul

Map prepared by Heather Francisco, Cartography Lab, University of Wisconsin, Madison, 2006.

Four

Out in Left Field

Feminist Movement and Civic Athletic Space

Parade Stadium, downtown Minneapolis, 1971. Softball players on two of the most distinctive Class AA teams in the nation shake hands, laughing, at the end of a well-played game. The Avantis of Minneapolis are a nationally ranked team of predominantly working-class white women who bear the reputation of being one of the "dykiest-looking" teams in the Midwest. They thrill to host the Motown Soul Sisters of Detroit, an African American team, also nationally ranked, and—the Avantis know from experience—source of fun times both on and off the field. In the stands, a small group of white, emerging feminists swoon over star athletes, turning them into icons of sexual self-determination. As the feminists leave the stadium, they practice the athletes' gaits and mannerisms and discuss the visible intimacy among team members. They decide to create Minnesota's first "out lesbian" recreational league softball team and name it the Wilder Ones.

For the feminists who would become the Wilder Ones, the Avantis modeled how to be "out lesbians": they played hard and looked tough in their baseball pants and black jackets, flagrantly defying middle-class gender norms. Prior to the gay and lesbian liberation movement, softball provided a visible arena of lesbian community when other arenas were hidden, exclusive, or absent. As Connie Harlan recalled of the 1950s and 1960s, "Back then, when you're new in town, the first thing you do is you look for the softball teams, because that's where you know you can find the lesbians."[1] Most top-caliber teams included many gay women among their members, but the Avantis stood out even among those teams: as Avanti Betty Hawes explained, "Well, we were *more* that way.

We were definitely more that way."[2] That lesbian spectacle is precisely what drew the Wilder Ones to the Avantis' games. But the Avantis had spent a decade modeling themselves after outstanding teams like the Motown Soul Sisters, *not* in order to learn how to be out lesbians but in order to become hard-hitting athletes who promoted new ways for women to move in the world. Ironically, not long after the feminist Wilder Ones "came out" on the ball field, they began to perceive the Avantis to be "terribly closeted."

> Horner Park, Chicago, August 1974. MS Lounge had defeated Why-Not-Inn again, and as was their tradition, they invited the losing team to the MS Lounge bar for drinks and free food. Members of the Chicago Women's Liberation Union's "Secret Storm" Outreach work group who were playing on the Why-Not-Inn team handed out copies of their socialist feminist newsletter to women in the park and decided it was time to finally take up MS Lounge on their invitation. Sponsored by a predominantly black lesbian bar, MS Lounge was the first "admittedly gay" team and the only black team in the Horner Park league. All summer, teams in the Horner Park women's recreational league had struggled to win gender and class equity from the Park District. Yet many of the teams in the league expressed discomfort with MS Lounge's hospitality. Thus, when Why-Not-Inn said "yes" to MS, the CWLU Secret Storm group hoped the summer's struggles had generated a little more solidarity among the women who used the parks. But they were nervous: Secret Storm's goal was not to promote out-lesbian politics but to build socialist feminism in working-class neighborhoods, and they hoped their alliance with MS Lounge would not alienate white, working-class players.

In April 1974, after several years of organizing with white and white ethnic women in high schools and junior colleges on Chicago's Northwest Side, women in the Outreach group of the CWLU learned that public parks had great potential as organizing spaces.[3] That spring, the gender discrimination endemic to Chicago's park system had turned violent as white men and women who played softball in Horner Park physically fought each other over their respective rights to the diamond. Outreach—calling themselves Secret Storm—entered the fray, seeing that the parks could be another space in which to connect with working-class women, catalyze activism around women's access to public space, and bring working-class women into socialist feminism more broadly. Secret Storm, that is, was not a team but a "work group" that quickly became dedicated to utilizing softball as an organizing tool. Unlike the Wilder Ones, they did not seek to build sexual identity or sexuality-based political community, but rather to replace capitalist production and reproduction with a more equitable, less sexist and classist system. Along with many of Chicago's grassroots activists, Outreach also believed that "you do the most when you organize within your own racial group."[4] But sports organizing, a time-worn labor union practice,[5] took on unanticipated dimensions for Secret Storm as they found themselves in an arena in which sexuality and race demanded explicit attention. The ball field brought together prior, white working-class women's softball cultures, white women newly resisting heterosexual oppressions, and out black lesbians. Over time, Secret Storm responded to the dynamics on the diamond. Just as their efforts transformed the gendered uses of public parks, so, too, did Secret Storm's experience in the parks deeply challenge the parameters of CWLU's initial socialist feminist mission.

This is a story about the establishment, during the 1960s and 1970s, of public spaces that gave new visibility to diverse lesbian subcultures. It is also a story about the establishment of spaces in which a variety of women publicly rebelled against gender conventions and heterosexism as part of an overt, feminist politics. Softball in public parks was an activity and location through which a wide range of political activism took place. By 1972, Title IX had federally mandated gender equity in educational facilities, including scholastic athletics, and Billie Jean King had already gone to the courts with Bobby Riggs. All over the country, women were seeking the right of their daughters to play in Little League. In that moment, thanks in part to the prior groundbreaking work of women like those who played for the Soul Sisters and Avantis during the 1960s, challenging the gender, race, and class exclusions of public parks made sense to women coming from countless different contexts. Through broadly based women's activism, these civic spaces became a common and powerful location in which women proliferated diverse and politically minded communities.

This chapter elucidates the ways that a variety of feminist interests emerged and took form in civic athletic space from the late 1960s through the mid-1970s. In some ways, it could seem as though women arrived on the ball field as members of distinct subcultural groups; by the mid-1970s, especially, participants made much of differences between gay women, feminists, and feminist lesbian presence on the fields.[6] Historical and spatial analysis tells a more interesting story, however. The softball diamond was not a given terrain for women, much less a static one; neither did already-formed subcultures simply visit that space. Instead, through the very effort to gain civic athletic space, women actually shaped the spatial contexts of softball; through that effort and in those spatial contexts, subcultures emerged and interacted. Women of an established, working-class softball culture inspired and challenged self-identified feminists in their methods of securing civic athletic spaces for women. Analyzing feminist engagements with civic athletic space underscores the particular role that lesbians played in the development of feminism and also reveals feminism's connections to gay women who did not consider themselves activists, much less feminists. Feminist and feminist lesbian groups, meanwhile, distinguished themselves from each other in part around different ideals for the public expression of gender and sexual identity, but analysis of their emergence reveals their common indebtedness to working-class subcultures. Thus, rather than positing concrete distance between various subcultures, the chapter highlights related strategies of taking up civic athletic space and the links between "groups" that may otherwise appear unconnected. Together, they broadly enhanced the presence and expression of women in civic spaces and fueled distinctly feminist politics.

Sexuality was central to softball within many different cultural contexts. Indeed, sexuality was central to conceptions and uses of civic park space, and thus played a major role in women's strategies of athletically claiming civic space. Homophobia and heterosexism along with race and class shaped all women's organizing efforts on the ball field, albeit differently: these dynamics shaped working-class cultures and gay women who "played it" but didn't "say it," as well as feminist lesbians who put an increasing emphasis on "out lesbian" sexuality. Homophobia also shaped the efforts of activists who did not consider sexuality to be their issue. One can distinguish different communities by the manner in which they negotiated sexuality on the ball field: some groups generated lesbian styles within public parks while at the same time using the multiple meanings of athletics to create styles that "family-minded" people did not have to read as lesbian; others insisted that their performance be read as lesbian. Regardless of strategy, women's activism turned the ball field into a space that could be variously public, democratic, feminist, family, lesbian, and socialist.

This perspective on public parks evidences the creative synergy among

groups formerly assumed to be disconnected. In showing the mutual rein-
forcement of feminist and lesbian feminist organizing, it challenges a sim-
plistic "gay-straight split" so common in historiographies of the era.
Additionally, in showing the intentional but often intentionally veiled collaboration of feminist organizers and working-class athletic subcultures, it
challenges the vast gulf that queer theory and feminist historiography have
posited between prior working-class gay women and Second Wave feminists. Emerging and ever-changing subcultures did differentiate themselves from each other in their uses of civic space, often forming distinctions around gender, sexuality, class, and race. But to the extent that all in
some measure challenged the gender and sexual hierarchies embedded in
civic athletic space, they did so by borrowing, copying, and modeling
themselves after each other in those shared public spaces.

From Detroit to Minneapolis to Chicago, public parks offered fields of
political possibilities as softball became a premier site for challenging
sexism across race, class, and sexuality. Feminist lesbians and socialist
feminists each drew inspiration from women who had already won some
portion of park space—indeed, they gravitated toward the parks because
they could see that something worthy of feminism was already happening
there. But as they took to the fields in the name of lesbian liberation and
feminism, they found themselves participating in far more diverse social
contexts than they had initially envisioned. The chapter begins with the
Avantis and Wilder Ones of Minneapolis to analyze the emergence of an
explicitly feminist lesbian subculture. The Wilder Ones used softball as an
activity through which to become *out* feminist lesbians. Even when they
modeled themselves on established, visible lesbian subcultures, occupying
ball parks as "out lesbians" gave new meanings to that civic space and
generated a new politicized sex/gender community. The chapter then
turns to CWLU's Outreach work group, Secret Storm. Secret Storm initially used softball as a vehicle with which to pull women into a socialist
feminist organization, not as a focus for sexual identity formation. But
once pressed to engage sexual diversity on the ball field, Secret Storm
participated in the establishment of a collective challenge to the oppressive technologies of gender primarily within white women's lives. They did
much less, however, to challenge the racial segregation of the parks and
the ways that gender and sexuality buttressed a system of racist oppression. The Wilder Ones and Secret Storm came to civic softball diamonds
with different intentions and, in many ways, they played different games.

Exploration of these differences within comparable spaces shows that women's activism inflected spaces with contested meanings. This makes it possible to see how, in turn, "feminist" and "out lesbian" emerged as particular social identities in relation to the locations of their emergence.

In practice, softball in the Twin Cities and Chicago overlapped little, but analyzing them together lends insight into national trends as well as the contingent and local nature of feminist formations. Although the Avantis and Soul Sisters traveled regionally and nationally, neither team recalled playing any Chicago teams.[7] Socialist feminists in Chicago and the Twin Cities communicated regularly around organizing strategies, but softball was not among the many things that women in the two urban areas shared with each other, nor did the Wilder Ones have any special awareness of CWLU sports organizing.[8] Instead, the Wilder Ones and Secret Storm each related themselves to national changes such as Title IX and the widespread emergence of out lesbian activism. It is most interesting to look at them together not as examples of an identical or conjoined process but because they reveal two different ways that feminist organizers interacted with softball, how those interactions constituted feminist activism, and finally, how softball thereby inflected feminism in the 1970s.

Playing It: The Dykiest-Looking Team in the Park

The Avantis, like the Motown Soul Sisters, were a nationally ranked team by the late 1960s, traveling to and often winning tournaments around the country. But in 1960, there were very few slow-pitch women's teams in the Twin Cities, and all but five of them were "recreational"; rarely did anyone see a competitive slow-pitch game anywhere in Minnesota, Illinois, or Michigan.[9] Few women growing up in Minnesota during the 1940s and 1950s had opportunities for competitive sport.[10] A small number of determined girls managed to play and develop skills nonetheless. Driven by lack of opportunities for girls, Toni Stone, an African American girl of St. Paul, practiced with boys until she earned invitations to all-male and mostly white baseball skills schools. By the mid-1950s, Stone was playing for Negro Major League teams in San Francisco, New Orleans, and Indianapolis. She influenced athletes who formed some of the best women's slow-pitch softball teams in the nation, such as the Dana Gardens of Cincinnati in the late 1950s. Her influence also made its way back to Minnesota, as local teams sought out models for promoting competitive softball throughout the upper Midwest. Still, virtually all the women who played on top-caliber (fast-pitch) adult women's softball teams had played on boys' teams as children: usually, they were so good that their boy teammates were happy to have them on the team; some had fathers who coached the teams; and some passed, for a little while, as boys.[11] These women provided a model of athleticism that bucked white, middle-class norms. In turn, beginning in the early 1960s, women who had been barred from competitive sports as girls took that model and ran with it, furthering the growth of women's competitive sport among adults with little prior experience.

In 1960, the Avantis were not yet a team but simply "a handful of marginally talented women," in the words of Betty Hawes, one of the team's cofounders. They were women who had given up athletics as youngsters because they had no effective support against the charges that competitive sport was unladylike, deviant, and lesbian. One day, at the company at which they earned a wage, a few of them talked about how they had never outgrown their desire to hit a ball into the outfield. They wanted to retrain their bodies, and they wanted a team. Co-worker and friend Merlin "Woody" Wood had played minor league baseball and believed a women's team could be good. He was willing to coach the women as long as their team would be called the Avantis, after his favorite Italian car.

The Avantis started out like the vast majority of women's slow-pitch teams in Minnesota: as a recreational team composed of women who worked for the same company. At that time, there were only five "Classic" (what later became AA) slow-pitch teams in the Twin Cities; most people assumed that slow-pitch ball should be a recreational, "entry-level" game requiring no athletic training. But some of the women on the fledgling Avantis wanted to practice skills and play harder—indeed, they thought of themselves as athletes, even if they hadn't yet been trained as athletes. They were happy to try plays that Coach Wood adapted from his experience playing in the baseball minor leagues, and he had a notion that the team could make it to nationals by 1962; he even bet the team that if they made it, he'd pay their way.[12] Hawes recalled,

Then, in '62, Woody said, "We're going to the world tournament," and we all almost fainted because we thought, "There's no way in hell!" But we did go, though. We played our first game, it was in Cincinnati. We played our first game against a North Carolina team, an all-black team, they were very big. We were there in our tennis shoes, but they were very gentle with us. They could have killed us. And at that time, the race situation was such that all we were hearing [from spectators and other teams] was, "Go out and beat those chick-aboos." At that time. I don't even know if we scored a run.[13]

The next year, the Avantis invited one of the best teams in the nation, the Dana Gardens of Cincinnati, to Minneapolis. As Woody put it, "It was to show people that women could really play softball. To show what slow-pitch could really be."[14] Though some white women played for the Dana Gardens in the early 1960s, and by the late 1960s nearly half the team was white, many people who were used to seeing only white people on the ball fields interpreted the Dana Gardens as a black team. Hawes recounted, "Those women were really big. We were very intimidated: they were *that* good. It was an all-black team, and they were very tough, *fine* ball players. In Minnesota, well, we had never seen anything like that."[15] Big, tough ball players, the Dana Gardens apparently defied whiteness—though many were white—in the very acts through which they defied middle-class gender norms. The Avantis, though uncertain about racial constructions, were certain about claiming the Dana Gardens as their first teachers of an aggressive style rarely seen in women's slow-pitch leagues of the upper Midwest. As the Avantis developed skills, friendship, and rivalry with teams like the Dana Gardens, the Soul Sisters, and other teams at national tournaments, their knack for "putting on a good show" increased. So did their reputation as a "tough" team. Many credit so-called black teams for giving them a positive image of both: to be tough and no less to be showy, flew in the face of everything most Avantis had been taught about being women.

Due in part to the success and spectator value of such groundbreaking teams, many people in the upper Midwest began to newly honor aggressive physical output in the context of women's games. But Avanti Jan DuBois recalled a familiar theme of the 1960s when she remarked, "On the ball field we were really tough. Off the ball field, we were just like anybody else."[16] In 1967, a Minneapolis newspaper titled a story on a local ball team, "Tom boys have more fun, but they enjoy being girls." Another headliner joked that softball didn't prevent women from "cleaning up" as "mother, wife, career girls."[17] As long as sport was a contained arena (that is, the ball field), it allowed women to play in a contradictory space that made visible, celebrated, yet also masked the full extent of their deviance from white middle-class heterosexual norms. Competitive athletes challenged those norms, usually not through overtly politicized statements but through their playing style, appearance, and their command of public space.

Leaving sexuality unspoken, the Avantis drew on positive models of "tough and showy" women to bolster their own resistance to homophobia. Many women on the team had experienced homophobia as youngsters who did not fashion themselves after dominant measures of femininity. And they noticed that virtually all ball players experienced homophobic discrimination if they were not somehow feminine *enough*. Coach Wood admitted that one of the reasons he helped start the team was "to counter the unfairness" that women experienced: the team, as a rule, would not discriminate against lesbians or women who looked like lesbians. But even his support strained with ambivalence. He recalled, "we never talked about the gay identity of 80 percent of the team, or the issues they faced related to that. But I always told them to conduct themselves like ladies. Maintaining a class act was very important."[18] Wood encouraged aggressive athleticism and tolerated butch appearance as long as players projected honorable and refined manners in public.

Conducting themselves "like ladies" off the field did not protect the Avantis from gaining a reputation as the dykiest team, and middle-class norms fed into that reputation, class acts notwithstanding. Even laudatory media labeled deviance by denying it: Minnesota's *Time Out* sports magazine ran a feature article on the Avantis that began, "If you envision a successful women's softball team to be something akin to a group of Wonder-Woman-like amazons, prepare to have one more dream shattered. The Avantis of Minneapolis, undoubtedly the most consistently powerful team in the history of Minnesota's slow-pitch softball, are successful indeed, but not the least bit amazonish."[19] When the Avantis took over the spaces of ball fields, they met with constructions of gender and class that together regulated the meanings and uses of public space. Dominant norms of the region signified bodies as they moved through various landscapes, coding them black, white, feminine, masculine, normal, queer.

Although the bounded ball field gave teams some room in which to present alternative ways of being women, the Avantis bucked even the more expansive gender norms of the diamond. When other women's teams in Minnesota still wore shorts, the Avantis introduced below-the-knee baseball pants formerly reserved for men. This made the team "look more serious about ball," according to DuBois, and also allowed them to occupy their space more aggressively. As Avanti Hollis Monnett put it, "We played in the natural baseball pants, where the other teams were in shorts, so we just tore up the diamond: slides, dives, you could do anything."[20] Only ten years earlier, the National Section for Girls and Women's Sports (NSGWS), bolstered by a team of physicians and parental experts, questioned if it was safe and becoming for girls and women to slide into base.[21] The NSGWS reflected common conservative boundaries around female athletes' use of space; the Avantis, Soul Sisters, and other teams rose to fame by breaking those very boundaries.

Other transgressions distinguished the Avantis from other teams in Minnesota. Monnett recalled that "the team was almost feared, because they recruited the bigger and better athletes. I mean, those women could really put it over the fence!" Avanti Linda Polley described tangible markers: "We had some big women. And the other teams, well, *we* didn't have our hair all permed and try to mask it." Woody, whom the team dubbed "Mary," was well aware that the class act and verbal silence did not mask the dyke image of the team, explaining, "We were the scapegoat, because [the other teams] all swept it under the rug. The other teams could point to us and say, 'oh, *that's* the gay team.' "[22] Although the Avantis' foremost goal was to play outstanding softball and spur the growth of the sport, they fulfilled that goal only by also challenging white, middle-class norms about gender, sexuality, race, and the uses of public space.

Even as "the gay team," the Avantis were role models for many people seeking new ways to become women—both women who sought new sex/ gender subcultures, and those who did not. Women's softball fast became the bread and butter of community recreation programs in Minnesota, and teams at all levels came to number in the hundreds by the late 1960s. Like the Soul Sisters, the Avantis worked hard to gain playing time for girls and women on good fields, they offered softball clinics for young girls, and they assisted in the creation of girls' leagues to ensure that girls would have a place and social support for playing softball at a more competitive level. While they espoused no explicit feminist agenda, they were part of the grassroots that fueled the passage of Title IX: even before 1972, girls in the Twin Cities had many opportunities to play competitive softball so that by 1972, gender equity in sports was not a foreign idea handed down by a distant government, but something that ordinary Minnesotans wanted in their everyday lives.

Saying It: Out Feminist Lesbians in the Park

As teams played in public parks throughout the cities, they inspired many women to challenge norms in new ways on the field and outside of sport altogether. In the late 1960s, Jo Devlin and her friends were among those who followed the Avantis, thirsting for public icons of lesbian life. They were well practiced at reading through contradictions in public images of women's sexuality and found models out there on the ball field, sometimes "piecing it together from just *scraps!*"[23] They perceived athletes to project sexual assertiveness, self-possession, sexual and gender "ease," and indifference to white, middle-class norms regulating feminine attire, mannerism, and use of public space. To some feminists newly coming out, athletes in fact modeled "how to be a lesbian." Thus, they consciously drew on aspects of gay women's softball culture as they developed their own distinctly feminist lesbian culture.

In the early 1970s, when no other recreational division team in Minneapolis overtly supported a gender-deviant appearance, the Wilder Ones publicly defined themselves as a bunch of lesbians, and they simultaneously became self-defined athletes—most for the first time in their lives. Across the United States, the number of women's recreational leagues swelled, and feminists joined what many referred to as "that old lesbian institution"; in that context, many newly and explicitly announced their lesbian status. The appropriateness of softball as a feminist lesbian activity was widely assumed. In Chicago, for example, the collective of black and white women who published *Lavender Woman* ran an ad in the paper's third issue announcing, "We meet every Sunday at the field behind the Art Institute to play lesbian softball."[24] By the mid-1970s, women everywhere were elaborating the implications of women's softball. In a 1976 article titled "Come Out Slugging," Atlanta feminist activist Vicki Gabriner wrote, "Athletics have long been significant in the lives of many lesbians." And yet, she acknowledged, "Most of us are still in the closet." The ball field offered an opportunity to change all that as, she asserted, "Sports is becoming a significant part of the lesbian feminist community." Her political agenda was inherently linked to a spatial question: "To build a lesbian movement, to fortify ourselves for survival in a hostile environment, to create massive social change, to create lesbian-feminist institutions, to build a power base, we need to ask ourselves: Where do lesbians hang out?"[25] Lesbians not only hung out in the civic spaces of ball parks, but they became visible and coherent by actively contesting the norms regulating those spaces.

In the Twin Cities in 1971, the idea to form an out lesbian team was born in part in the bars. As the Wilder Ones founder Jo Devlin recalled, "I was totally closeted at my job, and I desperately needed a place where I could be myself among lesbians. We were all going to the bars every night: we'd *close* the place! . . . Finally we realized we were drinking ourselves to death, and we needed something else." Out lesbian softball was also born in the softball stands: Devlin explained that "even though the double A teams were just a joy to watch, we realized that we didn't want so much to sit in the stands and *watch* those women play, as we wanted to *be* the players. So we just decided to become gorgeous softball dykes *ourselves!*"[26] But when it came time to put a team together in 1972, Devlin did not go to the bars or the parks, where women could be found who were already playing softball. Instead, she went to the new Lesbian Resource Center (LRC) that had opened that year. The LRC held daily rap groups and monthly coffeehouse-style entertainment: theater, readings, concerts, and folk singing. It was a great alternative to the bars, but Devlin and many others wanted more action, literally. In ways that the LRC and even Amazon Bookstore could not, softball could help women develop a positive physicality, use their bodies to take up civic space in new ways, and represent themselves increasingly publicly as feminist lesbians.

It wasn't hard coming up with willing players for the new, predominantly but not entirely white team: several Wilder Ones had attempted to play sports as children and quit, either because, as Carol La Favor put it, "I got teased mercilessly from the boys and the parents and everyone," or, as Nancy Cox recalled, "In high school, most of us [athletically inclined girls] got labeled lesbians. It was mostly because we did sports, the guys all said, 'they are a bunch of lesbians.' "[27] Twenty years later, these adults were only too happy to return to sports and, late in the spring of 1972, they went to the Park Board to register as the Wilder Ones, "after Laura Ingalls Wilder, you know from Minnesota history."[28] As they did so, they not only refused the homophobia that had kept them and most girls out of athletics, they also challenged the sexism and homophobia regulating civic space by taking up that space as women and as out lesbians.

Self-representation as an out lesbian team was a crucial step for the Wilder Ones in countering dominant norms. While the Avantis broke gender norms by wearing baseball pants and short hair and by playing a uniquely tough game, the Wilder Ones introduced explicitly feminist-identified gender defiance into the world of softball. Candace Margulies qualified what it meant, in the 1970s, to be out: "We weren't closeted, but we weren't making out on the field, either. We didn't have stickers or all those identifying things, merchandise that people use now to be out. But we did look very, very different from the other teams: hairy legs and short hair and our whole style and appearance. I don't know if that was the source of the unfriendliness we received, or if it was just for playing women's softball in Minnesota."[29] The Wilder Ones registered with the Park Board in 1972, and they did so as a decidedly lesbian team. Devlin recalled that the board periodically asked the Wilder Ones, " 'Do you really need to advertise that you're lesbians?' and we said 'yes!' and that's how it was. That's who we were." La Favor explained the practice in direct terms: "It was a very political thing, to play lesbian softball. There were dyke softball players *all over*, but to *say* it, to play *as* a lesbian team, was really making a statement."[30] Each game was an opportunity to develop "a sense of ourselves as lesbians in the world." Creating a new public culture thus involved advertising the nature of the team as widely as possible.[31]

The Wilder Ones and other similar teams countered sexism and the verbal silence surrounding lesbians in sport by developing a distinct gender style *and* playing style that came to signify "lesbian" and "feminist" together. The Wilder Ones perceived that in the recreational as well as the AA through C leagues, the "mostly straight teams with hairdos and nail polish" had "male coaches who would yell at them."[32] The truly liberatory team, they reasoned, would have no coaches and no male input; it would be non-authoritarian and non-hierarchical. In this configuration, hairy legs marked feminist, lesbian, athletic self-definition. Despite receiving "unfriendly" reactions, the Wilder Ones derived pleasure and power from their "whole style." They combined their modified appreciation of the Avantis' gender style with a specifically anticoach attitude to create the Wilder Ones' first team motto: "we play to have fun." On that team, everyone got to play. Margulies, for example, "stank" at softball, and her favorite position was right field, where nothing happened. "It was so relaxing," she said, "like standing out in nature." She loved the team in part because, "it was so nice that you could be a lousy player and still be on the team. The rare times that I did something right, like caught a ball or had a hit, everyone would just go crazy cheering and carrying me around on their shoulders. That felt really good."[33] Margulies was in good company on a team that boasted few practiced athletes, and thus, placing fun above competitive status was practical as well as consistent with feminist disdain for hierarchy.

That kind of fun was short-lived, however. After a year or two, the team wearied of "losing *every single game*," and they elected Devlin their first coach. It took some time on the field to separate dominant gender ideologies and socialization from winning strategies, to distinguish playing a good, hard game (which they wanted) from male aggression and patriarchal competitiveness (which they rejected). They instituted regular practices, and created a nonmacho mantra—"the ball is your friend"—to counter their physical hesitation on the field. While team members discovered that "we enjoyed running ourselves into the ground to become better ball players," an egalitarian ethic prevailed in attitude if not always in practice.[34] Margulies, reflecting memories of several narrators recalled, "I'd get pissed if Jo didn't put me in [to play] enough, because I felt really entitled to that."[35] Coach Devlin taught team members how to charge a ball, dive for a catch, and slide into base until they became a leading recreational division team whose new motto proclaimed, "We play to have fun, and winning is more fun than losing!" Using their bodies in new ways on the field, they publicized women's activism and gave particular shape to emerging feminism.

The public nature of civic softball diamonds rendered personal "body work"—learning how to use one's body, publicly, as a lesbian—highly political. Based on her experience with the Wilder Ones, Devlin wrote articles on "feminism and patriarchy and everything that used softball as a metaphor." But softball was more than a metaphor. For the Wilder Ones, softball practice *was* feminist praxis, and it was about "gaining a little *more space*, a little *more* room for striving." It was the literal play of the game— the running, hitting, throwing, striving, and the visibility—that for many women was "the best practice for being feminist, being a lesbian, being a lover, being a woman, being a teacher, everything that a woman could imagine herself being."[36] In the interest of having fun and winning, the Wilder Ones insisted on occupying public spaces in new ways. They thus used civic parks and crafted sexual and gender deviance within those spaces to construct a new public identity as feminist lesbians. Integrating their identities as softball dykes and feminists required creating more spaces in which women could act and also more ways for women to move through space. When the Park Board erected soccer goal posts in the fields where the Wilder Ones regularly practiced, three teammates "went out in the middle of the night and tore them down, like vigilantes."[37] The connection between liberation and territory was explicit: as Devlin put it, "softball was being alive: our togetherness, our physical activity, and being mouthy and demanding space from the Park Board."[38] Recreational softball reached ball players, their fans, families, and sponsoring businesses; it took place in public parks scattered through every neighborhood of the Twin Cities; it traveled regionally and received coverage in local papers. The Wilder Ones thus advertised their lesbian presence before a sizable audience.

As many feminists created feminist and lesbian teams, they turned sport into a context in which they could dismantle one very specific form of sexist oppression, namely, the norms and practices restricting women's movement. Rosemary Lundell, a soccer player in the 1970s, explained, "You know, we were taught *not* to yell, *not* to hit a ball, you had to walk a certain way—you know, there's a way lesbians walk, walking like you meant something—that's what we were taught *not* to do."[39] Feminist politics and lesbian liberation entailed learning a new body language that was practiced on a day-to-day, immediate, and geographic level. Each time the Wilder Ones walked onto the field, they practiced occupying a new space in a new way. Devlin graphically recalled, "We didn't wear bras, and we'd go floppin' around the bases, and men would go by and point at us and laugh at us, and we'd yell 'em out of the park, you know we'd just storm 'em completely. It was absolutely dramatic liberation that we were pulling off at that time."[40]

Narrators' language suggests that their feminist lesbian ideologies and identities derived in large part from a very embodied self and from the *enactment* of that self in and through newly emancipatory spaces. As Devlin put it, "We had a lot of body work to do, and softball was the ticket: we said, 'we're lesbians,' and we took a lot of shit for it, and it was well worth it. The difference was just declaring *our space*, just declaring *ourselves* for who we were." Space and self were thus intertwined and mediated through the body.[41] Claiming new spaces, taking up space, and moving aggressively within space: these were part and parcel of a new feminist and lesbian activism. Mari Stack denied that she was politically inclined during the 1970s, but she was proud of making "a *real* political statement" as part of the Wilder Ones. She explained, "I couldn't wait for the season to start, the first second you could get outside, to be *outside*. But it was scary at times, to say, 'this is who I am.' "[42] It was scary, and liberating, in part because self-definition for the Wilder Ones included fiercely defending their presence in public parks, and when harassed by passers-by, chasing them away, yelling and with bats in hand. Being an out lesbian team and a feminist team thus involved both "playing it" in new ways and "saying it" in new words. Feminism, then, was realized in part through newly politicized bodies performing in newly politicized spaces.

To be serious about athletics was to intrude on the very spaces that defined masculinity and heterosexuality. At the forefront of feminist and lesbian resistance, out lesbian teams refused the "female apologetic." That is, they refused to make the public assertion that they were heterosexual and subordinate to men—an assertion that has so often accompanied women's movement into formerly male-defined spheres.[43] By the mid-1970s, the strategy of playing out lesbian softball had spread widely. Cities such as Columbia, South Carolina, Lexington, Kentucky, Athens and Atlanta, Georgia, Providence, Rhode Island, San Francisco, Boston, Washington, D.C., and Los Angeles, to name a few, all boasted out lesbian teams. Park district leagues were not the only structure for out lesbian softball: in the early 1970s, San Francisco women's bars sponsored an entire league of out lesbian teams, and attendance at games sometimes approached 1,000. Out lesbian teams helped women represent themselves increasingly publicly, giving visibility to a growing movement culture that was changing gender norms and constituting feminism in the most ordinary places.

Hearing It: Felt Needs of the People in the Park

In spring 1974, the Outreach work group of the Chicago Women's Liberation Union seized on softball as a way to reach working-class white and white ethnic women and organize them to socialist feminism and to the CWLU. Because working-class women were already actively struggling for park space, Outreach correctly believed that challenging gender and class discrimination on the diamonds would be a productive organizing activity. Imagining their core constituency to be "working-class women and housewives," they published a newsletter called *Secret Storm* and distributed it to girls and women in the parks, helped set up new women's leagues, offered day care and skills clinics, and joined teams themselves.

Gender exclusions in the park district proved catalyzing indeed. Tricia Leja, for example, first came into contact with Outreach on the ball field, and she ended up becoming a CWLU organizer herself. She did not expect that other players would be so ready to protest the fact that they always got time on the worst playing fields made of gravel while men's teams got the grassy fields; as her team played and talked with other teams, she discovered that it was surprisingly easy to rally women to the cause.[44] Taking on the alias Secret Storm, Outreach organizers succeeded in winning playing time for scores of new ball players: by 1976, over 140 women played on teams that Secret Storm had organized.[45]

Sexuality, lesbianism, and race proved more important to organizing efforts than Secret Storm had anticipated. Initially, organizers did not publicly address sexuality or race, nor did they acknowledge their indebtedness to prior lesbian cultures built around public athletic spaces. But their organizing efforts helped them turn ball fields into locations in which women from a variety of social backgrounds met and formed sexually diverse and politically minded communities, and thus, after two years on the field, Secret Storm had come to define its core constituency as women who were "blue collar," "gay," "mothers," and/or "Third World." Nevertheless, race and sexuality introduced productive tensions in Secret Storm's organizing methods. Although Secret Storm activists early began to develop a feminist critique of heterosexism, they did not resolve homophobic and racist tensions within their own group or on the ball field before CWLU disbanded in 1976. A spatial analysis, with attention to sexuality, helps explain how homophobia and racism crucially shaped Secret Storm's outreach work on the ball fields.[46] In turn, it suggests that feminist activism did not simply encounter and grapple with a preexisting or static racism and homophobia; rather, feminist activism itself also produced constituencies with multiple, shifting, and conflicting investments in race and sexuality.

The women who formed CWLU's Outreach work group in 1972 were women who sought to develop a mass movement through organizing strategies based on "the felt needs of the people." Like the rest of CWLU and the Black Panther Party, Young Lords, Young Patriots, and La Gente, Outreach emphasized neighborhood organizing, using Chicago's multiply segregated social geography to reach particular constituencies.[47] Outreach most sought working-class, often white ethnic constituencies with whom members already had built connections.[48] Though they drew on a

Marxist theoretical base, they did not think Marxism accurately spoke to the condition of women, or women with kids, and they were concerned that socialist feminist discussion was too removed from everyday struggles to build a mass movement.[49] Offering rap groups, consciousness-raising groups, and regular educational forums to young white and white ethnic women in high schools and junior colleges in Chicago's northwest working-class neighborhoods, they found a receptive audience.[50] As Outreach explained their strategy to Union members, "The base of our work is outreach [which is] hanging around getting to know people; political and women's consciousness raising, developing people into self-conscious organizers. All our decisions on what to do . . . are based on what we learn are the real and felt needs of the women that we do our outreach with."[51] For Outreach, the everyday lives of "ordinary" women would be both the source and site of social movement.

In April 1974, Outreach learned of women's "real and felt needs" in civic, athletic space. One night that month, Michelle Ghishoff, manager of Chicago's Why-Not-Inn team, demanded that the men on one of Horner Park's softball diamonds honor her team's park permit for playing time. The ensuing fight left Ghishoff with a head cut requiring stitches and a strong desire to publicize the incident. As she later explained to *Chicago Daily News* columnist Mike Royko, one of the men on the field punched her in the face, hit her on the head with a baseball bat, and pushed her down. The man himself later told Royko, "These damn fucking women want to take over everything."[52] In addition to being the home of sixteen-inch softball, Chicago took some pride in the fierceness with which men and boys fought for possession of softball diamonds in parks, schoolyards, and empty lots; as Royko put it, "When it comes to possession of a softball diamond, a park permit is only 10 percent of the law. Brute force is the other 90 percent."[53] Scuffles for playing time, as an expected dimension of Chicago softball, suggested that scarce resources were at stake: not only park space but, even more so, the rites and rights of masculinity. Now, women were changing the terms of the game and what it meant to earn possession of the diamond.

In response to the well-publicized conflicts between white men's and women's teams at Horner Park, Outreach took on women's softball in Chicago's public parks as a new arena for organizing in May 1974. They retrospectively explained, "The neighborhood park districts offered us one of the few areas where housewives get together outside their homes, and women get together off the job."[54] As Secret Storm, they investigated the Park District. They experienced firsthand Horner Park's overt discrimination against women, and they saw the exciting possibilities of "waging an all-out struggle" around women's athletics in public parks.[55] Rinda West was one of the first CWLU women to join a Horner Park softball team in spring 1974. Of Secret Storm's origins, she recalled,

> We put out a newspaper called *Secret Storm*, which we would hand out in the parks. I guess the place we probably went to the most was Horner Park, it was white working-class. We also went to Kosciusko. . . . It was because there was a woman who was playing in a league in Horner Park who got into a fight with a man, an umpire I think it was. And she came to the Women's Union and said, 'This is outrageous, they don't have enough playing time for women.' . . . But she was, I don't know how she'd heard about the Women's Union. You know, feminism was in the air, and she was not intimidated by coming to a women's organization. So we started hanging out with them and inviting them to events, and then we started playing on teams.[56]

Hanging out with their constituency and playing on teams especially in Horner and Kosciusko Parks, Outreach and *Secret Storm* further publicized the gender discrimination of park softball league entry fees and the gross disparities in services provided to men's and women's teams.

In this new activity, Secret Storm drew on established, New Left organizing strategies, but their own work around softball greatly departed from New Left organizing in that it directly challenged the gendered order of civic space.[57] Like the Economic Research and Action Project (ERAP) and Chicago's own Rising Up Angry, Secret Storm believed in contacting less enfranchised people by finding them literally on the streets and in the parks. Some in the CWLU critiqued Secret Storm's methods, implicitly seeing them as too New Left.[58] As West put it, "I think that we were dismissed by some women as, 'Oh, they're just Rising Up Angry clones.' "[59] The predominantly white, middle-class men in Rising Up Angry themselves had adopted an old union organizing strategy when they used sports as a location for organizing and joined men's softball teams to have the opportunity to meet with working-class men. But in that context, sports *itself* was not a politicizing issue. Men's occupation of public athletic space was unquestioned; sports simply provided a venue in which men could converse about *other* issues, such as the workplace. In contrast, when Outreach joined women's softball teams, they not only found a place to meet women, they also entered an already contested location for the regulation of gender and sexuality. In taking up the formerly male spaces of softball, identified feminists and others challenged that regulation, directly addressing women's use of their own bodies in public parks. For Secret Storm, playing softball thus became a distinctly feminist strategy for changing the conditions of civic space.[60]

Secret Storm took up some of the same work that the Wilder Ones had found necessary. Like the Wilder Ones, they articulated a ball-friendly, gendered philosophy of sports: as one *Secret Storm* article explained, "We realize that there is a lot that happens in men's and boy's sports that we wouldn't want in our women's sports program. We think that teamwork, sharing what we know, and friendship are more important than competition. Sports should be fun and give people confidence, not be a threat to their ego." Also like the Wilder Ones, they offered weekly skills clinics. Learning to play was a radical act that went beyond the ball field: as *Secret Storm* put it, "Women deserve to have equal opportunity to enjoy sports, play the sports we like, and develop the strength and coordination of our body [sic] . . . knowing our strength can go a long way when someone tells us we can't do something because we're too weak." Speaking to women's experience in typically male-dominated geographies, the article concluded, "Being able to move quickly can do a lot for a woman on the streets these days."[61] Thus, Secret Storm consciously used athletics to invite women to more assertively occupy their bodies and public space.

But skills clinics were not enough. Just as norms of femininity and early lessons in heterosexuality had kept many girls off the ball field, normative heterosexuality and motherhood were keeping adult women off the ball field.[62] Secret Storm discovered that only about one in ten women playing softball had children. Some women with young children used the parks in the roles of wives watching their husbands' softball games or as mothers attending to their toddlers on the playground. While their position as mothers and wives gained them a legitimate admission ticket to the parks, that same position kept them off the ball fields as players.[63] Judy Kloiber was a white, middle-class woman who came to CWLU through Outreach's sports organizing. As a young housewife herself, she was sympathetic when women said they wanted to get jobs or play softball but could not afford child care for their children.[64] Impatient to reach working-class women and housewives, Secret Storm organized child care during Horner Park women's games, allowing more women to take up public park space in a new way, as players.[65] Adding child care to their organizing (a dimension largely absent from the Wilder Ones' practice), Secret Storm offered women with young children, like Tricia Leja, an opportunity to challenge this sexist arrangement of civic space.

Secret Storm activism included collecting stories from women who played (or who wanted to play) and printing them in the pages of *Secret Storm*. Many stories revolved around the compromises and costs of compulsory heterosexuality. Narratives such as the following became veritable tropes of the feminist reclamation of athletics: "They retired my [softball jersey] number when I was thirteen. . . . You see, at 13 I got interested in boys, and everybody knows boys don't like girls who might beat them. But if I had wanted to play, as I do now 18 years later, I would have found it very difficult."[66] And this: "Some of us 'know better' than to arm wrestle with our boyfriend because he goes crazy when we beat him. If we're children, we're told not to mess around because we'll get dirty. If we're older, we're told it's simply unfeminine. . . . High school girls may get laughed at or labeled tomboy for playing sports."[67] Secret Storm organizers also recalled how, when they were youths, being "boy crazy" required them to concede athletic space to males.[68] These common stories implied that a young woman's interest in athletics was not compatible with normative heterosexuality. Secret Storm circulated such stories to promote a feminist sensibility and challenge that norm.

Skills clinics, child care during softball games, and circulating stories, as well as direct confrontations with the Park District over women's playing times and the quality of the diamonds, all constituted feminist political organizing. These efforts brought more women to the playing field and supported the feminist consciousness that they developed as they took up civic space in new ways. But feminism was not all foreign to women who joined new teams. Secret Storm's work invited women to radical acts based on relatively familiar contexts and life experience. As West explained,

> The women were really responsive, because what we were saying, they'd heard it, it was in their lives. Whether [our Outreach work] had any lasting impact, who can say? But I think that we became a voice that allowed them to receive a feminist message that they couldn't hear from *Ms.* magazine or from whatever the other sources of information were at the time. Because we were there with them. And clearly we weren't any of the things that had been presented in the media as these horrifying images.[69]

Most women in Secret Storm's purview, even those who did not identify as feminists, could identify with experiences of gender hierarchies in every-day contexts, and they were more than ready to create arenas in which they could collectively challenge those hierarchies.

Despite the familiarity of gender struggles, mainstream media produced plenty of "horrifying images" of feminists in general so that even *Ms.* magazine could seem deviant and alien. But in civic, athletic space, sexism and lesbian baiting specifically and explicitly worked together to discourage women's sports and women's bodily autonomy in public. The female athlete in public (male) athletic space, that is, very well exemplified all that was "horrifying" about feminism. Secret Storm hoped to appeal to women and show that familiar and even ordinary women could play soft-ball—and thereby Secret Storm would construct an image of feminism that was not horrifying. To avoid alienating their constituency, they patently avoided printing the word *lesbian*. Based on their perception that "lesbianism is among the most threatening issues around," they "wanted to be careful about how publicly we come out in our outreach."[70] And yet, just as the ball field was a space that generated concerns about sexuality, "the people" themselves brought their own sexual interests to the field. Thus, if Secret Storm would build a movement of all possible women, they would have to publicly support women who chose to come out as lesbians, as well as those who feared lesbian associations.

The parks belied firm boundaries between openly lesbian teams and teams that did not clearly mark sexuality, and they also belied firm boundaries between "racial groups" and neighborhoods. Though Secret Storm had made a decision to work within "their own racial group," they had to address race as well as sexuality in ways they hadn't anticipated. In summer 1974, black women from the new MS Lounge lesbian bar formed a team; they registered in what they saw as the "lily white" Horner Park women's league because it still had openings by the time MS started looking for a league.[71] Doing so, MS Lounge challenged not only the silence around lesbian sexuality at Horner Park but also the white composition of the Horner Park league. In turn, organizing in the parks pushed Secret Storm to expand their perception of their constituency and argue for the possibility and necessity of building "a mass movement of women—a movement that unites all women that can be united . . . among non-white and working class women."[72]

MS Lounge joined Horner Park conscious of the fact that they would draw attention simply for being a black team, if not also for being sponsored by a lesbian bar. Marge Summit, owner of MS, asserted, "Not too many people liked being around them [blacks]. . . . We did make a statement with our team though."[73] Like the Soul Sisters, they faced hostility from umpires, as in the case of a call that—MS believed—erroneously cost them the recreational league championship in 1974, and it was not easy to build rapport with other teams in the league.[74] Nevertheless, whether in the interest of integration or simply in the spirit of good sports-person-ship, whenever MS won a game, they invited the losing team to their predominantly black lesbian bar for drinks and free food. Teams in the upper Midwest commonly (though not universally) invited each other to sponsoring establishments for postgame food and drinks.[75] But a team invitation to a black lesbian bar, or any gay bar, vastly departed from the norm; in 1974, it may have been unprecedented. Secret Storm politicized their own response when they finally went to MS toward the end of the summer as part of the Why-Not-Inn team: in their view, this was a gesture of solidarity across race and also an opportunity to make a lesbian-positive statement, perhaps even an occasion to add that to their overall political mission. They later asserted,

> We thought going [to MS Lounge] was pretty important for the teams and for the whole outreach effort at Horner. There were bad attitudes and tensions between Ms. [sic] and other teams, both because Ms. was admittedly gay and because they were black. While the contradictions were not solved, the season ended with more unity than it began with. We should also say that we paid a certain price for being tight with Ms. A lot of women were put off by it, but we felt that we handled it correctly.[76]

Secret Storm's statement reflects a carefully measured assessment. As socialists, they had a commitment to appeal to the masses. They perceived, however, that their response to MS alienated some women. Despite that admitted cost, Secret Storm argued for the correctness of enacting solidarity with an out lesbian black team.

Too much should not be made of Secret Storm "being tight" with MS, however. It was sharing park space with MS, and MS's invitation, that provided the opportunity for Secret Storm to envision solidarity across race and sexual identity. Witnessing the homophobia and racism leveled against MS did not prompt Secret Storm to campaign on behalf of that team or to directly organize around racism and homophobia. Indeed, they disavowed doing so when they asserted to CWLU, "We have never worked with a lesbian organization or felt the need to."[77] Secret Storm, that was to say, was not a lesbian organization, nor did they see MS as such. Thus, although they promoted the relevance of race and sexuality in the Union's larger mission, they also avoided their own identification with racism and homophobia and thereby ironically also affirmed their own status as white and not-lesbian.

It would be another year before Secret Storm printed the word *lesbian* in its newsletter, but the softball parks insistently proved to be a location in which women could and did become lesbians. Whatever the reasons that women joined softball teams, the activity had ramifications in their lives beyond the ball field. Judy Kloiber was only too happy to join Secret Storm because she loved sports but—as so many women experienced—her husband was not happy about it and her marriage quickly ended.[78] Kloiber had had enough of being a middle-class housewife, and the Union offered exciting new arenas of work until it dissolved a year later. During that year and in the context of the ball field, Kloiber met Leja, and the two raised seven children together. In so many cases, playing softball defied the rules of "compulsory heterosexuality"; some women changed those rules within their marriages to men, and some left their marriages altogether.

Softball organizing re-created not only ball fields but also bars as more sexually diverse and more visible social spaces.[79] As they occupied park space with other women in new ways, many women believed that the teams sponsored by MS Lounge and Augie's were the first "out lesbian groups" with which they had ever come in contact, even though organizations like Chicago Lesbian Liberation and the Lesbian Group (formerly called the Gay Group) of the CWLU, as well as *Lavender Woman* newspaper, had all been "out" for three years before the sports teams arrived on the scene. Teams sponsored by lesbian bars advertised not only "bar" but also "lesbian." Such signs helped the public "read" lesbian sexuality, but only a few years earlier, such signs were rare. Thus, it is a testament to the increased visibility of women's athletics, and to the impacts of feminism and lesbian liberation, that some remember Augie's and MS as being the first out lesbian groups.[80] It also reveals that outness had everything to do with location; being out in a lesbian periodical, or in a gay bar, or in an organization was not the same as being out on a lesbian softball team in a public park.

Outreach in public parks shifted Secret Storm's commitments as it exposed them to the complexity of sexuality in women's lives. The group increasingly encouraged interaction among teams who negotiated sex/gender expression as well as racial and class identity in public space in different ways (such as Why-Not-Inn and MS Lounge). By 1976, some members had integrated themselves into out lesbian spaces, such as Augie's bar. The work group began to explicitly state its more lesbian-positive values to CWLU, declaring, "We feel that our work is important because of the constituency we reach (working class, gays, housewives)." They even pressed CWLU to embrace these values, stating, "We reach a large number of women. . . . A large part of these women are blue collar; a fair amount are gay; many are mothers; some are Third World. *We are making contact with women the Union wants to reach.*"[81] They were not only putting to practice but also *teaching* the Union core principles of socialist feminism.

Nevertheless, Secret Storm as a group did not extol the value of being "out," nor did they create a place specifically for out lesbians. They left the task of creating out lesbian softball in Chicago to others, including CWLU's Lesbian Group. In 1975, the Lesbian Group renamed itself and its new newsletter *Blazing Star* and began organizing sports teams. Softball was taking the nation by storm, and it's possible to see Blazing Star as part of that storm.[82] It's also possible to see that storm as a product of feminist organizing and the popularization of feminist activism. Locally, if Secret Storm somewhat inadvertently landed on an old lesbian institution in the interest of building socialist feminists, Blazing Star appropriated Secret Storm's use of softball as an organizing tool in the interest of building feminist lesbians. They facilitated lesbian bar and business sponsorship of new, increasingly out lesbian teams, and they found new, racially diverse constituencies. In 1976, CWLU dissolved, but Blazing Star continued independently. Building a cooperative relationship with Rising Up Angry that provided outreach energy and printing capacity, Blazing Star created Chicago's premier bilingual publication oriented around socialist, feminist, Latina, and lesbian politics. With a small staff, *Blazing Star* lasted until 1986, all the while promoting out lesbian teams and developing a mass base for feminist, interracial, increasingly global, labor activism.

Playing What, Saying What?

These stories show women's negotiations with and resistance to hetero-normative regulations of civic space in specific historical and cultural contexts. A focus on ball fields reveals the deep extent to which emerging lesbian feminists in the late 1960s and early 1970s drew on the prior and ongoing activism of working-class lesbian and gender-deviant softball communities such as the Avantis. Then, both those who would "play it" and those who would "say it" paved the way for socialist feminists and women more commonly to assert their presence on formerly male-defined turf. While commercial spaces like bars or alternative spaces like dollar parties served particular and sometimes narrowly defined communities, civic spaces like the ball fields brought diverse women into contact with each other. Feminist and lesbian activism together helped turn civic athletic space into places in which more women could enact new politicized identities and challenge the heteronormative structures that regulated women's public autonomy and sexual self-determination.

Prior to the 1970s, a women's softball culture thrived as a civic "lesbian institution" in public space in part *because* lesbian athletes played by the "don't say it" rule. Self-censorship allowed athletic women's public self-promotion as norm breakers. In the 1960s, an increasing number of women and teams like the Avantis challenged prescriptions of femininity, letting their athletic performance be read by spectators as being as ambiguous—or contradictory—as it in fact was. They thus magnified gendered contests over the uses and users of softball parks. They *also* made these contests appear salient and winnable to other women who would claim feminist and lesbian identities and thereby build explicit liberation movements. Not only playing it but saying it in public parks simultaneously engaged the contest over uses of public space and reclaimed the right to unambiguous self-definition in those same spaces. In the context of widespread regulatory discourses, saying it was defiant and resistant, a *protest* in all senses of the word. In the context of feminist and lesbian liberation, women like those who played on the Wilder Ones could believe that that "playing it" was less liberated than "playing it *and* saying it."

Yet the cases offered here and in chapter 3 belie the idea that "saying it" represents absolute historical progress or liberation over playing it without saying it. As teams, the Soul Sisters, Avantis, Wilder Ones, and MS Lounge all engaged in public queer performance when they took over public, previously heteronormative, male-defined space. They celebrated their skills and bodies, and made no effort to hide the toughness, short hair, or winning records that signified lesbianism to themselves and to many observers, supporters and critics alike. Furthermore, sex and gender meanings were variously coded within and against constructions of race, class, and geography. Attention to historical and spatial contexts indicates that the performance and meanings of feminism, outness, queerness, and liberation were multiple, shifting, and at times contradictory; furthermore, feminist activism helped produce investments in particular constructions of race, class, and sexuality, even as it sought to challenge the social hierarchies embedded in civic space.

The Avantis, whose style was modeled in part on the Soul Sisters, did not call themselves "softball dykes," but in their assertive claims to public space, they provided a silhouette of the softball dykes the Wilder Ones would later become. The Wilder Ones, wanting to feel as free on the inside as the Avantis looked on the outside, to be "whole people" in all spaces, developed a more explicit, public stance as lesbian athletes committed to playing it and saying it. For them, "it" was a feminist lesbian identity. Modeling themselves on the Avantis, the Wilder Ones played a new game by developing embodied identities in the context of civic athletic space. Such interventions—then happening all over the country—changed the game for teams like the Avantis, too. More players on more teams came out as lesbians, and they had more lesbian-friendly bars to go to after games. For fifteen years the Avantis had cultivated intense unity off the field as well as on it, but by the mid-1970s, the team often divided after games, some players going to new lesbian venues with lesbians from other teams, and others going out to the traditional burger joints they had always enjoyed. Betty Hawes and Linda Polley, two Avantis who supported and missed the former unity of the team, each explained that, by the mid-1970s, "Women had more to choose from, and that was probably a good thing."[83]

Meanwhile, Secret Storm had a different feminist vision than the Wilder Ones. They were not on the ball field to come out and elaborate feminist lesbian publicity but to radicalize working-class women and housewives to socialist feminism. Sexuality and race, however, were ever-present in that space and in women's lives—indeed, all the more so as the act of taking up softball space broke open countless dimensions of heteronormative regulation. Playing softball fostered new autonomy and sexual self-determination for many women, and the diamonds themselves offered a full range of models for how women might make use of that autonomy while also exposing the homophobia and racism that made it difficult for women to do so. Secret Storm had captured white housewives' attention through struggles over park space: hundreds joined new teams, scores became intensely politicized in the process, and several joined CWLU. And then in 1976, CWLU dissolved. From an organizational standpoint, Secret Storm could no longer serve its purpose. As West sadly recalled, "We no longer had anything to organize them *to*."[84] But the ball field had created activists: it created lesbians and bisexual women and antiracist activists even among socialist feminists who disavowed identity politics. And just as the Union fell apart, Blazing Star stormed the fields with renewed intent. If Secret Storm never resolved the tensions around organizing methods and the significance of race and sexuality in the parks, Blazing Star had discovered that the parks were the ideal place in which to organize specifically around sexuality and race, even while offering a socialist feminist critique and vision in the pages of their bilingual newspaper. Arguably, Secret Storm's work set the stage for Blazing Star to use the ball fields as spaces in which to embrace lesbian sexuality as an integral part of a multiracial, global, socialist feminist organizing strategy.

This examination of feminist organizing in civic, athletic space reveals that a dynamic far more complex than a gay-straight split was at work when some feminists embraced an identity as lesbians and others did not. In histories of feminist activism that assert a gay-straight split, it appears as though gays and straights separated into different spaces *because* one group made sexuality an identity and the other did not. This spatial analysis, in contrast, reveals that *both* feminist and lesbian feminist groups—as well as groups that disavowed political motivations—necessarily engaged sexuality, homophobia, and lesbian issues when they occupied public ball fields. Civic athletic space led Secret Storm to take up not only gender equity and women's access to public space, but also women's use of their bodies, lesbian baiting and homophobia, and lesbian presence within their constituency. Likewise, socialist organizers were compelled to address sexuality and race in new ways even though they did not adopt an identity politics around those issues. Gay women's stake in claiming civic athletic space preceded and intertwined with both lesbian feminism and socialist feminism as they developed in space and over time. Lesbian feminists and socialist feminists did often distinguish themselves around different goals, to be sure. But this analysis refracts their different interests through the common space of the ball field to explain how that space gave *all* of its occupants a stake in constructions of race and sexuality. At the same time, this analysis shows that for feminists and lesbian feminists alike, activist strategies for addressing sexuality and gender did not derive from static sexual identities but from the embedded processes of occupying civic space. Alongside women's efforts to change the norms regulating their bodies in civic spaces, many women politicized "personal" issues through the creation of distinctly feminist institutions—such as shelters, health clinics, coffeehouses, and clubs—intended to simultaneously protect women from, engage with, and change, mainstream social institutions. Those feminist institutions are the subject of part III.

Part III

Politicizing
Place
and
Feminist
Institutions

Five

Finding the Limits of Women's Autonomy

Shelters, Health Clinics, and the Practice of Property

"**B**arefoot and pregnant in the kitchen" oprecisely described Eileen Hudon's circumstances in the early 1970s, her husband even taking her shoes to prevent her from leaving the house. Perhaps relatively few women's partners kept them literally barefoot and pregnant, but the phrase attested to the spatial dimensions of dominant domestic and sexual ideologies and to the fictive separation between public and private worlds.

During the 1960s and 1970s, many women in the United States challenged this separation by creating women's spaces that interfaced with public institutions to increase women's sexual, economic, and spatial autonomy. In particular, places that were primarily service-oriented, such as battered women's shelters and self-help health clinics, functioned as woman-centered hubs for feminist activists, introduced women's particular needs to mainstream society, and demonstrated the deep connections between public institutions and so-called private concerns such as domesticity and sexuality.[1] Such places thus also allowed women to discover and challenge the extent to which gender hierarchies were embedded in the built environment. Feminists created new spaces to offer previously unavailable services, and in the process, they changed the public landscape and feminism itself in unforeseeable ways. Through their activism in embedded environments, they learned new things about building politicized communities, but they also replicated some aspects of race and class hierarchies.

When activists established shelters for women needing to get away from violent partners, they pressured heteronormative social institutions to support and ensure women's bodily autonomy both at home and in the larger world. When they developed self-help health clinics, they worked toward women's autonomous control over their sexual and reproductive lives and pressured conventional medical institutions to provide better access to sexual health and reproductive choice. Grassroots activists put together sexual health, abortion, antirape, and antiviolence services to address immediate needs, and they also put together spaces out of which to offer such services. At first, feminist service spaces were almost always borrowed or rented and vulnerable to the vicissitudes of public opinion and local and national economies. The places were neither grand nor stable but, in the words of one of the founders of Women's Advocates Shelter, "We made do."[2] Shelters and clinics were among the signature stamps of women's movement. They arose organically in all parts of the country; communicated with other shelters and clinics throughout the United States, Canada, Europe, Australia, and New Zealand; and made a lasting impact on a wide range of public institutions. The institutionalization of feminist activism thus entailed building feminist networks and, at the same time, increasing involvement with mainstream social service agencies and funding sources.

This chapter analyzes two spaces that took shape as feminist interventions in a larger heteronormative public landscape: Women's Advocates battered women's shelter in St. Paul, and the house shared by the Feminist Women's Health Center and the Feminist Federal Credit Union on the boundary between Detroit and its northern suburbs. Women's Advocates formed in 1972 as a legal information hotline to help women with divorce procedures. The hotline quickly evolved into an informal shelter network run out of Advocates' own homes, and women thereby discovered the personal and political value of housing up to fifteen women and children under one roof. Equally, neighbors' hostile reactions to sheltering pushed activists to secure a formal shelter and thereby formalize Women's Advocates as a social service in 1974. The new shelter was open to women and children only, and its boundaries were fiercely guarded. Presuming their clients to be in heterosexual relationships, Women's Advocates' practice both evidenced and confronted the heteronormative, sexist organization of most public and domestic property. Advocates held public institutions such as law enforcement and emergency services partially responsible for male dominance and challenged them to protect women from sexual and bodily harm in their own homes. Ultimately, the related projects of securing public support for shelter, living together as service providers and clients within a shelter, and serving women's multiple needs beyond shelter led to an elaboration of coalitional ideology and practice.

In 1973, a handful of women established the Detroit Feminist Women's Health Center (FWHC) in a working-class neighborhood in Detroit. As part of the grassroots, "self-help" women's health movement and a member of a growing consortium of feminist health clinics in the United States, the Detroit clinic offered birth control, pregnancy testing, screening for sexually transmitted infections and diseases (STIS and STDS), early abortions, educational workshops on sexual health and self-exam, counseling, and resource referral.[3] By providing affordable and respectful sexual and reproductive health education and services, the health center challenged the ways that conventional medical institutions reinforced heteronormative, white male dominance. The FWHC supported itself on volunteer labor, earnings from speaking tours, and base-level charges for services.[4] Recognizing that women's sexual autonomy could require some financial autonomy, some of FWHC's founders also started one of the country's early Feminist Federal Credit Unions, and the two organizations shared building space for two years. With a rapidly growing clientele, the health center grew strong enough to maintain four directors and a paid staff of eighteen, including physicians and registered nurses. The FWHC relocated twice by 1978 and ran strong into the early 1980s. But whether women were teaching other women to use specula for pelvic self-exam or whether they were performing any variety of abortion procedures, they at once confronted the ways that medical practice, women's health care, and women's sexual autonomy were all related to place. Believing that women's own bodies were the first site of women's sexual health education and practice, they asserted that sexual health care did not require conventional doctors' offices or medical institutions. But just what constituted a "medical procedure" in this new rubric? Who were the providers, and who were the clients? Should and could women create specialized or public facilities for practices so deemed? The answers to these questions were not abstracted medical ideals; instead, they emerged under the contingencies of immediate spatial contexts. Like the women who opened Women's Advocates, FWHC activists built spaces and offered services in a context of internal and external economic and property systems; they had to fend off or earn support from city officials and neighbors; and their clientele and services changed in relation to the various properties that they could and could not secure. From the early to the late 1970s, these on-the-ground issues made feminist health clinics, the services they provided, the feminist constituencies they generated, and the lessons they learned far more conditional than many had envisioned.

To an extent that cannot be overestimated, the battered women's movement and the women's health movement emerged and took shape around the places of their practice. That dynamic also revealed the extent to which the "privacy" of a woman's body depended on privileges of race, class, and sexuality. Geographic and social topographies differentially distributed privacy, and women's efforts to build shelters and health clinics at times challenged such topographies but at other times reinforced them. The shelter in St. Paul and the health clinic in Detroit each moved several times over their first few years of operation, often in response to a less-than-welcoming "public" consisting of neighbors, police, zoning boards, conventional medical institutions, and countless other public agencies. The moves they made were part of the process of institutionalization, affecting outreach, clientele, and ultimate sense of mission, but in different ways. The establishment of a formal Women's Advocates shelter led to an increasingly coalitional response to race, class, and sexual hierarchies; the health center, on the other hand, could only survive by moving into increasingly suburban locations with restricted opportunities for multiracial and cross-class activism. Thus, the two cases offer two different examples of the impacts that spatial processes had on women's movement and feminism. Together, they evidence the historical contingencies and contexts that shaped women's activism and its multiple outcomes. Whether operating from rented or owned spaces, shelters and sexual health clinics alike had to interact with, be changed by, and demand changes from mainstream institutions to maintain "a place" for women.

Nothing so dramatically clarified the spatial dimensions of sexism and heteronormativity as women's efforts to run shelters and sexual health clinics. The resistance women encountered while attempting to meet immediate needs revealed the multiple mechanisms and public institutions —from service agencies and medical facilities to real estate and banks— that constructed women as the property of father, husband, and the state. Though many feminists believed that the first site of women's autonomy was women's own bodies, bodily autonomy often required reconfiguring larger landscapes to support and protect that autonomy. These efforts also clarified feminist interests and strategies; the setbacks and compromises, as well as the victories, shaped the very practices and conceptions of sexual autonomy, coalition, and institutionalization that now seem so integral to feminism itself.

From Fortress to Public Institution: Women's Advocates Shelter, St. Paul

Many of the founders of Women's Advocates first came together in the late 1960s through their involvement in the antiwar movement. In that movement, they developed a critique of a violent society, a critique that meshed well with their budding feminist consciousness. Another thing that those white women brought with them from the antiwar movement was a feeling of constant emergency and the need to act *now*—taking risks, creating protests, and taking over public and corporate spaces—to save people's lives. Building a women's shelter, it turned out, involved nothing less: doing so entailed a radical takeover of domestic space. Indeed, creating a place in which a woman could demand public protection, privacy, and the inviolability of her own body required disrupting long-standing heteronormative conceptions of public and private itself.

The founders of Women's Advocates organized to transform the gendered division between public and private by creating a domestic space that was intensely political. As primarily straight-identified women, they initially based their work on heterosexual models of relationships and their experience with social services and with women who sought divorce help or shelter reinforced their unexamined assumptions. It took years, in fact, for advocates to gain awareness of violence within relationships between women, and to this day, state-funded work against violence against women continues to conceptualize gender and violence in ways that imply lesbian relationships are outside of the system. But it was not due to advocates' naiveté alone that they—and the battered women's movement as a whole—were slow to recognize and address lesbian battering. Rather, as they developed "shelter" as a response to domestic violence, Women's Advocates first and foremost engaged the specifically heteronormative dimensions of women's oppression—though they did not name it in that way. It became increasingly clear to them that the notion of dichotomous public and private realms functioned to privilege men. The privatization of domestic space, in particular, isolated and confined women, reinforced men's "property rights" over them, and condoned violence as a private matter not subject to public intervention.[5] Neither social services nor legal practices had challenged the privatization of battering and its dependence on heteronormative divisions between public and domestic realms; in fact, many feminists argued, existing services contributed to the isolation of women experiencing domestic violence.[6] Normative conceptions of "home" as an apolitical space furthered women's invisibility. While women's liberation in general challenged this conception by asserting that "the personal is political,"[7] the battered women's movement in particular went further, both critiquing domestic norms *and* creating an alternative home-like space that women embraced as a site of political resistance.

Women's Advocates battered women's shelter worked to secure women's bodily autonomy in three ways. First, shelter generated a politicizing "domestic" space free of heteronormative violence. Second, Women's Advocates demanded that "public" institutions such as law enforcement agencies change to support that new space. Third, Women's Advocates developed coalitions to address problems of race and class hierarchy that emerged in the process of running a shelter. Far from cutting themselves off from people who did not share their feminist or leftist analyses, leaders in the battered women's movement engaged state agencies and capitalist funding sources to create a lasting, though imperfect network of institutions addressing domestic violence.

The founders of Women's Advocates emerged from one of many eclectic consciousness-raising collectives in the Twin Cities. They were "ten or so" heterosexual-identified white women in their mid-twenties to late thirties of working-class and middle-class backgrounds. They had in common prior work with the Honeywell Project that sought to prevent Honeywell's production of cluster bombs used in Vietnam.[8] Sharon Vaughan of St. Paul had gained local prominence through her activism in the Honeywell Project; she had also been active in the local Catholic left, but, recently divorced and with three children, she chafed at what she called "St. Paul's Catholic values" because they denied women accurate legal information related to marriage and divorce.[9] Minnesotans Monica Erler and Bernice Sisson each had years of traditional civic volunteer work behind them and a growing frustration with the lack of emergency services for women. Susan Ryan, a young VISTA volunteer from New York, was perhaps least tolerant of the "establishment," and demanded nothing less than community-based devotion to ending violence and hierarchy. These and other women came together to "do something" to improve the conditions of women's lives.

Upon learning that most female clients of the county legal assistance offices lacked basic legal rights information, especially regarding divorce and custody issues, the collective first created a divorce rights booklet for women and worked to distribute information about custody, child support, and name changes. Drawing on Ryan's VISTA program grants, they also established a telephone hotline, housed in space donated by the legal assistance office.[10] Countless women throughout Minnesota called the phone service, alerting workers to a deep problem: many women were battered in their homes, but most had no place to go and no financial resources. Though there were thirty-seven emergency shelters for men in the Twin Cities, the only place that a woman with children could receive emergency shelter—and for one night only—was in a motel booked through Emergency Social Services. Lack of safe shelter and legal recourse led this first group of activists to found Women's Advocates in March 1972, a nonprofit group of volunteers who provided a crisis line and legal advocacy for women in abusive relationships with men.[11] As contact with women increased, advocates began to develop a vision of "a place for women who 'need to get away right now.'"[12] Activists offered clients shelter in their own homes and apartments, and women and children crowded onto floors and couches. The experience was indeed politicizing for many, but it was a short-term solution, and its political impact was weakened by its relatively privatized nature. Thus arose the idea of a formal shelter; it would be "like home" but collectively run, and not one person's property.

In part, the opposition Women's Advocates faced prompted activists to envision wide-reaching, almost utopian change. Their early efforts to help battered women—such as housing women in their own homes and later building a formal shelter—were policed with neighborhood suspicion, evictions, and threats of lawsuits by men concerned with "men's rights." From the outset, therefore, advocates adopted a role as "protector" of women, usurping a prerogative conventionally belonging to fathers and husbands. But advocates also demanded a "response from the whole public community."[13] They envisioned "a house on every block" in which the whole neighborhood would be involved, "like McGruff houses for kids, only they would be shelters for women."[14] Such houses would not only act as zones of safety for women but would also signal neighborly intervention in battering, making visible a formerly privatized issue. Women's Advocates, then, offered a vision of a dramatically changed public landscape that would support an alternative domestic space.

In challenging heteronormative notions of "domesticity," and in nurturing the politicization of residents and staff, Women's Advocates shelter itself represented a concerted challenge to the boundary between public and private. Activists also challenged boundaries between "the movement" and the "mainstream." Like other social movements, the budding battered women's movement incorporated dramatic and at times militant acts aimed at radical social transformation. Unlike others, it aimed to take over "the home" and reappropriate it as a space safe for women.[15] Initially, Women's Advocates activists seemed to believe that the protection of women depended on constructing impenetrable walls between the shelter and the public world. But Women's Advocates constantly renegotiated those boundaries, forging new relationships with local police departments, batterers, the neighborhood, and the larger metropolitan community.

For the energetic founders of Women's Advocates, sheltering women was a logical extension of those social movements protesting institutionalized racism, class stratification, and U.S. colonization of other countries. By 1972, advocates with homes took on an increasing number of women needing shelter. While their homes functioned as a sort of underground shelter system, advocates and residents caught their first glimpse of alternative domesticity as a diversity of women and children, advocates, and clients "realized the importance of women being together in one house, sharing their experiences and getting support from one another."[16] This experience, along with a belief in participatory democracy, shared authority, and female empowerment, prompted Women's Advocates to insist on a governing structure in which all residents, as well as advocates, were members on the board of directors, and all members had voting rights.[17] Thus, formerly privatized individuals experienced, as a group, a shift from perceiving the world from within a nuclear family framework to strategizing about the world as a community under one roof. This shift in perception also encouraged a coalitional approach—seeking involvement from a diversity of politicized groups—that became an inherent and far-reaching aspect of the battered women's movement.

Advocates saw their direct action as a radical challenge to society. Many advocates opened up their homes to women facing all manner of crises. Sharon Vaughan, Women's Advocates' first director, explained that doing so was possible in part because early activists tended not to have male partners at the time. "I had kids, but I don't think I could have done any of [Women's Advocates work] with [my former husband]. . . . I didn't have to check in with anybody, to see if it was okay to have somebody sleep in my house."[18] Their work as shelterers and advocates thus took place in the space of their own "private" lives, even withstanding break-ins by armed men in search of their wives or girlfriends. As activists had for the civil rights and antiwar movements, many advocates believed that "taking risks and chances" was an integral part of "what you did for Women's Advocates."[19] More important, doing so convinced advocates that domestic norms and the privatization of nuclear households allowed rather than protected women from domestic violence. As longtime Women's Advocates volunteer Bernice Sisson explained, battering depended on "private homes" because "most batterers do not batter in front of others."[20] This perspective led to an intense focus on the boundary between outside and inside, as advocates tried to convert the exterior walls of their homes (and later the shelter) from barriers that *hide violence within* to barriers that *keep violence out*. Advocates at that time explicitly interpreted violence in gendered, heterosexual terms. They determined that the most important thing was that women be able to get to a space "free of violence," where they could "keep the man out" long enough to envision a further solution. Using their own homes, Women's Advocates filled requests to house thirty to forty women and children each month and joked about the times that women and children showed up at the door with the cat, the dog, and the dog's new litter of puppies.[21]

As if to confirm that Women's Advocates challenged the public order, backlash came from many fronts. After only a few months, one advocate was evicted from her apartment because neighbors complained that she was bringing too many women and children into what was supposed to be an adult-only property.[22] Advocates discovered that even their own "private" homes existed under a tangible net of public surveillance. Vaughan had to stop housing women and children in the home she owned: in her "homogenously white" neighborhood, neighbors noticed the many women of color and children coming and going at all times of the day and night, and they pressured local legislators to find out and put an end to "what is going on in there." At the same time, a men's rights group threatened to sue Vaughan for housing women and children only. She recalled, "I was really scared of them, because when all you have is a house, you know that's what you'll lose."[23] It was the "public"—neighbors, civic groups, legislators, and police—that seemed to secure (or deny) privacy in accordance with gendered, classist, and racist norms about the use of space. Housing women and children only, Vaughan broke local codes about the gender, as well as number, race, and ethnicity of residents, and thereby forfeited her "right" to the privacy of the home she owned.

The challenges of housing women in their own homes prompted Women's Advocates to transfer to a new location their ideals of communal living and their challenge to the links between domesticity and violence. By July 1974, Women's Advocates had raised enough funds through public agencies and private donors to purchase a large Victorian house on Grand Avenue, a short bus ride from downtown St. Paul.[24] Vaughan explained, "It wasn't really a neighborhood. There was a big apartment building next to us, and a rooming house on the other side. . . . That makes it a great place for a shelter: because it's very visible and public, but it's not right in the middle of a residential neighborhood."[25] As shelters opened around the country over the years, neighborhood acceptance proved to be critical to a shelter's survival. Shelters were commonly "pushed out" of their neighborhoods by angry neighbors, most often in white neighborhoods in which residents espoused homogeneity and longevity of property owners and occupants as well as an absence of "problems." Women's Advocates chose its block so well that within a decade, they owned and occupied three adjacent houses, and thereby gained an unchallenged presence in and influence over an area otherwise on its way to gentrification.

Central to the advocates' vision was the desire to make the shelter feel like "home," albeit a temporary one, rather than a treatment facility. In the 1970s, that meant "scrounging" for "castoff" furniture, "covering the tatters with brightly colored throws," and finding things "to help create a homey atmosphere."[26] They sanded wood floors, stripped off old paint, installed louvered shades and drapes over all the windows, and filled the house with plants. Although many proclaimed the shelter's beauty, Pat Murphy's affectionate comment lends particular meaning: "We made do. It was *never* a *show place*, it was a *home*. . . . It was ticky tacky right from the start."[27] The space implied that battered women could and should make a public claim on their right to "home." In the words of one former volunteer, "*Women* were not the ones who were crazy or needed to be institutionalized."[28]

To keep women safe in this new, politicized domesticity, advocates attempted to create a shelter that was impervious to intrusion. In the first year or two of the shelter's operation, there were a number of incidents in which violent men broke into the shelter.[29] Other scares included telephone bomb threats, and angry men pounding on doors and throwing rocks to break windows.[30] The sense of ever-present threat led advocates to take two actions: one involved building an elaborate security system around the house; the other involved pressuring the local police department to change its policies. Both measures reveal some of the ways that the movement perceived and analyzed patterns of violence against women, as well as methods for taking over domestic space and introducing it to the realm of public protest.

The house security system signaled Women's Advocates' determination to keep women inside safe even without public support, and it received a great deal of attention in local papers. A 1976 *Minneapolis Tribune* article began its description of the shelter, "Women's Advocates looks like most of the large old houses on Grand Avenue in St. Paul, except for the wire mesh over the door and the highly visible alarm system across every window."[31] Advocates attempted to control all the permeable elements of the house's boundary. They covered windows with heavy-duty mesh wiring and alarm systems, and they kept heavy drapes and shutters pulled across all windows at all times; they kept the front door closed and constantly checked to see that locks were secured. Because of the electronic alarm system, residents were required to notify a staff person before opening any outside doors or changing the position of any of the windows.[32] At the time, advocates saw no alternative to maintaining this system that sealed the shelter from any relationship to its neighbors as well as the rest of the outside world. The darkness of the house, the rules against touching windows, and the surveillance of passers-by were all intended to create security. Unwelcome intrusions only reinforced advocates' sense of dependence on a barrier that even the sun could not penetrate.

Women's Advocates did not intend, however, to reproduce the centuries-old model of the cloister as an impermeable, safe, and even chaste space. Advocates and residents alike sought relief from the intensity of the shelter, and sometimes relief could only come with getting out of the house at night. The place of choice was not the newly operating A Woman's Coffee House in Minneapolis. Instead, after house meetings, many residents and staff walked together up Grand Avenue to the nearby Noble Roman bar. The bar had been open less than a year when the shelter settled on Grand

Avenue, and it had quickly grown enormously popular with white and African American gay men and drag queens. A predominantly white group of lesbians also loved the Sunday cabaret-style shows at the bar and often contributed their own acts.[33] The occasional presence of lesbians at the bar did not change common perceptions that the Noble Roman was a bar for queer men, but residents and staff at Women's Advocates constituted another happy portion of the bar's clientele every weekend. According to advocate Pat Murphy, they loved going to a bar where "they knew they wouldn't be hassled by men."[34] Within walking distance of the shelter, the Noble Roman gay bar seemed to many residents to be a fine place to get away from it all. Differing from many articulations of lesbian separatism, Women's Advocates did not link heterosexuality with violence against women; they did not seek escape from heterosexual relations, nor from heterosociability in general. But at the Noble Roman, women felt themselves to be neither the object nor the property of men. Until it closed in 1976, the Noble Roman offered Women's Advocates a pressure valve and momentary escape from the boundedness of security at the shelter.

Ultimately, Women's Advocates staff grew critical of the ways they maintained the shelter's boundaries. Rules and alarm systems smacked of institutions and were thus at odds with their own vision of the shelter as home and private residence. Security rules implied that staff held exclusive power to draw the defining boundaries between inside and outside the shelter. In summer 1976, Pat Murphy returned from a visit to a working shelter in Toronto with a new vision of how a shelter could feel more like a safe home. The Toronto shelter, in Murphy's opinion, was staffed by women "just like the women at Women's Advocates—collective, smart, great politics, great women," and the "very big, old house" itself was "very like Women's Advocates' house." Residents similarly came from all walks of life, and included children of all ages. But the "feeling" of the house, compared to Women's Advocates, was like day compared to night:

There was such a sense of openness! The light! It was so light!... This place was wide open and the light was there and the doors were open and the windows were open.... There was clearly no sense of crisis going on.... And there was a foyer where men could come visit their girlfriends or visit with the kids.... There were no rules like we had about 'you can't tell him we're here' and all that kind of stuff. And the feeling in that house was so much better.... The staff weren't fearful, the women in that house were not fearful. They and their kids went outside, played outside, came and went and were not fearful. It was just like a home.

Suddenly to Murphy, the "feeling" at Women's Advocates stood in stark contrast: she saw Women's Advocates "all holed up against the fearful men out there. . . . it was like a fortress, a fortress holding women in, imprisoning them here, we have them in this little prison, and we're going to get the walls high enough and nobody's going to hurt us or them."[35]

Murphy's visit to the Toronto shelter prompted a reevaluation of the effects of Women's Advocates' security measures. To Murphy, it was apparent that living in a "fortress" where the walls can never be high enough actually contributed to a feeling of fear. She blamed advocates and staff for setting the fearful tone of the house: "*We* projected the need for that fear, with our rules: don't tell him you're here, don't give out the phone number . . . *We* projected that fear." Others agreed that the symbolism of an "open" house was crucial and wanted to project a message that "women are not here to hide, and that women can be here and do not need to be afraid, that this is safe, this is a good place."[36] Thus, Women's Advocates decided to open the house by publishing the address, opening the drapes, and letting in the light.[37] To go from "hiding behind a fortress" to being "open" required renegotiating Women's Advocates' relationship with the public and reconceptualizing the relationship between gender, space, and power: "letting in the light" was an act that irrefutably politicized a domestic space by opening it up to a new kind of engagement with the public world.

Advocates' struggle to gain police protection revealed the ways that law enforcement was organized to protect established hierarchies. From the moment Women's Advocates opened, activists demanded that the St. Paul Police Department change its practices to protect women against abusive men. With some regularity, thirty to forty residents and advocates would march down the hill to city hall to confront the mayor about Women's Advocates relationship with the police. They also showed up as a group at the police department to submit verbal and written complaints.[38] Nevertheless, police responses as late as September 1975 indicate that the police protected established notions of property and male power over wives rather than women's right to be free of violent assault. Chief of Police Rowan recorded an incident in which an officer dispatched to Women's Advocates found a man aggressively demanding "visiting privileges" with his children at the shelter. Rather than intervening in the escalating tension, the officer referred the couple to court arbitration and told the advocate on duty, "You're a woman's advocate, I'm a man's advocate." Notably, Rowan found no fault with the officer's behavior.[39] Advocates countered that police officers, as "public servants," had "no right" to be "partial" in their protection of any citizens.[40] Women's Advocates emphasized that their own primary function was to shelter and protect women, and that the police department should similarly bear *public* responsibility for ensuring the safety of everyone at Women's Advocates.[41]

Women's Advocates had to change normative assumptions about (male) property ownership to gain police protection, and eventually they did so. Police were initially unwilling to recognize Women's Advocates as a private property against which men could be considered trespassers; they assumed that even when women owned a property, men retained a right of forcible access to "their" women and children on that property. In mid-September 1975, Women's Advocates voiced their criticisms of the police department at a formal meeting with the department and Mayor Cohen of St. Paul.[42] During the meeting, Chief Rowan was "very concerned about the legal rights of men who wished access to their wives and children." Only after a representative from the City Attorney's Office determined that men do *not* have a "right" to "self-help" in seeking access to women or children and that a man may be considered "at the very least a trespasser on Women's Advocates' property," did the police department begin to take seriously their role in protecting the shelter.[43] Before this legal clarification, common notions of private property were essentially gendered. Not only did privacy protect male property owners from social surveillance, it also granted men rightful access to "their" women on *any* property. Women, though they might become property owners, could gain privacy against social surveillance and protection against intruders and trespassers only through protracted struggle with public agencies. By August 1976, the police department had adopted new policies to "relieve some of the difficulties," including "to give calls to your facility [Women's Advocates] a high priority designation."[44] Women's Advocates thereby successfully instituted an unprecedented relationship with the St. Paul Police Department, including winning the presence and input of advocates at officer training sessions and educating officers on domestic violence and the options available and unavailable to women.

While advocates tried to create a place that felt like home, their initial representation of violence as perpetrated by males outside and something that could be kept out crumbled in the face of their experience. At the shelter, women encountered violence among each other and in disciplining children. A simple gender analysis proved inadequate, as all women at the shelter were forced to grapple with complex and ubiquitous dynamics of violence and power. Residents, some of whom became advocates, helped Women's Advocates shape itself around the difference that race and class made in uses of space and in experimental solutions to domestic violence. Through practice, Women's Advocates gradually exposed and redressed the white, middle-class bias of the shelter's policies. As soon as advocates acknowledged the multiple ways that hierarchy shaped the interior (as well as exterior) of the house, they brought the meaning of violence and nonviolence under closer scrutiny.

Advocates created and posted a set of house rules, called "House Policy," to "protect everyone's safety." Despite their initial assumptions, they became aware of women's violent potential early on, through a few incidents in which clients verbally and/or physically attacked staff members. To address this, advocates created rules granting staff the right to evict anyone acting in a "violent or threatening" way. Staff thereby implied that they had the power to keep the shelter free of violence.[45] House Policy did not initially elaborate what would constitute "violent or threatening" behavior among women; the definition of and reason for prohibiting violent behavior among adults was self-evident to advocates, at least in the early years of operation. Initially, advocates put forth their lengthiest interpretation of violence *within* the house not under the "House Security" section but rather under the section called "House Policy Regarding Children." There, advocates stated,

> Violence is frequently a learned behavior. Children who grow up with it as part of family life and discipline may well incorporate it into their adult lifestyle. This is one of the reasons there is no violent discipline of children allowed during the time they are here. This includes spanking and slapping hands. The staff, especially the child care staff, are willing to work with women to find workable alternatives.

Vaughan retrospectively explained the Regarding Children policy as an instance in which staff imposed white, middle-class values on residents:

We had a rule that you couldn't spank children because that was a form of violence. And there wasn't any question in our minds that this was just. I remember [intervening]: a woman was whopping her kid, a woman of color who came from a really tough situation in her neighborhood, and she turned around and looked at me, and in this calm voice said, "It's normal to spank." Just like that. I never forgot that because, I thought, "well, what *is* normal?" So even the radical philosophy [about violence] was up for grabs. . . . She said, "I teach her to whip anybody who comes up to her, because otherwise she's going to get whipped." And I thought . . . "I have a daughter too, and why would this not be the way I raise my kids?" I thought a lot about the social context of violence and nonviolence, and how, well, we did a lot of things that, well, came from our own context, not necessarily from the women we served.[46]

"Violence" and "nonviolence" proved not to be self-explanatory or essential categories; rather, the terms were culturally and spatially specific, as were conceptions of gender and power.

Initially, advocates explained the relationship between power and violence such that violence stemmed almost exclusively from specific (and stereotypical) hierarchical power: men were more powerful than women, and adults more powerful than children. Some advocates also associated deviance from white, middle-class status (e.g., a woman of color from a "really tough neighborhood situation") with violence. As women in the shelter discovered that hierarchy, control, and violence were part of the *internal* dynamics shaping the shelter space, they revised their simple gender analysis and definition of violence to one that recognized hierarchies of class, ethnicity, race, and sexuality. Although shelter policy maintained the view that spanking constituted violence, Women's Advocates took the opportunity for transforming their own assumptions because, as Murphy put it, "You're not in an office seeing people for an hour. You're *living together*. So *all* of your cultural patterns and behaviors are there."[47] In distinction from most social services, the experience of living in the shelter thus launched this idealistic, if initially naive, group of activists into the forefront of emerging feminist practice around the multiple dimensions of social hierarchies.

Women's Advocates gave many residents and advocates alike their first "consciousness-raising" experience that was not segregated by race or class. As one resident wrote of her arrival at Women's Advocates in fall 1975,

I was given a bed the first chance I got I lay down to rest. . . . [later] I went downstairs and found that a woman named Manuella had prepared a fried chicken and potato dinner. There were ten or so women sitting around the table eating. . . . I felt pleased and part of the pleasure came from the fact that here were women from several different racial groups all sitting together and sharing. . . . Often one hears, "Really, that sounds just like my husband/boyfriend." The revelation is quick in coming that the woman is not alone in her situation.[48]

Consciousness raising came in the context of crisis and the successful mobilization for change in these women's lives. By 1978, residents had also helped increase public awareness of battering and of the movement created to stop battering. In that year, Minnesotan Ellen Pence, a leader in linking the battered women's movement with other movements, reflected, "Most people think there's more wife-beating than before. I don't think that's true. They also think because of women's liberation, women are getting more uppity so they're getting beaten up more. But it's just the opposite. Most of the women in shelters are not feminists. . . . They've just never had a place to go before."[49] Shelters like Women's Advocates became one place in which feminism extended beyond the lives of self-named activists to become a broader movement.

The shelter created an unparalleled opportunity for experiencing, confronting, analyzing, and changing racist dynamics within its own walls and within feminist activism. Changes did not happen over night: in the words of one white advocate, "it wasn't like we just opened the doors and in came women of color and we figured it out. It was a long, three-year process."[50] Early residents of the shelter—particularly women of color—felt they were largely on their own to deal with racism without the support and understanding of the (virtually all-white) staff.[51] Eileen Hudon was among those who thought that the staff "had no idea of the racism going on" among residents or between residents and staff, and even that at times, the staff "was instrumental in creating a division between white women and women of color at the shelter."[52] They perceived racism at the shelter to function similarly to racism in the wider society, but with one crucial difference: whereas most urban space was defined by racial segregation and established norms guiding race relations, the shelter brought otherwise segregated Chicana, Indian, black, and white women together under the same roof with an ethos of common struggle.[53] If at times residents did not trust staff to respond appropriately to perceptions of conflict between white women and women of color, women at the shelter nevertheless functioned as an unnamed coalition, learning about the ways that race, class, and (later) homophobia shaped all women's experience. Hudon herself explained,

> It was in shelters that I first started talking about racism. What does that have to do with battering? Or what does homophobia have to do with battering? Well, it all has to do with a woman's safety, that's all. If you can't say the word *homophobia*, or *lesbian*, if you don't understand a woman's community, how're you going to help? If you don't know what resources or powers are there, or what particular kind of dangers, or isolation, she has to deal with, then you're not doing your job.[54]

Residents revealed that every woman came for shelter with her own specific resources and challenges; advocates, therefore, needed to understand the cultural contexts that shaped residents' needs.

Women's Advocates could be a politicizing space for residents as well as advocates. Under one roof, many residents did not consider themselves feminists, nor even about to become feminists. But Women's Advocates was "a place to go" where individuals suddenly became part of a broad-based movement. Beyond supplying a roof, Women's Advocates addressed a long list of residents' needs: school arrangements for their children; visits to hospital emergency rooms; support from welfare, police, and courts; affordable, long-term housing; and retrieval of women's possessions from her former home.[55] Meeting those needs involved intervention in all manner of public agencies and institutions. After isolation and demoralization, Women's Advocates was a space that was both radicalizing and empowering for battered women across race and class differences, affirming that women had "the right to run their own lives." In early 1976, while talking with other residents and staff after her first day at the shelter, Lois remarked, "This is the first time I've felt like a human being. I've kept quiet for so long."[56] Many residents experienced life-changing moments of community and support, such as the celebration parties they held whenever a woman found an apartment after a long search. Among their liberating actions were the en masse marches to the St. Paul Police Department or down the hill to the capitol, where they interrupted legislative sessions to demand laws and programs to meet women's needs for safe domestic space.

Being together under one roof allowed residents to foster a movement that worked in practice to address hierarchies of race, class, gender, and sexuality. Some residents, like Beatrice during the shelter's second month of operation, quite vocally criticized staff for being "do-gooders," "liberals" who were separated from and "better than" residents.[57] Seeking additional feedback, Women's Advocates began to keep a Residents' Notebook in which residents could anonymously evaluate staff as well as bring up conflicts they wanted addressed. Activists throughout the country—including former shelter residents—expanded this innovative strategy over the next decade by incorporating battered women's needs assessment, service evaluation, and ideas for solutions to design increasingly effective shelter and advocacy programs. This accomplishment of the movement, too often overlooked in histories of radicalism, was based on innovative responses to difference and power. Through struggle, Women's Advocates became one place that gave concrete meaning to the idea of coalition.

A series of grueling house meetings and staff retreats, as well as residents' willingness to articulate their perceptions of racism at the shelter, led to a critical policy change in 1978. Women's Advocates would henceforth hire and maintain a staff that proportionally matched the ethnic and racial composition of the residents—at that time, 35 percent women of color.[58] The insistence on maintaining a staff that was racially and ethnically representative of residents arose initially out of the understanding that many women of color did not receive enough support or "safety" at the shelter. The original white staff was not aware of the specific challenges facing and resources available to Indian, Latina, Asian American, or black women. The meetings that resulted in Women's Advocates' new hiring policy did not simplistically envision that a black woman would best be served by a black advocate, or an Indian by an Indian. Rather, the policy, hinting at the value of coalition, was instated to draw *more* resources to the shelter and hold everyone accountable for being aware of the specific intersectional issues facing residents of color.[59]

Client feedback also eventually led Women's Advocates to address the reality of violence in lesbian relationships by the late 1970s. Prior to this, advocates presumed males to be the perpetrators of violence, and they presumed that sheltered women were in heterosexual relationships; even attending to issues of lesbian motherhood and custody did not interrupt Women's Advocates' preconceived notions. Increasingly, however, clients in lesbian relationships challenged the gendered, heteronormative boundaries on which the shelter was founded. Initially, the shelter movement throughout the United States responded to such challenges by creating a popular canon of stories about conflicts that resulted when each member of a lesbian couple sought protection from the shelter.[60] Though this lore was often based on actual situations, its frequent retelling posed women in lesbian relationships as inherently confusing subjects—insiders to the shelter by virtue of being women, outsiders to the shelter by virtue of not playing a "woman's role" according to heteronormative structures. Only slowly did Women's Advocates begin to revise definitions of gender and violence and alter shelter policies and interaction with other public agencies to serve women in relationships with women. By the 1980s, lesbian activists throughout the United States began to more directly demand that the battered women's movement better address the multiple social roots of violence among women.[61]

Although the establishment of Women's Advocates shelter did not prevent domestic violence, it did transform the public landscape not simply by adding a new space and service but by deeply challenging the ways that gender hierarchies were embedded in built environments and the social institutions that composed them. As Women's Advocates itself became a social institution in this changed public landscape, it became increasingly clear that an exclusive focus on shelters was a practical and political hindrance. Eileen Hudon, for example, was among those who figured out that antiviolence activists needed to continue to imaginatively tap constantly changing community resources to minimize violence against women in disparate contexts, from particular Indian reservations throughout the country to multi-ethnic or homogenously white neighborhoods in urban, suburban, and rural settings. In the first several years, however, shelters were uniquely constructive because collective political alliances were realized not only within but also *about* domestic space. From its inception, the shelter movement necessarily resisted a definition of "home" as a privatized, nuclear family space. The act of turning a private house into a shelter instead created a home built of collective action and made that "woman's place" an integral component of the "public" and "political" world.

Of Menstrual Extraction and Money: Self-Help in Detroit

In Detroit as well as in St. Paul, "private" living space proved to be both politicizing and generative of feminist institutions. The Feminist Women's Health Center originated with a flowering of feminist activism beginning in a Highland Park apartment cooperative in 1970. Initially an ad hoc collective interested in improving women's sexual health care and wresting control from sexist conventional medical institutions, the Detroit FWHC formalized as an organization alongside the Feminist Federal Credit Union when the two took up residence together in 1973. The health center would occupy three different locations in the next three years as it developed a range of services related to women's sexual autonomy and health. Tracing the FWHC's occupation of urban spaces reveals that although predicated on the belief that women's own bodies were authoritative, the women's health movement in fact took shape around much larger social geographies.

In 1970, a group of young white women who had grown up in working-class families turned an eighteen-unit apartment building in the Highland Park neighborhood into a domestic cooperative. Real estate in that transitional neighborhood was "wide open," and Valerie Angers and her husband made the down payment for the building. Though most of the people in the cooperative had participated in the antiwar movement, Angers pointed out that "most . . . were not 'movement people'" from Detroit's radical left; instead, "they were people like me who had a family, had a husband or a boyfriend," they were "all nose to the grindstone with school and raising children," and "they just thought this was a grand experiment to figure out how to free up our lives so that we could be the kind of people we thought we'd like to become."[62] They arranged child care cooperatively and arranged domesticity so that each woman had her own apartment regardless of her marital status, in large part to facilitate sexually open partnerships. The alternative domicile inspired Poor Woman's Paradise coffeehouse as discussed in chapter 2, and provided impetus for the first Feminist Women's Health Center in the Midwest as well as the nation's first Feminist Federal Credit Union.

In a transitional neighborhood and in a building owned rather than rented, interpersonal relationships and sexual passion, rather than threatening neighbors and landlords, initially contributed to movement proliferation. The building magnetically drew additional women who created resource centers, child care co-ops, graphics collectives, and other projects. As Angers recalled, "It was a little beehive of activity, and there was a lot of activity around Joanne and I [*sic*]. . . . You know how when you have sexual energy, you know, when you're very attracted to each other, you become very attrac*tive* to other people too? And people say, 'Oh my gosh, *we* want to do what you're doing! We want to be *with* you!' It was that kind of thing. We had found this new neat thing called lesbianism, and . . . we liked to start things."[63] From that apartment building, the women's health project and the credit union began to take form. Each sought to increase women's autonomy in part by making a woman's body and money her own private business.

On the third floor of the apartment co-op, tenants and friends began to talk about women's sexuality-related concerns and the virtual impossibility of "obtaining decent gynecological care in America, at any price." By early 1972, they constituted a project, the Detroit Women's Health Project, with the purpose of learning and teaching pelvic self-examination, pregnancy diagnosis, and a host of other topics. Miriam Frank wrote a regular self-help column, "Notes from the Speculum Underground," for *Fifth Estate* and the *Detroit Women's Press*; Carole Kellog, Jessie Glaberman, Carol Taub, Connie Cronin, Kay Otter, and many others offered workshops on a growing list of women's sexual health issues and practices.[64] Importantly, the Women's Health Project (whp) provided referrals for things such as rape counseling, gynecological care, and abortion clinics and was decidedly not "service oriented." The whp never examined women, as their purpose was rather "to show people how to do it themselves . . . show women how to examine themselves."[65] Their educational workshops traveled easily; they went to women's meetings in churches, schools, and apartments throughout the Detroit area and beyond. At the same time, some of these women (along with women elsewhere in the country) were preparing themselves to provide menstrual extractions and safe, early abortions. The possibility of offering services led to new questions about place of practice.

Issues of space and property affected grassroots women's health activism and the entire self-help movement from the outset. Chicago's Jane underground abortion service—arguably the premier model of self-help in feminist health care—offers one example of the relationships among space, sexuality, and institutionalized health care. Beginning in 1969, Jane utilized apartments and offices secretly and on a very temporary basis to keep the mission as hidden as possible. In learning to perform safe abortions themselves and by necessarily working "underground," the volunteer staff of Jane circumvented conventional medical facilities, federal laws preventing doctors from performing abortions, and exploitive abortion practitioners who profited from the law and a steady stream of women in desperate need. Before the legalization of abortion in 1972, Jane could not even consider establishing a permanent or institutional property from which to work.[66]

In contrast, when Los Angeles feminist activists Carol Downer and Lorraine Rothman created a "self-help clinic" the year before *Roe v. Wade* legalized abortion, they appeared to deemphasize the importance of "place."[67] This clinic immediately became a model for other sexual health activists around the country. As proponents like Cathy Courtney of Detroit explained, "The self-help clinic is not always a particular place. It is a concept and a set of techniques."[68] According to lore, the self-help movement "was born" at Everywoman's Bookstore in Los Angeles when Downer inserted a speculum into her vagina and invited those present to see her cervix. As the historian of medicine Judith Houck points out, Downer thereby made very public her very privates.[69] In theory, self-help could be taught anywhere women could gather: the proliferation of public women's spaces like bookstores certainly contributed to such gatherings, confirming that women did not need a literal clinic or even clinic-like facilities to practice or teach self-help examination. But in practice, the self-help clinic model institutionalized the establishment of feminist health centers throughout the United States and other countries. By 1972, the legalization of abortion allowed women all over the United States to expand their services toward the formation of facilities often called "Women's Choice" clinics. Women could and did establish countless above-ground clinics focused on women's sexual health, and many included a variety of abortion services. As women in Detroit and elsewhere discovered, however, the legal right to abortion did not guarantee that surrounding communities would give women's clinics a warm welcome.

In fact, the self-help clinic was *not* simply a concept but rather a stake claiming women's sexual autonomy in the public landscape. Whether in Cambridge, Tallahassee, or Detroit, such clinics were public places for the practice of women's sexual autonomy, and as such, they were vortexes in which social conflicts played out through property itself. Further, the clinic model was one already fraught with class distinction. When self-help health activists set up clinics, they rejected the "private practice" model of health service maintained by most physicians during the 1960s and 1970s. But neither could activists adopt wholesale the clinic model. In contrast to private practice, clinics—usually by virtue of being associated with well-funded institutions for medical training and research—offered care that was less expensive and less dependent on an ongoing relationship between patient and doctor. In many senses, then, clinics were both more "public" and less "private" due to the very structures that made them more accessible across class.[70] While self-help activists promoted accessibility as a goal for women's sexual health, few had the economic resources that would have buffered women's health clinics from certain kinds of public surveillance. As they discovered, clinic space was not easy to come by: space anywhere cost money and required the good graces of neighbors and city officials who could easily challenge a clinic's ability to stay open, much less provide sexual health services for a rapidly expanding clientele. Furthermore, all locations introduced issues of access for clientele and staff, and influenced what services would or could be offered. Spatial dynamics thus shaped the self-help movement, its "concept," and the ways that women envisioned and practiced sexual autonomy.

Although many of the proponents of self-help sexual health care were lesbian-identified women, the establishment of service-oriented clinics contributed to heteronormative bias within the nascent feminist health movement. Women who slept with women and women who slept with men may equally have found pelvic self-exam, home remedies for yeast infections, and discussions of orgasm and masturbation to be politicizing and revolutionizing. But feminist sexual health services and clinics took shape around particular needs created by heterosexual relationships in a sexist dominant culture: finding safe, accessible methods of birth control, abortion, and childbirth. The movement as a whole was slow to acknowledge that such issues were relevant to many lesbian-identified women.[71] Above all, the early movement failed to demand accessible care for lesbian-identified women, and thus feminist clinic spaces came to reinforce major contradictions within the movement. On one hand, lesbian-identified health activists promoted feminist health clinics as a solution to grossly homophobic conventional medical clinics and encouraged lesbians to seek regular care. Focused on practical matters, some feminist health practitioners even acknowledged that many lesbian-identified women had sexual contact with men, just as many straight-identified women slept with women, and thus had equal need of services related to heterosexual practices. On the other hand, these same activists often quipped that "heterosexuality is a serious health hazard for women at this point in time," and lesbians "don't have to use contraceptives," confirming that the cause and purpose of feminist health clinics was, in fact, heterosexuality.[72] When lesbian-identified women entered the realm of reproduction, feminist clinics adjusted to serve them, but in general, women's health clinics—like battered women's shelters—continued to be structured around heterosexual health.

In Detroit, the Feminist Women's Health Center became a service-oriented establishment in 1973 when Valerie Angers and Joanne Parrent rented a small house on Golden Gate (near Seven Mile Road) and Woodward. There, FWHC formed a place-based, symbiotic partnership between self-help health activism and feminist credit union activism. The Highland Park apartment cooperative had dissolved by 1972, and many women were seeking space for their various projects.[73] Most relied on tiny grants to run tiny spaces that burst at the seams with movement. The Women's Health Project, for example, for months held weekly educational sessions out of a small office paid for with earnings from benefits, traveling workshops, and a $500 grant from Robin Morgan's Sisterhood Is Powerful, Inc. fund.[74] Meanwhile, Cathy Courtney, who had studied with Downer at the L.A. Self-Help Clinic and had energetically led the Women's Health and Information Project at Central Michigan University in Mt. Pleasant, arrived on the Detroit scene in 1973 committed to building a stable, service-oriented clinic. She and other interested white women (many of them coming from the Highland Park apartment co-op and the WHP) held the first organizational meeting for a Detroit Feminist Women's Health Center.[75] In late 1973, Angers and Parrent opened their three-room house on Golden Gate to the FWHC, giving them a room for health procedures and a place to hang the all-important shingle.

The tiny house also provided an office for the first Feminist Federal Credit Union in the country. It made sense that the health center and credit union would emerge in the same space. The Feminist Federal Credit Union began in part out of a desire for a more stable women's space, as it seemed that such a space depended on removing financing decisions from public and paternal scrutiny. Importantly, the credit union claimed the self-help health movement as its model, initially calling itself a "women's self-help financial center." Credit union founders Angers and Parrent had gone to Self-Help Clinic meetings in Kentucky; Downer visited Detroit; and Angers and Parrent visited Downer's L.A. Self-Help Clinic. Although they shared an interest in revolutionizing women's sexuality and health care, Parrent and Angers saw feminist economic self-help as the first step toward anything else. The feminist credit union thus arose as a solution to a problem that its founders and virtually all the women they knew experienced: most banks required male signatures—a husband's or father's—on loans made to women and sometimes even on checking accounts; credit cards in women's names were virtually unheard of.[76] This was particularly vexing and even dangerous when women needed money for health care, abortions, or divorce. A women's credit union would provide "women's money for women's needs," allowing women to get loans from each other without male signatures.[77] Whether someone needed money to go to school, get divorced, or get an abortion, the credit union could be a means toward greater sexual and economic autonomy: her body and what she did with it would be her own business and not that of her husband, her father, or the state. Health projects, too, needed money if they were to evolve from "projects" to "centers"—that is, if they were to establish working clinics. Thus, it seemed almost natural that from their inception until early 1976, the Feminist Federal Credit Union and Feminist Women's Health Center shared space, paid rent together, moved together, and even collaborated in their practices to a surprising extent. Activists forged this bond through implicit acknowledgment that women's autonomy had to be purchased, but analysis of the self-help trajectory shows that women's privacy and autonomy were more deeply bound to class distinction than those activists realized.

"All you need is seven people and $65 to start a credit union," according to Angers. But you also need a willingness and ability to "interact with the mainstream": Parrent and Angers had to convince federal examiners that contrary to conventional banking wisdom, women were creditworthy; they had to explain to the Federal Credit Union Charter Agency "what *feminism* was in the first place"; and they had to show why "feminism" constituted a legitimate "common bond" that could be the basis of credit union membership.[78] The idea of an association-based credit union had a solid foundation: at that time, 17 percent of credit unions in the United States were associational rather than workplace-based. But when Parrent and Angers defined the membership bond as "anyone who has the goal of working for the improvement of the condition of women," Federal Credit

Union Charter Agency officials responded defensively, "but that could be 52 percent of the population!" Parrent, who pressed a motion to add "sisterhood" to the "brotherhood" of credit union language before two thousand members of the Michigan Credit Union Association, contrasted this kind of work with left, antiwar, and feminist activists who "just debated everything" within their own insular groups. "When we started the credit union and started interacting with the mainstream society, saying things like, 'You should acknowledge Sisters because we're *here!*' there was not only resistance to that but almost *shock* that we should ask or demand such a thing. To me that was very exciting because we were pushing against areas where you can see that you're forcing this society to think about and accept change."[79] When the Feminist Federal Credit Union (FFCU) received their federal charter in August 1973, they opened services with over $22,000 in federally insured loans from fifty-three eager members from diverse race and class backgrounds.[80]

Angers and Parrent credibly argued that feminism constituted a common bond by relying on the existence of already-established feminist organizations that would act as "sponsors" of the credit union. In response to agency concerns about an economically marginal and amorphous 52 percent of the population, the credit union initially restricted membership to anyone (male or female) who was a member of NOW or the Women's Liberation Coalition of Michigan. The Federal Credit Union Agency wrote this organization-based membership structure into the requirements for all future feminist credit unions, reinforcing the idea that a "feminist" is someone who belongs to a feminist organization. Many activists expressed frustration at this outcome. The Chicagoland Women's Federal Credit Union, in particular, argued that this requirement restricted membership and access in ways that were antithetical to the goal of helping women across race, class, and political identity.[81]

Although restricting, the required structure in itself promoted organizing, as women seeking loans joined one or more of these organizations to also join the credit union. In fact, organizing went both directions. Faye Roberts, Janette Salters, and Pam Carter, founders of WOMAN (Women's Organization to Mash Alcoholism and Narcotics, an inner-city addiction treatment program), convinced the credit union to include the National Black Feminist Organization (NBFO) in its list of sponsors: as they saw it, requiring membership in predominantly white feminist organizations undermined the credit union's claim to serve women broadly. Underscoring their point, Roberts, Salters, and Carter founded a Detroit chapter of the NBFO while looking into credit union assistance to support a stable space for WOMAN. Seemingly overnight, the credit union grew from hundreds to over two thousand members and assets approaching a million dollars, as it addressed a need acutely felt by women from all walks of life. Women set up feminist credit unions throughout the United States, with the two most common "sponsors" being NOW and the NBFO. The feminist credit union network grew so rapidly that it gained the attention of mainstream banking agencies and initiated another round of interaction between these feminists and conventional public institutions. Suddenly, women were a market, and bankers wanted in. Suddenly, that is, bankers came to the office (of sorts) of the expert, the Detroit FFCU, an institution that had "wonderful, wonderful loans" on its books.

At its first location in a small house on Golden Gate, the credit union shared a practical partnership with the health center, the former working out of one small office in front and the latter working in the other front room. Parrent and Angers lived in back. In telling ways, the practices of the FFCU and the FWHC blurred the line between public and private institutions. As Angers recalled,

> The banks would come talk to us in our flannel shirts and boots. . . . So we were sitting there in the credit union office. Being an artist, I had a very steady hand. The health center was doing these menstrual extractions—of course, they were early abortions—and they would call me back there and prep me and get me all cleaned up. I would insert the catheter through the os, because I had a very steady hand and you couldn't touch the vaginal wall, it had to be really clean. And I was really good at this. So there they were doing the menstrual extraction and I put the catheter in and they do the rest of it, and I go back to the front room where these two bankers were waiting because they wanted to talk to us about how to give loans to women. They were sitting there in the front room in their suits, and we were in the back room doing menstrual extraction. It was such a juxtaposition, about how our two worlds were so different, so apart. And yet, you know, we talked to the bankers, of course.[82]

As at Pride and Prejudice in Chicago, activist goals could not always be neatly delineated. Although health interests led to menstrual extraction and credit interests led to visits from men in suits, these practices shared the immediate terrain of women's bodies. Moreover, the Golden Gate house showed that these practices were interconnected not just by ideology but by intensely tangible, moment-to-moment activities.

Only a few months later, in March 1974, the credit union women and health activists opened the Women's Resource Center just around the corner at 18700 Woodward and moved in. Earlier outreach had revealed additional activist groups from all over the Detroit area, most of them meeting in women's homes. Many of them would constitute a core for the resource center: despite the small size of the center, soon more than thirteen different groups met there, including rap groups, the NBFO, a feminist food co-op, the credit union, and FWHC; the space housed activities, events, a reading library, medical and legal referral service, a community bulletin board, and a monthly newsletter.

The new resource center helped formalize the Feminist Women's Health Center, and women more definitively divided the health movement mission into two parts—one less and one more institutional. Their divergent trajectories were due in part to divergent goals and in large part to differential access to spaces that could serve as a public clinic.[83] The education-oriented Health Project handed over the goal of clinic formation to the Detroit Feminist Women's Health Center when it opened its services in the Women's Resource Center in March 1974. The Health Project reiterated its emphasis on educational rather than service-based self-help, and explained that in contrast to the FWHC Inc., "We are not an actual institution-type clinic. But we are doing things about women's health in Detroit on very little money, collectively."[84] Though women who had been involved in the original Women's Health Project group continued to offer self-help workshops in borrowed spaces for many more years, the project as an organization quickly and quietly disappeared in the shadow of FWHC.

In September 1974, with virtually guaranteed income, FWHC and FFCU vacated the Women's Resource Center in favor of a larger home at 2445 West Eight Mile Road.[85] The two groups rented the house for $235 per month and extensively renovated the property that had been vandalized and left vacant. There, FWHC enjoyed a whole floor to itself with a living room–style waiting room (also used for intake interviews and educational workshops) as well as another homey room for procedures, a nice bathroom, and a kitchen. This address quickly became another "hubbub, a beehive of activity." With a weekly food co-op, it served as another community center of sorts, where women could "get information about anything they needed."[86] The health center offered free pregnancy testing and counseling, free STD and STI screening, complete gynecological services and referral, early term abortion, pre-and postnatal care, nutritional and health counseling, and regular workshops on a vast range of topics from self-exam and birth control to menopause and meditation.

In both intentional and unintentional ways, the FWHC's establishment as a public service entailed greater public visibility. Soon the clinic found itself at the center of public conflicts over where, how, and under what authority health practitioners should serve women's sexual health needs. Indeed, as women around the country gained increasing sexual autonomy through the work of feminist health clinics, backlash initially emerged with as much focus on location and authority as on the meaning of sexual autonomy and reproductive choice. This process often discursively reconstructed clinics offering a wide variety of health services as "abortion clinics" and simultaneously constructed abortion as an evil if not literally illegal practice that tainted virtually all aspects of women's sexuality. Hence, women's sexuality and health care remained open to ongoing public censure.

The white, "blue-collar" neighborhood around the FFCU/FWHC house, called the Green Acres–Woodward neighborhood, was primarily residential but included a number of businesses and some vacant lots in the vicinity. A half-mile west of Woodward, the Eight Mile Road location had advantages: as Angers put it, "It was kind of a nice section, it was safe, and we always had wanted safety for the women using the services." The FWHC advertised a range of gynecological services (including early abortions) in local papers, and some neighbors constituted a portion of the clinic's growing clientele. But other neighbors, with a well-organized neighborhood association and access to public agencies, ultimately decided to drive the clinic away, claiming, "We neither want nor need these services," and "Detroit is a big city; they [the clinic] can go somewhere else."[87] Eight Mile Road defined the jurisdictional boundary between Detroit and *not*-Detroit, and many white residents near the boundary line solidified ideological distinctions by suggesting that if women's clinic services were needed anywhere, it was in *Detroit*, not *here*; thus, when they rejected the clinic in their own neighborhood, they simultaneously constructed a sexually deviant Detroit.

While mainstream and feminist presses alike celebrated the opening of the combined credit union/health center building, neighbors balked: the Feminist Food Co-op created parking problems when it operated on Saturday mornings, and even on weekdays health center clients occasionally blocked neighbors' driveways; there was too much traffic, supposedly leading to increased crime; something called a *Feminist Women's Health Center* would undoubtedly be an abortion clinic—would that reduce property values? These rumblings quickly reached zoning authorities. The FFCU and FWHC had only occupied the house for one month when the City of Detroit issued an order to "discontinue and desist in the use and occupancy of this building as a Credit Union and Health Center and restore it to its legal use as a one family dwelling and doctor's office as per permit dated May 14, 1936." The credit union wrote a letter of appeal, stating, "we have a quiet operation limited to credit union members only (90% women)." In early February 1975, the city granted a permit to extend the lease for one year, with pages of conditions including creating a parking lot behind the building and the provision that "this building shall be used only as a credit union and health center and shall not be used for a food distribution center or an on-site abortion clinic."[88] Before the year was over, the credit union announced its move to "the largest woman space ever," the exciting new Feminist Women's City Club, in downtown Detroit; by April 1976, the health center was left to fend for itself on Eight Mile.

In addition to running a clinic whose client volume was increasing almost 400 percent per year, health center workers spent the next year and a half trying to secure their place in the neighborhood.[89] They improved the property, met with neighbors, and attended zoning hearings. They circulated respectful letters to "Dear Green Acres Neighbors" and "Dear Gentlepeople," and they attended each monthly neighborhood association meeting in an effort to integrate themselves as citizens of Green Acres. They received permission from the nearby St. John's church to use eight spaces for staff parking, and they posted signs directing clients where to park. They also communicated with other clinics around the country facing similar challenges. The health center saw these as non-negotiable measures, inextricably connected to the clinic's ability to offer sexual health education and procedures for scores of women each week. And for a time, clinic directors believed they would earn the same rights enjoyed by other businesses in the neighborhood if they behaved like citizens and met neighbors' most explicitly stated demands, namely, those related to the physical property.

Neighbors, meanwhile, spent the year organizing against the clinic, buttressed by a growing regional and national backlash against abortion and women's self-help health care.[90] One neighbor, Pat Reese, spearheaded a petition that garnered sixty signatures in opposition to the health clinic, and others brought well-rehearsed arguments and statistics to zoning hearings in early June. Parking was still a problem—especially since the church, hearing from neighbors that FWHC was an abortion clinic, rescinded its offer of parking space. Neighbors told the zoning board that the clinic was neither wanted nor needed in the neighborhood. Lindy Offer testified that she and others had been "shocked and dismayed" to learn that the FWHC was "doing abortions practically in [our] backyards"; she was "willing to do anything" she could to evict the clinic. "Let one in and they'll be others," agreed one man, borrowing segregationist language to apply to a zoning conflict. "They can't be part of this Association," petitioners erroneously claimed, "they don't even pay rent."[91] The clinic, that is, was not *us*; it did not contribute to the neighborhood's health and stability but detracted from it. Businesses that drew questionable activities—such as the nefarious motel that neighbors had driven out two years earlier—could demolish property values and neighborhood coherence almost overnight if allowed to stay. Although the government-assisted red-lining/white flight phenomenon was one that reinforced white privilege, it was often with reluctance that white communities—particularly those without extra money—packed and moved farther out. Green Acres inhabitants had seen too much of that over the previous two decades, many of them feeling more pushed by "black Detroit" than pulled by working-class suburbs or inaccessible middle-class suburbs. With intensity, they appealed to zoning regulations in race-laden language to keep their backyards clean.

Attempting to mediate various sides of the conflict, the Green Acres–Woodward Civic Association Board held an additional meeting in October in which earlier complaints were reiterated. At least one board member was supportive of the clinic, arguing that she knew many women in the neighborhood who had used the service but who feared admitting it and had even signed the petition out of fear. Further, the association and zoning board had received letters in support of the clinic, and those should be considered as well. Others, however, supported the neighbors' petition. "If it was a house of prostitution," argued one board member, "we'd get them out."[92] Somehow, houses of prostitution and feminist self-help clinics that included abortion services required comparable neighborhood intervention. Having begun with complaints about parking problems, neighbors' charges against the clinic increasingly and explicitly linked women's sexual health and autonomy to practices (such as prostitution) that received consistent public condemnation as sexually immoral and threatening to public well-being.[93] Though abortion was legal, one of the ways it was publicly stigmatized was by suggesting that places that supported women's sexual autonomy (feminist health clinics) were equivalent to places fostering sexual immorality (houses of prostitution).[94]

City officials offered little help. In late June, William Levin, executive secretary of the Detroit Zoning Board, railed against the idea that "a bunch of girls could open a clinic, hire doctors, and give medical services to people." He insisted that they get a license for performing abortions, though he acknowledged that Michigan at that time had no licensure for free-standing clinics of this type. He suggested that the FWHC apply for rezoning as a "doctors' office run by doctors" with FWHC women as support staff. He advised the health center that *other* people on the board had strong anti-abortion sentiments, though he claimed that he himself was more "neutral," explaining, "Personally, I don't care if you're performing abortions or intercourse in that place."[95] Such "neutrality" hardly seemed supportive, reiterating the specter of a sexually deviant and publicly threatening household run by women. Clearly somebody—doctors or politicians or zoning officials—needed to take charge. As neighbors tried to get various city boards to take charge, so too did city boards appeal to each other for jurisdiction. In early October, the Detroit City Council directed jurisdiction to the Board of Zoning Appeals by sending the zoning board a collection of ads posted in local papers with a letter that inquired, "Attached is an advertisement for the Feminist Women's Health Center which advertises abortions. Do they have the authority to perform abortions at the moment?"[96] Thus, it was not just a question of who could take charge of "a bunch of girls," but equally, who had authority over *this property* and the activities within. As the locus of debates over what kind of public surveillance would appropriately regulate women's sexuality and the degree to which women's sexuality was or was not a private matter, the building itself came to spatially signify nothing less than women's bodies.

Neighbor and city official sentiment registered a high degree of discomfort over a women's clinic that offered abortion services as well as other services that increased women's control over their own sexual health. A self-help/women's choice clinic might just as well have been a house of prostitution; inside, women might as well perform intercourse as perform abortion. When attached to fixed, public locations, prostitution, intercourse, and abortion had something in common: formal and informal state mediation of urban landscapes did not prevent the occurrence of them as much as it circumscribed the places of their practice and thereby influenced (if not fully controlled) women's mobility and sexuality in ways that served race and class distinction. A place that supported women's sexual autonomy, unmediated by men or the state, disrupted the spatial dimensions of heteronormativity and sexism, helping provide alternatives to the "barefoot and pregnant in the kitchen" condition. Such a place intervened in the public landscape not only as a woman-run building but one that furthered women's sexual autonomy in all places. But although the building was woman-run, it was not ultimately woman-controlled, and in the end, the "public" forced FWHC to move.

As much as the zoning board acknowledged that they, as well as neighbors, found women's sexual autonomy to be quite threatening, the board ultimately denied FWHC's appeal on the technical grounds of parking problems because that was the only legitimate locus of their authority. In subsequent years, antichoice activists developed well-organized strategies to make abortions (and sometimes even birth control) more stigmatized and much less accessible despite the constitutional rights granted by *Roe v. Wade*. But in 1976, FWHC still had some legs to stand on. They argued that legally, it was not the zoning board's jurisdiction to demand abortion licensing, but rather, the state's. Legally, FWHC was *not* an "on-site abortion clinic," as was at issue in the original zoning permit. An on-site abortion clinic was one whose volume of abortions constituted 20 percent or more of its business, and the FWHC was a total health facility offering birth control, pregnancy tests, STI and STD screening, prenatal and postnatal care, pelvic exams, and sexual health education programs. What's more, other agencies would vouch for their legitimacy as a public health service: the Detroit Public Health Department contracted with FWHC to do STI/STD screening for them; the Michigan Cancer Foundation analyzed the Pap smears taken at the clinic, free of charge; the clinic was an integral member of the Southeastern Michigan Anti-rape Coalition; and the National Bicentennial Commission had donated two VISTA volunteers to the clinic. And, while many behaved otherwise, abortion *was* legal. The FWHC performed short-term abortions within the terms of the law and medical wisdom; doctors were always present, and difficult cases were referred to local hospitals. Parking was the only ground opponents of the clinic could stand on, and it was on that ground that the city ordered the health center at 2445 West Eight Mile Road to vacate the building in December 1976.[97]

Although connected to a nascent backlash against women's sexual autonomy, the parking lot problem was no mere smokescreen. For neighbors, the ever-increasing volume of traffic turned the clinic into a tangible nuisance.[98] In fact, responsibility for the parking lot was but a small manifestation of the conflicts arising from multiple feminist efforts to institutionalize women's space. The Feminist Federal Credit Union had promised to build the lot but ultimately abandoned its promise in the face of greater crises at their new home in the City Club. Over the parking lot and the City Club (discussed in chapter 6), the health center and credit union parted company.

From 1972 to 1975, the Women's Health Project and the emerging Feminist Women's Health Center each had been instrumental in publicizing the dangerous abuses of most abortion clinics and abortion referral agencies. For years, their concerns went unheeded until Cathy Courtney and others organized committees of women to investigate every clinic in Detroit that provided abortions. Tracking their findings in 1974 and 1975, a series of articles in the *Detroit Free Press* and the *Detroit News* urged Michigan's Governor Milliken to declare a "health emergency" until the Department of Public Health established licensing regulations for abortion clinics, and they also publicized the unethical practices of most referral agencies.[99] In February 1976, the Department of Public Health passed Standards and Licensing Rules and Regulations for all free-standing surgical outpatient facilities. They did so without consulting feminist health care providers on their content. In fact, they fully bypassed Public Act 274 of 1974, an act requiring the Michigan state legislature to form a joint committee and hold public hearings so that consumers, citizens, doctors, and other members of the public would have input in the matter.[100] The Department of Public Health and the state legislature exercised illegal autonomy (circumventing a legislated process of public input) in creating and passing the new standards. At the same time, the new standards undermined women's autonomy and privacy in sexual health matters by requiring "duplicate reporting of procedures" that requested clients' marital status and other "personal" information.

Though feminists themselves had pushed for regulation of abortion referrals and services, the new standards threatened to close all but two clinics providing abortions in the entire state of Michigan. New standards required six-foot-wide hallways, multiple examining rooms, recovery rooms, longer recovery times for patients, and longer postprocedure presence of doctors, among other things—all of which challenged small clinics like FWHC that provided low-cost, confidential abortions.[101] Unlike most small clinics, however, FWHC had the means to move to meet the new regulations. They found a new facility at 15251 West Eight Mile Road on the border between Detroit and Oak Park. Though they had to complete a series of appeals to rezone the building, the new space made it easy to meet the Department of Public Health Rules and Regulations: it had five examination rooms, a recovery area, a lab, and office as well as reception areas. Ambivalently pushed to greater institutionalization, FWHC reassured those on the mailing list that although the new clinic was admittedly "modern" and "more institutional than what we're used to," "all of us are scheming and brainstorming to make it comfortable, and all of us love our new home."[102]

Before the FWHC moved, some among its staff had predicted that the new regulations would lead to increased suburbanization combined with increased costs. Indeed, increased costs led many clinics to *choose* more suburban locations, leaving the inner city with little support in the way of feminist health care. As it turned out, some women who had received FWHC's self-help training were committed to serving "downtown black women," ensuring that at least for a year or so, FWHC would keep downtown in mind. Faye Roberts, Pam Carter, and Janette Salters, who ran the perpetually underfunded WOMAN center in Cass Corridor, were only too aware that the inner city had precious few sexual health resources for black women, and they turned to the FWHC for help. Of all the "free clinics" in Detroit, not a single one was set up to provide abortions for poor women who could not enter the "whole other world" of Eight Mile Road and beyond.[103] No downtown clinic provided safe, affordable sexual health care and abortions, and every clinic that did was located in the suburbs—Ferndale, Bloomfield, Deerfield, and so on.[104] Roberts, Salters, and Carter hoped to expand the services begun at WOMAN to eventually meet women's needs for sexual health services including abortion. They had discussed the possibility of the FWHC assisting with a collaboratively run downtown clinic, but it was not to be. At that time, the health center had its hands full with the Green Acres neighborhood challenge and was deep in conflict with other white feminists who were then setting up the City Club. Furthermore, the FWHC did not seem willing to relinquish directorship of a new clinic to these three less experienced women.

While FWHC offered educational and moral support, it was left to others to offer the practical and financial support needed to open a new downtown feminist health clinic. In fact, FWHC directors had developed an increasing sense that "the women we serve would not be comfortable" in many downtown locations.[105] To maintain their already-developed suburban base, and under pressure from regulations on clinic spaces, FWHC moved farther west on Eight Mile Road. Against its core values as a clinic providing accessible, respectful health care, FWHC thus became part of an urban topography in which bodily autonomy was an economic privilege, a topography that constituted poverty in part through differential distribution of privacy in matters of health care.

The suburbanization of feminist clinics impeded "dialogic encounters" and coalitional work across geographic distances and between very poor and working-class women in several ways. The suburban location of FWHC not only affected who might or might not have access to the clinic, it also influenced the *status* of those who might have a stake in determining the goals and services of the clinic. By 1977, a geometry of distance discursively positioned "inner-city" women—even when they were physically present— as outsiders to the project of building a clinic based on women's perceived needs within a still-contested terrain of public sentiment.

But Detroit's suburbs, it must be noted, inhered their own complex geometry that constituted dramatic race, class, ethnic, religious, political, and even sexual distinctions; these distinctions relied not only on discursive and literal distance from an "inner city" but also on separation between neighborhoods, often block to block. The new FWHC, located on a more culturally neutral, busy "dividing line," could not have known precisely what assemblage of persons would comprise the new clientele. While the clinic advertised its proximity to the Conant and Greenfield bus lines, directors' letters indicate that they expected to retain especially that portion of their former clientele who—as they put it—would *not* have "felt comfortable" in an inner-city location. Years earlier, that same liminal suburban location might have offered an opportunity to build a new clinic through quite interesting suburban coalitional conversation. But by 1977, due in part to the intervention of public institutions regulating women's health care, the clinic's survival depended on a kind of institutionalization that discouraged the unpredictable conflicts, divergences, and proliferations that emerge through democratic, boundary-crossing, coalitional work. And as an outpatient service, FWHC may have been less compelled, less moved, than a live-in women's shelter to discover what its own clients had to offer.

Conclusion

The movement against domestic violence came into being in part around the establishment of shelters for women who immediately needed to get away from violent partners. As Pat Murphy of Women's Advocates explained to the press, "The reason women who are battered continue to be battered is that they have no place to go. At least one or two or three or five or ten houses like this are needed in every town in the country."[106] The women's health movement, too, took shape around the places of its practice—women's health clinics designed to meet women's immediate need for "decent" gynecological care, sexual health education, birth control, and abortion. Shelters and clinics alike assumed the primacy of women's bodily and sexual autonomy, and thus took women's own bodies as the locus of control. But creating shelters and clinics entailed increasing interaction with mainstream public agencies and services, and these interactions dramatically shaped feminist practice and vision even as they also profoundly changed the larger public landscape. It was with ambivalence that activists met the resulting institutionalization of what began as a grassroots gathering.

By 1978, having received unprecedented state and national recognition of battering, activists had grown critical of all the bills and programs that provided only for more shelters and counseling: "The shelter thing is really a stop-gap remedy. We have to get to the point where women and children are safe in their homes and are not forced to leave."[107] Institutionalization threatened the radical potential of women-run communal, politicized households to challenge the heteronormative privatization of domestic space. Having worked on domestic violence issues coalitionally and within Indian communities in the Twin Cities and Minnesota since the late 1970s, Eileen Hudon argued that solutions have to be community-based because each community has particular cultural resources for addressing domestic violence. In Detroit, the establishment of a feminist self-help health clinic and a feminist self-help credit union went hand in hand, affirming (if not explicitly approving) that bodily autonomy had to be purchased. Around the country, wherever women established women's credit unions, they nodded toward the economics of the differential distribution of privacy and choice in matters of sexuality and health, and they sought to increase women's economic autonomy. The establishment of women's health clinics, as much as any other feminist institution, exposed the limits of that strategy. Not only did women's clinics—embedded as they were in complex social geographies—fail to escape public surveillance, they also failed to dismantle the ways that sexual health care was an arena for the constitution of class and race as well as gender hierarchies.

Attempting to respond to women's immediate needs by building sexual health clinics and shelters generated some of feminism's most important insights about coalitional work and the extent to which race, class, and sexual hierarchies affected women's movement. As Lisbet Wolf, director of Women's Advocates during the 1990s, recalled of her work with Women's Advocates in the 1970s, "It was absolutely the most transforming thing in my life, absolutely unique. We had nothing to model ourselves after. We did things right and we made devastating mistakes."[108] In the case of Women's Advocates, being "under one roof" made possible the mistakes and the learning; the space encouraged and constituted uneasy coalition, which—in a deeply embedded landscape—was the only possible kind. At the same time, public landscapes encouraged exclusions within the movement and inhibited uneasy coalition within movement spaces. In Detroit, for example, the Feminist Women's Health Center maneuvered within the city's segregation and various regulatory bodies (zoning boards, neighbors, and health boards), and managed to survive into the 1980s. But when seen alongside Women's Advocates, it becomes more clear that segregation and regulatory bodies directed the FWHC's "choices"; commonly, feminists and feminist spaces participated in institutionalized racism and class hierarchies even when they began with more egalitarian visions of public service.

While often reinforcing heterosexism and race and class hierarchies, shelters and sexual health clinics for women also challenged heteronormative and class- and race-laden conceptions of domesticity, public responsibility, sexuality, and private space. Feminist institutions like these in fact proved the inextricability of the personal and the larger political world in practice and on the ground, especially as the process of establishing them imbricated feminism with many of the hierarchies and exclusions of that larger world. Other kinds of feminist institutions like coffeehouses and clubs sought to offer lesbian-friendly, social, community space. Though they were not public institutions, they were no less political in intent and practice. Those community spaces are the subject of the next chapter.

six

If I Can't Dance Shirtless,
It's Not a Revolution

Coffeehouses, Clubs, and the Construction
of "All Women"

Imagine: two or three times a week hundreds of predominantly lesbian
women gathering for workshops, political organizing, dances, and concerts, *in a church*! It was like you had died and gone to lesbian heaven!
—Candace Margulies, Minneapolis, February 1994

The eyes of the women of the world are on Detroit tonight.—Gloria Steinem,
Detroit, April 9, 1976

I n 1975, Candace Margulies, the "young whipper-snapper" of local
feminist lesbian organizing in the Twin Cities, decided it was time for
lesbians to have a "nice place" in which to hold a regular coffeehouse
for educational and political programs, live music, and dances. She and
others involved in the Lesbian Resource Center (LRC) had tried to renovate the musty basement of the Chrysalis Women's Building where LRC
was then housed, but it proved impossible. "Fearful of the world which
was full of homophobia," she explained, they weren't sure if they could
hope for a lesbian-friendly response anywhere else: schools and park facilities were out of the question. As a Jewish woman, Margulies was not
looking to hold the coffeehouse in a church, but friends told her that
Plymouth Congregational Church in downtown Minneapolis had hosted
various progressive coffeehouses in the past. So it was that one day she
and Janet Dahlem found themselves following Pastor Bud Jones past the
church sanctuary and down the stairs to the basement social hall to have a

look at the space. "We were just wowed!" recalled Margulies. With a large linoleum floor, a low balcony on one end, and an adjacent kitchen, "it looked like paradise, the possibilities were endless!" Pastors Jones and Elaine Marsh "invited us to use the space to do whatever we wanted" every Friday and Saturday night and many Sunday evenings as well. It was the nicest place Margulies had ever imagined, and suddenly it was available to a group of feminist-identified lesbians for organizing, agitating, recreating, and whatever women might do in "women's space."[1]

Across the United States during the mid-1970s, feminist-identified women formed weekly or monthly coffeehouses oriented around concerts, dances, workshops and classes, organizing drives and fundraisers. As social spaces, they drew a broad spectrum of women—some activist-identified and some not—and they also often provided a hub for a range of political projects. Some coffeehouses used alternative restaurants or women's resource centers, but possibly the majority operated out of borrowed church spaces. A large set of factors was thus at work in creating the particular kind of place that women's coffeehouses became; issues of property, cultural capital, sexuality, and respectability were as formative of coffeehouses and "woman-space" as any preexisting feminist vision and philosophy. Most often in borrowed space, coffeehouses compelled women to work at securing ideal relations with their own potential constituents and also with a "public" outside: landlords, church pastors and congregations, feminist and mainstream journalists, and others. Such negotiations in themselves constituted new articulations of feminism, sexuality, and even the definition of *woman*. In the process, coffeehouses became key institutions of feminist movement itself.

In the interest of greater autonomy, some activists experimented with owned—not rented or borrowed—spaces in which to hold coffeehouse-like activities as well as activist-oriented services, such as health care. In 1976 a handful of young feminists in Detroit bought one of the finest historic buildings in the city, formerly home to the Women's City Club with its Progressive-era origins. While most women's spaces operated in the public's peripheral vision as well as on the margins of the economy, women intended the new *Feminist* Women's City Club to serve as a women's space that would command public attention. Thousands of women from Detroit's suburbs and women from the East and West Coasts attended the opening festivities of the new club. Women who had never paid much attention to feminist activism, and feminists who had never paid any attention to Detroit, all came to have a look at the "largest woman space ever to be owned and operated by feminists." Gloria Steinem theatrically opened the building by cutting a ribbon of $1 bills autographed by "famous feminists." Invited guests toured the magnificent building, feasted at a catered banquet, and danced to a live jazz band. The *Detroit Free Press* made much of the club's new incarnation as a place that would "offer services that members of the older club could scarcely have ever imagined occupying the premises: abortions and karate classes, for example."[2] With the Feminist Women's City Club, Detroit won the national feminist spotlight by elaborating on a vision that many women around the country shared. In part, the new City Club was imagined to be a coffeehouse writ large. It would almost be a world unto itself that combined coffeehouse-like activities with more market-driven functions: the building had a swimming pool, ballroom, conference rooms, offices, a cocktail lounge, a restaurant, feminist businesses, and even hotel rooms. There, it might have been assumed, women could really do "whatever [they] wanted." What's more, the Feminist Women's City Club explicitly advertised, "membership is inclusive, not exclusive, and is open to women of all races, classes, and political persuasions."[3]

As "the largest woman space ever," the City Club magnified the hopes and also the stresses experienced within many feminist spaces, and for that reason, it received more national attention than any other women's space at the time. Its founders had wanted the building to demonstrate that with pooled money, women could create an autonomous space and an autonomous economic system—a national feminist economic network. Women did not need to be apologetic beggars beholden to husbands or the goodwill of church congregations, nor need they be content with linoleum-floored church basements. Instead, women could purchase their own buildings and set their own terms for public admission. But in five months, the City Club project fell apart in financial crisis and controversy. Many women near and far claimed that hierarchical leadership and a $100 annual membership fee created barriers to women's participation, and they cringed at the *Detroit Free Press*'s celebratory quip that the grand opening of the City Club building proved that "feminism and capitalism can go comfortably hand in hand."[4] The nearly total erasure of lesbian existence—despite the fact that most of the founders of the club identified as lesbians or were in relationships with women—was another sign that all was not well. Though not at the mercy of ministers, the City Club was at the mercy of the market and a drastically divided urban geography.

A Woman's Coffee House, typical of women's spaces around the country at that time, and the Feminist Women's City Club, atypical in many respects, beautifully elucidated the strains of women's movement in the public world. This chapter analyzes these two predominantly white, lesbian-driven, feminist social spaces to show how the relationships between these women's spaces and larger public worlds influenced the constructions of race, class, sexuality, and ultimately feminism within those spaces and beyond. The Coffee House in Minneapolis and the City Club in Detroit, like most predominantly white coffeehouses and women's buildings throughout the United States, promised exciting new possibilities for coalition and purported to be "open to all women." Because they fell short, they were locations that invited widespread consideration of feminist practice and identity. They also invite a specifically historical consideration of how feminist movement became manifest within politicized social spaces. Although women of color actively participated in the Coffee House and in the City Club, each space was shaped around white, middle-class cultural imperatives. These locations thus offer examples through which we may better understand how a dynamic, empowering movement committed to egalitarianism, inclusivity, and antiracism could at times become hierarchical, narrow, and exclusionary. These examples show that white predominance was not simply a matter of local demography, nor was it due simply to faulty feminist thinking. Rather, it was a cultural problem that *took place* as women invested in the politics of space.

Lesbian Heaven, Open to All Women

After opening in 1975, A Woman's Coffee House in Minneapolis rapidly became a clearinghouse for many local grassroots feminist organizations and action groups, as did women's coffeehouses in so many other cities. At the Coffee House, recalled one of its founders, "People could see each other every single weekend, they were able to post announcements, hand out flyers, sell tickets, and just be able to feel that kind of energy and enthusiasm. It made for some pretty infectious optimism. We felt pretty good, pretty big! It was a tidal wave!"[5] Workshops, concerts, plays, and dances at the Coffee House furthered the growth of women's production companies, music groups, women's unions, health clinics, athletic leagues, bars, and literary journals, many of which became nationally known initially through coffeehouse networks spanning the country. As a place "open to all women" that revolved around education, organizing, and dancing, the Coffee House fostered new cultural formations that were unimaginable in more narrowly conceived feminist and/or lesbian spaces. As a place premised on lesbians' need to socialize, A Woman's Coffee House also contributed to the growth and visibility of a newly "out" lesbian culture.

As women created that "women's space," they simultaneously charged the categories "all women," "feminist," and "lesbian" with the power to represent a particular emerging movement. This process was always imbricated with the multiple meanings of the space itself. Women at the Coffee House "felt like it was their own," yet it was a borrowed church basement; women wanted it to be public enough for "all women," but private enough to exclude men; they wanted it to legitimize homoerotic and lesbian dancing, but not incur a reputation as a place for sex; women proudly distinguished the Coffee House from market-driven spaces, yet the church infused the Coffee House with white, middle-class connotations. The tensions between women's sexuality and constructions of public and private catalyzed women's activism and also was a source of conflict within feminism.

One could trace the roots of women's coffeehouses to the civil rights, antipoverty, and antiwar coffeehouses of the 1960s. After all, those earlier coffeehouses commonly operated out of church basements or borrowed space in countercultural or progressive eating establishments. Some made this connection explicit. When asked why Twin Cities feminists used church space, the founder of A Woman's Coffee House explained, "There is a long history of using churches for coffeehouses and progressive activities."[6] Many church congregations, too, opened the doors of their church to diverse groups as part of their larger social justice mission, and they often recognized women's coffeehouses in that capacity.

Those spatial and ideological congruences with earlier progressive movements were critical, but women's coffeehouses had their own distinct spatial-historical trajectory. Usually women did not seek churches first, but "*ended up* in" churches because "that's where [they] could get space."[7] Other possible spaces either discouraged broad-based public participation or would not permit women-only gatherings, much less a high degree of lesbian visibility. For example, Chicago's Mountain Moving Womyn's Coffeehouse opened in a cavernous, north-side storefront shared with a feminist crisis line in November 1975. When the rent increased in 1976, the coffeehouse moved to borrow a "known lesbian" space—the popular north-side Mama Peaches restaurant. When the restaurant closed in 1978, the coffeehouse could not afford a new commercial site and moved to a welcoming north-side Methodist church. Over the next twelve years, the coffeehouse moved to other churches on the North Side—the second another Methodist church, the third Lutheran.[8] At each church, initial welcome was followed by exile as church leadership changed, and yet the coffeehouse continued to choose north-side churches. Its fourth and last location until it closed in 2005 was the Metropolitan Community Church, founded on the principle of inclusivity across sexual orientation with an explicit goal of serving queer people of faith. Founders of A Woman's Coffee House in Minneapolis, too, had explored many other community spaces before resorting to church space; the coffeehouse had its roots in two successive locations of the Lesbian Resource Center, and founders initially hoped it could stay in such familiar, lesbian-friendly space.

A Woman's Coffee House began out of distinctly feminist-identified, lesbian desires in a landscape that had previously precluded openly lesbian gatherings. Prior to the mid-1970s, lesbians and feminists (whether lesbian, bi, or straight-identifying) in the Twin Cities had few choices for public, social space in which to assemble independently of men. As chapter 1 argues, there were only a handful of gay bars, and most gay and straight bars restricted women's presence in various ways. Women thus began to generate a variety of meeting grounds to encourage lesbian, feminist lesbian, and/or feminist activism and sexual self-determination. These included Amazon Bookstore, Chrysalis Women's Resource Center, the Women's School, and the Elizabeth Blackwell Women's Health Center, to name just a few tangible spaces that served overlapping lesbian and feminist interests. White-identified lesbians particularly came to seek yet another kind of community space—one that protected lesbians from violence, allowed them to develop their differences from heterosexuality, and affirmed the legitimacy of lesbian sexuality.

A Woman's Coffee House was born in lesbian space. In 1972, three white women opened the Lesbian Resource Center (LRC) in a small storefront space off Lyndale Avenue, claiming, "We have found that the Gay House, due to its male orientation, and existing women's groups, due to their straight orientation, have given us secondary, if any consideration."[9] That same year, LRC held the first lesbian pride parade in Minnesota—a nervous and rushed march two blocks down Lyndale Avenue and back—and it was also instrumental in the formation of the Wilder Ones softball team. It was at LRC that women created the much acclaimed lesbian literary journal, *So's Your Old Lady*, and the center also put out a monthly newsletter and calendar called *Le'sbeinformed*. Lavender Theater came together in and performed at LRC and also consistently contributed to the Noble Roman Sunday cabaret. The resource center generated the Shakopee Women's Prison Project, providing theater, book swaps, and softball games with women at the prison. And, on frequent Saturday nights, LRC held a "coffee-house"—most often, simply a gathering of women singing folk songs together. Soon after LRC moved into the Chrysalis building early in 1974, some women began to think of forming a "real" coffeehouse.[10]

When Candace Margulies, then twenty-one and actively involved at LRC as well as a member of the Wilder Ones softball team, initiated the Coffee House Collective, she was specific about her interests: "I wanted *lesbians* to have a *nice* place to go. I wanted *lesbians* to have a place that offered them a sense of legitimacy, and the kind of thing that heterosexual people have and enjoy: a place to go and dance and listen to music. And it was a much more consciously political place than the bars. . . . And no men! That was very exciting for women!"[11] She and others took for granted that the Coffee House would be a feminist space based on feminist programming and interests. But no one took for granted that they could build a feminist place in which "lesbian" was a comfortable norm.

A space for such a place was not easy to find: these young women had no capital for real estate, and no community center would host A Woman's Coffee House virtually for free and on all weekend nights. But when Margulies and Dahlem received welcome to use the church basement, even they could hardly foresee that in that space, hundreds of women between the ages of sixteen and eighty would give shape to feminist movement. Like similar spaces springing up throughout the United States, women made A Woman's Coffee House into an accessible, chemical-free meeting ground that many remember as the "pulse" and "life-blood" of feminist and feminist lesbian activity in the Twin Cities.[12] Two or three evenings a week, the church basement became a temporarily woman-only environment that fostered some of the most widespread features of women's activism in the 1970s: lesbian comedy, women's music, fundraisers for Wounded Knee legal defense and Indian custody cases, workshops on everything from health to auto mechanics, from global politics to socialism. Each night, following and underscoring the evening's more overtly political programs, the Coffee House held women's dances.

Although the Coffee House started as a distinctly lesbian vision, the Coffee House Collective came to articulate democratic inclusivity as a critical part of feminism. As soon as they began searching for community space, they stated that the Coffee House would be "open to all women," as were many other leftist women's spaces in the United States at that time. Holding the Coffee House somewhere other than the Lesbian Resource Center was thus a consequential decision, but it was not automatic. The collective had tried to *stay* in the Chrysalis building where LRC was housed, working to renovate Chrysalis's private but gritty and dank basement for Coffee House use until they discovered that it would be too expensive to meet fire codes. Matters of space, including negotiations with more public places such as Plymouth Congregational Church, shaped Coffee House demographics and feminist ideology from its inception.

In addition to being "open to all women," the Coffee House never used the word *lesbian* in its title or any of its promotional material. Elaine Marsh, one of the pastors, took a lead role in convincing the congregation to grant the space to A Woman's Coffee House, but she did not bring explicit visibility to its lesbian impetus. Toni McNaron, a white professor and regular Coffee House-goer, explained that "Marsh ensured that the word 'lesbian' was never used in those negotiations, because *she* never used that word." Marsh, along with Alice, her partner of many decades, led the church in its progressive orientation, but she also signaled that certain things—like women's sexuality—were not open to public, verbal articulation.[13] Members of the original Coffee House Collective now say they always had a political commitment to make the Coffee House open to all women, not just lesbian-identified women. Yet the early, seemingly self-evident decision to form a *woman's* coffeehouse rather than a lesbian coffeehouse coincided with acquisition of the Plymouth Congregational social hall and was only retrospectively embraced as a key to building a larger and more inclusive community space. Spatial politics thus not only shaped the Coffee House, but also the demographics of feminist activism and the development of feminist ideology.

The women who frequented A Woman's Coffee House were feminist-identified, and lesbians and bisexual women comprised the majority. They ranged widely in age from children to women in their sixties and older, though most were between twenty-two and thirty-five. Many had been active in the civil rights and antiwar movements, and many took part in progressive activism around gender, race, and class issues. Many were involved in local chemical dependency recovery programs or for other reasons sought that sober space. Regulars came from all parts of the Twin Cities, Iowa City, Madison, Chicago, Duluth, and rural points in between. Most earned a wage, though a handful were white-collar professionals. African American, Indian, Asian, and Latina women may have attended in slightly greater numbers than represented in the Twin Cities population generally (at 1 to 3 percent each).[14] Most women did not identify as Christian but had Christian cultural backgrounds; at the same time, Jewish women significantly contributed to leadership at the Coffee House.

Many early collective members, even those who had attended Plymouth Congregational as children, did not think of its basement social hall as a particularly Christian space or as a foundation of the dominant culture; for them, the space could temporarily be an areligious place of and about feminists and lesbians. Margulies, among others, looked at the space with a slightly more skeptical eye. As a Jewish woman, she acknowledged, the church felt "more alien" to her, and she felt "more *other*" in it, than most women who had grown up with Christian cultural privilege. But she was quick to add, "I think the concern was not so much that it was Christian, but that it was *straight*: a conservative institution. But we knew that even if they were homophobic, they were committed to doing good, that they had a *class of values*, that we felt some protection in." Though Christianity and churches generally might be associated with homophobia and anti-Semitism, Margulies relied on a shared "class of values"—feminism and progressive social politics—that Plymouth Congregational promoted and that promised a degree of "protection" not only for lesbians but for Jewish presence as well, even though the latter was not explicitly sought. Margulies's driving cause was to find a harassment-free space for lesbian organizing and dancing.

Many women appreciated that going to A *Woman's* Coffee House, and even creating affectional and erotic ties with women in that space, did not imply any certain sexual identity. Some feared that lesbianism was a threat to their job security. McNaron, though tenured at the University of Minnesota, recalled, "When the Coffee House opened, I was in my late thirties, and never in my life as a lesbian . . . I never had any place to go in public. . . . I never went to the Town House or a known lesbian space because I was afraid I'd lose my job if somebody saw me there." Karen Clark, a white lesbian then soon to enter public office as a Minnesota state representative, believed that "at that time, feminists and lesbians needed protection" from men in general, and from the FBI in particular, which held feminist groups throughout the United States under intense surveillance during the 1970s.[15] In practice, protection meant spatial and verbal discretion.

The physical layout of the church offered the Coffee House protection from intrusion. The discreet side door leading to the basement opened onto a front room in which women milled. A hallway stemmed from the front room and rounded a corner before leading to the social hall of the Coffee House itself. Coffee House workers set up a table at the head of the hallway, from which they not only collected donations and passed out flyers but also surveyed incoming people to ensure that they were (or were perceived to be) female and sober. Male journalists—and indeed, all reporters from mainstream papers—were summarily turned away. The Coffee House security system, relying as it did on the belief that gender was binary and transparent, may have magnified many participants' perception that drag queens, passing women, and other trans people would interfere with the Coffee House as a women's space. Lesbian-identified persons who passed as men were sometimes turned away at the door. Guarding against male intrusion entailed policing the gender expression of everyone at the Coffee House, as I discuss at greater length in the book's conclusion. But in the mid- to late 1970s, few Coffee House participants questioned the immutability of "woman" in women's space, and most felt protected by the interiority of the social hall.

The space inside conferred aesthetic and class legitimacy to the sexuality of the women who attended A Woman's Coffee House. By 1974, many women had begun to view existing lesbian-run spaces as "run down"; as one collective member put it, they had "an atmosphere that said, 'we aren't worth it.'" According to Margulies, the local Lesbian Resource Center was "a very depressing place, couches with springs coming out, it just had a terrible feeling to it. It was dark. *You really felt like a pervert going there.*"[16] The church basement, in contrast, had its own magnificent kitchen, a carefully crafted mezzanine, and good furniture; it was "bright," "vibrant," and "first rate."[17] Claiming this space for lesbian activities thus simultaneously transgressed and reinforced associations between "nice" places and respectability. Spaces signified class, race, and sexual status together; to inhabit an always already nice place like the predominantly white, middle-class Congregational Church was thus to demand lesbian legitimacy via common signifiers within dominant class and race hierarchies.

The social status of the church, and its socially progressive mission increased most women's sense of security at the Coffee House. McNaron well understood that "a lot of women who were otherwise fairly closeted felt comfortable there. And that was because of Elaine's leadership [in the Twin Cities]: there could be nothing more four-square than a church minister being behind this thing!" To a large extent, the Coffee House drew on the church's moral authority to further lesbian and homosocial interests in sexual self-determination and the formation of a publicly visible, feminist lesbian community.

The new feminist, lesbian space paradoxically gained its visibility in part through discretions carefully negotiated and mutually nurtured by the church and the Coffee House. Margulies recalled that the Coffee House Collective and the pastors at the church tacitly agreed "not to say this is a lesbian thing."[18] But neither was the predominantly lesbian nature of the Coffee House entirely hidden. According to Pastor Marsh, there was a "vocal contingent" of the congregation who did not approve of the Coffee House, but Marsh took hold of her leadership role, later explaining that the congregation felt, "It must be okay if *I* thought it was, and of course I did."[19] As a frequent participant in Coffee House functions, often giving workshops and Gertrude Stein readings, Marsh actively promoted the Coffee House to her congregation. She encouraged female church members, leaders, and board members to attend the Coffee House, where it was surely not lost on them that women were kissing each other. Marsh also led the church to grant slush funds to the Coffee House for major expenses, such as bringing in national artists like the ever-controversial radical lesbian separatist Alix Dobkin. "Saying it" and "not saying it" often seemed like two opposing political strategies for surviving a homophobic society. But in the case of the Coffee House, Marsh engaged both strategies simultaneously as she secured a steepled space in which women were free to express themselves intimately with each other. A Woman's Coffee House tremendously broadened the social, political, and spatial boundaries within which feminists imagined themselves and women's sexualities. At the same time, this example also reveals the ways that homophobia influenced the construction of the terms "all women," and "woman" in feminism. Like many feminist endeavors, the Coffee House was born of a distinctly lesbian vision; and, as in many gatherings of activist women, lesbian presence was partially masked. Indeed, it was because of homophobia that "lesbian" lurked behind "woman," "all women," and "feminist" in representations of the Coffee House as a "woman's" or "feminist" space.

The physical layout of the church space, as well as "not saying it," protected the Coffee House against certain kinds of opposition, and indeed, even enabled it to exist quite exuberantly. But the church space and verbal discretion also created barriers that were at odds with feminist antiracist and anticlassist commitments. With its hidden, side doorway, few women would accidentally happen upon the Coffee House *and* feel entitled to enter. Quite intentionally, most advertising occurred through word of mouth; print media ads were limited to feminist and lesbian newsletters. The Coffee House's reliance on word of mouth verbally and spatially created a limited, known social network: people comfortable in one kind of space heard and told about others that were similar in constituency. Though the Coffee House was located in one of Minneapolis's few mixed-race, mixed-class neighborhoods, it did not invite—nor was it even known to—its neighbors. Its physical setting and sociospatial practice of community building ensured that all who went possessed at least some degree of insider knowledge and entitlement.

The space as a whole—sometimes Coffee House, always at least partially church—realized a number of contradictions and compromises. Most women at the Coffee House reiterated Margulies's claim that the church social hall was a space in which "we could act so freely it felt like our own." But "our own" involved different things for different women. Many white lesbians who had grown up in Christian contexts easily distanced from Christianity as a "patriarchal institution," and they joked about their participation in an "establishment church," while at the same time taking its spaces as normative. Ironically, in 1975, few white Coffee House–goers emphasized the radical potential of churches, despite liberation theology, the importance of black churches to African American community organizing, the Catholic upheavals indicated by Vatican II, and the practice of socially progressive churches in general to foster coffeehouses, consciousness-raising, and antiwar activism. Some Jewish women participating in the Coffee House had a growing sense of potential connections between communities of faith and radical activism, as expressed in the concept of *tikkun olam*, but they rarely drew attention to the specifically Jewish sources of their insights.[20] Instead, they worked within spatial compromises. Laura Altman explained, "It was a social hall: it wasn't like there were crosses on the walls that we had to cover up." The Coffee House felt welcoming to her because it was lesbian-friendly, and also because "Candace, who was an outspoken Jewish lesbian, started it, and she was *always* there, so there was always going to be—[it was] not a Christian thing."[21] Alternatively, McNaron, a Southern-born woman, was more conscious of the extent to which *church* meant social legitimacy, and that allowed her to feel safe as a lesbian. Anna Stanley, an African American activist, put the church in a moral, political context of community organizing; without reference to religious faith, she often insisted that the Coffee House *should* be compelled by its church space to promote deeply coalitional action.[22]

Occupying church space affected the class appearance of the Coffee House. In keeping with socialist feminist desires to undo class hierarchies, admission was $1 (waivable), and refreshments cost 25 cents, so participants spent a fraction of what they would in commercial venues. But some felt that the church itself epitomized dominant social hierarchies. The church's stone and slate, rural gothic architecture refrained from the ostentatiousness of some churches, but its place within an urban geography told another story. The church was built in 1909 with additions in 1949, when its neighborhood was more homogenously white and upper middle-class; in 1966, the construction of I-94 divided the neighborhood and lowered property values on both sides of the freeway. The church, occupying a full block south of the freeway on the south end of downtown, thus stood as the sole reminder of the neighborhood's former prestige.[23] This prestige was spatially revived each Sunday, as congregants ritually reclaimed the church parking lot and surrounding streets with cars, gaits, manners, and styles that increasingly smacked of middle-class suburbia in the midst of this declining neighborhood.

Struggling against dominant social evaluations of their sexuality, feminists used the church to redefine their own sexuality and ways of being women. The church did not resemble spaces such as those in red-light districts, to which "sexually deviant" women were banished. At the Coffee House, separatism was a choice and a means toward self-representation. In that context, the Coffee House was a radical departure from gay bars which even longtime bar regulars described as "sleazy," "dingy," "ratty," "holes" in "dangerous" and "poorly lit" neighborhoods, and from straight bars, which discouraged women from entering unless escorted by men.[24] For those who liked the Coffee House, it was exhilarating to transgress the spatial boundaries between "deviant" and "respectable," and in so doing challenge dominant evaluations of feminist and lesbian sexualities. If dominant ideologies regulated women's access to public life, the church was a space like no other in that its "establishment" status suggested the racial and sexual legitimacy of its inhabitants and the privileges of whiteness.

Moving into the Coffee House in a church with nice facilities thus gave some lesbians a new kind of visibility and a new kind of space in which to recognize each other as a political community. Simultaneously, they challenged the ideology that homosexuality is socially unacceptable. As Margulies exclaimed, "Imagine: two or three times a week hundreds of predominantly lesbian women gathering for workshops, political organizing, dances, and concerts, *in a church!* It was like you had died and gone to lesbian heaven!" Lesbians' claim to a "lesbian heaven" transgressed some homophobic norms, but it did not revolutionize "heaven" itself or completely overturn the mechanisms through which access to "heaven" was related to sexuality. Furthermore, to claim a women's (feminist/lesbian) Coffee House in this mainstream church was not to undo a sexual system in which white women historically played the arbiters of respectability. When women of the Coffee House gained access to the church social hall by agreeing to "not say it," they invested in a locus of dominant cultural capital that perpetuated racist exclusion in its (often unspoken) assertion of sexual respectability.

Even in a diverse movement in which most members opposed racism, women's negotiations for privileged spaces replicated the harsh effects of whiteness, and this dynamic often played out in the enactment of sexual politics as well. If "run-down" and "dark" places implied sexual perversion, at A Woman's Coffee House, a lesbian did not have to "feel like" or be a pervert. Nor, however, was she automatically free of those charges simply for being in a "first-rate" place. When activists utilized (rather than subverted) concepts of respectability to create a new kind of feminist space, they ensured that issues of perversion and racial privilege would continue to be played out within those walls. In the mid-1970s, women debated such issues most directly in relation to dress codes, dancing, nudity, and the implications of bare breasts. Style and sexuality debates were widespread throughout the United States as feminists created new styles of dress, asserted the pleasure of dancing shirtless in semi-public and sometimes public spaces, and questioned whether eroticism was inherently sexist. These debates were linked to broader concerns about women's embodiment and the creation of new sexual politics, and they bore lasting implications for the Second Wave. Women's dances—and especially dancing shirtless—became a key way of claiming and enacting "women" as the subject of "women's space." Dances invited women to viscerally engage the politics of embodiment and the reality of difference, not simply between men and women but also among people who—most of the time —identified as female. Because they took *place*, women's dances thus became sites of multiple embodiments that complicated the category of "woman" and the possibility of "her" liberation. For those reasons, women's dances can and should be analyzed as a vehicle for understanding the ways that women formed spaces around cultural and racial hierarchies as well as gender and sexual hierarchies.

Debates about shirtless dancing came up at A Woman's Coffee House one muggy summer night in 1976. The Coffee House was packed with women, and it grew even hotter when the DJ nixed Cris Williamson ballads in favor of Motown's up-tempo Martha Reeves and the Vandellas. In the heat of the evening, "twelve or so" white women decided to take their shirts off, as they put it, "to be comfortable and happy."[25] These women had just arrived from a week at Maiden Rock Feminist Learning Center on women-owned land in rural Wisconsin. There they had worked and studied shirtless, a liberating experience for most of them.[26] Maiden Rock, like the Michigan Womyn's Music Festival that began in 1976, was a rural space in which women started to define "woman" and "women's space" through what women *did* in women's space "on the land": there, women went comfortably shirtless together. Full of energy and confidence, the Maiden Rock women introduced shirtless dancing to the Coffee House. After slight hesitation, a member of the Coffee House Collective made this request: "Women, we need to ask you to put your shirts back on, or we'll have to ask you to leave the dance. It's making some women uncomfortable."[27]

The formerly happy and shirtless women put their shirts back on and left, disgusted, later to locally publish a letter that they called a "feminist analysis" of the incident:

> For us still to need to raise the issue indicates just how much we have internalized society's stereotypic ideas of women. If we are ever to walk on city streets or work outdoors without shirts we obviously must first accept that option for ourselves and other women. The Coffee House seems like one of the only in-town settings where the myth of women's breasts being automatically arousing, hence always to be covered, could be tested and cast aside. . . . If we keep our shirts on, the only winner will be the patriarchal repressive society and he will have won without lifting a finger.[28]

The issue of repression was intimately connected to women's experience of sexual objectification and harassment—most commonly by men—in most public places. As spaces not quite public or private, women's coffeehouses generated a productive tension between sexual self-determination and rebellion. Dale Columbus recalled, "Dancing shirtless was an act of defiance. There were always two factions: one wanting to play by the rules and be real secure." But claiming women's space required *enacting* it *as such*, and thus, the other faction retorted, "Well, if we can't do it *here*, where *can* we do it?"[29]

Coffee House participants were indeed precariously poised: while the church space seemed to confer legitimacy and respectability to feminist and lesbian sexualities, it could do so only if participants also policed those emerging sexualities so that they produced at least the appearance of a congruent respectability. Though the Maiden Rock women initially felt defeated, most Coffee House participants recall that women subsequently danced shirtless "all the time."[30] As an acknowledged leader in the Coffee House Collective, Margulies offered an interpretation of the shirt conflict:

> I think a lot of what we were feeling was a result of heterosexism you know. We were determined not to appear to be having sex orgies down there. We were scared about the church members. We were just scared. . . . It wasn't the Michigan Womyn's Music Festival hundreds of miles away from civilization. People did continue to take their shirts off, they always did, and I think for those who did, it was a really precious option. But they always did it after midnight, when the coast was clear, when nobody's mother was still there.[31]

The Coffee House, along with other similar spaces throughout the United States, came to define women's space in part because there "many women felt safe enough to take their shirts off and dance with their shirts off."[32] Though the church space seemed to call for a kind of propriety or discretion, women's dances turned the Coffee House into a *women's place*, signaling freedom from sexual harassment. Concerns for legitimacy ("we didn't want people thinking we were having sex orgies down there"), safety ("we were living with heterosexism and we were scared"), and liberation ("for those who did it was a really precious option") did not go away. Instead, they were part and parcel of women's space, and they operated in a time/space nexus: the Coffee House was "ours" only during certain hours of the week, and it accommodated open sexual expression only at certain hours of the night.[33] As Margulies insisted, "It wasn't that we thought it was wrong or bad to take your shirts off," but doing so required careful consideration of the implications for women's movement.

At the Coffee House, dancers bumped smack into the ways that in public geographies, the female and the sexual were conflated.[34] How could feminists at the Coffee House recuperate a sense of sexual self-determination? Could (or should) they de-eroticize bare breasts in the church in order to dance shirtless and not imply sexual acts? Even when women wore clothes, the Coffee House *was*, for many, an erotically charged space; did women have to give that up in order to dance shirtless? For women to dance shirtless in that space was not simply to claim a right that men enjoyed. Rather, it was to suggest a whole new relationship among women's bodies, sexual arousal, and women's involvement with each others' bodies, and it was also to assert new conceptions of sacred and profane space. The place of the church compelled women to consider what bare breasts could mean in public, in spaces that signaled gender, race, class, sexual, and even religious hierarchies. Though many women felt safe at the Coffee House, that space also provided the possibility of their "trouble" as the theorist Judith Butler used the term; women inflected and exposed the meanings of bodies as they acted in and moved through social/spatial terrain. It was through those very practices that women laid claim to and defined women's space and simultaneously articulated feminist sexualities.

Whereas some women wanted the Coffee House to be free of the sexual objectification they associated with the oppression of women, others worked to distinguish the feminist sexuality made possible by women's space from heterosexist oppressions experienced elsewhere. Toni Mc-Naron, for example, felt that the Coffee House "was not a cruising space. Sexuality was absent there . . . you didn't go intending to pick up somebody or expecting that to happen to you."[35] On the other hand, Janet Dahlem claimed the space as one that offered the opportunity to create new sexual subjectivities, surmising,

> We all wanted everything to be different from how hets did it; so maybe for some of us this meant denying our sexuality. I think they want to say we didn't do it *the same way*. . . . I think sexuality and picking people up is *very* feminist . . . at the Coffee House, cruising styles were very feminized. We *all* looked at each other: who danced well, and who has a cute butt—not in any lewd way, but in a very loving and appreciative way. . . . Women pick up women to have

love, and men in straight bars pick up women to have sex. . . . You know, we didn't want [the Coffee House] to be a meat market.[36]

The Coffee House, that is, was not like straight spaces: it was neither sexist nor lewd but—as a women's space—was sexual and affirming. Founders and participants did not intend the Coffee House to be "about sex"—far from it. But it was in part through sex and sexuality, and the forging of new sexual subjectivities, that the Coffee House became women's space.

No one wanted the Coffee House to be a "meat market," but simply doing it "different from how hets did it" allowed white cultural assumptions about sexuality to remain in place. For this reason, dances at the Coffee House—sometimes more than other activities—could alienate as well as empower women of color. Anna Stanley perceived that especially as the Coffee House developed a younger clientele by the early 1980s, "sexuality had become the single defining issue." And wherever sexuality was treated as a singular issue, that is, one seemingly separate from race, Stanley asserted, "On the sexual plane, black women are treated like black men . . . we are viewed as pieces of meat, we are performers."[37] Stanley regularly participated in the Coffee House for years, but when she talked about the space, she invoked a history of racism and imperialism that marked black women's bodies as sexually accessible to whites; it was also a history that conjoined white property with dominant notions of respectability, putting African American women in compromised positions in relation to *that* property and its respectability.[38] In many public spaces, the sexuality of women of color was on stage, exploited in a "commodification of Otherness" (to use bell hooks' term) that reproduced white sexual agency as a dimension of racialized privilege in and access to public space.[39] The project of producing and guarding a sexually liberatory and non-oppressive *women's* place thus ran dangerously close to processes through which property itself came to be aligned with a seemingly uniform whiteness.

Of course clothing also carried great power, constructing the Coffee House as a movement-defining space and its participants as insiders or outsiders to that movement. As bids for feminist and lesbian cultural coherence, clothing exposed race, class, and gender hierarchies as surely as did the absence of clothes. Many women shaped style around clothing and haircuts that were previously unacceptable according to white middle-class norms of femininity. Dale Columbus recalled, "Nobody put a sign up at the Coffee House that said you can't come in unless your hair is two inches short . . . it was all unwritten, subtle. I remember people talking about how they hated the code, they had to sign a whole line of things about what you had to wear. . . . I never thought of it as a code then, I just thought that's what I had to do to be a dyke."[40] Within that emerging subculture, wearing pants rather than a skirt was one indication of a woman's refusal to participate in sexist norms. Clothing styles were among the most visible means through which women asserted feminist and lesbian sexualities: women searched for clothes that accentuated certain physical features, and that attracted attention around a new set of erotic markers. Some rebelled: the white artist and lesbian Jymme Golden recalled that she occasionally wore skirts, nylons, high heels, and lipstick to "throw people."[41] "Code," then, was about belonging in a place shaped in part by an emerging culture whose standards for membership were differentially distributed over a variety of persons and thus open to heated debate.

The dominant clothing style at the Coffee House—jeans, workboots, flannel or denim shirts, or T-shirts and vests—contributed to a construction of women's space and feminist sexuality that, while breaching some gender norms and asserting new erotics, still resonated with white middle-class privilege. This also seemed to mute differences among white participants, though participants regularly experienced those differences. Karen Clark couldn't get used to the blue jeans; as a white youngster growing up on a family farm and working with Chicano/a migrant laborers, she had instilled in her the idea that jeans were for *working* people, "and that was something you were *ashamed* of; you would never wear jeans *out*." As an adult, jeans were not, for her, a sign of "identification" with working-class people, but came closer to demonstrated class and race entitlement.[42]

Kim Hines, an African American playwright and performance artist, recalled the first time she went to the Coffee House. A white friend was taking her to this lesbian dance par excellence and advised her about proper attire: "You gotta look *good*. We get *dressed* for this." Hines was thrilled to be going to a place where she would meet and dance with other women. She explained,

So, okay. Well, you know, when *black* people go out, we get dressed *up*! So I got my pants all creased and I'm wearin' this blazer, you know and a little ascot, some jewelry, make-up, you know, I looked *good*! And I walked in the front door and saw all the people, and went, "Oh! Am I in the right place? Is this the Coffee House?" So, there I was, there they all were in all their—lumberjack shirts and all—you know, I quickly learned what was appropriate!

Having dressed to attract, Hines quickly learned that in that space, to be visible as a lesbian was to put on a lesbian style that was distinctly white.[43] As white women staked a claim to a place that legitimated lesbian sexuality and affirmed lesbian community, they maintained a "possessive investment" in the mutual constitution of lesbian and whiteness, and thereby also reified the Coffee House as a place that affirmed a seemingly singular white, middle-class culture despite the presence and influence of women of color and working-class women and despite differences among white, middle-class women.

"Appropriateness" marked the ability to plant a legitimate stake in defining a place. It depended not only on access to certain kinds of public space but also on subcultural and public knowledge of what local signs signify. But as Evelynn Hammonds reminds, "Black women have created whole worlds of sexual signs and signifiers, some of which align with those of whites and some of which do not. Nonetheless, they are worlds which always have to contend with the power that the white world has to invade, pathologize, and disrupt those worlds."[44] One of the ways that many women's spaces reproduced this power was by creating places in which the codes of sexuality and sexual agency refer to systems of white privilege: lesbians in or out of women's space could claim cultural visibility by appropriating jeans and work boots precisely because that very practice marked "lesbian" as youthful, white, and middle class, distinct from women of color and laborers. Women of color, in "dressed up" clothing, could not appropriate *that* sexuality any more easily than they could appropriate the prestige of whiteness. Nor could they very simply make readable and authoritative their own sexual signs and signifiers in a place created around white sexual agency.

This spatial process helped make many places purporting to be "open to all women" instead predominantly white, lesbian spaces. And the costs were high: while white feminists and lesbians enacted and brought new visibility to white female sexual self-determination within certain women's spaces, they maintained structures of cultural power that limited women of color's ability to give presence and visibility to the sexualities of women of color in those same spaces. Indeed, the authority of feminist and lesbian sexualities seemed to rely on whiteness not only to help secure privileged property, but simultaneously, to supply a normative definition of woman. Spatial hierarchies, then, tremendously influenced the development of sexual politics within women's spaces intended to be open to all women across race and class, and these emergent sexual politics in turn often reinforced the whiteness of feminism.

The Largest Woman Space Ever

While the Coffee House in Minneapolis drew on local emerging communities to help turn a semi-public church basement space into a nonmarket-driven hub of feminist and lesbian activism, the highly visible and for-profit Detroit Feminist Women's City Club depended on being able to convene a membership beyond Detroit. As feminist movement spread throughout Detroit, and as feminists there forged ties with women all over the country working on health clinics, credit unions, publishing, printing and graphics, theaters, coffeehouses, restaurants, and various other projects, Valerie Angers, Joanne Parrent, and others imagined "what it would be like to have a huge space to be able to do those kinds of things." By January 1976, they, along with a handful of women from the East and West Coasts, had figured out how eight women could take loans from the Feminist Federal Credit Union to buy the magnificent Women's City Club building in downtown Detroit for $200,000 cash and have another $50,000 cash on hand for renovations.

Feminist-oriented women's buildings were not new; one could easily trace their roots to the feminist-inspired settlement houses of the Progressive Era. In the early 1970s, feminists created women's buildings to serve as multi-use spaces often housing a great variety of projects, from health clinics and rape crisis centers to graphics collectives, from women's schools to art and theater collectives, day care centers to lesbian resource centers. They tended to be service-oriented and decidedly nonprofit; some availed themselves of government funding such as CEDA (Community and Economic Development Agency) grants, but all ran on a shoestring. Openly lesbian-friendly spaces especially skirted mainstream market relations out of necessity as well as by design. In Detroit between 1969 and 1972, the dynamic Michigan Women's Liberation Coalition had held gatherings of several hundred women in space borrowed from the downtown YWCA building. More humble and less visible to the public, between

1973 and 1976, the service-oriented Women's Resource Center and the event-oriented Women's Cultural Center had each offered short-lived, multi-use, lesbian-friendly spaces near the border between Detroit and its northern suburbs. With those preceding examples and the knowledge that women could manage their own credit and businesses, Angers, Parrent, and others imagined owning the expansive City Club building to affirm an expansive feminist movement; women would come from all over the United States and beyond to attend feminist events, take classes, and kindle the feminist revolution.[45]

The City Club would depart from most women's coffeehouses and feminist buildings to offer a new definition of women's space: it would not be on the margins but at the center of market relations; not borrowed, but owned; not nonprofit, but for profit and commanding public attention. Parts of the building would be open to men at certain hours or if escorted by women, and parts would be open to women only; women would not have to go home after evening programs, but could stay in the club's hotel. At the City Club, women would be fully in charge. The dream drew women from both coasts to act as directors, managers, and employees, but as quickly as women rushed to purchase and open the building, the Feminist Women's City Club entered crisis. It closed within five months, in debt and amid a nationwide storm of criticism. As Angers—who quickly left the club project to salvage the strained credit union—explained, "We just bit off way more than we could chew."[46] Though the City Club involved an atypical operating process and a new model of women's space, it replicated—indeed, magnified—many of the problems common to women's buildings and coffeehouse-like spaces throughout the United States.[47]

The Feminist Women's City Club in fact had additional ancestry in elite women's "city clubs" that had their own buildings—yet another Progressive Era model of women's space. The building itself had been a women's building ever since it was built in the decade of Detroit's pre-Depression prosperity, and its history was part of its appeal to those who would turn it into an openly *feminist* women's space. In 1924, Pewabic Tile founder Mary Chase Stratton and her architect husband designed the large building at the corner of Park Avenue and Elizabeth Street for a philanthropic group called the Women's City Club. Considered one of the finest "town club" buildings in the country, all seven stories contained niches and window sills adorned with the famous, multicolored tiles; even the Olympic-size swimming pool was laid in Pewabic tile, making it the only pool of its kind in the world.[48] Marble floors, drinking fountains, a circular staircase, wall murals, paneled lounges with wood-burning fireplaces, a ballroom with crystal chandeliers, and statues of Greek goddesses all contributed to the grandeur of the building. When the Depression crippled the livelihoods of Detroit's auto workers and left much of the city in shambles, the Women's City Club—its leadership largely composed of women from the Ford and other industry-owning families—continued to function without debt. The club came out of the Depression thriving, and membership numbers soared beyond seven thousand. The neighborhood surrounding the City Club, however, could not keep up with the club's wealthy stature and white flight out of Detroit. Between the mid-1950s and 1970, suburbanization and deindustrialization drained the inner city of its economy, and urban freeways dispersed formerly coherent communities. By the late 1960s, most of the businesses in the area had closed, leaving a boarded-up ghetto in their place. By 1970, with only a thousand members, the Women's Club could no longer afford to maintain the massive building; they tried to sell the building in 1973 and then again in 1975.[49]

Given the proliferation of feminist spaces and enterprises during the mid-1970s, and given the compromises required for most women's spaces, the possibilities of the City Club building must have seemed truly endless to Angers, Parrent, and other women near and far. But realizing the dream required creating a new financing and operating structure. According to Angers, "Getting the building came first: we said, 'well, we can form a network, we'll call it the Feminist Economic Network (FEN), and we can train women in how to open businesses, and we'll have wonderful meetings and we'll have seating for everyone when they come."[50] Without mentioning that the City Club building was the immediate impetus for FEN, they began to talk with others around the country. Nationally, at the time of the first FEN organizational meeting in New Haven in May 1975, there existed sixteen feminist credit unions, a handful of women's banks, over a hundred feminist health clinics, and countless feminist presses, bookstores, and restaurants; such ventures provided a pool of constituents who had created feminist institutions where none existed before. Many were interested in discussing a coordinated feminist economic credit organization to support the proliferation of feminist enterprises: representatives from nine credit unions—many with ties to health clinics—attended the first FEN meeting and the follow-up FEN conference in Detroit, November 28–29, 1975.[51] Parrent and Angers from Detroit; Lolly Hirsch of the Connecticut Self-Help Clinics; Laura Brown, Barbara Hoke, and Debbie Law from the Oakland FWHC; and Cathy Czarnik from Diana Press in Baltimore appointed themselves to FEN's Board of Directors.[52] Meanwhile, Detroit members eyed the City Club building: owned by women and filled with FEN-managed enterprises, it would go well beyond the coffeehouse-as-feminist-watering-hole model of women's space.

Barely moments after the Detroit FEN convention, the group calling itself "Detroit" mailed a veritable flurry of documents to FEN, to "Feminists," and to "Sisters of the Feminist Press," promoting the City Club building as a utopian space from which to institutionalize feminism throughout the country and beyond. "Obviously, [the City Club building] is the perfect place for FEN headquarters, as well as several other income-generating projects." They elaborated their vision to the FEN group:

> The things that came to our mind are the things that are probably in all of your minds: . . . the credit union office, legal self-help clinic, law offices, the *Monthly Regulator* office, an art gallery, a women's bookstore, culture caravan activities going on all the time, some sort of a membership structure . . . and of course, the FEN Institute where women from all around the country would come to work here, to learn here, and be able to stay in the hotel rooms upstairs and be able to eat in the wonderful women's restaurant and go swimming in the neat pool downstairs and have a drink at the end of the day in the women's cocktail lounge. Obviously it would make money and be fun and provide many salaried positions for women.

They further pointed out, "The ballroom happens to be egg-shaped" (or "ovum-shaped" as they wrote on their building blueprint), as if to confirm that it was "the perfect place for . . . FEN" with its own egg-shaped logo; the building itself, that is, provided the raison d'être of FEN.

Although some women around the country looked to FEN as a potential system of resource-sharing, FEN's direction and tactical practices developed around the stake that certain leaders placed in the City Club. "Detroit" was so sure of the building's success that, at the time they wrote the letters promoting it to FEN, they had already put down an offer to buy it for $200,000 cash.[53] They had sixty days in which to figure out how to finance the purchase, but they did it in twenty-one, fueled by their eager visions of what women could do in that woman space:

We thought that we could open a nice clothing store that would cater to the styles that feminists usually wear . . . a tailoring service where you could . . . have a suit made for you . . . we could set up a travel agency and a real estate agency. The travel agency would be, of course, where we would buy our airport tickets for going to . . . meetings and where people would make their arrangements for traveling to the Institute and traveling around.

In addition to the auditorium that would have "many moneymaking activities going on," the forty-six hotel rooms "will be in constant demand."[54] Annual membership fees of $100, as well, would help keep the club afloat. Leaders turned FEN into a for-profit holding company investing in feminist businesses: the businesses that women started in the building would be owned by FEN and the business-women members of FEN; a portion of their profits would pay into the mandatory cooperative structure of the City Club/FEN. Researching their options, these women who had started grassroots feminist credit unions and health clinics on a shoestring and from the ground up entered a heady new world in which people made money from money.[55] They briefly searched for some venture capitalists willing to invest in the initial down payment, but because "time was of the essence," they concluded that instead they had a "real sure source of money" in the Detroit Feminist Federal Credit Union. The FFCU would grant eight individuals personal loans of $30,000 each; those eight would buy the building and turn it over to FEN, and FEN would then bear responsibility for paying back the loan to the credit union.[56]

These discussions of financing evidence the shift in conceptualizing a "woman space" that occurred through the purchase process. Like humbler coffeehouses, the City Club began out of an interest in women's space that allowed women to interact in new ways, apart from the barriers and dangers of a sexist, homophobic public. Like localized feminist credit unions, FEN was to be a vehicle for circumventing mainstream banking institutions that were hostile toward women and for supporting women's efforts to create feminist enterprises. However, the scope of the project and the simple fact that the building cost $22,000 a month just to maintain led its directors to an increasing focus on a professional membership base. Simultaneously, they gave up two common features of women's space: low entrance fees with sliding scales, and activities (such as women's dances) that explicitly affirmed lesbian sexuality or—at the very least—generated open struggles around sexual politics among women.

In the conflicts over hierarchy and accessibility of the new "woman space," women simultaneously constructed a local/outsider divide related inconsistently to class-laden judgments: women from the coasts who came to work for the City Club did not like Detroit or the "skid row," "wino district" surrounding the City Club. Some locals, however, charged that directors from the West Coast did not respect the local credit union or understand Detroit's particular working-class ethos and therefore blithely indulged in destructive borrowing and spending sprees. As Angers put it,

> We weren't into that in Detroit. . . . Because Detroit, if you were from Detroit, you were probably . . . raised in a blue-collar neighborhood and you had to scrimp and save. You didn't have much money, and you learn how to do things on a shoestring. . . . And we had people coming in who wanted to spend money . . . redecorate, and bring people in to have a huge catered meal for all the bigwigs in Detroit and stuff, and we just didn't do things like that.[57]

Women involved in the City Club wrestled over how to imagine and locate themselves *and* feminism on the ground: would they build a club that invoked the once-elite status of the building and downtown Detroit? How would they position themselves and the club in relation to the recent class and race struggles that created one of the poorest urban areas in the United States?

Originally, founders had imagined that poor inner-city women and wealthy suburban women, white women and black women, would come together in that space. As the Feminist Federal Credit Union in Detroit and Women's Advocates in St. Paul had done, the City Club would engage with (rather than dismiss) the "mainstream." And, as the founders of Amazon Bookstore in Minneapolis and the Chicago Women's Liberation Union had duly noted by 1969, the radical feminist revolution needed to and did already include "ordinary suburban housewives." But economic necessity drove the directors of the Feminist Women's City Club to reach beyond a *known* constituency of feminist-identified activists. As they did so, they invested in a geography of race and class distinction within Detroit as well as between locals and outsiders, and the building itself seemed to solidify those constructions. On opening night, for example, Detroiter Jan Bennet commented to a reporter, "I'm surprised that the place is so magnificent. But I know that I definitely cannot afford the $100 membership fee. It seems like only downtown professional and business women will join." Tongue in cheek, she added, "But that's okay. They need a place, too."[58] Against the protests of many activist-identified women, City Club Director and Californian Laura Brown insisted that "$100 is not too much to pay for what the building has to offer," signaling that money would define the parameters of "woman" in that "woman space." Club women expected to be "inundated with membership applications" from "professional class women."[59] In fact, though, that class did not want to come downtown. As local Nan Antisdel put it, also on opening night, "I was very moved by the magnitude of the building. But . . . some of the dressed-up women . . . it seemed that they would probably go back to Birmingham [a wealthy suburb] without a second thought about joining the Club."[60] Antisdel's critique pointed to a devastating contradiction. The former elite Women's City Club had lost membership precisely because of white flight; by 1973, the old club had abandoned the neighborhood because, in Angers's words, "Nobody came down there anymore."[61]

Club leaders depended on an imagined community of middle- or upper-class "suburban women" as a necessary constituency, but such women proved to be a tough draw. According to City Club President Parrent, "suburban women" did not have the street smarts to feel safe in the City Club neighborhood. To secure that imagined constituency, the City Club armed its private security escorts with guns, only further alienating many women. Ironically, City Club directors explained this conflict through another polarized urban/suburban construction. Parrent, for example, claimed that "only the divisive women" criticized the guns; she argued that, in contrast, "*women off the street* love to see these women walking around with guns who look like they can really protect them."[62] Both "women off the street" and "suburban women" were fictive constructs, and it was on the latter that the club depended for economic survival.

Demanding a well-heeled membership, City Club rhetoric eclipsed actual feminists in the suburbs. The suburbs were indeed full of feminists. At their peak in the early 1970s, the local National Organization of Women and the Women's Liberation Coalition of Michigan each had had over a thousand members drawn predominantly from the suburbs. In the mid-1970s, as chapter 5 indicated, grassroots feminist-identified activism was participating in accelerated white flight at the very moment the City Club was opening; named feminist institutions like the Feminist Women's Health Center were establishing themselves farther from the inner city. Thus, the suburbs contained women involved in "women's lib" organizations, younger activists dedicated to grassroots change, and the increasingly policitized clients of services such as feminist health clinics. But watching the club lose tens of thousands of dollars a month, the editor of the City Club newsletter harshly criticized the hoped-for suburban members:

> Perhaps some of the members may not come in more often because of the supposedly "bad neighborhood" in which the Club is located. They knew that when they joined. . . . Members living in the suburbs also have to contend with the distance to the Club. Yeah, it's not close for many of us, but then neither is equality, strength, or freedom. If I'm not willing to drive the thirty miles from my home to the Club to work with or for my sisters, why should legislators or employers be willing to give an inch of their ivory towers to my sisters or me?[63]

With such exhortations, even women who founded the Feminist Women's City Club as a utopian woman space seemed to admit that downtown Detroit, and the historic building with its swimming pool, book clubs, proposed businesses, "culture caravan" activities, and of course its major debt, had become a duty, not a draw. In the process, the imagined suburban constituency had become stingy and alien, not sustaining and known.

An inner-city location, however, did not guarantee an inner-city membership base any more than it did a suburban one.[64] The club's greatest potential for connecting to its own immediate neighborhood rested on the FEN-run women's health clinic that the club opened to all women regardless of membership status. The City Club established the clinic as a true community service with the help of Faye Roberts, Janette Salters, and Pam Carter, the same women who had founded the Detroit National Black Feminist Organization (NBFO) and Women Organizing to Mash Alcohol and Narcotics (WOMAN), and who were intimately connected to the neighborhood. As did women everywhere, women who lived in the neighborhood and nearby Cass Corridor needed pregnancy testing, birth control and abortion counseling, treatment for STIs, and abortion services; no other downtown clinic offered such health services to poor women, and even mainstream institutions acknowledged the clinic's importance.[65] But conflicts over authority within the building compromised the health center. Already involved with residents of the neighborhood, Roberts, Salters, and Carter had expected to run their own clinic in the building, but instead, Deborah Law of Oakland became the clinic's director. FEN had also promised Roberts, Salters, and Carter a greater salary than they could have received working for the more suburban Feminist Women's Health Center, but the City Club's finances strained the clinic too much.

Further, the club's conflicts with the Feminist Women's Health Center ultimately played out over race. It wasn't long before the three women resigned from the club, explaining, "We don't want to be part of the hassles of the white feminists." They clarified that although they were "on good terms" with the City Club, conflicts among white women over the building and the clinic made their own position and leadership untenable.[66] The health clinic might have been the club's most revolutionary site, the project that functioned across race and class and spanned geographic divides by offering a service that the neighborhood itself needed; it might have been a space that constituted coalition, and in the process, it might have influenced the geographically based factors around which the women's health movement *and* the women's coffeehouse network developed. But the "woman space" of the City Club instead invoked the hierarchies of suburbanization and the failed dreams of urban renaissance. The fate of the health clinic was inextricably tied to that of the building.

When City Club directors pitched the club beyond a known feminist demographic and toward an imagined suburban base, they created a space more shaped by homophobia and racism than A Woman's Coffee House of Minneapolis. Although the Coffee House kept the word *lesbian* out of its title, it *was* a "lesbian heaven": women utilized the space specifically to affirm lesbian existence and allow women to enact new sexual politics through conflict as well as celebration. At the City Club, however, *the lesbian* really was reduced to a lurking specter. In truth, the immediate conflicts surrounding the club were not about lesbianism or homophobia but about capitalism and authoritarian leadership. But on the level of public image, lesbianism and homophobia were central players carried in on the shoulders of white flight and the effort to create a "national headquarters" for feminist institutions in a deeply divided urban landscape.

It required a high degree of manipulation to keep the lesbian hidden from view, especially given the club's significant lesbian leadership. The club even created an elaborate spatial routing of gender within the building, but one would have to look closely to see that it provided space for sexual intimacy between women and not between women and men. The first "guidelines" for the club, written up before the grand opening, stated that membership was only open to women but that members could bring female and male guests to the club.[67] The swimming pool specified distinct times for women only, women and children, and women, children, and men. "The public" was invited to shop at all stores on the first floor and also to eat at the cafeteria. The Cocktail Lounge would be open to members and female guests at all times, and to "escorted guests of either sex" on Wednesdays. The restaurant was divided to provide one section for members with female guests only, and one for members with guests of either sex. The fourth floor lounges were open to members with female or male guests. The hotel, on the fifth and sixth floors, would be available to members and female guests.[68] As subtle as it was in the original guidelines, subsequent brochures left the gender of members' hotel guests altogether unspoken.

Only a fairly intricate time-space map could plot the building's spaces and uses according to gender, and few observers fully understood the routing. One Detroit paper, for example, simply noted with amusement, "men are allowed in the Club if escorted by a woman."[69] The word *lesbian* did not appear in the club's newsletter, nor in its schedule of coffeehouse-like events; neither the club's brochure nor its policy of inclusivity mentioned sexuality. Explicitly lesbian-affirming businesses, such as Her Shelf bookstore, would have no place in the City Club's collection of feminist shops. Certain areas, at certain times, might have been open to women only, but no one publicly used the word *separatist* to describe them. In short, the club as a whole was not to be confused with lesbian heaven.

Unlike many specifically "women's spaces" around the country, the City Club was not a site for the assertion of sexuality-based constituencies. If potential members had wanted the club to be more separatist or less separatist in its gender policies, or more straight-appearing or more explicitly lesbian-affirming, no one publicly said so in the short time the club was open. Mainstream presses, too, raised no questions about sexuality at the club, with one exception. In a July 1976 article on the City Club's debts, the *Detroit News* reported that women variously connected to the project had "traded angry charges of lesbianism" that led to "fistfights among members" during the "stormy opening month" and ultimately to the club's financial crisis.[70] Given the club's struggles over everything else, the newspaper's salacious lesbian baiting seemed so bizarrely out of place that it earned no response.[71] And yet, catering to a presumed suburban respectability and perhaps also to an urban antiseparatist bent, the City Club effectively registered a silencing homophobia. There, any clear lesbian visibility looked like a "political persuasion" that threatened to drive others out of the building. While some Detroit feminists long argued against separatism on the grounds that it hindered coalition in class-identified struggles, the example of the City Club shows that sometimes refutation of separatism also came from an insistence that the lesbian did *not* lurk behind the "woman" in "woman space." In this, the City Club paralleled the rhetoric and exclusions of many feminist formations that hid homophobia behind calls for unity.

Late one night, five months after the club's opening, City Club directors packed a truck and drove away to California. FEN turned the building back over to the credit union and dissolved itself. Its failures were little different in kind, but very different in magnitude, from those that beset many attempted spaces "open to all women" throughout the country. City Club records show that founders did not take time to grasp the actual costs of running the building; they did not work out differences of spending style or leadership style; they did not take care to reconcile geographic, class, and race conflicts that emerged when "women from all over" worked together in one single building. They did not have time to build a membership base of "suburban women," but neither did they work in cooperation with existing feminist projects of Detroit such as WOMAN, the Health Center, Poor Woman's Paradise and the Cultural Center, and Her Shelf bookstore. Equally self-incriminating were the statements that FEN published to undergird the City Club's top-down financial and management practices.[72] One FEN statement asserted, for example, "We recognize democracy to be a patriarchal concept." FEN would have no elections or regional representation because "the underlying assumption of the election process is that everyone must work together even if they don't agree on the same goals and purposes."[73] Instead, FEN directors were self-appointed, and they happened to be the same women who ran the City Club: "Women who believe in the FEN vision—women who trust and respect and agree with each other."[74] At the City Club, there were directors and hired laborers; laborers were expected to put the club before personal interest in time clocks and paychecks, and directors made no pretense of collective leadership. As Parrent repeatedly asserted, "People committed to do the most work and take on the most responsibility will make the most (and final) decisions."[75] If—as Jo Freeman had famously written in 1970—structurelessness invited tyranny, FEN unapologetically demanded an authoritarian structure and total commitment to its leadership specifically in order to support its investment in the tangible and imagined space of the City Club building.

Despite incurring losses while attempting to sell the City Club building after FEN dissolved, the Feminist Federal Credit Union survived by reorganizing its splintered leadership and maintaining the faith of its members.[76] Finally in fall 1978, at the beginning of a development boom that some had hoped would be the renaissance of Detroit's inner city, FFCU sold the City Club building to Higgins Property, a development corporation. The credit union had also received a contingency-riddled offer from Women in Transition, a Detroit-based group aspiring to turn the building into a battered women's shelter. Sadly, FFCU explained to its members, "We had hoped to be able to sell to W.I.T. but there was no doubt that we had to take the offer with the best price and the least risk."[77] The "choice" between selling to a development corporation padded with government subsidies or to a volunteer- and donation-based, activist group struggling to finance shelter for women could not have been more emblematic of the challenges posed by the wider economy to the institutionalization of women's space.[78]

Conclusion

The magnitude of the City Club project was atypical among women's social spaces then proliferating throughout the United States, and so was the attention it received in the feminist press. Though sensationalist, published conversations about the City Club were crucial because all over the country, women were encountering the promises and implications of women's space, and the potentials and limitations of various ways of stabilizing some of feminism's most radical takeovers within a heteronormative, sexist, and racist public landscape. At least five nationally circulating feminist papers published a combined eighty pages of scathing copy on FEN and the City Club, including over fifty impassioned letters by readers near and far; countless groups throughout the country wrote memos announcing their formal disassociation from anything FEN-related.[79] Rare (and less visible to feminists) were more measured and forgiving analyses, such as that by Jan Prezzato of the alternative Detroit *Sun* who argued, "Intermediate steps exist between the present economic reality and Utopia, and ... gradations exist between profit-making structures like the City Club and rapacious corporate giants like GM and Standard Oil."[80] If FEN represented a peculiarly capitalist, antidemocratic ideology, it mattered to feminists because it was about securing "woman space," and all over the United States, women were figuring out *how* to *take place* in the interest of women's and human liberation. FEN came under fire because its focus was spectacularly material—not a philosophy or ideology but a goal literally embodied in the City Club—and because it was the "largest" (not the only) "woman space" that capitulated to capitalism rather than providing an alternative to it.

Against the City Club's particular manifestation of respectability, for-profit economics, and centralization of "the feminist movement," feminists around the country reaffirmed activism based on democratic participation, local flexibility, and rejection of capitalist relations. By its negative example, the City Club lent surprising confirmation to the practical link between women's coffeehouses and churches. Coffeehouses spatially articulated economic accessibility, lesbian community, and the drive to overcome race and class hierarchies. However, as this chapter demonstrates, women's coffeehouses in churches also came with a cost. While the particular histor-ical development of women's coffeehouses linked them so commonly to churches, the church space out of which they operated had substantive implications for women's movement, women's space, and the meanings of "feminist" and "all women."

The relationship between coffeehouses and churches in fact influenced more than feminist and lesbian activism; it also changed a broader public landscape, as both coffeehouses and churches existed within larger social contexts. In its heyday from 1976 to 1982, A Woman's Coffee House led Plymouth Congregational Church in its progressive social mission in sev-eral ways. Congregants who otherwise might have had little contact with overtly feminist and lesbian projects remember attending and being moved by Coffee House programs such as poetry readings, lectures, work-shops, and benefits, as well as concerts. At times, the Coffee House moved from the basement social hall to the church sanctuary itself, being invited by and inviting the congregation to share community rituals such as com-mitment ceremonies, baptisms, and funerals for Coffee House partici-pants. Congregants and Coffee House–goers filled the sanctuary to over-flowing, for example, when Pastor Elaine Marsh officiated a memorial service in 1978 for a lesbian couple killed in a car accident; while each of the two women's families had refused their daughters' relationship and held separate, private services, Plymouth Congregational's service af-firmed the community surrounding the women and acknowledged the church's own connection to and participation in that community. The church continued its outreach in other ways even after Marsh retired in

1983, becoming a consistent supporter of Quatrefoil GLBT Library in St. Paul, hosting countless queer events, and supporting antidiscrimination campaigns.

For their part, women of the Coffee House grew critical of the church space as their expectations and desires changed. By 1983, the Coffee House Collective had not a single remaining original member. New members brought a new core of values, and increasingly they vociferously demanded lesbian separatist space and adherence to anti-imperialist politics. In the process, *the lesbian* ironically came to define a white subject even more than it had in the mid-1970s. Attendance withered. In 1985, a "Coffee House community-wide discussion" revealed ongoing concern over place. Many voices chimed in to the recorded conversation: "We need more women coming!" "We need more *diversity*, and we have *got* to *get out of this church*! [applause] I mean, what are we doing in this kind of elitist institution?! [applause]" "Yeah, people think we're some kind of *club*!" Criticisms of church space continued at length until several women exclaimed, "We need a *bar*! [yeah, yeah!] You know, *our own bar*! [applause]." "I'm not a drinker, but that's the kind of space we need; something really social and inviting to *lots* of women! [cheers, loud applause]."[81]

That women in 1985 could imagine that a bar would fulfill their social and political needs hints at the impact the Coffee House made—and did not make—on the landscape of the Twin Cities. In those cities, it was thanks in part to feminist activism that women could imagine a bar as a liberated, not closeted or sexist place. But imagining that a bar would automatically have "more diversity" required glossing over a long history of racial segregation and class distinction in gay and straight bars alike. Despite unease, misgivings, and deteriorating relations with Plymouth Congregational, the dwindling and penny-poor Coffee House continued to meet irregularly at the church until finally closing its doors in 1988. Seven years later, in 1995, the original Coffee House Collective organized A Woman's Coffee House Twenty-Year Reunion, celebrated by over four hundred women thrilled to return to the very same church basement, home to their lesbian heaven.

As this chapter shows, the sites of women's movement engendered class, race, and sexual hierarchies; as women created coffeehouses and buildings "open to all women," they sometimes invested in those constructions as much as they resisted them. Focusing on the spaces of A Woman's Coffee House and the Feminist Women's City Club reveals the contentiousness of forging politicized communities in the public world and also helps explain how class, gender, sexuality, and race were actually constructed in everyday experience. It was in part through such experiences that feminist-identified activists in predominantly white women's spaces developed insight about the costs as well as potentials of defining woman-only space. In truth—as I will further discuss in the last chapter—the definition of woman was as contested as women's space. Naming a place by the presumed identity or status of its presumed occupants—women, for example—invited productive conflict as well as painful exclusions. These on-the-ground processes not only defined tangible spaces and their occupants but further, they composed feminism and its subject. Feminism itself, then, carries these legacies; just as feminist spaces were always contested, so, too, were and are the parameters of the movement.

Recognizing the Subject of Feminist Activism

I was still trying to find [women's liberation], and not knowing where to look. A friend of mine said she was going to a party at the University of Chicago, and there were going to be feminists there. . . . So I went over to the party. I had on my false eyelashes—well, that was like having Dolly *Parton* walk in, practically—and was just utterly and completely rejected. They were just *horrified*. You know, I had my [southern] accent and my big hair and my eyelashes.—Kathleen Thompson

One time I went [to A Woman's Coffee House] and I got kicked out. I was in male drag. They wouldn't let me in because I was a man. And I said, "I am not!" But, I was proud of that, because I knew I had done a good job.—Red Helbig

In 1969, Kathleen Thompson read *Notes from the Second Year* and immediately began to search for "women who were part of this movement." She thought she'd find them at a party at the University of Chicago, but to her surprise, she encountered unanticipated gender and cultural barriers: she was too southern, too feminine, too much "like Dolly Parton" to be welcomed at a northern feminist party where all of those things coded uneducated and unenlightened. Newly divorced, employed, and well-educated, Thompson had mobility. Months later she took the El from her South Side apartment to an unfamiliar neighborhood to find the office of the Chicago Women's Liberation Union. Decked in anti-imperialist posters, the office posed more barriers than invitations to someone who "still looked like a country singer," someone who simply wanted to "connect" with women who were "part of this movement."[1]

By most measures, Thompson had found the women's movement: she had read a highly influential radical feminist publication, she had attended a perfectly typical social gathering of movement-identified people, and she had even visited the office of the largest grassroots feminist organization in the United States. Paradoxically, however, the very venues in which she found women's liberation suggested an exclusive, not a popular movement; the self-definition that made them findable also created barriers for many "women . . . who are trying to connect." Along with literally countless women throughout the United States, Thompson went on to build the movement outside of those now well-known venues, ensuring that feminism would exceed its own boundaries.

Red Helbig was not exactly looking for the women's movement when she got turned away from A Woman's Coffee House one night in 1976. Nor did she expect to find herself completely "at home" in a feminist-identified space. But she did like to be with women, and the Coffee House offered interesting programs and good music. As a women's space, the Coffee House also proved to be an important indicator of how well Red could pass as a man, though it was not her intention to take that test *there*: as a lesbian, she expected welcome. Red had been involved in the gay and lesbian bar scene and in nascent gay liberation actions. Before she was even nineteen, she had passed as "old enough" at every bar and 3.2 joint catering to queers in the Twin Cities and had passed as male at some. She had proudly participated in each Pride event since the Twin Cities' first in 1972, had frequented Gay House, and had also visited the Lesbian Resource Center. But at the Coffee House, Red looked too much a man— exactly the category of persons kept out of that women-only space. Not to be brushed off, Red returned with some friends on Halloween. "I got in, but *first* of all, the first thing they told me was 'we don't let men in here.' . . . Anyway, eventually they let me in and a lot of people were staring at me because I'm sure they *did* think I was a man. I guess word got out though, and everybody calmed down."[2] Like Thompson in Chicago, Helbig had found one of the central hubs of feminist and feminist lesbian sociality in the Twin Cities. But as a lesbian who sometimes passed as a man, the moment she approached the door of that key venue, proprietors called into question her status as a movement participant. She, too, continued her work elsewhere, often in places that, although not commonly associated with feminism, helped build the movement.

A history of feminism without people like Kathleen Thompson and Red

Helbig (now Russ Helbig) would be an impoverished one. Thompson's Pride and Prejudice bookstore and living collective in Chicago gained little print documentation, but along with other spaces of this nature, it had a tremendous impact on the development of feminism not only while it operated but—through the continued activism of those connected to it— long after. Pride and Prejudice reminds us of the diverse range of feminist practice, its unruly and ad hoc nature, its connections to Latino/a activism, and its embeddedness in neighborhood geographies and varied agendas. Helbig's longtime occupation of bar space helped create women-friendly and lesbian-friendly public spaces, reminding us that feminist- and lesbian-identified demands to open public accommodations to women drew inspiration not only from the civil rights movement but also from queer efforts to build a public that was more open to women, men, and trans people across class, race, sexuality, and gender expression. Likewise, the Avantis and the Motown Soul Sisters softball teams, in Minneapolis and Detroit, respectively, engaged in activities that directly expanded opportunities for girls and women in sports as they publicly performed women's assertive, athletic occupation of civic space. When the feminist-identified Wilder Ones and CWLU's Secret Storm made softball diamonds the site of overt feminist-identified activism, they did so because they recognized that something attractive was *already* happening on the ball fields, and they followed the lead of softball-playing women who did not identify as feminists or as activists.

Thus, the history of feminism is a history not just of established institutions that bore the name "feminist" and left records to that effect. Feminism in fact was constituted through the historical connections between different sorts of spaces, and between people who eagerly identified as feminist, people who uncomfortably identified as feminist, and people who disavowed political identification altogether. This is not to say that we should see all spaces and people who created and contested them as "feminist"; rather, it is to argue that the movement was built by more than the people who embraced the name. The history of feminism, then, must seek to understand not only what was going on outside of feminist-identified arenas but, equally important, how feminists constructed and maintained borders around what counted as feminism in the story of the movement.

This book has sought to understand the ways that diverse people's interventions in the public landscape constituted feminist activism and gave shape to feminism as a mass social movement. Often with little capital, women claimed existing public spaces and built new ones in which women were welcomed, honored, and empowered to set the agenda. In the process, they formed activist communities and developed new feminist and lesbian sensibilities and politics. By doing so, they forever changed public space and public institutions, gaining new stature as participants in the larger political landscape. This spatial process also perpetuated and sometimes introduced social exclusions around race, class, sexuality, and gender expression, and those exclusions infused some of the most widely known manifestations of feminism despite many women's passionate desire for an integrated and welcoming movement. To a far greater extent than has been acknowledged, built environments were at the heart of widespread women's activism; diverse women's navigation of those environments, their collective and contested investments in them, and their variable access to them gave shape to the goals, strategies, and ideologies that we know generally as feminism.

The spatial practices exemplified in the stories of Thompson and Helbig reveal two aspects of gender construction—and gender-based exclusions—that were integral to the formation of the feminist subject. First, feminist spaces conjoined the gender of the feminist subject with race and class hierarchies; second, feminist spaces regulated gender *expression* as they produced their own boundaries. It might seem counterintuitive to suggest that women faced gender exclusions at the doors of the feminist movement. But in fact such exclusions shaped the contours of feminism as well as key challenges to it in the years since. On the surface, veteran feminists at the University of Chicago party seemed to reject Thompson simply because, with her false eyelashes and so forth, she appeared to "buy into" a sexist, objectifying, mainstream culture; she even modeled for glossy magazines and liked country music! But Thompson's gender expression—not only clothing but mannerisms, speech, and style of interaction—was shaped by region, race, and class; women in northern feminist spaces brought regional, race, and class hierarchies into play when they refused to see Thompson as a credible feminist. Alternatively, at A Woman's Coffee House, gender exclusion may have seemed more clear-cut: women-only space, by definition, simply required the exclusion of men. But it was not so simple to distinguish between women (who belonged) and not-women (who did not): in the women-only space of the Coffee House, "men's" clothes (jeans, work boots, T-shirts, or flannel shirts) usually enacted *woman* as a feminist and possibly lesbian subject; but that embrace of masculinity had definite limits that were made clear in the refusal to comprehend Red's "passing" gender expression as also *woman*. As spaces of feminist production, both the party and the Coffee House show that feminism constituted *woman* in large part through race and class constructs; furthermore, the difference between woman and man was not always easy to draw in the absence of rules regulating gender expression. In the historic emergence and consolidation of the feminist movement, feminist spaces depended on managing the boundaries of woman as much as the boundaries of place.

Feminist spaces such as the CWLU office, Women's Advocates, the Feminist Women's Health Center, and A Woman's Coffee House defined the parameters of feminist legibility as they consolidated their public reputation as "feminist." Applying Judith Butler's theoretical insights toward historical, spatial analysis, we might say this: feminist spaces—never truly spaces apart—generated their own cultural matrices to ensure the intelligibility of gender in those spaces. Although feminist spaces revised normative sex/gender practices, insofar as they composed *woman* as their subject—and indeed, as the subject of feminism—they perpetuated many of the exclusions and extinctions of the heterosexual matrix. Within feminism, then, "certain kinds of 'identities' cannot 'exist.'"[3] Spatial analysis, however, tells additional stories—stories in which feminist consolidation was never complete and always contested, stories in which feminist-identified spaces were only some among infinite sites of feminist activism, and stories that presage multiracial and transgender feminist activism.

Like feminist-identified spaces, archived manifestos and the records of named feminist organizations have created defined places in which historians may find feminism but simultaneously lose track of its popular reach. Women's liberation may well have been the most widespread social movement in the United States during the twentieth century, but the most clearly feminist-identified records do not reveal that feminism reached far beyond its most explicit proponents. Nor do they indicate how women, trans people, and men across sexuality, race, class, *and* political inclination built vehicles for this truly vast movement. Ironically, by focusing inquiry on the self-identified feminist institutions that perpetuated themselves as feminist in space and over time, our histories may overselect for the more boundary-policing aspects of feminism. But fortunately, the boundaries even of feminist-identified spaces were never neatly sealed: feminist spaces did intersect with spaces not so named, and people with multiple allegiances moved in and out of them, transforming them along the way. Feminism thereby extended beyond its named manifestations, produced by and spilling into the lives of many who disavowed feminist identification. These excesses are *also* where we might find feminist activism, the tangible "elsewheres" that are crucial to understanding the real breadth of the movement. We would do well, as historians, not to replicate the boundaries set by 1970s feminist institutions but to interrogate them as socially and historically constructed, a product of social movement dynamics that can be better understood through analyzing the contested ways in which women *took place.*

Feminist-identified spaces worked to define feminist legibility in part through the enactment of a female gender rooted in constructions of race, class, sexuality, and gender expression. From the mid-1960s through the 1970s, virtually all feminist-identified women at one time or another participated in—and loved—women-only space, and much movement-building thrived in the separate spaces in which women gathered to organize *as women.* Over time, "women's space" took on special salience, first as a specifically feminist phenomenon and later as an often lesbian and sometimes separatist phenomenon. But feminist spaces of every variety suggested the consolidation of *woman* as the subject of feminism, and they *all* delimited what passed as *feminist* to a far greater extent than has been acknowledged. In turn, feminists of color and emerging trans/gender activists have vitally critiqued this consolidation. Thus it is worth considering the ways that gender constructions and exclusions within feminist spaces imported assumptions about class, race, sexuality, and gender expression into feminism itself. Doing so indicates the possibility and necessity of reconceptualizing the parameters of feminist activism during the 1960s and 1970s.

Overtly feminist projects produced feminist legibility and gender expression partially through constructions of race and class. As discussed in chapter 1, feminist and lesbian efforts to influence bar patronage and create new women's bars vastly expanded women's opportunities to socialize at night without male escorts and also reduced the harshest effects of heteronormativity for African American and white women across class, gender expression, and sexuality. Yet in Chicago, as in many other cities, a named feminist agenda found itself in part through the patronage of bars that actively discriminated against people of color; simultaneously, African American bars rarely registered in the records of feminist publications or in the consciousness of white women. Though some white feminists and lesbians challenged overt racism, the most visible feminist-identified efforts around public accommodations often constituted "feminist" and "liberated lesbian" as a white, middle-class subject. Feminist-identified women's spaces such as coffeehouses participated in a similar dynamic, increasingly located as they were in neighborhoods that were more welcoming to white women than to women of color. In addition to neighborhood, racially coded aesthetics reinforced segregated, spatial identities: as Kim Hines and Karen Clark had discovered at A Woman's Coffee House in Minneapolis, "appropriate"—that is, legible—feminist and lesbian gender expression seemed to depend on styles associated with whiteness and middle-class privilege in which jeans did not denote "laboring" but rather, "going *out.*"

Activists inherited and transformed but often accepted and even utilized the race and class hierarchies structured within the built environment, and this furthered feminist consolidation around privileged mobilities and access to various spaces. Feminist subjectivity thus came into being not simply around ideology or political position, but equally as a space-specific construct. The constitution of feminism through the built environment thereby alienated many women of color and often precluded a multiracial agenda. No wonder, then, that by the 1980s, so many feminists rejected the center for the margins, and called for inhabiting a *metaphoric* "space off" and "elsewhere"; it had begun to appear as though on-the-ground manifestations of feminism inhibited the development of a powerfully integrated movement.[4] Feminist-identified spaces made these conflicts most clear and disturbing.

Still, emerging and ongoing criticisms of racial exclusions within feminism should not lead us to conclude that feminism simply was "white" or "middle class"; the story is far more complex than that. First, as many scholars have shown, women of color created and embraced a feminist identity from the beginning. Whether they critiqued or promoted women's space, lesbian space, and/or separatist space, they consistently challenged the reduction of "woman" and "feminist" to a white, gender-appropriate, middle-class-appearing subject, and they offered alternatives. Concepts such as "womanist" and "black feminist" interrupted white hegemony in feminism and also claimed a veritable and continuous tradition of activism among African American women.

There is a second and equally important dimension of race and space within the movement: even feminist spaces that defined themselves according to white, middle-class access sometimes depended on the ways in which women of color propelled the movement through multiple forms of activism—much of it without the label "feminist." For example, the African Americans in Detroit who won civic athletic space for women discernibly fueled self-proclaimed feminism. In fact, their actions to gain space for women in highly charged public contexts were almost indistinguishable from actions adopted by others who named their work feminist: the Motown Soul Sisters of Detroit, the Avantis and Wilder Ones of Minneapolis, and Why-Not-Inn, MS, and Secret Storm of Chicago all claimed physicality in civic athletic spaces for homosocial community and lesbian performativity. African American and predominantly working-class white teams that disavowed political motivation influenced women who embraced a feminist identity, though those connections were rarely publicly acknowledged and often intentionally erased. Thus, although the historical formation of the feminist subject did not include them, the African American women who developed resistant public cultures through softball in Detroit are significant to the history of feminist emergence and self-definition.

In addition to race and class hierarchies, the gender construction of feminist spaces also involved sexuality-based exclusions. This had been a persistent feature of feminism for nearly a century, but the terms changed dramatically in the 1970s. Prior appearances of unity among women in women's homosocial space had largely rested on heteronormative assumptions within and outside of the movement: while women in lesbian relationships had always been present in feminist circles, feminist homosociality and political activism at times garnered legitimacy in part by masking lesbian presence. Not surprisingly, feminist challenges to heteronormativity—especially in and through the creation of distinctly feminist space—continually shattered an already doubtful sexual unity. For nearly a century, feminism had included women's efforts to change normative sexual hierarchies; by the late 1960s, most if not all feminists sought to develop new ways of understanding women's sexual desires and intimacies, and many created women's spaces—"free space"—in which such matters could safely be engaged. All the while, conservative detractors of women's movement routinely charged all feminists as gender-deficient sexual deviants. In a long-standing homophobic culture, feminist space itself was always already sexually suspect. Ironically, homophobia posed a challenge to women's sexuality that feminists shared, but homophobia also contributed to the processes through which "women's space" increasingly became code for feminist-identified lesbian space.

In a sexist and homophobic culture, virtually all feminists defiantly participated in separate space in the 1960s and 1970s, though many also denied accusations of lesbianism. When women turned the relatively unstigmatized spaces of churches, schools, bookstores, and living rooms into "free space," they formed feminism but again often erased lesbian relevance. Simultaneously, in addition to bars, house parties, and softball diamonds, emerging feminist-identified lesbians and bi-attractional women also used these feminist "free" spaces to specifically nurture lesbian sociality and political development. That is, in the very spaces that feminists had long used as "free space," lesbians and bisexual women increasingly rejected the heteronormative performance of being sexually unmarked. By the early 1970s, many women's spaces that served as hubs of a movement—like coffeehouses, cafés, bookstores, and resource centers of all kinds—shaped and were shaped by lesbian interests and norms. But homophobia also shaped these spaces. Often, lesbians named even the most lesbian-affirming spaces with the label "women" rather than "lesbian." In Minneapolis, A Woman's Coffee House was compelled to use "Woman" to secure its church space; in Chicago, "for security reasons," the Lesbian Feminist Center used the Women's Center sign formerly hung at Pride and Prejudice; in Detroit, the untenability of separatism swayed the meaning of "woman" at Poor Woman's Paradise and the Feminist Women's City Club. Thus, while lesbians often led the creation of woman-friendly space in a homophobic culture, simultaneously a homophobic culture imported lesbian specters into women's space and ultimately made "women's space" code for "lesbian space."

As an increasing number of women's spaces became associated with lesbian interests, many straight and bisexual feminists found their relationship to *woman* to be newly problematic. Kathleen Thompson, whose bookstore was dubbed by others as the "Women's Center," found that although the sign literally stayed the same, its meaning changed when its location changed. At its new home, the sign did not invite her; rather, "woman" indicated a lesbian and preferably separatist subject—though not without contest. In truth, when activists attempted to solidify boundaries, they often just revealed the shifting terrain on which they stood. For example, in 1975, Alix Dobkin performed at the Women's Center (a.k.a. Lesbian Feminist Center), and at one point in her performance asked everyone who was not a lesbian to leave the space so that she could play one song to lesbians only. As Dobkin amiably explained, "I tested this controversial and troublesome policy at the LFC and it lasted only a few months. It was a short-lived practice because I got into too much trouble with lesbians and their straight or undecided friends. To me it seemed a straightforward and simple choice."[5] This story has become a bit of the lore of women's space and Chicago's infamous "internal" conflicts. Narrators who told it to me believed that lesbian feminist spaces—especially ones with a Women's Center sign out front—should not openly exclude women or tacitly demand that they pass as lesbian; the attempt to do so threatened to make women's relationship to *woman* and to women newly suspect.

In addition to race and sexuality, feminist spaces regulated gender expression to consolidate the subject of feminism. The dynamics surrounding gender expression were not limited to women-*only* spaces, such as women's dances, coffeehouses, and festivals, but those kinds of spaces helped make gender expression within feminism more apparent and more contested; women-only spaces could be at once tremendously liberating and revolutionary for some and rigidly exclusionary for others. As discussed, within some feminist-identified spaces, women performed *woman* through clothing and behavioral styles that resisted mainstream norms of femininity; false eyelashes were out, and so was fem identity. At the same time, many feminists in women's spaces shunned certain forms of masculinity (measured within white, middle-class gender rubrics). Although androgyny was very much in vogue in predominantly white feminist spaces as well as in the larger youth culture of the era, androgyny did not mean illegible or ambiguous gender: women's spaces especially depended on participants marking themselves as female, often also as feminist-identified, and sometimes as lesbian-identified. This coding—androgyny within female and feminist legibility—helped constitute feminist space and empowered "feminist" in that space. Such empowerment was no small achievement against a heteronormativity that asserted that *all* feminists were irrefutably gender deviant. Feminist spaces offered an alternative construction: woman was not something less than man; feminist and lesbian not something less than woman, but something more; women were worthy not despite but because of their womanhood, their rejection of normative subservience, and their difference from men.[6]

Coffeehouses and festivals, especially, exuberantly extended already common but radical practices of women's liberation in feminist space: at women-only coffeehouses and festivals, women danced together and developed new aesthetics about women's worth, women's bodies, women's intimacies, and women's "ways of being" with each other. To some extent, coffeehouses and festivals affirmed diverse women in their sexual desires, and doing so interrupted oppressive gender and sexual norms as powerfully as any other form of feminist activism. Though they did so incompletely, feminist-identified women's spaces were among the first to respond when disability activists demanded changes in built environments and social attitudes; though usually predominantly white, such spaces could be more embracing and less hostile toward women of color than predominantly white mainstream public spaces; they also often honored women whose shape, size, age, and ability departed from dominant "beauty" standards. Women-only spaces thereby allowed many women to experience community and sexual and bodily pleasure in being a woman, against the sexism, homophobia, harassment, and violence that many experienced elsewhere.[7] That experience helped radicalize more than a few women, equipping them to demand more egalitarian public spaces and social institutions. It is no wonder, then, that women-only coffeehouses and festivals popped up everywhere in the United States by the mid-1970s. In the upper Midwest, 1975 and 1976 saw the founding of A Woman's Coffee House in Minneapolis, Mountain Moving Womyn's Coffeehouse in Chicago, and the first national women-only music festival near Mt. Pleasant, Michigan.[8]

As vital as they were, women-only spaces made bodies and gender expression together key credentials of belonging and—by the same token —a source of alienation and exclusion. Women-only spaces continued the feminist consolidation of *woman* in part by excluding *man*. But what about those who were not different enough from man?[9] Red Helbig was admitted to A Woman's Coffee House on Halloween when she agreed to enter the costume contest. Red recalled, "I didn't feel like I was in costume, it certainly wasn't my intention. But I won the stupid contest I didn't want to enter. . . . For me, really, dressing in real drag would be dressing as a woman. And that would be excruciating. I wouldn't do it."[10] Red's passing, lesbian-identified, masculine gender expression disrupted a feminist aesthetic that depended on the ability to discern who was woman and who was not. The Coffee House recovered itself as women-only space by signifying Red's style as "costume," making it more like "code," albeit temporarily. The prevalent Coffee House code resisted white, middle-class norms of femininity but was yet inflected to allow *most* women to affirm their status (i.e., to comfortably pass) as women; code thereby also excluded passing women and retracted the possibility of their gender expression. That is, women-only spaces empowered *woman* in part through their very refusal to recognize women who appeared not woman enough in those spaces. However, continued contests over women-only space in fact proved that gender was impossible to determine in the absence of rules regulating gender expression as well as anatomies. Women's spaces and the unspoken rules of gender expression that helped construct them thus powerfully set the stage for emerging feminist critiques of gender essentialism within feminism.

Women-only space further exposed the fact that women not only produced masculinity (to use Judith Halberstam's formulation) but also produced men. By the late 1970s, countless coffeehouses and festivals defined their space through policies focused on male children; without acknowledging it, such spaces thereby also turned male children into another regulated element of women's gender expression. The Michigan Womyn's Music Festival helped popularize the issue beginning in 1976. The festival was not actually "hundreds of miles away from civilization" as Candace Margulies quipped, but fairly near Mt. Pleasant, Lansing, Grand Rapids, Flint, Detroit, and not far from Chicago.[11] Women from all over the United States and elsewhere attempted to influence its women-only policy. The Mt. Pleasant women who planned the festival (called the We Want the Music Collective) divided early. Those advocating for scheduled child care and for building alliances with a local mixed-gender, alternative political community earned the label "dissidents." News of conflict spread fast. Cathy Courtney of Detroit, for example, recalled discussing the matter with some "dissidents" she met at a Holly Near and Meg Christian concert in Ann Arbor months before the festival, and the question traveled the women's concert and coffeehouse circuit throughout the United States.[12]

Courtney had a direct stake in the issue: the festival collective had asked the Feminist Women's Health Center of Detroit to run the Health Tent and offer self-help workshops at the festival. The FWHC agreed to go on the condition that *if* the festival were to be "woman-separatist," it *must* be inclusive of *all* women—including mothers. Later, they noticed an asterisk on the festival brochure reading, "*Request: women only concert, no male children." When the FWHC charged that this policy was "counterrevolutionary," the festival collective apologized: the brochure was misleading, the asterisk applied *only* to Alix Dobkin's forty-five-minute set, it did *not* apply to the *whole* festival. Courtney angrily recounted, "I called the Collective and gave criticism and asked why the fuck did they allow Alix Dobkin to pull this shit?"[13] Ultimately, the FWHC attended in order to promote women's health awareness, provide necessary care for immediate health problems, and also influence the way women's space was conceived through that national festival. As the festival evolved into the annual Michigan Womyn's Music Festival, organizers instituted scheduled child care to make the festival more inclusive of women, but eventually also arranged a separate "camp" for boy children. At "Michigan," the definition of womyn-only space—and the preservation of gender-appropriate mothers—came to depend on separating boys from "girls' space."[14]

By the late 1970s, countless coffeehouses and festivals defined women-only space in part through policies that excluded boys altogether. Some charged that excluding male children reinforced race and class hierarchies.[15] Others found new ways to legitimate that exclusion. At Mountain Moving in Chicago, for example, the permissible age of boy children went from eight in 1978, to six, to four, and ultimately to two years old. Answering persistent conflict, co-producer Kathy Munzer explained that it was a ten- or eleven-year-old girl who convinced Mountain Moving producers of the rightness of the "no boy rule":

> This girl, Camillia, actually joined the collective. She was very mature for her age, God bless her. She was like, "you know what, little boys bother little girls and run after them." So we actually made it, because of Camillia, that only boys two and under could come. Because she said that "boys nurse until they are two, but after that, forget it." And so that was based on Camillia.[16]

The use of a child—a child presented as less ideological and therefore more truthful than adults—to legitimate an exclusionary practice indicates just how contested those practices were, even if they were also widespread. From exactly those contests emerged new articulations of the ways that *woman* could not simply be defined as an autonomous being but existed in relation to others: her children, her family, and her communities. Although some women could purchase a degree of temporary autonomy from them, others could not.[17] Women-only space, then, did not remove gender, gender expression, and other social hierarchies, but often depended on them.

Providing tools for ongoing critiques of racism and class and gender exclusions, and also providing ongoing sites of contestation that indicate the necessity of those critiques, feminist activism continues to emerge and transform through on-the-ground contestations. In 1992, the Michigan Womyn's Music Festival (MWMF)—the largest women-only space in the country—made explicit its infamous womyn-identified, womyn-born, womyn-only policy. Trans and intersex advocates across race, class, gender, sexuality, and also age—many of them feminist-identified—were ready for movement. The next summer, they situated a new space called Camp Trans, for "humyn-born humyns," outside the borders of MWMF. With the addition of Camp Trans, "Michigan" became a richly contested, highly publicized site in which the parameters of feminism continued to evolve.[18] Since that time, trans inclusivity has been a topic of conversation not only at Camp Trans but within MWMF as well. A large number of MWMF participants have also made a point to spend time at Camp Trans, out of interest and solidarity; at the same time, though MWMF has hosted discussions on trans inclusion, trans-people were never invited to participate in those discussions. Although camp borders and boundaries were thus incommensurate, traversable by some but not by others, fourteen years of conversation and activism finally eroded MWMF's long-standing fence: in 2006, for the first time, trans people freely entered MWMF, welcomed (implicitly) with a new statement: "the festival has no policy barring any woman."[19]

In 2003, shortly after I interviewed her, Alix Dobkin invited me to attend a performance at Mountain Moving that she was to share with the young gender activist and spokenword artist Alix Olson. "We call it the Alix show," she enthusiastically chirped, revealing her admiration of Olson and the pleasure of sharing shows with her: "It's great! She's kind of my protégé, so we really bridge the generations." Dobkin, outspoken advocate of gender separatism, doing shows all over the country with a leading queer artist who more often tours with trans people—great indeed! The day before the Mountain Moving event, Dobkin had to cancel, leaving Olson to perform solo in a church sanctuary truly packed with women, most of whom were in their forties and fifties. Though they had arrived expecting to hear Dobkin, they became a highly appreciative audience, enthusiastic about Olson's feminist, queer, and distinctly pro–gender-queer message.

But I could tell the story of what became the Alix Olson show differently. Inside the church sanctuary–turned–concert hall, eagerness to hear Olson mitigated the disappointment of Dobkin's cancellation: after all, this audience had still decided to pay the $15 charge for the show. Outside the doors, however, something complicated was taking place. As I stood near the entrance before the show, I watched as women my age and older, some of whom could probably pass as male in many places, streamed in the doors. I wondered what part of *me* told the coffeehouse producers that I, too, was a woman who belonged in that women-only space. I also watched as coffeehouse bouncers turned away a handful of young gender-queers and tranny boys—Olson's fans—who wanted to see the show and hand out flyers for an upcoming drag king cabaret. I wondered what allegedly made them, in their early twenties and wearing men's clothes, more threatening than I, in my forties and wearing men's clothes. I recalled my conversation with one of the coffeehouse producers months earlier: "From the beginning, Mountain Moving has been womyn-born-womyn only," she explained, "but we never had to *say* it until the recent kind of transgender stuff going on within the gay and lesbian community."[20] Did women-only space depend on a gender expression that is legible as *woman* only when combined with specific generational and political codes? Is that why I passed? Thirty years earlier, some North Side lesbian bars had required African American women to display "like five kinds of ID" to gain entrance. Would feminist spaces continue to broker the signs and identities of feminism by excluding some while admitting others? What kinds of ID would a young queer, still facing a sexist and homophobic public landscape, have to show to prove that ze respected the struggles of an earlier era and saw something of current value in feminist space?

The contours of feminist subjectivity are undoubtedly changing, in part due to the creation of queer feminist spaces that are not predicated on female anatomy or identity, and hopefully also not on generational, racial, or class-based signifiers. It is in fact rare for feminist spaces to maintain rigidly woman-identified, female-only boundaries. But as the Michigan Womyn's Music Festival and the recently closed Mountain Moving reveal, even the most rigidly defined feminist sites are and have always been intersections composed of the meetings, collisions, and exchanges of older and newer activist formations. The spaces of our everyday lives, quite apart from named feminist institutions, also consist of such rich intersections. When recognized as such, they serve as perfect reminders that earlier feminist activism helped make more recent gender-activism and trans-activism, as well as antiracist and class-conscious activism both *possible* and *necessary*. Sites of contestation can often be productive sites of connection, coalition, and collaboration. In addition, they still provide useful lenses for understanding the exclusions, transformations, and the continued popular reach of feminist activism.

Notes

1 Author interview, Eileen Hudon (Minneapolis, October 6, 1997), speaker's emphasis.

2 American Indian women had been active in the organizations of the 1960s and early 1970s that resisted police brutality, forced sterilization, and further encroachment on Indian lands and that built programs to educate and empower Indian youth, and so on. Women were among the founders of AIM, among the participants in well-publicized direct action takeovers, and provided leadership and legwork to gain legal support for Indian men arrested for those takeovers. Thus, when Women of All Red Nations (WARN) formed in 1974, it was self-evident that all of those issues were "women's issues." What WARN and other distinctly feminist groups added, however, was a critique of gender relations and sexism within Native communities and organizations like AIM, as well as the gendered dimensions of U.S. dominance over Native Nations.

3 Baxandall and Gordon, eds., *Dear Sisters*, 1. Also see Rosen, *The World Split Open*; Evans, *Tidal Wave*; internationally, Freedman, *No Turning Back*.

4 Author interview, Hudon.

5 The three other women involved with Hudon were Wanda Weyous, Leslie Snow, and Norma Heider. Funding for Women of All Nations came in part through legislation mandating the provision of a Native women's shelter. State Representative Karen Clark wrote and pushed the bill. Author interview, Hudon; author interview, Karen Clark (St. Paul, September 30, 1995).

6 As feminist and cultural geographers have argued, space influences social interaction and helps constitute gender, race, sexuality, class, age, ability, nationality, and other forms of social status. Even public spaces have been composed of barriers, prohibitions, and exclusions that not only direct traffic but

ascribe status to social actors; they tell people who may go where and whether being there signifies ownership or trespass. The alleged "democratic public sphere"—always a built environment—has thus rarely if ever been fully democratic or fully public. On the democratic public sphere, Habermas, *The Structural Transformation of the Public Sphere*. Feminist critiques include Fraser, "Rethinking the Public Sphere"; Fraser, *Unruly Practices*; Massey, *Space, Place, and Gender*; Rose, *Feminism and Geography*; Domosh and Seager, *Putting Women in Place*; McDowell, *Gender, Identity and Place*; Low and Smith, eds., *The Politics of Public Space*; Harvey, *Justice, Nature and the Geography of Difference*; Evans, "Women's History and Political Theory"; Landes, *Women and the Public Sphere in the Age of the French Revolution*; Soja, *Postmodern Geographies*; and Lefebvre, *The Production of Space*.

7 Many historians have analyzed the contributions of the Victorian era to these processes. Walkowitz, *City of Dreadful Delight*; Wilson, *The Sphinx in the City*; Stansell, *City of Women*; Sklar, *Florence Kelly and the Nation's Work*; Hewitt and Lebsock, eds., *Visible Women*; Domosh, "Those 'gorgeous incongruities'"; Deutsch, *Women and the City*; Spain, *Gendered Spaces*; and Ryan, *Women in Public*.

8 When women's athletics was not altogether denied, it was circumscribed by rules limiting women's physicality and by keeping women's bodies and sports out of public view. Disch and Kane, "When a Looker Is Really a Bitch"; Messner and Sabo, eds., *Sport, Men, and the Gender Order*; Cahn, *Coming on Strong*; Festle, *Playing Nice*.

9 Many women did rent apartments in their own name throughout the entire twentieth century. However, as narrators for this project experienced, many also faced challenges and harassment as they did so: landlords frequently inquired about marital status, and many turned "single" women away. Single mothers, women in relationships with women, working-class and poor women, and women of color were especially vulnerable to such discrimination.

10 Activists and theorists such as Barbara Smith, Audre Lorde, Adrienne Rich, and Monique Wittig linked feminism and lesbianism as each fundamentally challenges the nuclear family structures at the heart of capitalism. Historical analyses that view lesbian participation as integral to feminism include Rupp and Taylor, *Survival in the Doldrums*; Estelle Freedman "Separatism as a Strategy"; Rupp, "Sexuality and Politics in the Early Twentieth Century"; and Rupp, *A Desired Past*.

11 I attempt to use historically and locally accurate terms of sexual preference and subjectivity. I do not, for example, use the term *transgender*, even for narrators who *now* identify themselves that way or as FTM or MTF, because the term was not in use during the 1960s and 1970s. However, my use of the term *queer* does not always follow historical practices; instead, borrowing from a more recent usage within the fields of history of sexuality and queer theory, I often use *queer* as an adjective to describe spaces in which various people of non-normative gender/sex gathered and also to describe groupings

of variously non-normative gender/sex people. For example, I write of "queer women" who created house parties in Detroit, as well as the more individual terms by which they described themselves at the time. In other ways, the term *queer* speaks to the historic absence of "sexual identity" as a universal concept. See Howard, *Men Like That*; Johnson, " 'Quare Studies' "; Omosupe, "Black/Lesbian/Bulldagger"; Hammonds, "Black (W)holes."

12 For critiques of the common (masculinist) declension narrative, see D'Emilio, "Placing Gay in the Sixties," from which I draw the term "good 1960s, bad 1970s"; Gosse and Moser, *The World the Sixties Made*.

13 Focusing on what women did and not just what they thought, a few syntheses have provided invaluable frameworks for comprehending a vast movement. Sara Evans's *Personal Politics* places the origins of the Second Wave in the Southern civil rights movement and the New Left. More recently, Evans's *Tidal Wave* argues that the concept "the personal is political" expressed contradictions at the heart of Second Wave feminism: the concept empowered women to challenge inequities in previously privatized realms, and also to develop political legitimacy; yet this same concept led to "repeated episodes of fragmentation and self-destruction" by encouraging dogmatic emphasis on purity of ideology, lifestyle, and identity. Fortunately, feminism also compels its own ongoing rebirths. Evans, *Tidal Wave*, 4 and passim. Alice Echols's *Daring to Be Bad* not only seeks to better understand "radical feminism" and distinguish it from "cultural feminism" but also to answer the question, "how did radical feminism come to be eclipsed by cultural feminism?" Echols argues that the radical, society-changing potential of feminism in the late 1960s was compromised by narrower, more personal interests (cultural feminism) toward the mid-1970s (7 and passim.). Like Evans, Wini Breines begins with the Southern civil rights movement; acknowledging that the "unity" of that period was always suspect, Breines narrates a "coming apart" of white and black women and the formation of separate (though related) white socialist and black socialist feminisms in the 1970s. In Breines's analysis, identity politics proved an important challenge that, finally by the 1980s, led to a reshaping of feminism itself. Breines, *The Trouble Between Us*. Also see Valk, *Sisterhood and Separatism*. Other syntheses of feminist movement include Rosen, *The World Split Open*, and Freedman, *No Turning Back*.

14 This narrative hegemony largely left it to theorists to develop a "post-identitarian" scholarship resisting the traps of identity-based movements; the post-identitarian scholarship of Judith Butler, Judith Halberstam, and others, is partly motivated by a desire to overcome the identity emphasis of the "bad 1970s." Although not a historical study, Barbara Ryan's edited collection, *Identity Politics in the Women's Movement*, offers a useful collection of key contemporaneous and recent essays.

15 Women's activism itself motivated profound exploration of how one finds oneself in community, and how one knows one's place *and* who one's "people" are. As Audre Lorde declared, "Without community there is no liberation. . . . But

community must not mean a shedding of our difference, nor the pathetic pretense that these differences do not exist." Lorde, *Sister Outsider*, 112. Judith Butler articulates an ethical imperative to admit connection despite apparent difference, writing of "the constitutive sociality of the self" in *Undoing Gender*, 19.

16 Alice Echols, for example, nicely illuminates the ways that feminists rejected the enforced aspect of heterosexuality and instead politicized bisexuality and "natural polymorphous sexuality"; indeed, Echols recounts, they often fell in love with each other quite apart from lesbian identity per se. Sara Evans, too, offers a lively discussion of the ways that activists developed intimacies—including sexual intimacy—among each other and acknowledges that lesbians were not a new and problematic force but had long been the backbone of feminism. Echols, *Daring to Be Bad*, 210–211; Evans, *Tidal Wave*, 49–53.

17 In one of the first major syntheses of the movement, Echols argued, "The 'gay-straight split,' in particular, crippled the movement." Echols discussed the Furies and Radicalesbians to demonstrate the "enormously divisive" impact of lesbianism. Though claiming that the Furies were "hermetic," their example comes to represent "the gay-straight split" for the whole movement in Echols's work and in many that followed (*Daring to Be Bad*, 204, 210–241). In 2006, Breines qualified Echols's claim about crippling the movement, but left intact a link between lesbianism and splitting: "this ['crippling'] did not hold true for all organizations. . . . Lesbianism ruptured some groups, created anger and divisions in others, and was absorbed in some, although not without a great deal of talk and confrontation" (*The Trouble Between Us*, 105–106). These works acknowledge that heterosexual women's discomforts and fears exacerbated tensions around sexuality. But by claiming that lesbianism (why not compulsory heterosexuality or homophobia?) was divisive, they reify "the gay-straight split" as a nearly universal effect caused by the politicization of lesbian identity. Other works replicating the paradigms of "the gay-straight split" and the divisiveness of lesbian identity include Ruth Rosen's synthesis, which states, for example, "by 1972, a 'gay-straight split' affected nearly every women's liberation group" (*The World Split Open*, 171–172); and "The gay-straight split fragmented 'the sisterhood,' creating various kinds of hierarchies that excluded many women" (174). Also see Brownmiller, *In Our Time*, 173–179.

18 I am indebted to John Howard's work on homosexuality in Mississippi. By building an analytical framework around homosexual desire, *Men Like That* does not depend on *gay identity*, but rather historicizes multiple queer formations and their place in local, regional, and national contexts. Other queer theorists and historians have demonstrated that gay identity is historically and culturally specific. Black queer scholarship has more specifically critiqued the white middle-class privilege inherent in representations of "gay identity," "coming out," and even "queer." Howard, *Men Like That*; Butler, *Gender Trouble*; Halberstam, *In a Queer Time and Place*; D'Emilio, "Capitalism and Gay Identity," and *Lost Prophet*; Vicinus, *Intimate Friends*; Chauncey, *Gay New York*; Manalansan, *Global Divas*; Boag, *Same Sex Affairs*; Hammonds, "Black

(W)holes"; Johnson, "'Quare' Studies"; and Ross, "Beyond the Closet as a Raceless Paradigm." Works that understand queer sexuality through a spatial analysis include Bell and Valentine, *Mapping Desire*; Colomina, ed., *Sexuality and Space*; Beemyn, ed., *Creating a Place for Ourselves*; Ingram, Bouthillette, and Retter, eds., *Queers in Space*; Patton and Sanchez-Eppler, eds., *Queer Diasporas*.

19 At different times in history, marginalized peoples have changed the status quo in part through the use of covert separate spaces in which to establish group-ness around common concerns and goals. See, for example, Evans and Boyte, *Free Spaces*; Payne, *I've Got the Light of Freedom*; Boyd, *Wide Open Town*; Freedman, "Separatism as a Strategy"; and Rupp and Taylor, *Survival in the Doldrums*.

20 Allen, *Free Space*; Evans and Boyte, *Free Spaces*.

21 Gluck, "Whose Feminism, Whose History?"; Roth, *Separate Roads to Feminism*; Collier-Thomas and Franklin, eds., *Sisters in the Struggle*; Springer, *Living for the Revolution*; Ezekial, *Feminism in the Heartland*; Cobble, *The Other Women's Movement*; Washington, "We Started from Different Ends of the Spectrum"; Bricker, "'Triple Jeopardy'"; Baxandall, "Revisioning the Women's Liberation Movement's Narrative." As historians have shown, it would be hard to find another movement of the 1960s and 1970s that was as concerned with its own race and class politics as was feminism. The Combahee River Collective's "Black Feminist Statement" laid the intellectual ground for feminists to subsequently critique models of women's gender and sexual liberation that left race and class hierarchies intact. Cade, *The Black Woman*; Moraga and Anzaldúa, eds., *This Bridge Called My Back*; Anzaldúa and Keating, eds., *This Bridge We Call Home*; and Breines, *The Trouble Between Us*, offers the first sustained inquiry into race conflict growing out of a multiracial civil rights activism and growing into feminism. Valk, *Sisterhood and Separatism*; Thompson, *A Promise and a Way of Life*; Evans, *Personal Politics* and *Tidal Wave*.

22 Ezekial, *Feminism in the Heartland*. Ezekial's analysis of feminism in the small city of Dayton, Ohio, explicitly challenges two assumptions of the prior, nearly exclusive focus on East or West Coast cities: first, that feminism in the heartland was a watered-down, milquetoast (liberal) version of big-city (radical) feminism; and second, that heartland feminism offered a derivative microcosm of urban East Coast feminism in dynamics, agendas, and chronology. Instead, Ezekial argues, feminism in Dayton developed its own trajectory, priorities, and strategies, thereby revising the history of the Second Wave.

23 Ezekial's work on feminism "in the heartland" and Howard's work on queer Mississippi each argue that histories based exclusively on urban narratives are incomplete at best. The weight of urban-based historiography has presumed too much universality and often implies an outdated metropol-to-hinterland model of culture flow—what Halberstam has called metronormativity. The vast majority of works in history of sexuality and the history of feminism have

adopted not simply urban perspectives, but specifically East and West Coast perspectives—reifying what might be (less poetically) called bicoastal-normativity. Through their lens, the entire Midwest constitutes not the heartland but a hinterland.

24 Author interview, Judy Sayad (June 26, 2003); Seligman, *Block by Block*; Keating, *Building Chicago*; Hirsch, *Making the Second Ghetto*.

25 People in most of those groups took classes from Saul Alinsky in the 1960s; no doubt Alinsky learned as much from them as they from him. Author interviews: David Hernandez (Chicago, June 29, 2004), Estelle Carole (Chicago, June 30, 2004), Sayad, and Vivian Rothstein (July 17, 2003); Boyte, *Backyard Revolution*.

26 White flight took place most dramatically during the 1950s and early 1960s; by the early 1970s, especially on the North Side, gentrification pushed Latino/a, black, American Indian, and poor whites out of urban neighborhoods within a mile of Lake Michigan and replaced them with white majorities—usually first with young, alternative or upwardly mobile, well-educated whites without children or other dependents. De Genova, *Working the Boundaries*; LaGrand, *Indian Metropolis*; Ramos-Zayas, *National Performances*.

27 Between 1967 and 1977, Detroit lost over 110,000 jobs, simultaneously losing earnings taxes, corporate taxes, mortgages, property taxes, investment and development, entertainment, tourism, and other sources of revenue. In 1966, 22,000 whites left the city, but in the last five months of 1967 alone, 67,000 fled. In 1968, 80,000 left, and in 1969, 46,000. Ultimately 1.4 million whites left. By the mid-1990s, the city was 80 percent black, and almost all suburbs were more than 90 percent white. Hartigan, *Racial Situations*; U.S. Kerner Commission, *Report*; Sugrue, *The Origins of the Urban Crisis*; Thompson, *Whose Detroit?*; Kenyon, *Dreaming Suburbia*; Farley, Danziger, and Holzer, *Detroit Divided*.

28 "Distress" is measured according to rates of poverty, joblessness, extremely high school drop-out rates, and other indicators. Hartigan, *Racial Situations*, 9. Also see Hartigan, "Locating White Detroit," 180–213.

29 Labor organizing in Detroit often spanned neighborhood and race boundaries, building across place and race. Volumes could be written about the last century of women's labor activism in Detroit, something I leave to other scholars.

30 The Twin Cities enjoyed national leadership in electronics, medical products, machinery, milling and food processing, and printing. In the 1970s, the Twin Cities had sixteen *Fortune* 500 companies (including 3M, Honeywell, Pillsbury, and General Mills). From the 1950s through the 1970s, local corporations and small businesses regularly "gave back" to local funding structures for health, welfare, and education. Smith, *Minneapolis-St. Paul*; Vance, *Inside the Minnesota Experiment*.

31 Farm women of the nonpartisan league left a legacy of radical, socialist-leaning women's activism that continued in later peace movements and notable fig-

ures like Meridel Le Sueur and Rachel Tilsen. Starr, "Fighting for a Future"; Faue, *Community of Suffering and Struggle*; Evans and Nelson, *Wage Justice*; Rosheim, *The Other Minneapolis*; Adams and VanDrasek, *Minneapolis-St. Paul*; Mason and Lacey, *Women's History Tour of the Twin Cities*.

32 In *Claiming the City*, Mary Wingerd offers a highly relevant discussion of the history of St. Paul's civic identity, showing the impact of Catholicism on that city's politics.

33 Certeau, *The Practice of Everyday Life*.

34 As the work of Alessandro Portelli suggests, historical accuracy may be measured in many ways. Understanding the meanings people made of events requires paying attention if and when people's memories—collectively or individually—alter recorded "facts" about time and place. Portelli, *The Death of Luigi Trastulli and Other Stories*.

35 Author interview, Janet Dahlem (Minneapolis, March 7, 1994).

36 Author interviews: Pat Murphy (St. Paul, January 22, 1998), Bernice Sisson (St. Paul, January 22, 1998), and Lois Severson (Shafer, Minn., June 15, 1998).

37 Kennedy and Davis's history of lesbian community in Buffalo argues that the effort to maintain bar space constituted "pre-political" activism that laid the groundwork for the later gay and lesbian liberation movement. The works of John D'Emilio and Nan Boyd see activism around bars as directly political and dialectically linked to the homophile movement of the 1950s and 1960s. Kennedy and Davis, *Boots of Leather*; D'Emilio, *Sexual Politics, Sexual Communities*; Boyd, *Wide Open Town*.

38 Stein, "The Year of the Lustful Lesbian"; Duggan and Hunter, *Sex Wars*; Seidman, "Identity Politics in a 'Postmodern' Gay Culture"; Case, "Toward a Butch-Femme Aesthetic"; and Feinberg, *Stone Butch Blues* holds feminism partly responsible for driving butch and fem women underground. Other works offer more nuanced discussions of class-based conflict between butch-femme and trans cultures on the one hand, and the homophile and feminist movements on the other. Kennedy and Davis, *Boots of Leather*; Boyd, *Wide Open Town*; Feinberg, *Transgender Warriors*. In *Shameless*, Arlene Stein suggests that debates about lesbian sex and sexual visibility became more heated and multivocal in the 1980s, partly in response to a 1970s still characterized by feminist rejection of sexual objectification.

39 Just as spaces and the communities that peopled them were variously accessible to historical actors, so they were variously accessible to me as a historian, an academic, and a white queer Midwestern woman. Additionally, because many spaces and groups left relatively little historical documentation, simply finding them often required a great deal of persistence. Once I identified a site of potential interest, I looked for names associated with that location, often relying on the grapevine; for example, archived documentary sources did not yield any names of people involved with Pride and Prejudice Books in Chicago, but I could easily tap into existing feminist bookselling networks and let it be known that I was seeking people who might know anything about the erst-

while store. Similarly, archival research provided no contacts for the Motown Soul Sisters, so I called countless people—strangers to me—involved in community recreation and girls' athletic programs, told them I was looking for anyone who knew anything about the Motown Soul Sisters, and waited. By the time someone gave me leads for potential narrators, those narrators had usually already heard of me and this project.

40 To this day, much scholarship conceptualizes both public space and sexuality in ways that render women all but invisible or, equally erroneous, materially powerless, sexually inscrutable, and perpetually domesticated. In Manuel Castell's often-cited analysis (*The City and the Grassroots*), while gay men build visible enclaves to advertise sexual subjectivity, lesbians instead "establish social and interpersonal networks. . . . Lesbians are placeless . . . and tend to create their own rich, inner world." The belief that lesbians and women are placeless and lack sexual assertion continues to show up as guiding premises in major studies such as *The Sexual Organization of the City* (Laumann et al., eds.). In that work, authors asserted that "lesbians have tended to be more residentially diffuse" than gay men who have more economic power to colonize visible real estate. What's more, gay men create "visible" urban enclaves in part to foster environments for sexual encounters, whereas lesbians use their own "diffuse" (invisible?) spaces for "emotional relationships" and "a variety of household and socializing activities." Castells, *The City and the Grassroots*, 140; Laumann et al., eds., *The Sexual Organization of the City*, 95–101. Feminist scholars have critiqued such gendered erasures. Adler and Brenner, "Gender and Space: Lesbians and Gay Men in the City"; Rose, *Feminism and Geography*. Alexandra Chasin offers a sustained analysis of the gay and lesbian liberation movement's relationship to commercialism in *Selling Out*.

41 Because my interviews spanned a number of years, and the activism in question also spanned a number of years, I do not quantify ages. However, I can loosely say that at the time narrators engaged in the activism discussed, most were in their twenties but many were in their thirties; quite a few were in their teens, their forties, or their fifties. Interviews involved a combination of life history and open-ended questions. I conducted the majority in person with one narrator at a time, in tape-recorded sessions lasting one to three hours, at a location of their choosing. I conducted a number of phone interviews as well: sometimes these were initial conversations to ascertain mutual interest, or sometimes follow-up interviews seeking clarification or elaboration. I conducted phone interviews with narrators if it was not feasible for me to travel to them. (A surprisingly small number within my potential pool of subjects have relocated outside of the Midwest, the majority still living in the Midwest though not necessarily in the city focused on in the interview.) Narrators always granted permission to audiotape interviews, although in two cases in which narrators wanted to meet at dance clubs, and in one case in which a group of narrators wanted to meet together at a bar, I decided against taping. Four narrators did not want me to use their real names or asked me to use a

pseudonym. I initiated most interviews topically (e.g., "I would like to learn more about the team") and directly asked about space if and when narrators brought it up.

42 Castells, *The City and the Grassroots*; Lauria and Knopp, "Toward an Analysis of the Role of Gay Communities"; Warner, ed., *Fear of a Queer Planet*, introduction; Escoffier, "The Political Economy of the Closet"; Chasin, *Selling Out*.

43 Low, Taplin, and Scheld, *Rethinking Urban Parks*.

◄(One)► Claiming the Nighttime Marketplace

The title of this chapter comes from the author's interview with Jean Niklaus Tretter (St. Paul, July 2, 1996).

1 *Goldflower Feminist Newsletter* 1.2 (February 1972).

2 One sees hints of feminist emergence in the bar-based and homophile organizing in Nan Alamilla Boyd's study of queer San Francisco. In particular, Boyd reveals that even as the Daughters of Bilitis adopted a gender-assimilationist, homophile, and feminist orientation, they recognized bars as critical sites for organizing. Boyd, *Wide Open Town*.

3 Historians have shown that the gay/lesbian liberation movement cut its teeth on efforts to resist homophobic control of bar space as early as the 1940s. See Boyd, *Wide Open Town*; Kennedy and Davis, *Boots of Leather, Slippers of Gold*; D'Emilio, *Sexual Politics, Sexual Communities*; Chauncey, *Gay New York*. Marc Stein shows the emergence of gay public culture through a greater variety of locations in *City of Sisterly and Brotherly Loves*.

4 Stein, "The Year of the Lustful Lesbian"; Case, "Toward a Butch-Fem Aesthetic"; Seidman, "Identity Politics in a 'Postmodern' Gay Culture"; Duggan and Hunter, *Sex Wars*. Alternatively, Kennedy and Davis present a historical analysis of political consciousness as feminist lesbians veered away from butch-fem aesthetics in *Boots of Leather, Slippers of Gold*. Feinberg's *Stone Butch Blues* suggests that feminism as well as economic recession and other factors were responsible for destroying the public life of butch women and trans-people; Feinberg's *Transgender Warriors* argues for the contributions that feminism made to gender liberation.

5 In the Twin Cities, African American women occasionally went to licensed white gay bars as individuals and with white friends but never in large groups. Particularly by the mid-1960s, after the new I-94 freeway displaced the black speakeasy-rich neighborhood of Old Rondo in St. Paul, house parties provided the predominant venue for gatherings of black queers. I have discovered very little written or oral information about those spaces and do not include them in my analysis.

6 Cultural and feminist geographers and theorists have argued that liberal (and Habermasian) notions of democratic accessibility in fact *depend* on such exclusions.

7 Among African American women in Detroit, the terms *stud* and *fem* named

gender expression and sexual intimacies formed primarily with other women. Women who did not mark their gender as stud or fem gained the dubious distinction of being "sooners." According to some, sooners were "like a dog, a mixed breed," and others joked that *sooner* meant "sooner be had than be gotten." Bulldagger was also in common parlance as a term that sometimes (though not always) registered stigma. Few women at that time named them-selves lesbians, though many who did not then do so now, decisively using the term *lesbian* alongside *stud* and *fem* to signal a political stance and sexual orientation toward women. Author interviews: Antoenette Foster, Peggy, An-dromeda, Yvonne Roundtree (Detroit, June 24, 2001).

8 The largest and longest-lasting clubs depended on drawing a sexually mixed clientele for their viability. Bingo's, for example, was a drag club, and the Pink Lady was a strip club, each offering entertainment for an ostensibly "straight" clientele of men and heterosexual couples. Nevertheless, black queers com-prised a steady clientele.

9 White bars were numerous enough to take shape around class distinctions among white lesbians, but all were hostile to black patrons. Author interviews, Roundtree, Foster, Peggy, E. Marie. Rochella Thorpe documents white bars and the minimal black presence within them in "The Changing Face of De-troit's Lesbian Bars," and "'A house where queers go.'" Notably, white lesbians in Detroit only began owning their own bars in the mid-1970s.

10 Author interviews: Roundtree, Foster. On changing urban demographics, see Sugrue, *Origins of the Urban Crisis*; Kenyon, *Dreaming Suburbia*; Farley, Dan-ziger, and Holzer, *Detroit Divided*; Hartigan, *Racial Situations*; Moon, *Untold Tales, Unsung Heroes*.

11 Retzloff, "Detroit"; Retzloff, "'Seer or Queer'?"; Retzloff, personal communica-tion to author, March 29, 2006.

12 Several African American women I interviewed recounted their own and others' stories of being taken to a gay bar for the first time by their brothers, fathers, or fathers of their children. This also shows up in many of the inter-views that Thorpe conducted with black women in Detroit. Roey Thorpe Collection, Human Sexuality Collection, Cornell University.

13 Author interview, Roundtree.

14 Several women expressed greater outrage that gay bashers "broke in" to George's Inca Room and raped a woman *inside* the bar than they did over bashing that occurred on the streets. Author interview, Foster, E. Marie, Peggy, Roundtree.

15 Concurring, E. Marie simply stated, "We would get beat up a lot." Author interviews, Foster, E. Marie.

16 Kennedy and Davis argue that this dynamic was a critical aspect of "prepoliti-cal" lesbian consciousness and activism between the 1930s and 1960s. Fein-berg's *Stone Butch Blues* also showed that butch women's response to violence outside of lesbian bars ritually constituted community.

17 Author interview, Foster.

18 This public culture was distinct from a more private sexual expression. As Peggy put it, "You had studs and you had fems. And everything in the middle was a sooner. Now, when they got *home* it might have been a little *different*." Thus, sooners were those who *publicly* suggested that some portion of gender expression was mutable, and they served as reminders that people's gender practice always included invention and slippage across commercial and domestic realms.

19 Author interviews: Peggy, Roundtree, Foster.

20 Quote from Antoenette Foster, in recorded conversation with Roundtree, Peggy, E. Marie, and Andromeda.

21 On the Motown Record Company and its relationship to Detroit, see Smith, *Dancing in the Streets*.

22 A great deal of black community organizing took place in regular but unlicensed after-hours clubs known as "blind pigs." In addition to offering casual social space, blind pigs supported political work and the redistribution of resources through sharing food, purchase of drinks, sex work, and numbers running. Georgakas and Surkin, *Detroit: I Do Mind Dying*; Thompson, *Whose Detroit?* An extensive analysis of sexuality and black women's alternative economies is in Blair, *African American Women's Sex Work*. On the historical development of blind pigs in Detroit, see Wolcott, *Remaking Respectability*.

23 During the 1940s and 1950s, Ruth Ellis and Babe Franklin's house was known to black queers throughout the upper Midwest as "the gay spot." Ellis and Franklin were the first African American women to own their own business in Detroit (a printing shop) and among a tiny percentage of black women who owned their own house. Unsurpassed as a stable location, the gay spot provided a model of queer hospitality across gender that poorer women in poorer neighborhoods continued during the 1960s and 1970s. Author interviews; Thorpe, "'A house where queers go'"; Welbon, *Living with Pride*.

24 Author interview, Foster.

25 Author interview, Peggy.

26 Author interview, Foster and group conversation.

27 Fine, *Violence in the Model City*; Sugrue, *The Origins of the Urban Crisis*; and Kenyon, *Dreaming Suburbia*.

28 Author interview, Roundtree.

29 Author interview, Foster. For her, house parties were a way to offer the community the shelter she had been offered as a youth in need, and she extended hospitality beyond the event of the party itself.

30 At that time, many black activists described the inner city of Detroit as an internal colony whose borders were sealed by an almost all-white police force. The Shrine of the Black Madonna, along with Temple of Islam Number One and the meeting places of the League of Revolutionary Black Workers and the Black Panther Party, reached outward into a larger world. They redistributed resources among poor blacks, organized labor, and gained access to the politics of City Hall. By the early 1970s, these centers of activism had redrawn the

terrain of everyday life by opening up new economic opportunities for blacks, but in their condemnation of homosexuality, they left black lesbians walking a careful line. E. Frances White, "Africa on My Mind"; Georgakas and Surkin, *Detroit, I Do Mind Dying*; Thompson, *Whose Detroit?*

31 Author interviews, Foster, E. Marie, Roundtree, Peggy, Andromeda. Also Thorpe, "'A house where queers go,'" and "The Changing Face."

32 Author interview, Foster. Historian Heather Thompson details the relationship between Detroit activists and federal responses, in *Whose Detroit?* Also see Young and Wheeler, *Hardstuff.*

33 By the same token, before the mid-1970s, many black lesbians had not heard of white lesbian existence. Softball had provided one route through which a few African American women—if they were members of predominantly white teams—received invitations to otherwise white bars. Author interviews; Thorpe interviews, Roey Thorpe Collection; Welbon, *Living with Pride.*

34 Author interview, Foster.

35 Author interviews, Foster, Roundtree, Peggy, E. Marie.

36 Quote from Jo Devlin, written communication to author, 1998. Community historian Jean Niklaus Tretter collected stories of St. Paul speakeasies dating back to the 1920s that gay men and occasionally women frequented. During the 1940s, Kirmser's downtown St. Paul bar was straight by day and "underground queer" by night. Whereas there was only one licensed queer bar in St. Paul between World War II and 1960, Minneapolis counted a number of gay bars during the 1940s, 1950s, and 1960s. Local lore embraces the term "Jewish Mafia" even while acknowledging that this "mafia" refers to only three men who owned and protected the largest gay clubs. Brown, *The Evening Crowd at Kirmser's*; author interview, Tretter.

37 Quote from Richard Bosard. Scott Paulson interview with Richard Bosard (October 31, 1993), Scott Paulson Collection, Minneapolis Historical Society.

38 For many gay-identified men, the Viking Room was *too* nice: "full of ribbon clerks, fashionable and pretentious faggots who worked for peanuts in Dayton's department store next door, bored-looking fellows who sit around in vested shirts and countless Mona neckties, drinking martinis." As Brown concluded, "the Viking Room was too high class for us." Brown, *Evening Crowd at Kirmser's*, 8.

39 The tiny 19 Bar (a 3.2 joint), near the south end of Loring Park, was one exception and was known to be friendly to drag queens and butches. Gay men and drag queens were also at increased risk of harassment and bashing when traveling to and from gay bars and within gay cruising areas such as Loring Park in Minneapolis and Rice Park in St. Paul. Drag queens may have been most likely to be bashed, but among queers, they had the reputation of coming to others' aid. Young lesbians often sought them out for protection. Annie Lealos, for example, recalled, "If I were ever in a fight, and could have somebody with me, it would be a drag queen. Not somebody with two black belts, but a drag queen." Author interview, Annie Lealos (Minneapolis, November

10, 1995); also see Myslik, "Renegotiating the Social/Sexual Identities of Places."

40 Author phone interview, Dorothy F. (July 16, 1994).

41 From the late 1950s to 1965, Sutton's was on Marquette and 5th.

42 Author interview, Dorothy F.; author interview, Donna M. (Minneapolis, September 10, 1995).

43 In contrast to most lesbians, the sex/gender expression of passing women—who might now be seen as trans—was consistently masculine; many women who "read them out" found that a particularly attractive quality. Sutton's maintained its dress code into the early 1970s, longer than any other bar. Other queer bars that enforced gender codes included Persian Palms, the Dug Out, and the Dome, all bars that were gone by the mid-1960s. Author interviews, Russ (formerly Red) Helbig (Shafer, Minn., December 4, 1995) and Ida Swearingen (Minneapolis, July 12, 1995); Millet, *Lost Twin Cities*.

44 Kennedy and Davis, *Boots of Leather*; Feinberg, *Stone Butch Blues*; Boyd, *Wide Open Town*.

45 Shirley Heyer, Amazon Bookstore talk, June 24, 1994.

46 Jo Devlin, Amazon Bookstore talk, June 24, 1994, speaker's emphasis.

47 The Dug Out and Persian Palms were the most popular among them. The sweep of the era left behind only the Happy Hour (a back section of the Gay 90s, which was at that time straight) and the 19 Bar in Loring Park.

48 Author interviews: Barb Hamilton (Minneapolis, November 19, 1995), Jeanne LaBore (Minneapolis, November 18, 1995, and phone, September 28, 1998), Jo Devlin (Minneapolis, July 26, 1995, and letter to author, September 29, 1998), Lealos, Tretter.

49 Author phone interview with Connie Harlan (September 16, 1998). Occasionally, women rented unused upper floors of existing clubs in north Minneapolis.

50 Author interviews: Swearingen, Harlan, Heyer, Amazon Bookstore talk, June 24, 1994.

51 Author phone interview, Harlan.

52 Author interview, Helbig, Tretter, Hollis Monnett.

53 Honey, deceased in 1993, became a local legend for her continuous efforts to maintain at least one women's space in the cities, ranging from her own usually short-lived bars to private lesbian after-hours clubs in which poker and numbers running constituted part of the pleasure of a night out. From the late 1950s through the mid-1960s, Honey ran Honey's on the outskirts of Shoreview, a small town ten miles north of the Twin Cities. Always lesbian-friendly, the bar sported a lesbian pool team that played in tournaments throughout the urban area.

54 One favorite was the D 'n' O, a straight-by-day, gay-by-night neighborhood bar very close to the Town House. The Belmont was notorious among lesbians as a "terrible" place, but lesbians went there in the early 1970s until the owner turned it into a strip club. In the mid-1970s, the Noble Roman was popular among lesbians and gay men and also straight women from the nearby bat-

tered women's shelter who enjoyed being at a bar in which male patrons left them alone.

55 The Selby-Dale and Old Rondo neighborhood was the geographic and economic heart of St. Paul's African American community. Old Rondo was sustained by markets, barbers, speakeasies, tailors, and other businesses between the 1920s and the mid-1960s and was destroyed when I-94 replaced Rondo Avenue. Fairbanks, *The Days of Rondo*; Craton and Schwab, *Ghosts Along the Freeway*; author phone interview, Senator Alan Spear (Minneapolis, August 30, 1996).

56 Bar manager Greg Weiss had gambled away the Town House's tax money. Convincing Jewell that he could make the Town House successful, he printed flyers advertising "The Town House: A New Gay Bar in St. Paul," and distributed them to Minneapolis gay bars and the gay and student neighborhoods of Loring Park, Powderhorn, and the West Bank. Author interviews, Kelly Jewell (St. Paul, October 15, 1996, and phone interview, September 9, 1998), Monnett.

57 See also Barbara Weightman's investigation of the layout of bars in the United States, 1977–1979, showing that women's bars provided more seating than men's bars. "Gay Bars as Private Places."

58 Author phone interview, Harlan.

59 This narrative parallels another. The establishment that preceded the Town House, the White House restaurant, dated back to the 1940s. With its menu of lobster, shrimp, steak, and also standard fare of hamburgers and sandwiches, the restaurant catered to a casual lunch crowd and fancier dinner crowd. Hollis Monnett and Marty Bergman, who bought the Town House in 1983, recounted how, frequently, elderly couples entered the Town House surprised and amused, "and they'll say this is where they had their wedding dinner." The narrative's power rests in referencing a heterosexual ritual of church/state legitimacy, along with the implication that elderly heterosexual couples express friendly acceptance of the fact that the place of their wedding dinner now caters to queer lovers. Author interview, Monnett.

60 Author interview, LaBore.

61 Author interview, Hamilton.

62 Author interview, LaBore.

63 Author interview, Sara Henderson (Minneapolis, September 18, 1995).

64 Author interview, Monnett.

65 Katie Gilmartin offers a relevant analysis of gender and class distinction among lesbians in Denver, "We Weren't Bar People."

66 *Goldflower*, 3.2 (July 1974); author interview, Diane Como (Golden Valley, Minn., September 6, 1996).

67 Karen Browne and Cindy Hansen of the Lesbian Resource Center and Gay Community Services initiated the legal aspect of the protest. The gay rights ordinance of St. Paul, passed in 1974, did not receive broad public attention until late 1977 when Anita Bryant's "target city" campaign targeted St. Paul to repeal the ordinance. Gays and lesbians together put all their energy into

fighting Bryant and the repeal. April 1978, when the popular vote repealed the gay rights ordinance, goes down in collective gay and lesbian memory as "one of gay Minnesota's darkest hours." Author interview, Tretter.

68 Jo Devlin, letter to author (September 29, 1998); author phone interview, LaBore; author interview, Tretter and phone interview (June 21, 1998).

69 Most women, in fact, when asked a second time, agreed with Tretter's assessment. Author interviews, Jewell, Monnett.

70 At the Midget Inn on Kedzie, "You walked back and there was a stairway upstairs and that's where all the gay people were. Women. It was a gay woman thing. . . . And when it got raided, you jumped out the second floor window and you took off running. . . . So, you were smart: you always took money in your shoes, to bail somebody out. You'd take inventory: who got caught, did anybody in our group get caught? Okay, let's go bail 'em out." Author interview, Marge Summit (Chicago, October 24, 2004).

71 Author interview, Ra (Chicago, June 29, 2004), speaker's emphasis.

72 Section 192-8, Municipal Code of the City of Chicago (1964).

73 Author interview, Summit.

74 For decades prior to the mid-1960s, police had arrested persons for "disorderly conduct," a vague charge often applied to cross-dressing as well as homosexual dancing and other gender deviance in public. In 1965, Illinois became one of the first states to decriminalize consensual adult homosex in private.

75 *City of Chicago v. Wilson*, No. 49229, slip. op. at 4 (Illinois, May 26, 1978). When challenged in the 1970s, the city listed four objectives of the ordinance: "1) to protect citizens from being misled or defrauded; 2) to aid in the description and detection of criminals; 3) to prevent crimes in washrooms; and 4) to prevent inherently anti-social conduct." The city further declared, "The State does have an interest in maintaining the integrity of the two sexes," and also refuted equal protection for transsexuals, stating, "because the United States Supreme Court has not recognized any 'liberty' interest in alternative sexual orientations we may not entertain equal protection arguments based on any but the two traditional sexual classifications." City argument to Illinois Supreme Court in *City of Chicago v. Wallace*, (1978) 44 Illinois Appellate 3rd at 626, 357 N.E.2d at 1342. The case that overturned the ordinance in 1978, *Chicago v. Wallace*, involved two MTF transsexuals who had been arrested in 1974 when they walked out of a café after breakfast one morning. *Chicago v. Wallace* repealed the code to allow transsexuals to complete the therapeutic aspects of sex reassignment but did not specifically grant freedom of gender expression to all persons.

76 Author interview, Lori (Chicago, June 21, 2003).

77 Author interview, Summit.

78 Attorney Renee Hanover was one of the lawyers most prominently involved in fighting for the rights of drag queens and cross-dressing gays and lesbians during the 1960s and early 1970s. In late 1972, Cook County Circuit Court Judge Jack Sperling announced that he would declare Code 192-8 unconstitu-

tional, but this could not be done without winning a court case to that effect, and that he left up to others. For contemporaneous reports, *Chicago Gay Crusader*, June 1973; *Chicago Gay Crusader*, September 1973.

79 Until 1924, Calumet City was known as West Hammond, Illinois. Separated from Hammond, Indiana, by State Line Road, saloons and brothels settled on the Illinois side before, during, and after Prohibition.

80 The first concerted effort to close Calumet City gay bars occurred in 1972 when Mayor Robert Stefaniak made a clean-up mission part of his mayoral campaign. The sweep closed many bars on "Sin Strip" on and near State Line Road, but within months, new bars opened.

81 The Velvet Heart had a small, nearly unmarked entrance but inside, as Irene Lee described it, "It was like a big old airplane hangar: two or three thousand women" along with some men and drag queens met there on Saturday nights. Elizabeth Tocci considers her Club 307 to be the first gay-owned gay bar in Chicago; it opened in 1963. Doubtless there were others, but community historians generally agree that the vast majority of gay bars were owned by straight men; gay men did not open gay bars until the mid- to late 1960s, and— with the exception of the Lost and Found—lesbians did not open women's bars in Chicago until 1971. Author interview, Irene Lee, Whitewater, Wisconsin, October 10, 2004.

82 U.S. Bureau of the Census, *Census of Population and Housing, 1960, 1970, 1980*, Illinois, Calumet City.

83 Chicago also offered easy access to the gay-inflected resort town of Saugatuck, Michigan. Between the 1930s and 1960, ferries made the two-hour trip to and from Saugatuck several times a day, making the town more accessible from Chicago than it was from Detroit. Much like Cherry Grove, Fire Island, in New York, Saugatuck welcomed middle- and upper-class men, but independent women took excursions there as well.

84 Author interviews: Vernita Gray (Chicago, June 20, 2003), Jackie Anderson (Chicago, July 12, 2003).

85 Author interview, Gray.

86 Author interview, Gray.

87 Mayor Daley encouraged police intervention in South and West Side civil rights activism when it pushed the boundaries of segregation, but in other matters, his "machine" looked the other way. Rich historical analyses of Daley's impact on the South Side include Cohen and Taylor, *American Pharaoh*; Grimshaw, *Bitter Fruit*.

88 The *Chicago Defender* silence on black queer happenings during the 1960s departed from earlier practices. For the 1940s and 1950s, Allen Drexel ("Before Paris Burned") shows the bemused attention that massive black queer events on the South Side garnered in *Chicago Defender*, *Jet*, and *Ebony* magazines. Kevin Mumford (*Interzones*) offers extensive analysis of queer activities in Chicago black neighborhoods and interzones during the 1920s and 1930s. Kevin Mumford, *Interzones*.

89 Papers covered the raid and arrest of 109 people at Louis Gage's Fun Lounge on Mannheim Road, publishing the names of those working in the public school system. The *Sun Times* published the addresses of twelve people in education and quoted assistant superintendent of county schools, "The school code clearly provides for dismissal of teachers in cases of extreme low moral character breaking the law." Only one educator kept his post; one was suspended, one granted a leave of absence, and all others resigned. Others arrested included several post office clerks from O'Hare airport and two civilian employees of the Chicago police force. Fifty people altogether lost their jobs, and community members connect at least two suicides to the arrests. "Area Teachers Among 109 Seized in Raid on Vice Den," *Chicago Sun-Times*, April 26, 1964, 1, 4. See also "Teacher, 1 of 8 Seized in Vice Raid, Quits," *Chicago Tribune*, April 26, 1964, 1, 2; "School Districts Acting Against 9 Teachers in Narcotics Raid," *Chicago Daily News*, April 27, 1964; "Ogilvie Seeks to Kill Vice Den's License," *Sun-Times*, April 27, 1964, 3; "Area Educators Off Jobs After Arrests in Raid," *Chicago Sun-Times*, April 28, 1964, 4.

90 Compelling analyses of differential harassment and media coverage during the late nineteenth and early twentieth centuries are found in Boag, *Same-Sex Affairs*; Duggan, *Sapphic Slashers*. On Progressive-era efforts to concentrate vice in black neighborhoods, see Mumford, *Interzones*, and Chauncey, *Gay New York*.

91 "Alternative to the bars" was an oft-repeated phrase through the 1970s, as is evidenced in *Lavender Woman, Chicago Lesbian Liberation,* and *Blazing Star.* However, the discussion in Chicago did not focus on chemical dependency until the early 1980s. Quote from Michal (formerly Michelle) Brody in Brody, ed., *Are We There Yet?*, 6.

92 Prior to that time, the Mattachine Society, Daughters of Bilitis, and One all had active chapters in Chicago. They held meetings with speakers, published newsletters, created referral services to local lawyers and doctors, intervened in antigay arrests, and attempted to persuade the police department to ease up. When CGL formed, the idea of direct action, protests, and takeovers was so antithetical to Mattachine that the various groups met to discuss whether alliance was possible given their strategic differences. After this meeting, CGL became the Chicago Gay Alliance, a group that always included a small percentage of lesbians even after the formation of the Women's Caucus.

93 Gray was among the women of color who moved to Hyde Park to attend the University of Chicago but quickly grew too busy to go to school. Gray offered her home phone to CGA and found herself providing shelter for countless queer teens who had run away or been kicked out of their homes. E. Kitch Childs (1937–93) was earning her doctorate at University of Chicago at the time she helped found CGL. One of the first African American women to earn a doctorate from the University of Chicago, she also testified for the gay and lesbian rights ordinance introduced to the Chicago City Council in 1973, practiced clinical psychology in Oakland, Calif., from 1973 to 1990, published

in feminist ethics, and continued to be an activist about racism, poverty, AIDS/HIV, and sexism. Margaret Sloan (later Margaret Sloan-Hunter, 1947–2004) was co-founder of the National Black Feminist Organization (NFBO), coeditor of *Ms.* magazine, and author of *Black and Lavender* and other poetry collections.

94 Lavender Woman Press Collective published Chicago's first and one of the country's longer-lasting lesbian newspapers, *Lavender Woman* (1971–76).

95 Vernita Gray, written communication to author, November 8, 2004.

96 In May 1970, King's Ransom became one of the first gay bars to allow same-sex dancing. Many men involved in the pickets to allow same-sex dancing at the Normandy bar believe it was their activism that led King's Ransom to change its policy. However, it was likely the success of ladies' night that led King's Ransom to lead in allowing same-sex dancing when other bars remained cautious. See, for example, Jack Rinella interview with Vernita Gray, August 1, 1995 (Gerber/Hart Library, Chicago).

97 Brody, *Are We There Yet?*, 5.

98 Author interview, Ra.

99 The 1972 Chicago Lesbian Liberation survey sought feedback on all Chicago bars but received "insufficient data" for Other You. Women frequented other, predominantly male and drag queen–oriented clubs in convenient neighborhoods such as Trip (in the heart of the Loop), and Baton (very near north), but these, too, were unfamiliar to most CLL women.

100 Other "dyke bars" at the time included the long-standing Lost and Found, and Sue and Nan's.

101 Brody, *Are We There Yet?*, 5. Gray, Pope, and Lee also confirmed that the group never considered black bars.

102 Author interview, Gray.

103 Author interview, Anderson. Anderson considers herself a womanist, butch-identified lesbian who likes fem styles on feminine women. Though involved with feminist activism during the 1970s, she resisted identifying with the term *feminist*—because she perceived it as white and its concerns narrow—until 1983 when she read an article by Andrea Dworkin who, she explained, "was the first white feminist to make sense to me."

104 Quote from Brody, *Are We There Yet,?* 6. As the group grew and as meetings were increasingly held in white neighborhoods, the percentage of women of color in the group decreased. For about seven months between late 1970 and summer 1971, the Women's Caucus used meeting space in the downtown community center run by CGA. CLL advertised its existence in local alternative and feminist papers with predominantly white readership such as *SEED* and the CWLU Newsletter.

105 In spring 1974, the CLL began to chafe at being in a church, and moved to the nearby Liberty Hall—also known as Wobbly Hall—at 2440 North Lincoln.

106 *Lavender Woman*, September 1972, 2. Jack, the owner of the Up North, reportedly served great food and welcomed (white) women as much as men to the bar.

107 Author interview, Gray.

108 Two months later, the newsletter promoted the In-Between bar—in the mixed neighborhood on Halsted between Belmont and Addison—as another place women liked to go after CLL meetings. *Lavender Woman*, November 1972, 3.

109 Mears, "I'm Hurt . . . I'm Angry," 4.

110 For example, Irene Lee, who had grown up going to South Side and Calumet City bars before moving to the North Side, characterized Chez Ron's as a bar serving "mostly old world dykes." Nancy Katz, who grew up on the South Side but became a North Side lesbian activist while still in her teens, noted, "The Lost and Found was for old-school lesbians. That was their place. We would go but there were tensions sometimes. I think the older lesbians looked askance at the younger political lesbians." Author interviews, Nancy Katz (Chicago, July 12, 2003), Lee.

111 Chicago Lesbian Liberation conducted the survey in November 1972 and published it in *Lavender Woman* in January 1973. The survey advertised beyond *LW*'s readership: conducting it was strategic, as women circulated the surveys in bars and other places where lesbians gathered. (*Lavender Woman*, January 1973, 13, "A Bar . . . is a bar . . . is a bar . . . is a bar?")

112 *Lavender Woman*, January 1973, emphasis in original. The "obituary" claimed that Chez Ron's was Mafia run, male-dominated, had no windows, served cheap drinks, and did not "love" women. See also Kennedy and Edwards, "Lesbian Head Changes," 9.

113 Chicago Lesbian Liberation and the Lavender Woman Collective were distinct organizations, and CLL had its own newsletter. However, both groups continued to meet in the same space on Monday nights until 1974 when CLL moved first to Wobbly Hall and then to the Lesbian Feminist Center.

114 Beginning in 1973, pleas in *Lavender Woman* indicate the decreasing popularity of meetings, though a very small staff managed to produce the publication until 1976. Also see Jack Rinella interview with Vernita Gray (August 1, 1995), courtesy of Gerber/Hart Library and Archive.

115 MS Lounge, formerly PQ's (Paul Quinn's), was located at 661 North Clark. It was not Summit's goal to reach out to a feminist clientele; indeed, she believed that feminists stayed away from MS Lounge. She held "feminist" to be synonymous with "radical separatist," while she herself insisted on welcoming her gay male friends to the bar. She called the bar MS (pronounced as Ms.) because those were her initials, while acknowledging that the name appealed because "everybody started using Ms." She created bar T-shirts that read, "We've come a long way, Baby: MS Lounge," in which the M of MS wore high heels. Author interview, Summit.

116 "Follow-up on 'ripped off on 50-cent night,'" CLL *Newsletter* 1.3 (April 4, 1974): n.p.

117 CK's (C.K.'s Carol Kappa) opened early in 1974, on Diversey near Southport.

118 Author interview, Summit.

119 These included Irene Lee, Penny Pope, Loretta Mears, Shawn Reynolds, Ver-

nita Gray, and others. Author phone interview with Penny Pope (September 2004). Author interview with Vernita Gray alludes to same effort, as do Loretta Mears's letters to *Lavender Woman*.

120 According to Mears, "We were told at the door that each of us needed five IDs. About a month later, a group of six of us returned. This time only one of us was white and the reaction was even more hostile." Mears, letter to *Lavender Woman*, June 1975. Also see *Lavender Woman*, April 1975.

121 As Gray tells it, "One of my friends, a black friend and I, were going to the North Side to go to one of those—Augies or CK's. And when we got there, Shawn was a heavy girl, a big girl. [They said] 'We're not letting you gorillas in this bar.' So we said '*what*!?' 'You gorillas—' '*what*!? you *gorillas*!?'" Author interview, Gray.

122 The Illinois Liquor Commission issued a citation against CK's for discriminating against black women. Though Kappa signed an admission of racist discrimination on April 14, 1975, the commission dismissed her citation in May rather than issuing the short license suspension that lawyers on all sides expected. Several women believed that "a payoff is a likely explanation for what happened." See Mears's letter.

123 Mears, letter to *Lavender Woman*, June 1975. Also see *Lavender Woman*, April 1975.

124 From CK's inauspicious start as an antiblack bar, Gray asserted that "in the end, it was *the* black lesbian bar: that was their total clientele, primarily African American and Hispanic." Jackie Anderson explained, "We just started going, and if we show up in enough critical mass, the white people leave and it becomes a black bar. Except for the white people who want to hang with black people, basically it becomes a black bar. It was just a matter of a lot of people deciding we were going to go there." Author interviews, Anderson, Gray. Carol Kappa was fatally shot while closing her bar in April 1984. Though the gunshot was reported as "accidental" and self-inflicted, most narrators suspect that Kappa was murdered.

125 Author interviews: Anderson, Gray. Pat McCombs became a central organizer of Chicago Gay Pride. She started a house party network in the early 1970s, and a South Side black queer group. She has helped put on the Michigan Womyn's Music Festival since the late 1970s, and also started a Chicago lesbian-only group in 1982 that hosts several major events each year.

126 Chicago's largest African American gathering is the annual Bud Billiken parade on the second Saturday of August since 1929. Drawing hundreds of thousands of people, the parade began as a promotion of the *Chicago Defender* and its delivery boys. Author Willard Motley, under the pen name Bud Billiken, wrote a weekly column in the newspaper's children's section. The name Billiken references a Chinese god of happiness and good health, patron of beauty, and guardian of children.

127 Quote from author interview, Gray.

◄{ *Two* }► Building Community in the Marketplace

The title of this chapter is taken from the author's interview with Kathleen Thompson (Chicago, June 30, 2004).

1   See, for example, Cox, *Storefront Revolution*; Boyte, *The Backyard Revolution*; Case and Taylor, eds., *Co-ops, Communes and Collectives*. Historians have argued that the countercultural ventures of the 1960s provided a foundation for ongoing radical transformation through the 1970s and into the 1980s. Mendel-Reyes, *Reclaiming Democracy*; and Gosse and Moser, eds., *The World the Sixties Made*.

2   Author interview, Cheri Register (Minneapolis, August 29, 1996).

3   Other historical works have shown the shared ideological roots of distinguishable progressive movements of the era. See, for example, Breines, *The Great Refusal*; Anderson, *The Movement and the Sixties*; Echols, *Daring to Be Bad*; Evans, *Personal Politics*; Schulz, *Going South*.

4   In Chicago: Pride and Prejudice (North Halsted) 1969–72; Helen Palmer's (Armitage) 1975; New Feminist Bookstore (1525 E. 53rd Street), 1976; Jane Addams Books (5 South Wabash) 1977–78; Women and Children First 1978–present. Attesting to the differences between social movement commerce and conventional commerce, marketing histories of women's bookstores in Chicago don't "see" most bookstores and cite Women and Children First as the only (or second, after Jane Addams) women's bookstore to exist in Chicago during the 1970s. See, for example, Barrett, "Women and Children First."

5   Author interview, Andra Medea (Chicago, June 29, 2004).

6   Amazon Bookstore is one of the most well-known women's bookstores in the country, but the few published (brief) histories of the bookstore gloss its first four years. The most extensive account of the operations of Amazon as a collective and cooperative business (beginning around 1972 and focusing on the years 1975–85) can be found in Zahniser, "Feminist Collectives."

7   Alison Bechdel lived in St. Paul at the time she created *Dykes to Watch Out For*, and drew Madwimmin Books in her cartoon according to photographs she took of Amazon Bookstore at its Loring Park location (1985–98). Until 2002, Madwimmin Books provided the core location around which *Dykes to Watch Out For* revolved. While Amazon Bookstore still survives, Bechdel's cartoon accurately reflected the reality for most independent booksellers when it depicted Madwimmin being driven out of business in 2002 by "Buns 'n' Noodle" and "Medusa.com." Bechdel's cartoons were first published in 1983, and Firebrand published the first bound collection in 1986.

8   Amazon Bookstore has been located at various places in Minneapolis from June 1970 to the present. Quote is from author interview with Register. The founders of Amazon, Rosina Richter and Julie Morse, joined more conservative cohorts during the 1980s. Neither has offered (to the media or to academic researchers) public comments on their prior lives as leaders of feminist

activism in the Twin Cities. My history of the early Amazon years is based on interviews conducted with others involved in Amazon and on postings and articles in *Female Liberation*, *Goldflower*, and *Le'sbeinformed*.

9 Author phone interview, Don Olson (July 22, 1996). Olson was one of the founders of the Twin Cities food co-op movement and is one of its mainstays to this day. See Cox, *Storefront Revolution*.

10 For example, in Houston, Polkie Anderson (then editor of *Point Blank Times* feminist newsletter), impatient with Houston's lack of a feminist bookstore, decided to purchase books from the new feminist distribution company Daughters, Inc., and sell them out of her garage along with other print media of interest to women. See Adams, "Built Out of Books."

11 Grant, "Building Community-Based Coalitions from Academe." On volunteer labor, for example, *Her Shelf Letters* to mailing list, September and November 1976.

12 Author interview, Register; Richter, *Female Liberation Newsletter*, 1, 1 (1969).

13 Female Liberation began in 1969 as a rap group called the Women's Collective. The collective's first project was to start a medical referral service, the Women's Counseling Service. In 1970, the collective split, one group staying with the Counseling Service and one group becoming Female Liberation. Myriad work groups collected under the umbrella of the Female Liberation Group (FLG). "Suburban women" built FLG's Women Against Male Supremacy group that successfully lobbied local papers to have gender specificity removed from want ads. Despite some women's desire to turn *Female Liberation Newsletter* into communication central, work groups operated on an ad hoc and independent basis. The Twin Cities Women's Union also functioned as an umbrella for a variety of work groups around alternative primary and secondary education, labor, health, theater, and women's "free schools." Author interview, Barbara Sandstrom-Tilson (Minneapolis, August 25, 1995); *Female Liberation Newsletter*; *Twin Cities Women's Union* newsletter.

14 Author interview, Register.

15 At that time, the four-member Meechee Dojo collective operated on religious and martial styles of discipline and separatist purity; it held the fascination and disdain of self-identified feminists around the Twin Cities for modeling an uncompromising lifestyle. Author interviews: Janet Dahlem (Minneapolis, March 7, 1994), Register.

16 3240 Cedar Avenue South, Minneapolis.

17 Lesbian Resource Center, 710 West 22nd Street, Minneapolis.

18 Koivisto, "Honoring Women Who Honor Women."

19 According to narrators, LRC received occasional harassment from people wandering by. More frequently, police shone their flashlights into the center at night to "see what was going on in there." In response, the LRC kept its door locked. Author interviews: Jo Devlin (Minneapolis, July 26, 1995), Candace Margulies (Minneapolis, February 21, 1994), Diane Como (Golden Valley, Minn., September 5, 1996).

20 The Lesbian Resource Center published its own calendar and nationally cir-

culating newsletter, *Le'sbeinformed*. LRC spawned Lavender Theater, a troupe that put on plays at Shakopee Women's Prison and later at the Noble Roman bar; a book exchange and softball games with Shakopee Women's Prison; and *So's Your Old Lady* feminist literary magazine. Coffeehouses held at LRC ultimately inspired the creation of A Woman's Coffee House, discussed at length in chapter 6.

21 Amazon Bookstore was at 2607 Hennepin Avenue by October 1974.

22 Author interview, Como.

23 Author interviews: Janet Dahlem (Minneapolis, March 7, 1994); Karen Clark (Minneapolis, February 18, 1994, and St. Paul, September 30, 1995). On FBI surveillance of the women's movement generally, see Rosen, *The World Split Open*, On COINTELPRO and harassment of black nationalism in Detroit, see Georgakas and Surkin, *Detroit, I Do Mind Dying*. On COINTELPRO, see Churchill and Vander Wall, eds., *The COINTELPRO Papers*.

24 Quote from author interview, Dahlem. Author interviews: Clark, Como.

25 Hanson and Browne left Amazon to Como and Carlson in spring 1974. As a parting gift, Hanson gave Amazon $1,000 to hire a coordinator. The job went to Como, providing stability to the business and inviting tension in the collective over the distribution of power. On Amazon Bookstore as "the meeting place," author interviews: Como, Jo Devlin (Minneapolis, July 26, 1995), Clark (Minneapolis, February 19, 1994), Dahlem.

26 Zahniser interview with Como, "Feminist Collectives," 118.

27 To name a few popular ventures: Circle of the Witch all-women's theater collective; At the Foot of the Mountain feminist theater collective; the Lesbian Resource Center and Chrysalis women's center; Women's Advocates, Calamity J. construction and contracting service, Duck Type Printing; Persimmon Productions; Full Cycle natural foods restaurant. The University of Minnesota's Women's Studies program formalized in 1977, a product of nearly a decade of feminist organizing on campus and the proliferation of scholarship by and about women throughout many academic disciplines.

28 Amazon's book buyers accepted that they served a predominantly white clientele. Even by the mid-1990s, buyer Donna Niles assumed whiteness: "I stock one-quarter of what I stocked at Lambda [in Washington, D.C.] in Women of Color literature, because of the population." However, Amazon always sold more Native American literature than the D.C. bookstore. Quoted in Matthesen, "Amazon Celebrates Silver Anniversary."

29 Amazon moved to the gentrifying neighborhood of Loring Park in 1985, where it was successful enough to outgrow that attractive space. In 1998, Amazon moved to 4432 Chicago Avenue.

30 Author interview, Jim Schulz (Chicago, June 29, 2004).

31 The original four members ranged in age from twenty-three to thirty. Thompson had been working on a graduate degree in English literature at Northwestern; Lucina Kathmann was teaching philosophy at Barat College of the Sacred Heart and dancing with the South Side Women's Dance Collective that she

helped found; Patricca was finishing a Ph.D. in philosophy and religion at University of Chicago and teaching theater at Loyola; Schulz had just finished a Ph.D. in philosophy at University of Chicago and was starting a teaching job in Milwaukee. Susan Bradford, the other cofounder of the Dance Collective, joined Pride and Prejudice almost immediately, moving the Dance Collective up with her.

32 Author interviews, Schulz, Nick Patricca (Chicago, June 29, 2004).

33 Author phone interview, Kathleen Thompson (July 22, 2003). At a minimum, the core of the collective also included Thompson's brothers, Paul and Mike, and sister, Sara, all up from Oklahoma; Susan Bradford; and Howell Langford, a philosopher friend of Schulz's.

34 Pride and Prejudice was located at 3322 N. Halsted in Chicago from 1969 to 1973. Quote is from author interview, David Hernandez (Chicago, June 29, 2004).

35 New York Radical Women focused on rap groups and zap actions. *Notes from the First Year* (1968) included Anne Koedt's essay, "The Myth of the Vaginal Orgasm," which was among the most influential pieces to come from and produce the movement. The *Notes* series ended with the *Third Year*.

36 Author phone interview, Thompson.

37 Author interview, Thompson (Chicago, September 20, 2003).

38 Author interview, Patricca.

39 Author interview, Schulz.

40 The living collective did have limits, however: Kidd, a Vietnam War veteran, was shown to the door for not deferring to feminist practices or for acting too masculinist. Some of the men in the collective remember that "the women" made the decision, but "the women" themselves were far from unanimous about the eviction. The eviction caused its own kind of damage, and such drastic measures were not repeated until 1973 when the Women's Center moved and lesbian separatists took it over.

41 Author interview, Schulz.

42 Author interviews with Thompson (phone, July 22, 2003, and Chicago, September 20, 2003).

43 Author interviews; Patricca, Schulz.

44 The police station was called Town Hall and was a focus for a great deal of political activism against graft, police brutality, and harassment of gays.

45 The alternative but predominantly white newcomers helped pave the way for capitalist commercialization that outpriced them as well as earlier, poorer inhabitants by 1980. By the mid-1980s, the neighborhood had become an upwardly mobile theater district; in the early 1990s, Chicago officially designated a section of the neighborhood as Boy's Town, recognizing its concentration of gay male enterprises and relative affluence. By the late 1990s, Boy's Town was outpricing gay men; now, wealthy, predominantly white heterosexual couples have considerable sway in neighborhood development.

46 During the 1960s, city officials recognized problems of poverty in the neigh-

borhoods of Lakeview and Uptown. Partly in response to community groups who put organized pressure on slum lords, Chicago initiated the Model Cities Program in the Uptown neighborhood in 1967. The program contributed to population decline in the neighborhood, as it enabled some to move out, but failed to reverse the rapid deterioration of housing. Beginning in 1970, American Indians made the most active demands for improved housing, tenants' rights, and even land reclamation in the Uptown area. Lakeview also bore the signs of discriminatory housing practices and the loss of manufacturing jobs in the late 1960s, but it had not reached the same state of deterioration when longtime inhabitants, young newcomers, and developers began staking the area with their distinctive markers. LaGrand, *Indian Metropolis*.

47 Author interview, David Hernandez.

48 In 1963, the original Hull House complex on South Halsted was demolished to make room for the University of Illinois (Chicago campus). The Jane Addams Hull House organization established two new community centers in then-impoverished neighborhoods: one at 3139 North Broadway in the Lakeview neighborhood, and one on Wilson in Uptown. The Lakeview location (1963–2002) offered child care, arts, theater, swimming, legal resources, English language classes, and other services vital to the neighborhood. Additionally, Hull House established many small storefront resource centers. The Hull House organization never formally called the storefront on Roscoe the Spanish Outpost, but the people who lived and worked there did. At the Outpost, people could learn about tenants' rights, employment, health care, and so on. VISTA volunteers there taught English as a second language and worked with youth to develop practical skills, self-esteem, and community.

49 Police shot and killed Aracelis Baez after the first Puerto Rican Day parade held in Humboldt Park. Locals referred to the ensuing riots as the Division Street Uprising, to emphasize protest not just of police brutality but also of racist discrimination embedded in the very structure of Chicago's economy. The uprising initiated the formation of countless community organizing projects to address poverty, housing, violence, education, and so forth. Author interview, Hernandez. Scholarly works that discuss the culture and politics of Puerto Rican organizing in Chicago include Perez, *The Near Northwest Side Story*, and Ramos-Zayas, *National Performances*.

50 Author interview, Hernandez.

51 Author interview, Hernandez.

52 Vesely and Hernandez also used their own apartment as community space with an open door.

53 Author interview, Thompson (September 20, 2003).

54 The five from La Gente all worked on *Roscoe Street Blues* in the basement of Pride and Prejudice, including a teenager representing the Young Lords. Author interviews; Hernandez, Thompson (July 22, 2003), Schulz, Patricca.

55 Thompson recalled, "When the men's rap group was going on, the women would tiptoe past it as the storms raged, and go into the kitchen and eaves-

drop." Author interviews: Thompson (July 22, 2003), Schulz, Patricca, Hernandez.

56 Author interviews: Schulz, Thompson (July 22, 2003), Medea.

57 Author interviews: Thompson (July 22, 2003, quotes), Hernandez, Patricca, Schulz.

58 Thompson was so unfamiliar with the North Side when Patricca found the Pride and Prejudice building that she did not realize the CWLU office that she had visited only months earlier was just around the corner. Elaine Wessel, who was actively involved in the CWLU, is one of few people who recalled Pride and Prejudice when asked about Chicago's women's bookstores. "Around 1970 there was a woman who had a bookstore which was around the corner from where the Women's Union office was located. . . . I went there for the books. There were occasionally meetings there that I was involved in." Author interviews; Thompson, Elaine Wessel (Chicago, June 19, 2003).

59 Lucina Kathmann, written communication to author (August 11, 2004). Author interview, Kathleen Thompson (Chicago, June 30, 2004). Kathmann, who had more direct contact with the CWLU than anyone else in the house, described the tensions: "They said people at our house 'would test any woman's urine.' I think they meant at any hour of the day or night, whether or not she had money or a good story."

60 See Kaplan, *The Story of Jane*.

61 La Dolores, a resource center focused on Latina needs, opened its doors a few blocks south in 1974; it also advertised in lesbian publications.

62 Author interviews: Schulz, Patricca.

63 Kathmann, written communication to author.

64 Author interview, Jude Vesely (August 24, 2004). As narratives, oral histories are products and producers of collective memory that, even when inaccurate, provide insight into the meanings narrators made of their activism. See Portelli, *The Death of Luigi Trastulli and Other Stories*.

65 One knew men's politics by their berets: "At that time all the men in all the groups were wearing their berets—black or brown berets and so forth—and then the gays started wearing berets too, they crocheted their own berets in purples and lavenders." Author interview, Hernandez.

66 As a commune, the space also drew the attention of graduate and undergraduate sociology researchers at Northwestern University and the University of Chicago. The collective perceived them to be young, naive, and primarily interested in discovering rampant sexual relationships and drug use. Collective members tell stories of toying with the ever-present researchers, inventing an extraordinary array of household sexual liaisons and earnestly offering nonsensical political theories. Author interviews: Thompson, Schulz, Patricca.

67 Author interview, Schulz.

68 Author interview, Thompson (July 22, 2003). This was a common request of the times. For example, in 1974, the Washington, D.C.–based journal and collective, *Off Our Backs*, agreed to explore the possibility of women in Chi-

cago starting a "sister *oob* collective" when a D.C. member relocated to Chicago. As they wrote nearly a year later, "It seemed to be a precedent-setting endeavor to try to develop a working relationship between two groups of women 1,000 miles apart" (*Off Our Backs*, September/October 1975, 1). By December 1975, tensions between the two groups were high, and the D.C. group explained, "It was initially planned that women interested in joining the Chicago *oob* collective would write to DC discussing their politics." The Chicago collective rejected the idea and the relationship ended (*Off Our Backs*, December 1975, 1).

69 Polly Connolly, a member of the Socialist Worker's Party, also lived in a house that was a gathering spot for activists from all over the country. Marge Witty, a dance and living collective member, helped launch feminist psychotherapeutic theory and clinical practice. Eve was a leader in Native American activism around both tenants' rights and Indian land reclamation, especially around the Nike missile sites.

70 *Against Rape*, based on primary research conducted entirely by the authors, was the first feminist book published on rape, shortly followed by Brownmiller, *Against Our Will*. Medea founded Chimera in 1970, the first women's self-defense school in Chicago.

71 "Chicago's Lesbian Feminist Center," *Lavender Woman*, June 1974, 3. The LFC collective included two women who had lived at Pride and Prejudice: Thompson's sister, Sara, and Joan Capra of the Family of Woman band. The center maintained a lending library and a small collection of books for sale, counseling and referral services, and rap groups, all on volunteer labor.

72 Author interview, Kathleen Thompson (Chicago, June 31, 2004). Divisions were indeed painful. Thompson's sister had a personal and political interest in establishing the Lesbian Feminist Center, but understood Thompson's investment in maintaining a more open women's center; Thompson also understood the desire for lesbian-separatist space though rejected the "credentialing" that went with narrower definitions of community.

73 Jack Rinella interview with Vernita Gray (August 1, 1995), courtesy of Gerber/Hart Library and Archive. Women of color, however, have contributed to feminist theories and practice of separatism. Among Chicago activists, philosopher Anderson, "Separatism, Feminism, and the Betrayal of Reform." Loretta Mears was convinced that "there was no way to deal with racism and classism as issues as long as women put all their energy into men, or even most of their energy into men. Because dark men and white men all have an investment in keeping things the way they are with women." Brody, "Interview with Loretta Mears," in Brody, *Are We There Yet?*, 130.

74 Author interview, Medea. Following two years of devastating research interviewing and receiving letters from hundreds of women who had experienced rape, Thompson and Medea's book tour also exhausted both women's physical health, as journalists and talk-show hosts scoffed at the concept of violence against women.

75 Susan B's restaurant was located at 3730 N. Broadway in Chicago from 1973 to 1975. Quote from author phone interview, Thompson (July 22, 2003).

76 Author interview, Thompson (September 20, 2003).

77 Susan B's served one meat soup and one vegetarian soup each day. Later, Hundseth added salad and a dessert fruit soup. Quotes from *Chicago Magazine* (July 1975); author interview, Thompson.

78 Rossinow, *The Politics of Authenticity*.

79 Vernita Gray, written communication to author (August 20, 2004).

80 In fact, the first published call to boycott MS Lounge appeared in the same issue of the CLL newsletter that celebrated Susan B. Anthony's 154th birthday and her namesake North Side restaurant. CLL *Newsletter* (March 1974).

81 Author interview, Thompson (September 20, 2003), speaker's emphasis.

82 *Lavender Woman*, "Women's Businesses Close," August 1975. Author interview with Thompson.

83 A "sister" collective, Chicago *off our backs*, began in October 1974 "to try to develop a working relationship between two groups of women 1,000 miles apart," and to "represent the feelings, politics, and activities of women in the Midwest" (*Off Our Backs*, September–October 1975, 1). The Chicago collective only had a small handful of participants, and only two or three women contributed news pieces. They cited lack of an office as a barrier to internal communication and membership growth (*Off Our Backs*, July 1975).

84 "rumor has it," by jacy—Chicago (*Off Our Backs*, July 1975, 22) (punctuation and lowercase in original).

85 *Off Our Backs* published a follow-up article, "more susan b's," in September–October 1975, 17. The situation was a turning point for Chicago *off our backs*, leading them to conclude that their own collective process did not support accountable feminist journalism; furthermore, the relationship between the D.C. group and the Chicago collective was fraught with conflict over Chicago's autonomy and D.C.'s control. The "sister collective" therewith disbanded. *Off Our Backs*, December 1975, 1, 26–27.

86 Poor Woman's Paradise was located at 926 Seven Mile Road in Detroit from March 1974 to June 1975. Quote from Askins, "Non-Sexist and Non-Populated."

87 Minneapolis feminists also tried their hand at the restaurant business with the Full Cycle natural foods restaurant. More than the food sold; Full Cycle enjoyed momentary popularity as the location for the filming of the lesbian soap opera *Toklas, Minnesota*. As its name suggests, *Toklas, Minnesota* played on common desires to make somehow real an imaginary lesbian landscape peopled with semifictional and historical lesbian figures.

88 Author phone interviews: Denise Dorsz (October 26, 2003), Valerie Angers (July 22, 2005).

89 Author phone interview, Dorsz.

90 The Women's Liberation Coalition, with over 2,000 members, was Michigan's largest grassroots direct action feminist organization (it later changed its name to the Women's Liberation Group, because they were not technically a

coalition). They had a small office and mailing address at 5705 Woodward Avenue, and, for several months in 1971, the coalition held regular mass meetings at the inner city YWCA (2230 Witherall), enabling several hundred women to organize together in a public venue. The Detroit chapter of NOW also had around 2,000 members but held meetings at various churches or in women's homes. Some local organizations printed newsletters discussing organization functions for those on the mailing list. Detroit Daughters of Bilitis met in women's homes, primarily concentrated in the affluent Dearborn suburb, and occasionally held picnics in public parks. The Detroit American Indian Center (360 John R.) offered stable meeting grounds that greatly contributed to women's organizing around local and regional Native American concerns. Newsletters of Women's Liberation Coalition, NOW Detroit Chapter, Detroit Daughters of Bilitis, North American Indian Association of Detroit; see also the short run of *Womankind* (1971), and the alternative presses *Fifth Estate, Sun, South End*, and *Inner City Voice*.

91 For example, *Lesbian Connection* was published in East Lansing; *Spectre* was published by the Ann Arbor Revolutionary Lesbians; Ann Arbor was also home to *Purple Star Journal of Radicalesbians* (1971) and *Lesbian Lipservice* (1975–76); *Mountain Rush* was published in Mt. Pleasant.

92 Whereas African American women had been involved in media production through African American radio and newspapers since the mid-1960s, white women did not enter media production in Michigan until the early 1970s. The first women's radio show operated from Wayne State's radio station beginning in the summer of 1971: "All Together Now" (WDET-FM 101.9), a weekly show, was written, directed, and engineered by women. This group also ran the Women's Radio Workshop. "Gayly Speaking" radio show ran in 1974–75. In 1975, white feminists produced "Why Aren't We Laughing?" on WABX-FM, and also created a group called More Air Time for Women that demanded the expansion of the existing show as well as integration of women into regular programming (1975). New in 1972, feminist TV media included "A Woman's Place" ("The only show in Michigan produced by women") on WTVS, produced and moderated by Marj Jackson Levin, a NOW activist. Announcements were run in *Moving Out, Womankind, Detroit Sun*, and *Fifth Estate*. On structural conditions and public policy between 1940 and 1975, see Fine, *Violence in the Model City*, Sugrue, *The Origins of the Urban Crisis*.

93 *Moving Out* 4.2 (1974). I discuss the Women's Resource Center and Credit Union at greater length in chapter 5.

94 First announcement of Poor Woman's Paradise (before it was named), *Moving Out* 4.1 (1974).

95 Gloria Dyc, quoted in Askins, "Non-Sexist and Non-Populated."

96 Denise Dorsz, quoted in Askins, "Non-Sexist and Non-Populated."

97 Near the University of Minnesota's West Bank, free university classes at the Riverside Café focused on everything from the war and imperialism to homosexuality, and many classes drew a hundred students every evening, far sur-

passing the restaurant's typical clientele. In Chicago, the Heartland Café in Rogers Park and the Blue Gargoyle in Hyde Park drew leftist and antiwar activists for teach-ins and free university classes. In Detroit, the Artist's Workshop Free University focused on music and poetry, and several venues near Wayne State functioned as leftist meeting grounds.

98 Author phone interview, Dorsz. The area between McNichols (Six Mile) and Eight Mile was incongruous and changing rapidly with white flight.

99 Author phone interview, Dorsz.

100 Quoted in Askins, "Non-Sexist and Non-Populated."

101 Poor Woman's Paradise, 926–927 Seven Mile Road; the Women's Cultural Center, 927 Seven Mile Road; The Women's Resource Center, 18700 Woodward Avenue.

102 European Americans began settling the Highland Park area in the early 1800s. It was incorporated as a village in 1889 and a city in 1917. The Ford plant in Highland Park, built between 1909 and 1920, was famous for giving birth to the modern assembly line and the $5 a day wage. By 1927, however, Ford moved auto production to the massive River Rouge Plant, limiting the Highland Park Plant to truck and tractor manufacturing. Meanwhile, the city of Detroit grew to completely surround Highland Park (excepting its southeastern edge, which borders the similarly independent city of Hamtramck). In the mid- 1950s, Ford converted most of the once-productive Highland Park plant to office headquarters. It is now known on the historic registry as Model T Plaza.

103 Before the Ford plant closed to manufacturing, virtually no blacks lived in Highland Park. In 1960, the U.S. Bureau of the Census listed 29,900 whites, 7,947 blacks, and 216 "other" persons living in Highland Park. In 1970, the Bureau of the Census listed 13,126 whites and 13,108 blacks. During the 1960s, 6.9 percent of the population left Highland Park. Nearly 30 percent of the population left during the 1970s. By 1980, the Bureau of the Census listed 3,977 whites, 23,443 blacks, and 489 other nonwhite persons living in Highland Park. U.S. Bureau of the Census, *Census of Population and Housing, 1960, 1970, 1980*, Michigan: Highland Park.

104 Quote from Edna Ewell Watson, in Georgakas and Surkin, *Detroit, I Do Mind Dying*, 223. By the 1980s, Highland Park was ranked as one of the cities with the highest crime rates in the nation. Most scholarly works on Detroit all but ignore Highland Park, as though the jurisdictional independence of Detroit and Highland Park reflects absolute independence. Georgakas and Surkin is one of the few exceptions.

105 NBFO listing in *Moving Out* 4.1 (1974).

106 Author phone interview, Dorsz, speaker's emphasis.

107 Heather Thompson discusses these dynamics in *Whose Detroit?* esp. 170–172. Also see interview with Edna Ewell Watson in Georgakas and Surkin, *Detroit, I Do Mind Dying*, 221–227; interview with Marian Kramer in Mast, *Detroit Lives*, 104–107.

108 Author interview, Angers; this is discussed further in chapter 5.

109 Edna Ewell Watson, for example, was centrally involved in the League of Revolutionary Black Workers during the late 1960s. The home she shared with John Watson was "one of the home bases for the movement . . . housing hungry and traveling comrades," and it was also under constant police and FBI surveillance. Frustrated with male dominance and homophobia in the League, she incorporated "radical black feminism into [her] political thinking" and believed that "gender issues needed articulation within the League if it was to achieve its agenda of liberation." Moving out on her own in 1974, she later wrote, "My immediate need was to get a permanent home and a modicum of economic independence. . . . I focused on preparing my children for surviving in a hostile society and trying to protect my sons from an America determined to cast all black men as the designated suspect." By the mid-1970s, Watson was organizing primarily with women (while Peter Wenger, a jazz musician and red diaper baby from New York, nannied the children that Watson raised with Ivy Riley). She relied on and helped build a feminism focused on coalition between grassroots community organizers, health workers, educators, and civic leaders at all levels. Watson interview in Georgakas and Surkin, *Detroit, I Do Mind Dying*, 222. On John Watson and the League of Revolutionary Black Workers, see Georgakas and Surkin, *Detroit, I Do Mind Dying*; and Thompson, *Whose Detroit?*

110 In Detroit, NOW was an organization composed of predominantly white women that included a handful of African American women. In the early 1970s, NOW held centralized meetings in downtown churches that brought together NOW committees that spread about the urban and suburban area. By the mid-1970s, suburban chapters operated more autonomously and centralized meetings waned in attendance, diversity, and function. *NOW Newsletter, Detroit* (1970–77).

111 "Women on the left" is Dorsz's phrase. On the "working women's movement," Jane Slaughter, written communication to author (June 27, 2003).

112 Wendy Thompson, interview by Freda Coodin, *Labor Notes*, October 2002. Some branches of auto plants had long hired women for "women's work." The Turnstead plant, for example, produced seat cushions, and thus employed women to sew. Most plants, however, employed no women, particularly as auto workers. General Motors was notoriously the last to hire women.

113 The year 1975 saw the biggest downturn in production leading to the loss of women's jobs at Detroit plants, sparking another massive wave of women's activism that also fed into organizing against sexual harassment. Jane Slaughter, written communication to author; Thompson interview, *Labor Notes*, October 2002.

114 Author phone interview, Dorsz.

115 Countless once-a-week women's coffeehouses beginning in the early 1970s propelled and were propelled by women's music. Minneapolis and Chicago both had lesbian feminist bands, feminist rock bands, and production companies, and Chicago generated the country's oldest women's music distribution company. On the development of women's music, festivals, production

and recording companies, see Mosbacher, *Radical Harmonies*; Morris, *Eden Built by Eves*.

116 Author phone interview, Dorsz. Dorsz initially explained Poor Woman's Paradise's musical choices in chronological terms: the coffeehouse existed "pre–the first music festival . . . pre–women's music. The timing was, it was way before women's culture and women's music really got going."

117 Family of Woman wrote a letter to *Moving Out*: "We are the Family of Woman, Lesbian-Feminist Musicians. . . . We are the only band we know of that demands to be billed as lesbian feminists. . . . This is not Show Business or Cock Rock for us. . . . We refuse to play bars or clubs because of who most of the club owners are. We play only women's concerts because we are not background music for other activities. . . . We operate as a collective. Four musicians, a lesbian sound technician, and a lesbian business manager. Our fee for doing concerts is adjustable. . . . We want all women's groups to be able to afford us" (*Moving Out* 4.1 [1974]: 6–7); Poor Woman's Paradise's first ad ran in the same issue. The band had played at fundraisers for Minneapolis's Lesbian Resource Center a year earlier. On Family of Woman in Minneapolis, see planning memo of the Lesbian Service Center (1973).

118 Verta Taylor and Leila Rupp provide a brief discussion of the political significance of "women's music" in "Women's Culture and Lesbian Feminist Activism."

119 *Her Shelf Calendar*, January and February 1977.

120 Author phone interview, Alix Dobkin. Before that concert, Dobkin held a "public (for all women) get together" so she could "get to know the lesbian community." *Her Shelf Newsletter*, November 1980.

121 Askins, "Non-Sexist and Non-Populated."

122 Author phone interview, Dorsz.

123 Dorsz quote from Askins, "Non-Sexist and Non-Populated."

124 Dorsz, quoted in Askins, "Non-Sexist and Non-Populated."

125 In May 1976, Irene Mariposa and Anna Tursich opened the more separatist Her Shelf "wimmin's bookstore" at 2 Highland, Highland Park. Her Shelf offered books and items "by wimmin," discussion groups, poetry sharing, live music, and occasionally movies. The bookstore increasingly defined itself as a lesbian separatist space through its programming. In 1980, for example, the bookstore formalized a "Lesbian Learning Institute (For Lesbians Only)," consisting of a variety of classes held at the bookstore and at women's homes; the bookstore also coordinated a directory of lesbian "skills and resources" to "keep lesbian/feminist money in the women's community where it belongs." *Her Shelf Newsletter and Community Calendar*, 1976–80.

126 Beth Brant has written numerous poetry and short story collections, including *Mohawk Trail* and *Food and Spirits: Stories*. She also edited *A Gathering of Spirit: A Collection by North American Indian Women*.

127 Askins, "Non-Sexist and Non-Populated."

128 Author interview, Penny Pope and Irene Lee (Whitewater, Wisc., October 10, 2004).

129 For histories offering a nuanced understanding of separatism(s) in relation to a broader movement, see, for example, Rudy, "Radical Feminism, Lesbian Separatism, and Queer Theory," 191–200. Contemporaneously and since, Alix Dobkin wrote prolifically about the necessity of separatism to feminism in her regular column, "Minstrel Blood," published first by *Outlines* and later by *Off Our Backs*. Historians have also argued that separatism, far from dividing the movement, has kept it going, for example, Rupp and Taylor, *Survival in the Doldrums*; Freedman, "Separatism as a Strategy," 512–528. Anne Valk (*Sisterhood and Separatism*), alternatively, argues that even when women separated into race or sexuality-defined groups, they mutually influenced feminism.

◄(*Three*)► Playgrounds and Women's Movement

The chapter title comes from an interview with Virginia Lawrence (Detroit, June 6, 2000).

1 This argument is central to Smith, *Dancing in the Streets*. Also see Georgakas and Surkin, *Detroit, I Do Mind Dying*; Watson, ed., *Paradise Valley Days*; Mast, ed., *Detroit Lives*.

2 Prior to the mid-1960s, the only high-caliber women's softball was the fast-pitch game. Its availability varied by location. The Twin Cities and other areas sported a handful of outstanding fast-pitch teams, but it was nonexistent in most Midwestern towns, all but inaccessible to African American women living in Detroit, and not widespread enough to support elaborate national tournaments. Beginning in the early 1960s, athletes began to develop women's slow-pitch—distinguished in part by the higher arc of the pitched ball—as a highly athletic and widespread endeavor. Cities such as Cincinnati and Cleveland led the development, and between 1962 and 1968, women throughout the Midwest exponentially expanded the number of women's leagues; teams participating in the highest level of national slow-pitch tournaments went from sixteen to over a hundred.

3 Author interview, Charlotte Howza (Detroit, October 13, 2000).

4 Author phone interview, Jan Chapman Sanders (June 21, 2000).

5 Author phone interview, Virginia Lawrence (June 6, 2000).

6 Author interview, Jackie Huggins (Detroit, October 13, 2000).

7 Low, Taplin, and Scheld, *Rethinking Urban Parks*; Solomon, *American Playgrounds*.

8 Most softball teams in the top women's league were predominantly or entirely white. But for the few white and Chicana women who played for the Soul Sisters, and the few women of color who played for otherwise white teams, softball was an avenue through which women across race not only shared park space but occasionally shared other social spaces, such as segregated bars.

9 Kane, "Resistance/Transformation of the Oppositional Binary"; Messner, *Taking the Field*; Messner and Sabo, eds., *Sport, Men, and the Gender Order*.

10 On debates over the safety of women's athletics, see Cahn, *Coming on Strong*.

11 Author interview, Howza.

12 Author interview, Barbara Hardison (Madison Heights, Detroit, June 25, 2001).

13 Author phone interview, Charlotte Howza (May 23, 2001).

14 Author interview, Victoria Lollar (Detroit, October 13, 2000).

15 Author interview, Huggins.

16 Author interview, Jackie Huggins, Victoria Lollar, Charlotte Howza, Virginia Wyat (Detroit, October 13, 2000).

17 Gissendanner, "African American Women and Competitive Sport"; Cahn, *Coming on Strong*.

18 Author interview, Virginia Lawrence (Detroit, June 25, 2001).

19 Author interview, Jan Chapman Sanders (Cohoctan, Mich., June 22, 2001).

20 The *Michigan Chronicle* paid scant (if any) attention to girls' and women's athletics in general; teams such as the Motown Soul Sisters were not to be found in the pages of that paper even during their most active years between the late 1960s and mid-1970s.

21 Inkster was thus the first Detroit suburb with a significant African American population; during the 1960s and 1970s, Inkster's racial demographic remained fairly consistent with African Americans constituting just under and whites constituting just over half the population. U.S. Bureau of the Census, *Census of Population and Housing, 1960, 1970*, Inkster. Also see Kenyon, *Dreaming Suburbia*.

22 Author phone interview, Chapman Sanders (June 22, 2001). Chapman Sanders specifically lived on Mayberry Grand in a triangle also bounded by Grand and Warren Avenues. "Eight Mile" meant two contradictory things: Eight Mile was a black neighborhood (between Wyoming and Livernois) that African Americans had settled in the 1920s, building modest homes ten miles distant from the city. As Chapman Sanders's narrative suggests, one had to go through a lot of white territory to reach Eight Mile. Eight Mile Road is the dividing line between Detroit and its northern suburbs where, in the 1960s and 1970s, virtually no blacks lived. Just as narrators in 1920 talked of Eight Mile as the opportunity to live in "dream homes out in the country," Chapman Sanders reflected that the Eight Mile suburban boundary demarked "a whole other country." On the early development of Eight Mile, see Sugrue, *Origins of the Urban Crisis*, 39–40.

23 Many scholars and citizens have discussed the urban renewal plan as part of an effort to marginalize Detroit's African Americans. See Fine, *Violence in the Model City*, and Sugrue, *Origins of the Urban Crisis*. Marsha Mickens oral history in Moon, *Untold Tales, Unsung Heroes*, 362.

24 Watson, ed., *Paradise Valley Days*; Wolcott, *Remaking Respectability*.

25 During the 1950s, unlike many other large U.S. cities, Detroit had built relatively few public housing units, but the largest—Brewster, Jeffries, and Douglass—were high-density, inner-city, black-only complexes. The Detroit Housing Commission unabashedly approved of segregation in public housing and

unapologetically underwrote racist discrimination in private housing outside of the inner city. See Sugrue, *Origins of the Urban Crisis*.

26 The freeway also fractured the already poor white neighborhood of Briggs. Fine, *Violence in the Model City*, 61–62; Hartigan, *Racial Situations*.

27 Author interview, Lawrence. The Detroit NAACP sued Detroit over the city's policy of racial segregation in public housing and won the suit in 1956. Officially, the city opened public housing, but desegregation was slow to nonexistent: by August 1960, Smith Homes were 96 percent white, Herman Gardens 98 percent white, Parkside and Charles Homes over 94 percent white; Jeffries was 86 percent black and Brewster, Douglass, and Sojourner Truth Homes were all black. Detroit Commission on Community Relations, 1960 *Annual Report*, Appendix A. *Michigan Chronicle*, September 28, 1957; *Saturday Evening Post*, October 19, 1957; *Detroit News*, August 18, 1959. See also Sugrue, *Origins of the Urban Crisis*, 306.

28 Author interview, Lawrence (June 25, 2001).

29 Northwestern Playfield. The neighborhood was dissected by both I-96 and I-94. Author interview, Chapman Sanders (June 22, 2001).

30 Suzanne E. Smith offers a history of this production in *Dancing in the Streets*.

31 The *Illustrated News* was founded in 1960 by James Cleage, radical minister of the Central Congregational Church on Linwood Avenue.

32 Smith, *Dancing in the Streets*; Georgakas and Sturkin, *Detroit: I Do Mind Dying*; Thompson, *Whose Detroit?* Also see Griffin, "Conflict and Chorus"; Phillip Brian Harper, "Nationalism and Social Division in Black Arts Poetry of the 1960s."

33 Author interview, Hardison. The rioting in fact had begun some twelve hours earlier. Many Detroiters criticized the government for the media blackout that endangered people who would have stayed away had they known about the riots. Fine, *Violence in the Model City*, 184–188.

34 Fine, *Violence in the Model City*, 296–301, and *Time Magazine*, August 4, 1967.

35 Sanders interrupted her Detroit narrative with a narrative about her experiences of the riots at Fisk University. She believed that neither riot was a "race riot" in that neither literally pitted blacks and whites against each other. However, both riots clearly incited racist violence. Author interview, Chapman Sanders.

36 See, in particular, Marilyn S. Johnson, on discourses surrounding the 1943 Detroit riots, "Gender, Race and Rumors: Re-Examining the 1943 Race Riots," 252–277; Thompson, *Whose Detroit?*; Wolcott, *Remaking Respectability*.

37 Author interview, Eleanor Josaitis (Detroit, June 25, 2001).

38 Warren, "Community Dissensus."

39 Author interview, Howza; also Huggins, Lollar, Chapman Sanders (June 22, 2001).

40 Many historians have noted that Gordy was an integrationist who, though sympathetic to Black Power, placed value on being "practical" and shied away

from radical politics while seeking an ever greater share of the white market. While histories of Motown Records and the relationship between Motown and Black Power are numerous, Suzanne Smith uniquely delves into the Detroit context, arguing that the emergence and cultural politics of Motown cannot be understood apart from the politics of Detroit. Smith, *Dancing in the Streets.* Also see Ward, *Just My Soul Responding,* esp. 393–400; Early, *One Nation Under a Groove;* Gordy, *To Be Loved.*

41 Author phone interview, Chapman Sanders (June 21, 2000).

42 Hamtramck is one of two technically independent villages (along with Highland Park), jurisdictionally separate islands located within the larger borders of the city of Detroit. Conant Gardens, originally a mile north of Jayne Field (near Seven Mile Road adjacent to the Fenelon neighborhood), became a middle-class black neighborhood during the early 1940s, as well-to-do blacks sought to move away from inner-city ghettos. White resistance to integrated suburbs in that area began with the Seven Mile–Fenelon Improvement Association, which formed in June 1941 to oppose the Sojourner Truth housing project. Black families began to move into the project in February 1942, greeted by huge signs and white protestors demanding, "We want white tenants in our white community." Over 1,000 people were drawn into what came to be called the Sojourner Truth riots, in which over 40 were injured, 220 arrested, and 106 blacks and 3 whites held for trial. See Sugrue, *The Origins of the Urban Crisis,* 73–74.

43 Author interviews: Huggins, Howza, Lollar, Wyat; and author phone interview, Howza.

44 Motown Records continued to sponsor the team even after the company moved to Los Angeles in 1973. Motown started a new team in L.A., also called the Motown Soul Sisters, that lasted for two years. In 1974, the national softball finals were held in northern California, and Motown not only paid the Detroit Soul Sisters' airfare to the tournament but also paid for them to spend a few days in L.A. playing with the L.A. team and vacationing. The Detroit Soul Sisters fondly remember the trip and Motown's generosity, but it was one of the last acts of loyalty that the record company paid to the Detroit-based team, as the company departed ever farther from Detroit by the mid-1970s. The L.A. team, lacking community-based origins, a determined coach, and a defiant set of players, never went far. The Detroit team began to decline in the mid-1970s, and most cite the departure of Motown and lack of money as one very concrete hardship.

45 Following the 1967 riots, countless activist groups came into being around efforts to build a healthy city. Many developed in coalition with existent groups such as the Dodge Revolutionary Union Movement, a grassroots black auto-workers' union, radical churches, and black nationalist groups. One group proposed a central Black Communications System and Black Arts and Education Program. Its authors explained, "We are attempting to raise the aspirations . . . of these youth by making available to them knowledge of Black

achievements [worldwide]. Only by instilling a positive racial pride in these youth can we hope to convince them of . . . working for constructive change . . . rather than plotting for the system's destruction." This group distributed their proposal to all levels of government, city service organizations, and the UAW. Black Arts and Educational Program, UAW Recreation Department, Box 5, Folder 3, Walter Reuther Archive.

46 Author interview, Huggins.

47 Demands to the city for youth facilities raised the specter of continued unrest. One proposal argued, "When the school systems of River Rouge and Ecorse terminate their year, this releases approximately 4,600 youth into the cities. The youth facilities in both cities are nearly non-existent." "Rationale for Summer Programs," UAW Recreation Department, Box 5, Folder 3, Walter Reuther Archive.

48 Smith, *Dancing in the Streets*, 135.

49 For historical analyses of the ambivalent reception of black athletes, see Bass, *Not the Triumph But the Struggle*; Hartmann, *Race, Culture, and the Revolt of the Black Athlete*.

50 On the scholarly reification and production of the invisibility of black women's sexuality, see Hammonds, "Black (W)holes and the Geometry of Black Female Sexuality."

51 Full Truth Unity Fellowship of Christ African American Gay and Lesbian Church was begun in 1989 and is Detroit's oldest black gay and lesbian congregation. It formed in part to serve African Americans with AIDS and their partners and loved ones. In the mid-1990s, Full Truth Unity split as additional gay and lesbian congregations formed in the city, and the original congregation retained the name Full Truth Fellowship of Christ.

52 Author interviews: Antoenette Foster, Yvonne Rountree, E. Marie, Beverly, Andromeda, Peggy (Detroit, June 24, 2001).

53 Author interview, E. Marie.

54 Author interviews: Jackie Huggins, Barbara Hardison, Victoria Lollar (Madison Heights, June 25, 2001).

55 Author interviews, Huggins, Hardison, Lollar.

56 Author interview, Hardison, speaker's emphasis.

57 Author interview, Huggins.

58 Author interview, Huggins.

59 Author phone interview, Chapman Sanders (June 21, 2000).

60 Author interview, Virginia West (Detroit, October 13, 2000).

61 Author phone interview, Howza.

62 Author interviews: Howza, West, Lollar.

63 Author interview, Huggins.

64 1974 Detroit News segment, on "married women playing softball," focused on Virginia Wyat and Charlotte Howza and two women from other teams.

65 Author interview, Hardison. Recounted and confirmed also by Victoria Lollar and Jackie Huggins.

66 Author phone interview, Chapman Sanders (June 21, 2000); author phone interview, Howza; author interview, Hardison.
67 Author phone interview, Chapman Sanders (June 21, 2000).
68 Author interviews: Huggins, Hardison, Lollar.
69 Author interview, Hardison.
70 Author phone interview, Howza.
71 Author interview, Huggins.
72 Author phone interview, Rujeania Vance (November 17, 2003), speaker's emphasis.
73 Author phone interview, Chapman Sanders (June 21, 2000).
74 Author interview, Linda Joseph (Minneapolis, June 30, 1998).
75 Author phone interview, Howza.
76 Author interview, Betty Hawes (Circle Pines, Minn., July 14, 1998).
77 Author interview, Joseph.
78 Author interview, Hawes, and briefly joined by Sandy. Coach Merlin Wood and Linda Joseph expressed similar sentiments.
79 Author phone interview, Lawrence.
80 Author interview, Hollis Monnett (St. Paul, Minnesota, October 10, 1996).
81 Author interview, Marty Bergman (St. Paul, Minnesota, October 15, 1996).
82 Author interview, Hawes.
83 Author interview, Joseph.
84 Author interview, Hawes; author phone interview, Merlin Wood (October 30, 1996 and June 28, 1998).

◄ Four ► Feminist Movement and Athletic Space

1 Author interview, Connie Harlan (Minneapolis, September 16, 1995).
2 Author interview, Betty Hawes (Circle Pines, Minnesota, July 14, 1998).
3 The Chicago Women's Liberation Union formed in 1969 as an umbrella organization conceived to support a fluid array of women's activism generated by focused chapters and work groups spread throughout the city. Virtually every work group— from the Jane abortion service and many women's health initiatives to the Women's Liberation School and the Graphics Collective—focused on reaching women and promoting feminist, socialist politics while also working to change the immediate conditions of women's lives. Strobel, "When Sisterhood Was Blooming" (unpublished manuscript in author's possession; used by permission of Peg Strobel).
4 Author phone interviews: Judy Sayad (June 26, 2003), Vivien Rothstein (July 17, 2003); author interview, Rinda West (Chicago, June 19, 2003).
5 As early as 1910, unions have used recreation as a way to build community and activist subcultures among workers. In that decade, Chicago's Trade Union League even had a women's hockey team. Also see Daniel Katz's study of the ILGWU between the 1920s–and 1940s.
6 Zipter, *Diamonds Are a Dyke's Best Friend*; Cole, "Ethnographic Sub/versions."

7 In general, Chicago softball stayed in Chicago, in part due to the distinctive nature of the sixteen-inch ball game that many played. The size of the standard softball has changed many times during the last century, and at times the size of the ball has been gendered, a larger ball being a "women's" ball. Since the 1960s, ten inches (circumference) has been the standard for most softball outside of Chicago and even much of the game within Chicago.

8 The CWLU and the Twin Cities Women's Union (TCWU) each established women's health clinics, women's schools, graphics collectives, and cultural production groups. Minneapolis's socialist Alive 'n' Truckin' theater group performed in Chicago for several CWLU events, and Chicago's Women's Liberation Rock Band performed in the Twin Cities for occasions such as the opening of the Elizabeth Blackwell Health Clinic. The TCWU did not organize around sports at all.

9 In most parts of the country, league levels are based on expected practice time outside of games, as well as relative record of the teams. "Recreational" teams have no practice time outside of the games they play. The significant rule difference between fast- and slow-pitch has to do with the arc of the pitched ball. A good fast-pitch could prevent most batters from making a good hit, and thus, as long as most girls lacked consistent athletic training, very few women could play fast-pitch at all. In addition to being a more accessible game, slow-pitch was more defensively oriented than fast-pitch; those who promoted it (including many fast-pitch players who changed to slow-pitch by the late 1960s) said that it could incorporate a more complex strategy because more hits meant more fielding opportunities. For these and other gender-bound reasons, women's slow-pitch came to eclipse fast-pitch by the early 1970s; in the 1990s, fast-pitch made a significant comeback in girls' and women's leagues.

10 Enke, "Pioneers, Players, and Politicos."

11 Enke, "Pioneers, Players, and Politicos."

12 The original team divided over the decision to "go classic": team members who wanted to stay recreational stayed with a co-coach, while the Avantis stayed with Woody.

13 Author interview, Hawes.

14 Author interview, Merlin Wood (June 29, 1998).

15 Author interview, Hawes.

16 Author interview, Jan DuBois (Crystal, Minn., October 20, 1996).

17 Respectively, *Bloomington Sun*, July 1967; *Minneapolis Tribune*, August 27, 1968.

18 Author interview, Wood. Betty Hawes concurred with this origin narrative.

19 *Time Out*, February–March 1977 (no author cited).

20 Author interview, DuBois, Hollis Monnett (St. Paul, October 19, 1996).

21 Thorough historical, gender, and cultural discussion of the National Section on Girls and Women's Sports and other similar national organizations that have attempted to promote and regulate girls and women's sports since 1927 may be found in Cahn, *Coming on Strong*, and Festle, *Playing Nice*.

22 Author interviews: Monnett, Wood, Linda Polley (Minneapolis, June 30, 1998).

23 Author interview, Jo Devlin (Minneapolis, July 26, 1995).

24 *Lavender Woman*, 3 (May 1973). The first issue was published November 1972.

25 Gabriner, "Come Out Slugging!"

26 Author interview, Devlin.

27 Author phone interview, Carol La Favor (July 13, 1998), and Nancy Cox (July 12, 1998).

28 Author interview, Devlin.

29 Author phone interview, Candace Margulies (July 11, 1998).

30 Author phone interview, La Favor, speaker's emphasis.

31 Author interview, Devlin.

32 Author phone interview, Margulies.

33 Author phone interview, Margulies.

34 Author interview, Devlin.

35 Author interview, Margulies.

36 Author interview, Devlin.

37 Author phone interview, Margulies.

38 Author interview, Devlin.

39 Author interview, Rosemary Lundell (Minneapolis, December 20, 1995), speaker's emphasis. In the upper Midwest during the 1970s, soccer was relatively unpopular, and formal programs for girls and women were nonexistent. Women informally organized leagues during the late 1970s.

40 Author interview, Devlin.

41 Author interview, Devlin. Here I owe much to Susan Cahn for offering insightful comments on space, self, and embodiment in this context.

42 Author phone interview, Mari Stack (July 16, 1998), speaker's emphasis.

43 On the female apologetic in male space, see Disch and Kane, "When a Looker Is Really a Bitch," 108–143.

44 Strobel, "When Sisterhood Was Blooming."

45 Secret Storm focused most heavily on Horner Park but also directed organizing energies to Kosciusko, Wells, Wrightwood, and Hamlin Parks.

46 Women had struggled to articulate a place for "gay liberation" in the CWLU's political mission since its founding in 1969. In November 1970, gay liberation was the topic of one of the Union's "citywide" meetings in which all the work groups of the Union participated. In spring 1971, the Liberation School (a CWLU workgroup) offered a course called "Women's Liberation Is a Lesbian Plot," designed to counter lesbian baiting within the women's movement by positively acknowledging lesbian participation, leadership, and legitimacy. In 1972, women formed the Gay Group, with the explicit goal of adding lesbian liberation to the CWLU's statement of Political Principles. (The new section of the statement read, "We will struggle . . . against sexism . . . and for the liberation of all homosexuals, especially lesbians.") Despite the new statement, the Union as a whole failed to develop a strong stance on homophobia and heterosexism as impediments to all women's liberation. Frustrated by this, the

Gay Group revived in 1974 as the Lesbian Group. As Union member Elaine Wessel recalled, the Lesbian Group "had more to do with reminding people that lesbians existed, rather than dealing with actual sexual issues," and those reminders included "lesbian organizing *within* CWLU." Just a few weeks later, without intending to focus on lesbian existence, Outreach stumbled across the softball field as a key location for this struggle. CWLU Gay Educational (September 1972); Wessel's chronology notes on the history of the Gay Group; both in CHS, CWLU, Box 13 (Gay Group 1969–76). Author interview, Elaine Wessel (Chicago, June 19, 2003).

47 As Judy Sayad explained, "In the city of Chicago, you identified neighborhoods because neighborhoods were the key to identifying a working-class base. That was more effective than finding people with a certain position in the economy. . . . So in CWLU, the locals instinctively knew how to organize by neighborhood." Author phone interview, Sayad.

48 Many had contact with working-class and/or white ethnic constituencies through paid employment, such as Rinda West who taught at Oakton Community College, or through their own backgrounds in Chicago. While the Union's various projects served untold thousands of women across race and class, CWLU activists and other organizations in Chicago tended to organize "within their own racial groups."

49 Outreach offered this critique as part of their defense of their own organizing strategy in all of their annual self-evaluations. Also discussed in Strobel, "When Sisterhood Was Blooming."

50 Judy Sayad was among the youth looking for alternatives: growing up in Cicero, she was first "organized by SDS [Students for a Democratic Society]" at fourteen years old; shortly after, Vivien Rothstein introduced her to the Women's Liberation Union. Sayad believed that CWLU involvement interrupted gendered life patterns: she had the feeling that where she grew up, "it was rare to be fifteen and not be pregnant." Author phone interview, Sayad. In its first year, Outreach facilitated the formation of classes, workshops, and activist coalitions at Schurz High School, Alvernia High School, Oakton Community College, Wright College, Southwest College, and Moraine Valley College. Several people from these schools joined CWLU, as well. CWLU Conference (1973), Evaluation, CHS, Box 8/4-6; author interview, West; author phone interview, Rothstein.

51 This strategy was shared by a number of New Left community organizing groups, such as the Economic Research and Action Project of Students for a Democratic Society and Chicago's own Rising Up Angry collective. Quote from CWLU Conference (fall 1974), Outreach Self-Evaluation.

52 Royko, "Going to Bat for Feminism"; Royko, "And in this Corner . . ."

53 Royko, "Going to Bat for Feminism."

54 CWLU Conference (1976), Outreach Self-Evaluation.

55 Davenport, "Go to Bat for Feminism"; CWLU Conference (fall 1974), Outreach Self-Evaluation.

56 Author interview, West. There was a great deal of debate within CWLU over whether or not Outreach sought out Ghishoff first or whether she came to the Union first. The conflict reflected uncertainties about organizing strategies: what were the appropriate ways to build connections with working-class women? What were appropriate activities? While Outreach argued that years of "listening to the people" led them to discover their arenas of action including the parks, some in the Union accused Outreach of going "hunting" to find Ghishoff or, alternatively, that Ghishoff "fell into their laps." Documentary evidence does not resolve the question, nor have my interviews, as narrators tend to repeat one or another "side" as they were recorded in contemporaneous CWLU meeting minutes. However, interviews did reveal the fact Ghishoff was friends with CWLU member Susan Davenport and the initial contact occurred casually in the context of an already developed friendship. Thus, the question as Union members and meeting minutes phrased it (who contacted whom first) was a bit misleading and a distraction from the real debate at hand over theory versus practice.

57 Outreach shared strategy, belief, and resources with Rising Up Angry. Like Angry, Outreach thought it made sense to reach beyond one's own small world of politicos. Secret Storm used Angry's typewriter and graphics to print Secret Storm. (Angry's equipment had long been shared with feminist groups, to such an extent that some people considered the house in which it resided to be the "Black Mariah house" after the name of a feminist periodical published there during the mid-1970s.) Secret Storm spelled out its relationship to RUA as though it needed explaining to the rest of the Union. "The basis of the relationship has been running into them, especially in our high school work. They also play on some of the teams . . . They also have offered to distribute Secret Storm and they display it prominently in their office. The also publicize other union events in their office and they've been real good about coming to our fund raisers. As we do more sports stuff, we are going to have to work out a more definite relationship with Angry (they do a lot of sports outreach)." CWLU Conference (fall 1974), Outreach Self-Evaluation.

58 Some in the Union critiqued Outreach's methods on other grounds: "hanging out" until a rap group gelled was too random; Outreach failed to offer women a clear education in Marxist theory; claiming softball—a working-class pastime—as an organizing tool was simply holier-than-thou bourgeois frivolity, comparable to lesbian vanguardism. Author interviews: West, Sayad, Estelle Carole (Chicago, June 30, 2004); Evaluation/History of the CWLU, CHS, CWLU Box 2/5-6.

59 Many in CWLU saw Rising Up Angry as too closely linked to the parts of SDS and ERAP that had alienated women activists in the late 1960s and early 1970s. At least since 1967, women had critiqued SDS for valorizing this kind of public work above others. Organizing in the streets required male privilege, because women on the streets were neither safe nor taken seriously. At the same time, the organizing that SDS women did with women inside apartment complexes

to build tenants' unions and day care cooperatives did not "count" despite contributing to institutional and community change. It must be noted, however, that Rising Up Angry took feminism seriously and contributed to CWLU actions and fundraisers. As historian Sara Evans has argued, women's marginalization in SDS and their own organizing successes encouraged them to form separate feminist organizations and build a women's liberation movement. Evans's *Personal Politics* focuses on women's activism in SDS and ERAP and offers a gender analysis of the organizational dismissal of their work. The CWLU conflict had deeper roots as well. West continued, "There was a huge and nasty ideological struggle that was brewing in the Union from late '74 until the time that the union disbanded. And we were seen as the faction that advocated practice without theory. And there were the others who were the heavy theory people. And we of course looked down on them, because they didn't have any activist base. But there were *lots* of work groups that *did* really, that had really good *practice*." Author interview, West.

60 That fall, tensions mounted within CWLU over the legitimacy of certain work groups. Left-sectarian groups among Chicago activists became involved with the Union and attacked feminism, sexuality, and homosexuality as bourgeois concerns. Whether those groups wanted to merge with the Union or destroy it is unclear; what is clear is that those groups felt that to achieve their own vision of revolution, they would have to go through the Union one way or another, because CWLU was one of the largest, most diverse effective activist groups in Chicago, if not in the country. To no one's liking, the Union spent increasing energy over the next two years debating whether homosexuality was compatible with socialist revolution. Author interviews: Carole, Wessel. CWLU Conference Minutes (November 17, 1974) records the beginning of this conflict (CHS, CWLU Box 13). Also, Evaluation/History of the CWLU records the ultimate fracture of the Union. CHS, CWLU Box 2.

61 "Women's Liberation Builds Strong Bodies," *Secret Storm*, summer 1975.

62 Echoing Jan Chapman Sanders, *Secret Storm* quoted a young woman early learning spatial constraint and domesticity: "All my brothers love sports. So do I and my two sisters, but every one thinks that girls are nuts. And *they make us stay home a lot while the boys get to play ball.* That makes me really mad." "Women's Liberation Builds Strong Bodies in Many Ways," *Secret Storm*, summer 1975, emphasis added.

63 Being a wife and/or mother kept women off the fields and in the home in other ways, too, as Betty Hawes of the Avantis pointed out: "Of those who played ball, most were single, so they didn't have to go home and cook dinner." Author interview, Hawes.

64 Kloiber had really hoped that universal child care would become a stronger part of CWLU's agenda in general, but the Union at that time was struggling to withstand sectarian challenges and lost its ability to focus on practical campaigns. Strobel, "When Sisterhood Was Blooming."

65 While taking childcare on themselves, Secret Storm also criticized the Park

District for sexism in the area of child care: "All the park district has to do is *provide child care* and take half the interest in women that they take in men and boys, and then the parks might really serve all the citizens of Chicago." "Women Talk Back," *Secret Storm*, summer 1974. For many women, the sports teams came to represent a way "to be able to get out of the house (some for the first time without their husbands!)." Quote from Secret Storm Report, CWLU Conference (1976).

66 "Women's Sports Struggle Continues," *Secret Storm*, spring 1975.

67 Ibid.

68 For example, as a child, Rinda West assumed she would join a professional baseball team when she grew up. In junior high school, she became "boy crazy" and gave up sports with conscious awareness that an interest in athletics would compromise her status with boys. Author interview, West.

69 Author interview, West; emphasis added.

70 Secret Storm report, 1975.

71 The owner of MS, Marge Summit, referred to Horner Park as "lily white." Author interview, Marge Summit (Chicago, October 24, 2004).

72 CWLU Conference (fall 1974), Outreach Self-Evaluation.

73 Written communication from Marge Summit to author (December 29, 2004), ellipsis in original.

74 Author interview, Summit.

75 This was particularly common in the Twin Cities during the 1960s and early 1970s. Most often, teams went to one another's sponsoring club. Among the AA teams during the 1960s, Hofbrau Haus and Jennings Red Coach Inn sponsored leading teams and were among the most popular postgame hangouts. For most of its lifetime, the Avantis preferred to play without sponsorship, but from 1970 to 1972, they enjoyed the sponsorship of Mr. Days bar in northeast Minneapolis and greatly enjoyed the clubhouse that Mr. Day allowed the team to build above the bar. Alone of all teams to have their own clubhouse, the Avantis turned the unlicensed, unadvertised space into a place for invited softball players from all over to gather, drink beer, listen to music, and play pool.

76 CWLU Conference (fall 1974), Secret Storm Self-Evaluation. MS written as Ms. in CWLU docs.

77 CWLU Conference (fall 1974), Secret Storm Self-Evaluation. In 1972, when the Gay Group (as it was then named) incorporated lesbian liberation into CWLU's political principles, each work group henceforth had to address "lesbian issues" in their annual self-evaluations. Thus, question 4 of the self-evaluation read, "How does your group deal with lesbian issues? Does your group have lesbian and/or straight members? and/or work with groups that do?" This evaluation structure encouraged work groups to acknowledge "lesbians" and "lesbian issues," but also reinforced the view that sexual orientation was a "lesbian issue." The Gay Group initially contributed to this view, by suggesting that CWLU's focus on reproductive issues confirmed the Union's commitment to heterosex-

uality and erasure of lesbians—as though lesbians did not have reproductive concerns. CWLU Gay Educational (September 1972).

78 Strobel, "When Sisterhood Was Blooming."

79 Rinda West began hanging out at Augie's lesbian bar because the bar sponsored a team in the Horner Park League. By 1975, Augie's sponsored a volleyball team, a basketball team, and a softball team.

80 Author interview, West.

81 Secret Storm, CWLU Conference (1976), emphasis in original.

82 Softball as "that old lesbian institution" comes from author interview, Janet Dahlem (Minneapolis, March 7, 1994) and is also historicized as such in Chicago activist and journalist Zipter, *Diamonds Are a Dyke's Best Friend*, and historian Cahn, *Coming on Strong*.

83 All narrators offered essentially the same explanation; Polley and Hawes used the same words. Author interviews: Hawes, Polley. A similar dynamic affected the Soul Sisters by 1976, with the team splintering around interest in and expectations of lesbian socializing off the field. Author interviews, Jan Chapman Sanders (June 22, 2001), Jackie Huggins.

84 Author interview, West.

⊰(Five)⊱ Limits of Women's Autonomy

1 Feminists have long argued that domestic space, far from being a woman's place, has taken shape firmly within male-dominated social structures. In the United States, ideals originating in the early nineteenth century suggest that the privacy of domestic space is a (white, middle- or upper-class, heterosexual) male right, based on the inviolability of his property, including his domicile, his wife, and his progenitors; as owner, he protects his wife's social and sexual status and the purity of his bloodline. Gordon, *Heroes of their Own Lives*; Schneider, "The Violence of Privacy"; Kozol, "Media, Nationalism, and the Question of Feminist Influence." Challenging the historiographic reification of "separate spheres" and the dichotomy between "public" and "private," see Kerber, "Separate Spheres, Female Worlds, Women's Place." On systems that accord property and privacy to males and not females, see Dobash and Dobash, *Violence Against Wives*; Karlsen, *The Devil in the Shape of a Woman*. On privacy accorded to heterosexuals and denied to homosexuals, see Thomas, "Beyond the Privacy Principle," specifically discussing *Bowers v. Hardwick*.

2 Author interview, Pat Murphy (St. Paul, January 2, 1998).

3 The Detroit clinic was built on the "self-help" model established at a Los Angeles Feminist Women's Health Center. Archived documents count Detroit FWHC as the sixth, seventh, or ninth FWHC in the country. Others included, in California: Los Angeles FWHC, Orange County FWHC, Chico FWHC, Oakland FWHC, San Diego Womancare; Jacksonville, Florida FWHC; Tallahassee FWHC; Salt Lake City FWHC; Cambridge Women's Community Health; Atlanta FWHC; and Connecticut Self-Help Clinics.

4 Directors included Cathy Courtney, Jacqueline Stefko, Camilla Cracchiolo, and Christine Hennel.

5 With respect to legal definitions, see Schneider, "The Affirmative Dimensions of Douglas' Privacy," in *He Shall Not Pass This Way*, 978.

6 See Pence and Shepard, "Integrating Feminist Theory and Practice," 282–298.

7 On the relationship of this idea to women's liberation, see Evans, *Personal Politics*.

8 The best study of the Honeywell Project to date is Brockman, "Social Movement Perspectives and Dynamics."

9 Author interview, Sarah Rice Vaughan (October 24, 1996).

10 Early forms of antirape organizations were similar in their reliance on borrowed, minimal space. See Matthews, *Confronting Rape*.

11 Women's Advocates received two VISTA volunteer positions to help staff the operation.

12 Letter of Women's Advocates to "friends," in seek of support for a "Women's House," March 11, 1973.

13 Bernice Sisson, letter, November 1976, to subscribers to Women's Advocates newsletter. A study released by the Community Planning Organization similarly concluded that "physical abuse to women is a serious problem affecting not only the individual woman, but the entire community in which she lives. The problem needs to be acknowledged as a public rather than a private problem." Quoted in Women's Advocates newsletter, November 1976.

14 Author interview, Susan Ryan (Minneapolis, September 8, 1997). Women's Advocates developed this ideal while advocates were housing women in their own homes, beginning in 1972. See Vaughan, "Where It All Began"; Women's Advocates, *Women's Advocates*.

15 Women Strike for Peace was another, earlier movement that confronted the U.S. political and military machinery based on the desires of "housewives" to raise healthy children. Swerdlow, *Women Strike for Peace*.

16 Swerdlow, *Women Strike for Peace*, 6. Also author interviews: Murphy, Bernice Sisson (St. Paul, January 22, 1998), Lois Severson (Shafer, Minn., June 15, 1998).

17 In keeping with laws of incorporation, Women's Advocates had to create a governing structure and by-laws in 1972, but they did not have to replicate conventional structures. Their by-laws granted voting rights to paid staff, volunteers, and "any adult who is being or has been housed by Women's Advocates." Amended June 6, 1975, Article III of bylaws stated, "There is but one class of member, and all members have voting rights." Notes on By-laws meeting, January 9, 1973; March 19, 1975; and June 6, 1975. Women's Advocates Box 1, Minnesota Historical Society.

18 Author interview, Vaughan.

19 Author interviews: Murphy, Lisbet Wolf (April 15, 1998).

20 Author interviews: Murphy, Sisson.

21 Advocates received requests to place forty to eighty women and children each

month; thus they housed roughly half the number of total requests. *Women's Advocates* newsletter, July 1974.

22 Women's Advocates at that time housed its phone line, as well as women, in that apartment. Author interviews: Vaughan, Ryan, Severson. *Women's Advocates* newsletter (August 1973).

23 Author interview, Vaughan.

24 *Women's Advocates* newsletter, March 1974. On funding, author interview, Vaughan.

25 Author interview, Vaughan.

26 *Women's Advocates* newsletter, August 1974.

27 Author interview, Murphy.

28 Author interview, Sisson. Despite advocates' best efforts, institutional trappings encroached on the home, through physical alterations and policy. Sheltering twenty women plus children and occasional pets took a toll on the quaint, less durable furnishings. Advocates conceded that linoleum, institutional bedroom furniture, and commercial-grade appliances would "last" and ultimately keep the house in good repair. Author interview, Murphy; Women's Advocates, *Women's Advocates*, 13.

29 In a six-week phone log for fall 1974, advocates entered over twenty notes about men violently threatening residents and former residents. Still, entries on male violence comprised only about 2 percent of all phone log entries. Women's Advocates, Box 1, Minnesota Historical Society.

30 Paula Brookmire, "Haven for the Battered," *Milwaukee Journal*, August 8, 1976; Linda Picone, "Battered Women: Haven Is a Help," *Minneapolis Tribune*, February 1, 1976; Women's Advocates report to R. H. Rowan, Chief of Police, City of St. Paul (September 30, 1975); *Women's Advocates* newsletter, September 1975 and October 1975; Vaughan, "Where It All Began"; author interviews, Wolf, Murphy, Severson.

31 Picone, "Battered Women: Haven Is a Help," with the subtitle, "Battered: Security Is Essential." Also see Brookmire, "Haven for the Battered."

32 Women's Advocates House Policy (August 1975).

33 For example, the Lavender Theater troupe, a project connected to the Lesbian Resource Center of Minneapolis, often performed at the Noble Roman. Other lesbian-identified women enjoyed the bar, particularly on Sundays when the bar held cabaret-style shows with magicians, ventriloquists, fire dancers, and full-scale theater productions. The bar was also notable for attracting African American men and mixed-race gay male couples. By all accounts, however, it was a "men's bar" in the words of owner Mary Kester, who also explained that she didn't ever know or get to know any of the (apparently few) lesbians who patronized the bar. Author phone interview, Mary Kester (October 12, 1996), Jean Tretter (June 23, 1998); author interview, BJ Metzger and DJ Monroe (St. Paul, August 15, 1996). *Le'sbeinformed* newsletters from 1974 and 1975 note performances of Lavender Theater at the Noble Roman.

34 Author interviews: Murphy, Severson.

35 Author interview, Murphy. Also *Women's Advocates* newsletter, August 1976.
36 Author interview, Sisson.
37 *Women's Advocates* newsletter, September 1976.
38 Author interviews: Murphy, Sisson, Vaughan. First documented report of joint resident/staff efforts, *Women's Advocates* newsletter, June/July 1975.
39 R. H. Rowan, Chief of Police, and Wilfred E. DuGas, Captain, to Maryann Hruby (September 3, 1975).
40 Maryann Hruby to Internal Affairs Department, St. Paul Police Department, September 14, 1975.
41 R. H. Rowan, Chief of Police, and Sergeant L. T. Benson, to Sharon Vaughan, May 16, 1975; Sharon Vaughan to the Department of Police, City of St. Paul, June 5, 1975; Women's Advocates letter to R. H. Rowan, Chief of Police, City of St. Paul, September 30, 1975. And see Women's Advocates to Department of Police, June 5, 1975.
42 Year-long report of Monica Erler, September 29, 1975. Women's Advocates collection, Minnesota Historical Center Archives.
43 *Women's Advocates* newsletter, October 1975. Indeed, it seems that the department held such "responsibility" within a notion of male protection and "permissible violence" in which officers newly adopted the use of force and threats against batterers who disturbed Women's Advocates. For example, a letter from Chief Rowan to Women's Advocates (September 1975) mentions that Rowan talked to the parole officer of one of the men who had repeatedly and violently harassed Women's Advocates (without police intervention). Rowan explained, "[The parole officer] had a discussion with [the harasser] as a result of my request, and has informed me that he felt he had created enough of a threat that [the harasser] would curtail his previous activities."
44 Letter, Women's Advocates to R. H. Rowan, September 30, 1975, demanded: "That any call from Women's Advocates regarding threatened violence be given *top priority* and that the response be *fast* and *considerate*. That the Grand Avenue Squad check [Women's Advocates] throughout the night on an ongoing basis, and . . . the foot patrolman's beat to include Women's Advocates. That there be greater availability of police records and reports made by Women's Advocates. That Women's Advocates be allowed input into the next scheduled in-service training programs for the St. Paul Police Department, in order to make all the police officers aware of what we are trying to do." The police wrote a formal and favorable response eleven months later, in the letter of St. Paul Police Department to Dorothea Scott of Women's Advocates, August 26, 1976.
45 Women's Advocates House Policy, August 1975.
46 Bernice Sisson recounted a very similar experience that caused her to question the cultural context of discipline and violence (author interview).
47 Murphy and others also noted that staff expectations about the superiority of "whole grains, alfalfa sprouts, and recycling," as opposed to "meat, sweet potato pie, chips and pop," imposed class-laden values on residents. Author interview, Murphy.

48 "The Eye of the Storm . . . Thoughts of a Resident," *Women's Advocates* newsletter, November 1975.

49 Ellen Pence, HRA and State Coordinator of Battered Women's Programs for the Corrections Department, quoted in Suzanne Perry, "Beaten Women Reach for Shelter, But Little Is Left," *Minneapolis Star*, September 19, 1978, 1A, 2A.

50 Author interview, Murphy.

51 There was one woman of color—a former client—on Women's Advocates staff when the shelter opened. Residents of color, however, retrospectively represent shelter staff as "white," either because they had no contact with the shelter's only African American staff member, or because they experienced the shelter as a place that, nonetheless, felt "white."

52 Quote from author interview, Eileen Hudon (September 22, 1997).

53 From the moment advocates began sheltering women in their own homes, residents impressed on them that "battered women are *all* women." Author interviews: Hudon, Vaughan, Sisson.

54 Author interview, Hudon.

55 *Women's Advocates* newsletter (November 1976); author interviews: Murphy, Sisson.

56 Quoted in staff diary, selection reprinted in *Women's Advocates* newsletter, February–March 1976.

57 House log, Pat Murphy's notes, November 13, 1974.

58 During 1978, Women's Advocates records show adult residents: 64 percent white (193), 36 percent minority (108), with 24 percent African American, 6 percent Indian, and 6 percent Latina. Women's Advocates Personnel Committee notes, July 25, 1978.

59 Intersectionality is Kimberlé Williams Crenshaw's term, see "Mapping the Margins."

60 This intervention is part of what led activists to rethink concepts of battering, violence, power, and control in the context of intimate partnerships and also seek solutions beyond shelter. Nevertheless, although the movement challenged the extent to which gender hierarchy inhered in heterosexual relationships, as a whole it has not yet deeply challenged heteronormative bias. Many state-funded agencies working against violence against women continue to be structured around heteronormative assumptions that imply that lesbians are indeed outside the system. Narrators who worked at shelters in all three urban areas brought up this conundrum, and it appears in published commentary ostensibly designed to improve shelter services for women in lesbian relationships. Another popular trope revolves around battered lesbians who could not seek shelter because their batterer was on the staff at the shelter. Author interviews: Susan McConnell, Beth O'Neil, and Eileen Kreutz (July 10, 2005); author interviews: Murphy, Sisson, Vaughan. Also see Lobel, *Naming the Violence*; McClennen and Gunther, eds., *A Professional's Guide to Understanding Gay and Lesbian Domestic Violence*; Kaschak, *Intimate Betrayal*.

61 This topic is addressed in Girshick, *Woman-To-Woman Sexual Violence*; Bishop, *The Response of Domestic Violence Shelters*; Coal, "Escorting Lesbian Domestic Violence Out of the Closet."

62 Author interview, Valerie Angers (July 22, 2005).

63 Between 1970 and 1972, Angers started child care centers, was instrumental in getting the YWCA space for the Women's Liberation Coalition of Michigan, and co-created a nationally circulating booklet titled "Stop Rape," among other things. Author interview, Angers.

64 Topics included the Menstrual Cycle and Menstrual Cramps, Abortion Procedures, Nutrition, Meat Substitutes, Mental Health, Menopause, Vaginal Infections/Bladder Infections, Drugs and Alcohol, Birth Control/Alternatives to Pill and IUD, Herbal Medicine, Massage, Body Attitudes, Childbirth/ Technology of Midwifery, Midwifery Slideshow, Relaxation, Female Orgasm/Masturbation, Homeopathy, Yoga, Acupuncture and Acupressure, Medical Aspects of Rape, Writing About Health, and so on. List compiled from "Dear Sisters," letter written by Miriam Frank for the Women's Health Project, April 6, 1974, FWHC Collection, Box 2, Folder 42.

65 Frank, "Dear Sisters."

66 Kaplan, *The Story of Jane.*

67 Many women involved in the Feminist Women's Health Center network traced the origins of the self-help movement to the first FWHC, formed in 1971 in Los Angeles by Carol Downer and Lorraine Rothman. They credit Downer for being the "mother" of the self-help movement. Rothman is acknowledged as the inventor of the menstrual extraction kit that contributed to a relatively easy procedure of early abortion. The L.A. clinic was a leader in the movement in that it was one of the first establishments that offered workshops to women from all over the country who themselves were promoting self-help health care techniques in their own localities. But the movement owes equally to other grassroots sources, such as Jane in Chicago, the Boston Women's Health Collective, the 1970 international distribution of mimeographed copies of *Our Bodies, Our Selves,* and the much more local efforts of groups such as the Detroit Women's Health Project—groups that rarely established clinics but operated through borrowed spaces.

68 "Women's 'Self-Help' Clinic Opens Today in Detroit," *Daily Tribune* (Royal Oak, Mich.), March 1, 1974, 7.

69 Judith Houck, personal communication to author (October 7, 2005); Ruzek, *The Women's Health Movement*; Morgen, *Into Our Own Hands.*

70 I owe thanks to Judith Houck for clarifying this relationship.

71 Elaine Wessel, "A View from the Loop," and author interview, Elaine Wessel (Chicago, June 19, 2003). The health work of the Chicago Women's Liberation Union, Elizabeth Blackwell Women's Health Center in Minneapolis, and Detroit's FWHC all came under criticism for being heterosexually oriented and alienating to lesbians. Each group responded in part by offering special workshops or discussions focused on "lesbian health" that in many ways reinforced

an already constructed distinction. Initially, critics leveled a twofold, contradictory charge: clinics were too focused on reproductive issues ("straight women's issues"), and clinics assumed that reproductive issues were inherently heterosexual. For all its fits and starts, this is precisely the process through which activists clarified relevant lesbian health care that went beyond but included reproductive concerns.

72 Frances Hornstein, "Lesbian Health Care" (n.d.). Hornstein was deeply involved with the Los Angeles FWHC. This piece, written in 1973 or 1974 and circulated widely among women setting up health clinics, discussed the already prevalent "myths" and "differences" among feminist health care workers about the relationship between sexual practice and feminist health care. These myths and differences grew apparent in the context of feminist health clinics.

73 Sexually open partnerships proved more complicated in practice than in theory. The male partners and husbands of the women in the building never fully moved in, though many had fixed up their own apartments. Their ambivalence not only resulted in an apartment cooperative almost entirely inhabited by women and children but also led members to conclude that the experiment, though wonderful for raising children, was not working well enough to continue.

74 The office was located at 8344 Second Avenue. Listed in Frank, "Women's Health," 7.

75 Other women present at the initial meeting included Cathy Courtney, Valerie Angers, Joanne Parrent, Barbara Sutton, and Mary Lempke. Notes from founding meeting, FWHC Collection, Box 2, Folder 1.

76 The Equal Credit Opportunity Act (ECOA, 15 U.S.C. 1691 et seq.) passed the Senate in 1973 and became law in October 1974, largely in response to feminist pressure, including the existence of feminist credit unions. The act "prohibits creditors from discriminating against credit applicants on the basis of race, color, religion, national origin, sex, marital status, age, or because an applicant receives income from a public institution." It did not successfully eliminate discrimination against women seeking loans and sometimes even checking accounts in their own name. It was many more years before lending institutions in progressive states considered gender and marital status to be minor factors in determining credit-worthiness, and lending institutions continue to treat race, color, national origin, and welfare status as major factors.

77 As the FFCU stated, "The field of money and finance is male-dominated, mystifying, and outrageously discriminatory against women. It is not enough merely to pressure that male-dominated system into throwing us crumbs of credit. We must create and control our own financial institutions, set up specifically to meet the needs of women. We need a feminist credit union in order to support each other in our attempts to free ourselves to lead more independent, healthier lives." "Feminist Credit Union," *Her-Self*, 2.5 (September 1973), 3. The idea that women constituted a community that should keep its resources to itself rather than losing them to outsiders has been reiterated

as activism in many forms throughout the United States well through the 1990s. For example, in Detroit in 1980, Her Shelf bookstore attempted to catalog "skills and resources" owned and produced by lesbians so that women could "keep lesbian/feminist money in the women's community where it belongs." *Hershelf Bookstore Newsletter,* February 1980.

78 Author interviews: Angers, Joanne Parrent (July 21, 2005).

79 Author interview, Parrent.

80 The FFCU's Board of Directors was also a diverse group in terms of race and class background.

81 See, for example, Doran, "Breaking Out of the Nest-Egg Mold."

82 Author interview, Angers.

83 For years, many women from the Women's Health Project continued the original mission of offering self-help workshops at a variety of woman-oriented locations such as, by 1976, Her Shelf bookstore in Highland Park.

84 The project wrote a letter explaining to "Sisters" far and wide who had asked for information about how to start a women's clinic, "The Detroit Women's Health Project is not at this time putting a clinic together. The Feminist Women's Health Center, Inc., 18700 Woodward, Detroit, is specifically focused on setting up a clinic, along the model of the Los Angeles clinic." Frank, "Dear Sisters," FWHC Collection, Walter Reuther Archive.

85 The conflicted and cooperative management by the various Women's Resource Center groups did not work. The Health Center and Credit Union preferred to run their own place for their own purposes anyway.

86 Author interview, Angers.

87 "Report on Green Acres Board Meeting held on October 13, 1976," FWHC Collection, Box 1, Folder 3.

88 The original lease was signed by Jacqueline Stefko, for the FWHC, and by Joanne Parrent, for the FFCU. City of Detroit Board of Zoning Letter, November 25, 1974; FFCU Letter to Board of Zoning Appeals, December 18, 1974; Board of Zoning Letter of Approval, February 7, 1975. All files in FWHC Collection, Box 1, Folder 1. The contemporaneous news article that drew popular attention may have been Bunnell, "A Health Clinic and a Credit Union for Women."

89 FWHC Board of Directors Summary (1975–76) shows a steady "Increase in Medical Services" going from 94 women seen in April 1975 to 391 in March 1976. FWHC Collection, Box 2, Folder 7.

90 Conventional medical establishments participated in this backlash, often most clearly by reasserting their own medical authority while challenging women's ability to direct health clinics whether or not those health clinics utilized the services of people with medical degrees. At the same time, conventional medical facilities did respond to the obvious demand for respectful gynecological care. For example, Slater, "Health Center Under Fire"; Lee, "Feminist Target."

91 "Zoning Report" on June 8 neighborhood hearing, FWHC Board Meeting, July 8, 1976. Also "Dear Sisters" letter to Women Acting Together to Combat Harassment, July 8, 1976. FWHC Collection, Box 1, Folder 3.

92 "Report on Green Acres Board Meeting held on October 13, 1976." FWHC Collection, Box 1, Folder 3.

93 Kevin Mumford argues convincingly that obsession with interracial relations and a demand for racially segregated cities specifically motivated Progressive era reform as much as concern about sexual deviance generally. Historical studies of prostitution, urbanity, the state, and morality are numerous. See, for example, Kunzel, *Fallen Women, Problem Girls*; Rosen, *The Lost Sisterhood*; Gilfoyle, *City of Eros*; Walkowitz, *Prostitution and Victorian Society*; Symanski, *The Immoral Landscape*. To date, one of the best reviews of this literature is Gilfoyle, "Prostitutes in History."

94 As historian Kevin Mumford has argued of Progressive era reform, public forces did not work to eliminate sex trade but instead pushed it "elsewhere," out of white neighborhoods and into "interzones" and red-light districts. Mumford, *Interzones*.

95 FWHC letter to Sandy Mullins, Urban Law and Housing, re: June 29 and July 1 meetings with Zoning Board and William Levin, July 20, 1976. FWHC Collection, Box 1, Folder 3.

96 Letter of Detroit City Council to Board of Zoning Appeals (October 5, 1976). FWHC Collection, Box 1, Folder 4.

97 Blair, "City Orders Feminist Health Center to Close"; Morse, "Abortion Center Sues on Zoning."

98 FWHC suspected, but never managed to prove, that tire-slashing incidents were the work of angry neighbors. FWHC Collection, Box 1, Folder 10.

99 For example, one article exposed the corruption of twenty-eight Detroit phone directory listings for abortion referrals. Lucille DeView, "Abortion Referral Agencies under Fire," *Detroit News*, September 14, 1975, 1D, 13D.

100 Michigan Public Act 274 of 1974, also known as Senate Bill 888.

101 Many argued that such "medically unindicated stipulations were designed to harass abortion clinics and raise costs." Full discussion of regulations and impacts is found in Detroit Coalition for Abortion Regulations, "Press Statement," December 21, 1975. FWHC Collection, Box 9, Folder 7. Contributing to a backlash directed at accessible abortions were decreases in many forms of welfare. In November 1975, the Michigan legislature passed a bill preventing Medicaid from covering abortions. Detroit hospitals registered an increase in septic abortions during the three days that the bill was in effect. Michigan's attorney general overturned the bill on a technicality, leaving the strategy open to future use by antichoice activists. *The Sun*, March 11, 1976, 27, 30.

102 Feminist Women's Health Center Newsletter, June 1977, 1.

103 The free clinic movement powerfully took many forms in Chicago, the Twin Cities, and Detroit, as elsewhere in the country, during the 1960s. But because many women seeking respectful gynecological care found most free clinics inspiring but sexist (sometimes known as "the AMA with long hair and beards"), they worked to establish specific women's free clinics—such as the Elizabeth Blackwell Women's Health Center in Minneapolis. Only in the mid-

to late 1970s did feminists begin to make significant inroads into the standard practices and assumptions of "free clinics."

104 The records of suburban free clinics show their predominant customer base to be "young white women." Detroit-area clinic services and statistics pamphlet, FWHC Collection.

105 Deborah Miller (FWHC director), quoted in Cowan and Pack, "The Controversy at FEN," 11.

106 Murphy, in *Minneapolis Tribune*, February 1, 1976.

107 Marlene Travis, chairperson of State Task Force on Battering, in *Minneapolis Star*, September 19, 1978.

108 Author interview, Lisbet Wolf (April 15, 1998).

⟨ Six ⟩ Coffeehouses, Clubs, and "All Women"

The first epigraph at the beginning of this chapter is from the author's interview with Candace Margulies (Minneapolis, February 21, 1994); the second is a quote from Gloria Steinem at the opening of the Feminist Women's City Club on April 9, 1976 (quoted in Williams, "A Downtown Center Pulls It All Together").

1 All quotes from author interview, Candace Margulies (Minneapolis, February 21, 1994). Other sources include author interviews: Candace Margulies (June 2, 2001); Janet Dahlem (Minneapolis, March 7, 1994); *Le'sbeinformed*, December 1975; "Dear Women," letter from Candace Margulies, December 1, 1975, circulated to the community through Lesbian Resource Center, Chrysalis Women's Building, Amazon Bookstore.

2 Askins, "Old Lady, New Life."

3 *Moving Out*, 6, 2 (1976), 6.

4 *Feminist Flyer*, the newsletter of the Feminist Women's City Club, included among its columns one titled "Building a Club," and the next titled "Building an Empire." *Detroit Free Press*, April 9, 1976, 2-B.

5 Author interview, Margulies.

6 Quote from author interview, Margulies; also author interviews: Dahlem, Alix Dobkin (May 20, 2003), author phone interview, Kathy Munzer (June 16, 2003).

7 Author interview, Dahlem.

8 In late 1978, Mountain Moving moved to a Methodist church on School Street, where it stayed for nearly a decade. It then moved to a Methodist church in the Rogers Park neighborhood, then Ebenezer Lutheran Church, and finally Summerdale Metropolitan Community Church in the Andersonville neighborhood.

9 *Gold Flower* (Minneapolis), December 1972.

10 The Chrysalis Women's House, with the assistance of a federal grant, acquired a Victorian house on Stevens Avenue in south Minneapolis in 1973. It housed Chrysalis Resource Center, an organization providing counseling programs on women's health, economics, housing, single motherhood, and chemical de-

pendency treatment programs; the Lesbian Resource Center beginning in 1974; the socialist-inspired Lesbian Feminist Organizing Committee beginning in 1975; and the Black Women's Room in 1976. Chrysalis hoped that the presence of the Lesbian Resource Center would mitigate against homophobia within Chrysalis and signal that the building was a lesbian-affirming space; at the same time, Chrysalis expressed concern that if LRC hung its sign on the building, it would scare too many women away from Chrysalis. Chrysalis had also hoped that the Black Women's Room would mitigate against the white predominance of Chrysalis's clientele, but the Black Women's Room was perhaps too short-lived to have that impact. Chrysalis did ultimately succeed in expanding its service base, after years of coalitional outreach and program-building. Author interviews: Karen Starr (Minneapolis, September 28, 1995), Jo Devlin (Minneapolis, July 26, 1995), Paula Westerlund (Red Wing, September 29, 1995), Anna Stanley (St. Paul, September 25, 1995), Karen Clark (Minneapolis, September 30, 1995).

11 Author interview, Margulies, speaker's emphasis.

12 Minnesota led the nation in the development of chemical-dependency recovery programs. By 1975, programs tailored to specific populations—such as Christopher Street for gays and lesbians—had already become a well-established part of the Twin Cities landscape. The recovery movement in fact shaped much feminist activism as early as 1972; the Wilder Ones softball team, for example, started in part out of a sense that "drinking ourselves to death" was not a desirable way to live lesbian lives. Thus, in Minnesota, no one questioned that A Woman's Coffee House would be "chem-free" from the outset. Many women in fact came to the Twin Cities from East and West Coast cities specifically *because* there they could participate in both recovery programs *and* sober feminist lesbian social spaces. It was not until the late 1970s that the movement reached into feminist coffeehouses and lesbian activism in other parts of the country. Memories of the first several years of the Michigan Womyn's Music Festival, for example, revolve around sharing pot and acid as much as around sharing women's music. By the early 1980s, women's coffeehouses and music festivals throughout the United States had become synonymous with chem-free space. Author interviews: Ida Swearingen (Minneapolis, July 12, 1995), Dahlem.

13 Author interview, Toni McNaron (Minneapolis, January 25, 1994). Also author interview with Margulies.

14 This perception is shared by most narrators, but no one ever attempted to conduct a Coffee House census based on racial identity.

15 Author interview, Clark. The FBI's ostensible explanation for the surveillance revolved around a number of women who had "gone underground" to avoid arrest and were believed to be harbored by feminist groups.

16 Author interview, Margulies, emphasis added.

17 Quotes from author interviews: Jackie Urbanovik (Minneapolis, August 30, 1995), Clark, and Dahlem.

18 author interview, Margulies.

19 Elaine Marsh letter to author (August 4, 1994).

20 Notably, many of these women, after coming out as lesbians through places like the Coffee House, formed groups to sort out "what it meant to be a lesbian in the Jewish community, and to be a Jew in the lesbian community"; coming out as Jewish lesbians, they then helped create the Twin Cities' first gay/lesbian-affirming Jewish congregation. On this trend nationally, see Alpert, *Like Bread on the Seder Plate*. On unnamed Jewish presence in radical activism, see Kaye/Kantrowitz, "Jews in the U.S."

21 Author interview, Laura Altman [pseudonym] (May 28, 2001).

22 Author interview, Stanley.

23 Minnesota Census 1950–59, 1960–69, 1970–79; Conn, *Symbolism in Stone and Glass*.

24 John Howard notes that the terms *sleazy* and *dangerous* not only refer to aesthetic taste and geographic safety but also imply that in gay bars, *too much* sexual display and intercourse were taking place and made a space (e.g., a bathroom) sleazy and dangerous to white, middle-class lesbian sensibilities of the 1970s. Within gay male parlance, *dingy* carries a specifically racialized valiance: a "dinge queen" is a white person who fetishizes and pursues only men of color. John Howard, personal communication with author (October 7, 2002).

25 Letter published in *So's Your Old Lady* and *Le'sbeinformed*, both September 1976.

26 Author interview, Gerry Perrin (Lakewood, Minn., September 20, 1995).

27 Author interview, McNaron.

28 Letter, *So's Your Old Lady* and *Le'sbeinformed*, September 1976.

29 Author interview, Dale Columbus (Minneapolis, February 23, 1994).

30 Interview, Dahlem; also Margulies, Sara Henderson (Minneapolis, September 18, 1995), Urbanovik, Columbus, Perrin, Maude Allen (Minneapolis, September 21, 1995), Jeanne LaBore (October 25, 1995), Robin Holzman (Minneapolis, October 12, 1995).

31 Author interview, Margulies.

32 Author interview, Margulies.

33 A similar dynamic may be seen in bars that function as neighborhood watering holes before 8 pm and function as gay bars after 9 pm.

34 Monique Wittig contended that *language* conflates the female (and not the male) with the sexual. Here I offer an instance in which we may see sociospatial geographies doing just that. See Wittig, "One Is Not Born a Woman."

35 Author interview, McNaron.

36 Author interview, Dahlem.

37 Author interview, Stanley.

38 On the challenges of asserting black respectability against dominant, white supremacy, see White, *Dark Continent of Our Bodies*; Carby, "It Be's Dat Way Sometime," and *Reconstructing Womanhood*; Giddings, *When and Where I*

Enter; Hammonds, "Black (W)holes" and "Toward a Genealogy of Black Female Sexuality"; Higgenbotham, *Righteous Discontent.*

39 The "commodification of Otherness" comes from bell hooks, "Selling Hot Pussy." Historical works that analyze the mutual constitution of race, sexuality, and white dominance include Hale, *Making Whiteness*; Ross, *Manning the Race*; Johnson, *Roaring Camp*; Duggan, *Sapphic Slashers*; Mitchell, *Coyote Nation*; Hall, "'The Mind that Burns in Each Body'"; Pascoe, "Miscegenation Law, Court Cases, and Ideologies of 'Race'"; Stoler, *Race and the Education of Desire*; Fausto-Sterling, "Gender, Race and Nation"; Briggs, "The Race of Hysteria"; Somerville, "Scientific Racism and the Invention of the Homosexual Body."

40 Author interview, Columbus.

41 Author interview, Jymme Golden (Minneapolis, July 8, 1994).

42 Author interview, Clark.

43 Author interview, Kim Hines (December 4, 1995). On the in/visibility of black female sexuality and lesbians, see Omosupe, "Black/Lesbian/Bulldagger"; Hammonds, "Black (W)holes." Also see Peake, "'Race' and Sexuality"; and hooks, *Black Looks.*

44 Hammonds, "Black (W)holes," 138, drawing also on Spillers, "Mama's Baby, Papa's Maybe."

45 Founders' initial visions of the City Club may be appropriately understood in the context of this longer history of women's buildings. As narrators and the documentary evidence indicate, interest in acquiring the City Club as a former Women's Club and converting it to a decidedly Feminist Women's Club motivated the creation of a capitalist financial operating system, the Feminist Economic Network. Alternatively, Alice Echols, one of few Second Wave historians to consider FEN and the City Club, placed this bit of Detroit history in the context of an ideology that she called "cultural feminism." In her narrative, the City Club is an outgrowth of FEN, rather than a catalyst, but both are manifestations of cultural feminism's insular ideology. Echols, *Daring to Be Bad*, 276–282 and passim.

46 Author interview, Valerie Angers (July 22, 2005).

47 Contemporaneous feminist accounts of the City Club debacle were almost uniformly vehement in their attacks of FEN and City Club leaders; many at the time thought it necessary to disassociate from FEN to preserve and move forward with a more left-oriented feminist movement. It should also be noted that all narrators now speak critically of FEN/City Club: not only women who voiced the most critical objections but also those who helped create or who believed in the project at the time.

48 Mary Chase Stratton invented the glaze that made Pewabic Tile famous. Though many have tried to reproduce the glaze, none have succeeded.

49 The Women's City Club continued to function, meeting at the Belle Isle Boat Club and waiting to relocate to the much-awaited Renaissance Center upon its completion. Information on the City Club building is gathered from Silloway

and Company Real Estate listing documents pertaining to 2110 Park Avenue; Eleanor Breitmeyer, "Women's City Club Put Up for Sale," *Detroit News*, 3A (undated clipping); Fast, "Herstory"; Williams, "A Downtown Center Pulls It All Together"; and numerous FEN memos (December 1975), all available in FWHC Collection, Box 5, Folder 32.

50 Author interview, Angers.

51 "Economic Network," *Her-Self*, 4.3 (July 1975), 5.

52 At those meetings, it was already apparent that FEN leaders preferred self-appointment and disapproved of elections and regional representation; they also hoped FEN would encompass all feminist businesses in the country. Those who disagreed with FEN left, some rejecting the whole endeavor that seemed predicated on capitalist means and ends.

53 The offer was contingent on FEN figuring out within sixty days how to finance the purchase and "come up with a package of why this would work." "One of our First Investments," to FEN Sowing Circle from Detroit, December 10, 1975 (within the letter, the author refers to the date of writing as December 11; this date is confirmed by the date of the offer on the building: December 11); "First Week's Gossip," December 11, 1975. FWHC Collection, Box 5, Folder 32.

54 "General Communications" to the FEN Sowing Circle from Joanne, Valerie, Connye, and Beverly, January 1, 1976. FWHC Collection, Box 5, Folder 32.

55 As "Detroit" explained, they had learned that "private insurance companies and pension plans are prone to investing in holding companies and that of course is what we are." They also learned about "venture capitalists, who are not necessarily rich but who know rich people: they apparently are real American dreamers and might be excited by our bringing ourselves up from the bootstraps." "General Communications," passim.

56 This arrangement was to circumvent federal laws prohibiting credit unions from loaning to corporations. FEN's relationship with the Feminist Federal Credit Union strained from the start. Some in the credit union felt that FEN took advantage of the FFCU for ends antithetical to the credit union's original mission. In the heat of the moment, the FFCU Board of Directors compromised its decision-making process, deferring to Parrent and Angers who had worked tirelessly and without pay for two years to build the credit union from the ground up. Three of the eight women requesting loans in fact were on the Board of Directors. Beyond the board, very few credit union members had enough information about the nature of the loans to make an informed vote. The FEN loan totaled a risky 25 percent of the credit union's assets, and once the loans had been made, FEN drained money out of the FFCU much faster than promised. FEN further snubbed the FFCU when, during the grand opening celebrations of the City Club, FEN called its own security guards and the Detroit police to remove forty or so women connected to the credit union from the building. From FEN's perspective, the credit union women (whom they named "dissidents") threatened to ransack files in offices throughout the building and thus constituted a legitimate security threat. The credit union

women, for their part, felt they had legitimate reason to gather the operating papers of FEN and the City Club as related to the loan. The day following the melee, FEN let the credit union back into the building and into its own office. But whatever graces FEN had with the FFCU were lost, and less than a month after the City Club opened, Detroit FFCU withdrew from FEN, moved the FFCU offices out of the City Club, and ceased association with FEN. Quotes from "General Communications." Additional sources include author interview, Angers; Cowan and Peck, "The Controversy at FEN"; Moira, "FEN: Do the Facts Speak for Themselves?"; Barry, "F. E. N."; Robinson, "FEN Again."

57 Author interview, Angers.
58 *Her-Self*, May 1976, 14.
59 *Detroit Free Press*, April 9, 1976, 2-B.
60 *Her-Self*, May 1976, 14.
61 Author interviews: Joanne Parrent (July 21, 2005), Angers.
62 Quoted in *Her-Self*, May 1976, 14.
63 "Editorial Comment," *Feminist Flyer*, 2 (July 1976), 2. Abruptly changing its tone, the next month the club initiated an upbeat membership drive proposing a huge range of entertainment and special activities, asking for volunteer work from members, and effusively praising the women who found fulfillment working sixteen-hour days running the building, praising members, and praising women in general. *Feminist Flyer*, 3 (August 1976), 2.
64 Like the Detroit and Ann Arbor feminists who lodged the original critiques of the City Club's exclusive aura, feminists from afar used that fact to attack the club. *Off Our Backs*, for example, quoted Laura Brown's assertion to the *Detroit Free Press* that "this [building] is the beginning of the feminist economic revolution," to which *Off Our Backs* smugly commented, "And besides, the pool is a fine place to cool off after a hard day in the sweatshops." Moira, "Economic Briefs and Beefs." Though few directly participated in FEN events, the City Club, or in Detroit politics, feminists from all over the country had a high investment in the implications that the City Club would have for the definition, goals, and future of feminism. In response to critics, club leaders made much of the fact that they allowed young women without money to work as interns or as lifeguards until they had earned the membership fee. Williams, "A Downtown Center Pulls It All Together."
65 McDonald, "Alternative Health Care." Although the article praised the health clinic for meeting important public health needs, it was nevertheless published in a column titled, "For Women Only," testifying to the marginal status of women's health within mainstream medical communities at that time.
66 Quoted in Prezzato, "Update," *Detroit Sun*, July 1976, 5, 25. City Club leaders— three of whom had come from the Oakland, California, FWHC—named the City Club clinic the Downtown Detroit Women's Feminist Health Center, making use of the "good reputations" of FWHC. Precisely at the time that the Eight Mile Road clinic was embroiled in conflicts with their neighbors, the City Club clinic name created confusion over whether the Detroit FWHC had

moved downtown. FWHC directors, meanwhile, feared losing their majority white clientele as well as their smaller black clientele, and they filed and won a lawsuit demanding that the downtown clinic change its name. They also wrote letters to the presses, "We wish to clarify that we are in no way associated with their facility . . . or any future named clinic operating out of 2110 Park Ave. in Detroit." The City Club health clinic changed its name to Michigan Feminist Health Care. "Dear Friends," quote from letter from Cathy Courtney, *Her-Self*, 5.4 (August–September 1976), 2. Against charges of racism, one director of FWHC all but blamed Roberts, Carter, and Salters for caring about salary, retorting, "Are we racist because we don't have any black women working here now? They were the ones who were unwilling at the time to work for the subsistence salaries the Detroit FWHC pays. Don't call us racist because they don't want to work here" (Deborah Miller, quoted in *Her-Self* 5.2 [May 1976]: 11).

67 The brochure further explained, "Members will be accepted on the basis of compliance with club rules and standards, including responsibility for the conduct of their guests and support of the basic tenets of feminism." Feminist Women's City Club brochure (spring 1976).

68 "Guidelines for Feminist Women's City Club," 1–2. FWHC Collection, Box 1, Folder 53.

69 Williams, "A Downtown Center Pulls It All Together."

70 Slater, "Conflict Clouds Feminist Club's Finances, Future." The *Detroit Free Press* reported on the "female pushing-and-shoving melee which erupted" at the end of opening weekend, indicating that the fight made visible the conflict between the Feminist Economic Network and "dissident" members of the FFCU who opposed FEN's practices, leading federal auditors to audit the credit union. The *Free Press*'s sensationalist account of the "brawl" contrasted nicely with its characterization of the "low-key atmosphere" pervading the last-minute renovations only the previous week: "There was no haste, no shouting, as one imagined there might have been if men had been handling things." *Detroit Free Press*, April 9, 1976, 2-B; Watson, "US Is Auditing Feminist Credit Union."

71 The reference to "accusations of lesbianism" had its place, in fact, in a wave of hateful diatribes against gays and gay pride that mainstream papers published during June and July of that same summer.

72 Feminist news accounts at the time, and the scant feminist historiographic attention paid to the matter, have focused on the antidemocratic, capitalist ideology of FEN as a national organization and have glossed its connection to the City Club. The Detroit chapter of FEN itself underplayed this connection, promoting FEN as an organization that began purely out of ideology. But my analysis of FEN papers and interviews reveals that virtually all of FEN's offending statements were designed around purchase and management of the City Club building. That is, the building motivated the elaboration and tactical practices of FEN. An alternative analysis that sees cultural feminist ideology as the motivation behind FEN and the City Club, see Echols, *Daring to Be Bad*, 276–282.

73 A draft of the FEN Herstory, for example, described City Club leaders' observations that feminist projects operating on democratic principles and through collectives were the "unhappiest" and "least effective."

74 Parrent became president of the City Club, Laura Brown of Oakland became director, Debbie Law of Oakland became director of the women's clinic within the building, and Barbara Hoke of Oakland was personnel director. In the flurry of communications about purchasing the building, FEN leaders failed to formalize, ratify, or distribute FEN by-laws; as they later explained, "The other things that we've been sending out to you are more of a priority." They drafted the FEN founding history six days after putting an offer on the building and retrospectively asserted that at the founding Connecticut meeting seven months earlier, "Everyone agreed that the Network should see to it that Feminist credit unions were chartered until there was one to serve Feminists all over the world." "General Communications" to FEN Sowing Circle, from Joanne, Valerie, Connye, and Beverly, January 1, 1976; Connye Harper, "Draft of Statement of FEN for the Feminist Movement," December 15, 1975; Joanne Parrent and Connye Harper, "Sowing the Seeds of Feminist Economic Revolution: A Statement on the Feminist Economic Network: Its Herstory, Structure, and Goals," n.d. Related, dated drafts suggest that this was written in early January 1976.

75 As Joanne Parrent explained to critics, "We [the building directors] came together to give everything we had, every ounce of energy, every bit of money, every skill we knew, and every resource we could imagine to create something that would benefit women in this community and inspire women to take on new and imaginative projects throughout the globe." Parrent, letter to Belita Cowan and Cheryl Peck, quoted in *Off Our Backs* 6.10 (January 31, 1977): 16.

76 Of the original board members who approved the FEN loans, three resigned, two were "removed," and three stayed on. Membership pressed for and received open discussion, accountability, and election of a new board. "Alternative Report" from "Concerned Credit Union Officers and Members," signed by fifteen people, including Cathy Courtney (January 1977). The credit union paid no dividends and ceased normal lending practices. Ultimately the FFCU applied for a stabilization grant and initiated a massive letter-writing campaign by women indicating their support for the FFCU. In spring 1978, recognizing the support of FFCU members and the credit union's viability, the National Credit Union Administration approved section 208 stabilization grant assistance. FFCU immediately restored its normal lending policy, and the following year paid out dividends. "Annual Meeting Recap," *Financing Feminism*, spring 1978; "Good News to Members," summer 1978. All in FFCU Portfolio, American Radicalism Collection, Michigan State University.

77 "FFCU Sells 2110 Park!" *Financing Feminism*, fall 1978.

78 Women did not conclude that large women's buildings were out of the question; as if to prove their viability, Parrent left Detroit in 1977 to work at the new, arts workshop–oriented Los Angeles Women's Building. Angers joined

the Women's Building in 1979 to direct its Feminist Studio Workshop. But in contrast to the City Club, the Women's Building eked out its existence on the margins of the economy, relying on volunteer labor and fees for classes. Each of the two buildings it successively occupied were in relatively desolate warehouse districts, and they cost a fraction of what the City Club cost to maintain. Operating from 1976 to 1991, the Women's Building was exceptional in its longevity but was not immune to larger structural factors. The Feminist Studio Workshop, for example, closed after three years due to the increasing financial stress of the era.

79 Carole Downer of the L.A. Feminist Women's Health Center circulated a seventeen-page memo disassociating the Oakland FWHC from the wider FWHC body and refusing support of FEN. The Women's Community Health Center in Cambridge, Massachusetts, issued a position paper that not only censured FEN for its handling of power, its management of the City Club, and its lack of accountability, but also put under fire three Detroit-based groups for compromising the goals of democratic participation and coalition: the Detroit FFCU, the health center within the City Club building, and the Detroit FWHC. *Off Our Backs* and *Big Mama Rag* were the two most widely circulating national papers at the time, each of which carried several substantial and countless short pieces on FEN. *Her-Self*, an Ann Arbor–based paper that specialized in women's health issues, earned national prominence with its extensive coverage of the events surrounding FEN; after the seventeen-page Cowan and Peck article lambasting FEN, scores of people requested subscriptions to *Her-Self*, and others requested an additional five to twenty copies of the article to "distribute widely." Also see particularly *Big Mama Rag*, 4.7 (August 1976): 4.

80 Prezzato, "War Between the Sisters," *The Sun*, May 20, 1976, 27.

81 A Woman's Coffee House community-wide meeting (February 9, 1985), emphasis in original. Thanks to Maude Allen for making this tape available to me.

Conclusion

The first epigraph at the beginning of the Conclusion is from the author's interview with Kathleen Thompson (July 22, 2003); the second epigraph is from the author's interview with Red Helbig (Shafer, Minn., December 4, 1995).

1 Author interview, Thompson.

2 Author interview, Red Helbig (Shafer, Minn., December 4, 1995). Within a few years of that interview, Red Helbig became Russ Helbig. Author phone interview, Russ Helbig (September 17, 1998). I use feminine pronouns in this narrative because Red was not "passing" but seeking entrance as a woman. In other historic contexts or instances in Red's life between the 1970s and early 1990s, masculine or gender-neutral pronouns (*ze*, *hir*) would be more accurate. At the time of our interview in 1998, Russ consistently identified as male.

Thus, my context-specific use of feminine pronouns to describe his history at the Coffee House feels somewhat compromising and lends further weight to the validity of gender-neutral pronouns.

3 Butler famously theorized the heterosexual matrix through which gender is performed and made intelligible; this matrix naturalizes heterosexuality in part by requiring "that certain kinds of 'identities' cannot 'exist'—that is, those in which gender does not follow from sex and those in which the practices of desire do not 'follow' from either sex or gender." Butler, *Gender Trouble*, 19.

4 The mid-1980s saw an outpouring of spatial imaginaries and spatial metaphors to describe ways of conceiving viable feminist interventions in theory and practice. Theresa de Lauretis popularized "elsewheres" and "spaces off," while margins, interstices, and of course borders also gained salience. De Lauretis, *Technologies of Gender*; hooks, *Feminist Theory*; Mohanty, "Cartographies of Struggle"; Modleski, "Feminism and the Power of Interpretation"; Martin, "What's Home Got to Do with It?"

5 Author interviews: Alix Dobkin (May 20, 2003). Nancy Katz (July 12, 2003); Alix Dobkin, "Minstrel Blood: A Song for Lesbians Only."

6 For a materialist feminist critique of theoretical constructions of woman during the 1970s, see Wittig, "One Is Not Born a Woman."

7 Philosopher Kathy Rudy, resisting the recent valorization of public action and visibility, has argued that the feminist revolutions concerning women's intimacies and sexualities were no less revolutionary for being "personal" and taking place in spaces often considered "private." Rudy, "Radical Feminism, Lesbian Separatism, and Queer Theory."

8 The first national festival in 1974, the National Women's Music Festival, held in Champaign, Illinois, did not exclude men, and it has not done so in any of its three successive locations (Bloomington, Indiana, and more recently, Muncie). Between 1974 and 1979, at least six major new festivals were created; between 1980 and 1989, at least eleven; and during the 1990s, at least ten. According to festival historian Bonnie Morris, over twenty major festivals took place each summer during the 1990s. Literally countless smaller festivals emerged, sometimes only lasting one to five years, but drawing hundreds of women. Morris, *Eden Built by Eves*.

9 During the 1970s, many women involved in women-only coffeehouses expressed fear of intrusion by men and transsexual women; in their view at the time, transsexual women were "really men" because they had allegedly grown up with male privilege. This sense of ongoing harassment from men and fear of transsexual women amplified many women's feeling that women's spaces offered strength against inevitable harassment, objectification, and violence; simultaneously, the space and the exclusions solidified—for some—a sense of women as different from men. In the 1970s and 1980s, many coffeehouses and festivals registered explicit fear of MTF people as men hiding in women's bodies. Since the late 1990s, as a direct result of trans activism, a majority of Michigan Womyn's Music Festival participants believe that the festival should

admit MTF people as women-identified people, and more express concern about FTM people as male-identified and testosterone-laden. On research related to attitudes about gender at MWMF, see Barber, "Fish vs. Mammals"; and Koyama, "Whose Feminism Is It Anyway?"

10 Author interviews: Red Helbig, Russ Helbig.

11 Author interview, Candace Margulies (February 21, 1994).

12 Cathy Courtney, "Herstory of Detroit's Relationship to We Want the Music Collective Music Festival (WWTM)," September 1977. FWHC Collection, Box 2, Folder 23.

13 Ibid. Alix Dobkin regularly pushed local communities to define their upper limits of exclusion toward separate space. Author interviews, Margulies, Dobkin; Dobkin, "Minstrel Blood: A Song for Lesbians Only."

14 The policy was a defining one for many. Nancy Katz of Chicago recalled, "When Michigan started to have a separate camp for boys . . . I went to the first three [festivals], and I thought they were wonderful and I loved being in women's space, but I just wouldn't go back after that." Author interview, Nancy Katz (Chicago, July 12, 2003).

15 Author interviews: Anna Stanley (St. Paul, September 29, 1995), Katz.

16 Author phone interview, Kathy Munzer (June 16, 2003).

17 Mountain Moving co-producer Jackie Anderson, an African American woman and advocate of gender separatism as a philosophy and spatial practice, supported the coffeehouse's policies. She acknowledged that separate spaces were predominantly white and hoped that separate space would become more accessible to a greater diversity of women. Over the years, a handful of women of color occupied leadership positions at Mountain Moving, but signs of tension around white predominance persisted. When Munzer explained the mission of the coffeehouse, she initiated the topic of racial diversity: "We've tried over the years to be more diverse and to reach out to more women of color, too. To let them know it's not just—we've always been on the North Side—but to let them know it's not just, we always, over the years, we've always had like a women of color event in February. It's one of our goals, to try to have as many diverse cultural events as we can, different cultures and stuff." Author interviews: Jackie Anderson (Chicago, July 12, 2003), Munzer.

18 A large number of women who attend MWMF also visit Camp Trans. According to research conducted since 1993, a majority of MWMF participants support Camp Trans in its ability to keep questions of gender liberation open, rather than shutting them down with a single answer. For that reason, MWMF likely owes its own survival in part to Camp Trans. Survey of 1993 festival attendees: 80 percent advocated for continued exclusion of men and FTM persons. But 73 percent favored welcoming MTF and trans women, representing a significant change from the mid-1970s when most proponents of women-only space believed that the presence of MTF people would disrupt the perceived safety of woman-only space.

19 See, for example, Emilia Lombardi, "Michigan Women's Music Festival Ends

Policy of Discrimination against Trans Women," Listmgr@nwsa.org (accessed August 22, 2006), www.camp-trans.org; and Koyama, "Whose Feminism Is It Anyway?"

20 Echoing a common defense of MWMF's policy, she believed that the younger generation of gender queers "doesn't understand" the sexism that made women-only space—and feminism—necessary. Munzer has been a member of Mountain Moving Collective since 1981. Author phone interview, Munzer. See also Barber, "Fish vs. Mammals."

Bibliography

Author Interviews

Maude Allen, Minneapolis, September 21, 1995

Laura Altman (pseudonym), May 28, 2001

Jackie Anderson, July 12, 2003, Chicago

Andromeda, Detroit, June 24, 2001

Valerie Angers, July 22, 2005

Antiga, Minneapolis, October 18, 1995

Sandra Aronen, Minneapolis, October 21, 1995

Marty Bergman, St. Paul, October 15, 1996

Beverly, Detroit, June 24, 2001

Martha Boesing, Minneapolis, July 7, 1995

Lois Carlson, Minneapolis, October 15, 1996

Estelle Carole, Chicago, June 30, 2004

Jan Chapman Sanders, Cohoctan, Mich., June 22, 2001;
    phone interview, June 21, 2000

Karen Clark, Minneapolis, February 18, 1994; St. Paul, September 30, 1995

Dale Columbus, Minneapolis, February 23, 1994

Diane Como, Golden Valley, Minn., September 5, 1996

Nancy Cox, phone interview, July 12, 1998

Janet Dahlem, Minneapolis, March 7, 1994, and July 19, 1995;
    phone interview, July 6, 1998

Jo Devlin, Minneapolis, July 26, 1995

Alix Dobkin, May 20, 2003

Denise Dorsz, phone interview, October 26, 2003

Margaret Dousset, Minneapolis, October 6, 1995

Jan DuBois, Crystal, Minn., October 20, 1996

E. Marie, Detroit, June 24, 2001

Jean Eckerly, Golden Valley, October 8, 1995

Dorothy F., phone interview, July 16, 1994

Antoenette Foster, Detroit, June 24, 2001

Ellie Ghostly, phone interview, June 23, 1998

Jymme Golden, Minneapolis, July 8, 1994

Vernita Gray, Chicago, June 20, 2003

Jo Haberman, Minneapolis, August 8, 1995

Barb Hamilton, Minneapolis, November 19, 1995

Barbara Hardison, Madison Heights (Detroit), June 25, 2001

Connie Harlan, Minneapolis, September 10, 1995, and September 16, 1995; phone
    interview, September 16, 1998

Betty Hawes, briefly joined by Sandy, Circle Pines, Minn., July 14, 1998

Ellen Hawley, Minneapolis, August 8, 1995

Jo Heiner, Minneapolis, October 6, 1995

Red Helbig, Shafer, Minn., December 4, 1995; Russ Helbig, phone interview, Sep-
    tember 1998

Sara Henderson, Minneapolis, September 18, 1995

David Hernandez, Chicago, June 29, 2004

Leyla Hill (pseudonym), Minneapolis, September 14, 1994

Kim Hines, Minneapolis, October 1, 1995, and December 4, 1995

Patty Holman, Minneapolis, September 10, 1995

Robin Holzman, Minneapolis, October 12, 1995

Charlotte Howza, phone interview, May 23, 2001; Detroit, October 13, 2000

Eileen Hudon, Minneapolis, September 22, 1997, and October 6, 1997

Jackie Huggins, Barbara Hardison, and Victoria Lollar, Madison Heights,
    June 25, 2001

Jackie Huggins, Charlotte Howza, Victoria Lollar, Virginia Wyat, Detroit,
    October 13, 2000

Eloise Jaegger, Crystal, Minnesota, October 14, 1996

Kelly Jewell, St Paul, October 16, 1996; phone interview, September 9, 1998

Eleanor Josaitis, Detroit, June 25, 2001

Linda Joseph, Minneapolis, June 30, 1998

Nancy Katz, Chicago, July 12, 2003

Polly Kellog, Minneapolis, December 2, 1995

Mary Kester, phone interview, October 12, 1996

Frances Kidd, Minneapolis, October 12, 1996

Jeanne LaBore, Minneapolis, October 25, 1995, November 18, 1995, and
    September 27, 1998; phone interview, December 1998

Carole La Favor, phone interview, July 13, 1998

Virginia Lawrence, Detroit, June 25, 2001; phone interview, June 6, 2000

Annie Lealos, Minneapolis, November 10, 1995

Victoria Lollar, Madison Heights, Mich., June 25, 2001, and Detroit,
    October 13, 2000

Rosemary Lundell, Minneapolis, December 20, 1995

Jan Magrane, Minneapolis, July 20, 1995

Candace Margulies, February 21, 1994, December 2, 1995, and June 2, 2001,
    Minneapolis; phone interview, July 11, 1998

Susan McConnell, Beth O'Neil, and Eileen Kreutz, July 10, 2005

Toni McNaron, Minneapolis, January 25, 1994, and September 17, 1997

Andra Medea, Chicago, June 29, 2004

Donna Mellem, Minneapolis, September 10, 1995; phone interview, October 21, 1995

BJ Metzger and DJ Monroe, St. Paul, August 15, 1996

Hollis Monnett, St. Paul, October 10, 1996

Nancy Montgomery, phone interview, July 5, 1998

Rosie Morin, phone interview, September 22, 1998

Kathy Munzer, phone interview, June 16, 2003

Pat Murphy, St. Paul, January 22, 1998

Judith Neimi, St. Paul, December 5, 1995

Barb Northway, phone interview, June 25, 1998

Mary O., Minneapolis, September 16, 1995

Don Olson, July 22, 1996

Sandy Pappus, St. Paul, October 20, 1995

Joanne Parrent, July 21, 2005

Nick Patricca, Chicago, June 29, 2004

Joan Paulson, Forest Lake, Minn., July 2, 1998

Peggy, Detroit, June 24, 2001

Joyce Peltzer, Minneapolis, October 2, 1995

Gerry Perrin, Lakewood, Minn., September 20, 1995

Linda Polley, Minneapolis, June 30, 1998

Penny Pope and Irene Lee, Whitewater, Wisc., October 10, 2004

Ra, Chicago, October 24, 2004

Ann Reed, Minneapolis, September 27, 1995

Cheri Register, Minneapolis, August 29, 1996

Carol Robertshaw, phone interview, August 17, 1995

Vivien Rothstein, July 17, 2003

Yvonne Roundtree, Detroit, June 24, 2001

Chris Rouse, Minneapolis, September 20, 1995

Pat Rouse, Minneapolis, September 20, 199

Dolly Ruark, phone interview, September 17, 1996

Susan Ryan, Minneapolis, September 8, 1997

Barbara Sandstrom-Tilson, Minneapolis, August 25, 1995

Judy Sayad, phone interview, June 26, 2003

Jim Schulz, Chicago, June 29, 2004

Claire Selkurt, Minneapolis, November 10, 1995

Lois Severson, Shafer, Minn., June 15, 1998

Bernice Sisson, St. Paul, January 22, 1998

Allan Spear, phone interview, August 30, 1996

Mari Stack, phone interview, July 16, 1998

Anna Stanley, St. Paul, September 25, 1995

Karen Starr, Minneapolis, September 28, 1995

Annalee Stewart, Minneapolis, September 10, 1995, and St. Paul, September 13, 1995

Marge Summit, Chicago, October 24, 2004

Ida Swearingen, Minneapolis, July 12, 1995

Susan Terry, Minneapolis, November 6, 1995

Kathleen Thompson, Chicago, September 20, 2003, June 30, 2004, and June 31, 2004; phone interview, July 22, 2003

Jean Niklaus Tretter, St. Paul, July 2, 1996; phone interview, June 23, 1998

Jackie Urbanovik, Minneapolis, August 30, 1995

Rujeania Vance, phone interview, November 17, 2003

Susan Vass, Minneapolis, October 21, 1996

Sharon Rice Vaughan, St. Paul, October 24, 1996

Jude Vesely, phone interview, August 24, 2004

Janice Wagar, Minneapolis, September 10, 1995

Elaine Wessel, Chicago, June 19, 2003

Rinda West, Chicago, June 19, 2003

Virginia West, Detroit, October 13, 2000

Paula Westerlund, Red Wing, September 29, 1995

Lisbet Wolf, St. Paul, April 15, 1998

Donna Wood, phone interview, June 29, 1998

Merlin (Woody) Wood, October 30, 1996, and June 28, 1998

Kerry Woodward, phone interview, July 9, 1996

Mary Z., St. Paul, December 2, 1995

Published Sources

Adams, John, and Barbara VanDrasek. *Minneapolis-St. Paul: People, Place, and Public Life*. Minneapolis: University of Minnesota Press, 1993.

Adams, Kate. "Built Out of Books: Lesbian Energy and Feminist Ideology in Alternative Publishing." *Journal of Homosexuality* 34.3–4 (1998): 113–141.

Adler, Sy, and Johanna Brenner. "Gender and Space: Lesbians and Gay Men in the City." *International Journal of Urban and Regional Research* 16 (1992): 24–34.

Allen, Pamela. *Free Space: A Perspective on the Small Group in Women's Liberation*. New York: Times Change Press, 1970.

Alpert, Rebecca. *Like Bread on the Seder Plate: Jewish Lesbians and the Transformation of Tradition*. New York: Columbia University Press, 1997.

Anderson, Jackie. "Separatism, Feminism, and the Betrayal of Reform." *Signs* 19.2 (1994): 437–448.

Anderson, Terry. *The Movement and the Sixties: Protest in America from Greensboro to Wounded Knee*. New York: Oxford University Press, 1995.

Anzaldúa, Gloria, and Analouise Keating, eds. *This Bridge We Call Home: Radical Visions for Transformation*. New York: Routledge, 2002.

Askins, John. "Non-Sexist and Non-Populated." *Detroit Free Press*, July 9, 1975, 3-B.

——. "Old Lady, New Life: A Club for 'Today's Woman.'" *Detroit Free Press*, April 9, 1976, 1-B.

Barber, Amy. "Fish vs. Mammals: Second Wave Feminism, Transgender Activism, and the MWMF's Womyn-Born Womyn Only Policy Debates." Graduate seminar paper, University of Wisconsin, 2005.

Barrett, Nina. "Women and Children First: The Evolution of a Specialty Market." *Publishers Weekly*, March 27, 1987, 26–27.

Barry, Kathy. "F. E. N." *Off Our Backs*, January 31, 1977.

Bass, Amy. *Not the Triumph But the Struggle: The 1968 Olympics and the Making of the Black Athlete*. Minneapolis: University of Minnesota Press, 2002.

Baxandall, Rosalyn. "Re-visioning the Women's Liberation Movement's Narrative: Early Second Wave African American Feminists." *Feminist Studies* 27.1 (2001): 225–245.

Baxandall, Rosalyn, and Linda Gordon, eds. *Dear Sisters: Dispatches from the Women's Liberation Movement*. New York: Basic Books, 2001.

Beemyn, Brett, ed. *Creating a Place for Ourselves: Lesbian, Gay, and Bisexual Community Histories*. New York: Routledge, 1997.

Bell, David, and Gill Valentine, eds. *Mapping Desire: Geographies of Sexuality*. London: Routledge, 1995.

Birrell, Susan, and Cheryl Cole, eds. *Women Sport, and Culture*. Champaign, Ill.: Human Kinetics, 1994.

Bishop, Lisa. *The Response of Domestic Violence Shelters to Victims of Lesbian Battering: A Survey*. Psy.D. diss., Indiana State University, 1991.

Blair, Betty J. "City Orders Feminist Health Center to Close." *Detroit News*, December 10, 1976, D 1–2.

Blair, Cynthia. "Vicious Commerce: African American Women's Sex Work and the Transformation of Urban Space in Chicago, 1850–1915." Ph.D. diss., Harvard University, 1999.

Boag, Peter. *Same Sex Affairs: Constructing and Controlling Homosexuality in the Pacific Northwest*. Berkeley: University of California Press, 2003.

Boyd, Nan Alamilla. *Wide Open Town: A History of Queer San Francisco to 1965*. Berkeley: University of California Press, 2003.

Boyte, Harry C. *The Backyard Revolution: Understanding the New Citizen Movement*. Philadelphia: Temple University Press, 1980.

Breines, Wini. *The Great Refusal: Community and Organization in the New Left, 1962–1968*. New Brunswick, N.J.: Rutgers University Press, 1989.

——. *The Trouble Between Us: An Uneasy History of White and Black and Women in the Feminist Movement*. New York: Oxford University Press, 2006.

Bricker, Kristen Anderson. "'Triple Jeopardy': Black Women and the Growth of Feminist Consciousness in SNCC, 1964–1975." In *Still Lifting, Still Climbing:*

Contemporary African American Women's Activism, ed. Kimberly Springer. New York: New York University Press, 1999: 49–69.

Briggs, Laura. "The Race of Hysteria: 'Overcivilization' and the 'Savage' Woman in Late Nineteenth-Century Obstetrics and Gynecology." *American Quarterly* 52.2 (2000): 246–273.

Brockman, Vicky Lynn. "Social Movement Perspectives and Dynamics: A Study of the Honeywell Project and WAMM [Women Against Military Madness]." Ph.D. diss., University of Minnesota, 1998.

Brody, Michal. *Are We There Yet? A Continuing History of Lavender Woman, A Chicago Lesbian Newspaper 1971–1976.* Iowa City: Aunt Lute Books, 1985.

Brown, Elaine. *A Taste of Power: A Black Woman's Story.* New York: Pantheon, 1992.

Brown, Ricardo. *The Evening Crowd at Kirmser's: A Gay Life in the 1940s.* Minneapolis: University of Minnesota Press, 2001.

Brownmiller, Susan. *Against Our Will: Men, Women, and Rape.* New York: Simon and Schuster, 1975.

——. *In Our Time: Memoir of A Revolution.* New York: Dial, 1999.

Bunnell, Sandra. "A Health Clinic and a Credit Union for Women." *Detroit Free Press,* November 17, 1974.

Butler, Judith. *Gender Trouble: Feminism and the Subvervision of Identity.* New York: Routledge, 1990.

——. *Bodies That Matter: On the Discursive Limits* of Sex. New York: Routledge, 1993.

——. *Excitable Speech: A Politics of the Performative.* New York: Routledge, 1997.

——. *Undoing Gender.* New York: Routledge, 2004.

Cade, Toni, ed. *The Black Woman: An Anthology.* New York: Signet, 1970.

Cahn, Susan K. *Coming on Strong: Gender and Sexuality in Twentieth-Century Women's Sport.* New York: Free Press, 1994.

Carby, Hazel, " 'It Be's Dat Way Sometime': The Sexual Politics of Women's Blues." *Radical America* 20.4 (1986): 238–249.

——. *Reconstructing Womanhood: The Emergence of the Afro-American Woman Novelist.* New York: Oxford University Press, 1987.

Carroll, Peter N. *It Seemed Like Nothing Happened: The Tragedy and Promise of America in the 1970s.* New York: Holt, Reinhart, and Winston, 1982.

Case, John, and Rosemary C. R. Taylor, eds. *Co-ops, Communes and Collectives: Experiments in Social Change in the 1960s and 1970s.* New York: Pantheon, 1979.

Case, Sue-Ellen. "Toward a Butch-Femme Aesthetic." In *The Lesbian and Gay Studies Reader,* ed. Henry Abelove, Michèle Aina Barale, and David M. Halperin. New York: Routledge, 1993: 294–306.

Castells, Manuel. *The City and the Grassroots.* Berkeley: University of California Press, 1983.

Celine. "FEN, Credit Unions, and the Capitalist System." *Off Our Backs,* September 30, 1976, 4.

Certeau, Michel de. *The Practice of Everyday Life.* Berkeley: University of California Press, 1984.

Chasin, Alexandra. *Selling Out: The Gay and Lesbian Movement Goes to Market.* New York: Palgrave, 2000.

Chauncey, George. *Gay New York: Gender, Urban Culture, and the Making of the Gay World 1890–1940.* New York: Basic Books, 1994.

Churchill, Ward, and Jim Vander Wall, eds. *The COINTELPRO Papers.* Cambridge, Mass.: South End, 2002.

Coal, Carol. "Escorting Lesbian Domestic Violence Out of the Closet: Can Current Paradigms Embrace All Those Who Are Wounded?" Master of Social Work thesis, California State University, Long Beach, 1998.

Cobble, Dorothy Sue. *The Other Women's Movement: Workplace Justice and Social Rights in Modern America.* Princeton, N.J.: Princeton University Press, 2004.

Cohen, Adam, and Elizabeth Taylor. *American Pharaoh: Mayor Richard J. Daley— His Battle for Chicago and the Nation.* New York: Little, Brown, 2000.

Cole, Cheryl. "Ethnographic Sub/versions: Culture–Identity–Politics." Ph.D. diss., University of Iowa, 1992.

Collier-Thomas, Bettye, and V. P. Franklin, eds. *Sisters in the Struggle: African American Women in the Civil Rights-Black Power Movement.* New York: New York University Press, 2001.

Collins, Patricia Hill. *Black Sexual Politics: African Americans, Gender, and the New Racism.* New York: Routledge, 2004.

Colomina, Beatriz, ed. *Sexuality and Space.* New York: Princeton Architectural Press, 1992.

Combahee River Collective. "A Black Feminist Statement." In *All the Women Are White, All the Blacks Are Men, But Some of Us Are Brave,* ed. Gloria T. Hull, Patricia Bell-Scott, and Barbara Smith. New York: Feminist Press, 1982.

Conn, Howard J. *Symbolism in Stone and Glass: A Description of Plymouth Congregational Church, Minneapolis, Minnesota.* Minneapolis: Plymouth Congregational Church, 1949.

Cowan, Belita, and Cheryl Peck. "The Controversy at FEN, the City Club, and the Credit Union." *Her-Self* 5.2 (May 1976).

Cox, Craig. *Storefront Revolution: Food Co-ops and the Counter Culture.* New Brunswick, N.J.: Rutgers University Press, 1994.

Craton, Christine, and Tim Schwab. *Ghosts Along the Freeway.* Videocassette. Produced by Craton and Schwab. Ben Lomond, Calif.: Video Project, 1991.

Crenshaw, Kimberlé Williams. "Mapping the Margins: Intersectionality, Identity Politics, and Violence Against Women of Color." In *Critical Race Theory: The Key Writings that Formed the Movement,* ed. Kimberlé Crenshaw, Neil Gotanda, Garry Peller, and Kendall Thomas. New York: W. W. Norton, 1995.

Davenport, Suzanne. "Go to Bat for Feminism." *CWLU Newsletter,* May 1974.

Davis, Angela. *Angela Davis: An Autobiography.* New York: Bantam, 1974.

De Genova, Nicholas. *Working the Boundaries: Race, Space, and "Illegality" in Mexican Chicago.* Durham: Duke University Press, 2005.

De Lauretis, Teresa. *Technologies of Gender: Essays on Theory, Film and Fiction.* London: Macmillan, 1987.

D'Emilio, John. "Capitalism and Gay Identity." In *Powers of Desire: The Politics of Sexuality*, ed. Ann Barr Snitow, Christine Stansell, and Sharon Thompson. New York: Monthly Review Press, 1983: 100–113.

———. *Sexual Politics, Sexual Communities: The Making of a Homosexual Minority in the United States, 1940–1970.* Chicago: University of Chicago Press, 1983.

———. "Placing Gay in the Sixties." In *Long Time Gone: Sixties America Then and Now*, ed. Alexander Bloom. New York: Oxford University Press, 2001.

———. *Lost Prophet: The Life and Times of Bayard Rustin.* Chicago: University of Chicago Press, 2003.

Detroit Commission on Community Relations. *Annual Report.* Detroit: Commission on Community Relations, 1960.

Deutsch, Sarah. *Women and the City: Gender, Space, and Power in Boston, 1870–1940.* New York: Oxford University Press, 2002.

DeView, Lucille. "Abortion Referral Agencies under Fire." *Detroit News*, September 14, 1975, 1D, 13D.

Disch, Lisa, and Mary Jo Kane. "When a Looker Is Really a Bitch: Lisa Olson, Sport, and the Heterosexual Matrix." In *Reading Sport: Critical Essays on Power and Representation*, ed. Susan Birrell and Mary G. McDonald. Boston: Northeastern University Press, 2000: 108–143.

Dobash, R. Emerson, and Russell P. Dobash. *Violence Against Wives: The Case Against Patriarchy.* New York: Free Press, 1979.

———. *Women, Violence, and Social Change.* London: Routledge, 1992.

Dobkin, Alix. "Minstrel Blood: A Song for Lesbians Only." *Outlines*, May 20, 1998.

———. "Minstrel Blood: The Emperor's New Gender." *Off Our Backs*, April 2002.

Domosh, Mona. "Those 'Gorgeous Incongruities': Polite Politics and Public Space on the Streets of Nineteenth-Century New York City." *Annals of the Association of American Geographers* 88.2 (1998): 209–226.

Domosh, Mona, and Joni Seager. *Putting Women in Place: Feminist Geographers Make Sense of the World.* New York: Guilford, 2001.

Doran, Bernadette. "Breaking Out of the Nest-Egg Mold: Feminists Hatch Chicago's First Women's Credit Union." *Chicago Reader* (February 6, 1976), 7–8.

Drexel, Allen. "Before Paris Burned: Race, Class, and Male Homosexuality on the Chicago South Side, 1935–1960." In *Creating a Place for Ourselves: Lesbian, Gay, and Bisexual Community Histories*, ed. Brett Beemyn. New York: Routledge, 1997: 119–144.

Duggan, Lisa. *Sapphic Slashers: Sex, Violence, and American Modernity.* Durham: Duke University Press, 2000.

Duggan, Lisa, and Nan Hunter. *Sex Wars: Sexual Dissent and Political Culture.* New York: Routledge, 1995.

Duncan, Nancy. "Renegotiating Gender and Sexuality in Public and Private Spaces." In *Body Space: Destabilizing Geographies of Gender and Sexuality*, ed. Nancy Duncan. New York: Routledge, 1996.

Early, Gerald. *One Nation Under a Groove: Motown and American Culture.* New York: Ecco, 1995.

Echols, Alice. *Daring to be Bad: Radical Feminism in America, 1967–1975.* Minneapolis: University of Minnesota Press, 1989.

Enke, Anne. "Pioneers, Players, and Politicos: Women's Softball in Minnesota." *Minnesota History* 58.4 (winter 2002–3).

Escoffier, Jeffrey. "The Political Economy of the Closet." In *Homo Economics: Capitalism, Community, and Lesbian and Gay Life,* ed. Amy Gluckman and Betsy Reed. New York: Routledge, 1997.

Evans, Sara M. *Personal Politics; The Roots of Women's Liberation in the Civil Rights Movement and the New Left.* New York: Knopf, 1979.

———. "Women's History and Political Theory: Toward a Feminist Approach to Public Life." In *Visible Women,* ed. Nancy A. Hewitt and Suzanne Lebsock. Urbana: University of Illinois Press, 1993.

———. *Tidal Wave: How Women Changed History at Century's End.* New York: Free Press, 2003.

Evans, Sara, and Harry Boyte. *Free Spaces: The Sources of Democratic Change in America.* New York: Harper and Row, 1986.

Evans, Sara and Barbara J. Nelson. *Wage Justice: Comparable Worth and the Paradox of Technocratic Reform.* Chicago: University of Chicago Press, 1989.

Ezekial, Judith. *Feminism in the Heartland.* Columbus: Ohio State University Press, 2002.

Faderman, Lillian. *Odd Girls and Twilight Lovers: A History of Lesbian Life in Twentieth Century America.* New York: Columbia University Press, 1991.

Fairbanks, Evelyn. *The Days of Rondo.* Minneapolis: Minnesota Historical Society Press, 1990.

Farley, Reynolds, Sheldon Danziger, and Harry J. Holzer. *Detroit Divided.* New York: Russell Sage, 2000.

Fast, Marcia. "Herstory." *Feminist Flyer,* July 1976, 1.

Faue, Elizabeth. *Community of Suffering and Struggle: Women, Men, and the Labor Movement in Minneapolis, 1915–1945.* Chapel Hill: University of North Carolina Press, 1991.

Fausto-Sterling, Anne. "Gender, Race, and Nation: The Comparative Anatomy of 'Hottentot' Women in Europe, 1815–1817." In *Deviant Bodies,* ed. Jennifer Terry and Jacqueline Urla. Bloomington: Indiana University Press, 1995.

Feinberg, Leslie. *Transgender Warriors: Making History from Joan of Arc to Ru Paul.* Boston: Beacon, 1986.

———. *Stone Butch Blues.* Ithaca. N.Y.: Firebrand, 1993.

Ferguson, Philipson, Diamond, Quinby, Vance, Snitow. "The Feminist Sexuality Debates." *Signs* 10.1 (1984): 102–135.

Ferree, Myra Marx, and Beth B. Hess. *Controversy and Coalition: The New Feminist Movement across Three Decades of Change.* New York: Twayne, 1994.

Festle, Mary Jo. *Playing Nice: Politics and Apologies in Women's Sports.* New York: Columbia University Press, 1996.

Fine, Sidney. *Violence in the Model City: The Cavanagh Administration, Race Relations, and the Detroit Riot of 1967.* Ann Arbor: University of Michigan Press, 1989.

Firestone, Shulamith, ed. "When Women Rap about Sex." In *Notes from the First Year.* New York: New York Radical Women, 1968.

Frank, Miriam. "Women's Health." *Fifth Estate* 8.2 (April 28–May 11, 1973).

Fraser, Nancy. *Unruly Practices: Power, Discourse, and Gender in Contemporary Social Theory.* Minneapolis: University of Minnesota Press, 1989.

——. "Rethinking the Public Sphere: A Contribution to the Critique of Actually Existing Democracy." In *Habermas and the Public Sphere*, ed. Craig Calhoun. Cambridge, Mass.: MIT Press, 1992.

Freedman, Estelle. "Separatism as a Strategy: Female Institution Building and American Feminism." *Feminist Studies* 5.3 (fall 1979): 512–528.

——. *No Turning Back: The History of Feminism and the Future of Women.* New York: Ballantine, 2002.

Freeman, Jo. *The Politics of Women's Liberation.* New York: Longman, 1975.

Gabriner, Vicki. "Come Out Slugging!" *Quest: A Feminist Quarterly* 11.3 (1976): 52–57.

Gardner, Carol Brooks. *Passing By: Gender and Public Harassment.* Berkeley: University of California Press, 1995.

Georgakas, Dan, and Marvin Surkin. *Detroit, I Do Mind Dying: A Study in Urban Revolution.* New York: St. Martin's Press, 1975.

Giddings, Paula. *When and Where I Enter: The Impact of Black Women on Race and Sex in America.* New York: William Morrow, 1984.

Gilfoyle, Timothy. *City of Eros: New York City, Prostitution, and the Commercialization of Sex, 1790–1920.* New York: Norton, 1992.

——. "Prostitutes in History: From Parables of Pornography to Metaphors of Modernity." *American Historical Review* 104.1 (February 1999): 117–141.

Gilmartin, Katie. "We Weren't Bar People: Middle-Class Lesbian Identities and Cultural Spaces." *GLQ* 3 (1996): 1–51.

Girshick, Lori. *Woman-to-Woman Sexual Violence: Does She Call It Rape?* Boston: Northeastern University Press, 2002.

Gissendanner, Cindy Himes. "African American Women and Competitive Sport, 1920–1960." In *Women, Sport, and Culture*, ed. Susan Birrell and Cheryl Cole. Urbana: University of Illinois Press, 1994: 81–92.

Gitlin, Todd. *The Sixties: Years of Hope, Days of Rage.* New York: Bantam, 1987.

Gluck, Sherna Berger. "Whose Feminism, Whose History? Reflections on Excavating the History of (the) U.S. Women's Movement(s)." In *Community Activism and Feminist Politics*, ed. Nancy Naples. New York: Routledge, 1998.

Gordon, Linda. *Heroes of their Own Lives: The Politics and History of Family Violence, Boston, 1880–1960.* New York: Viking, 1988.

Gordy, Berry. *To Be Loved: The Music, the Magic, the Memories of Motown: An Autobiography.* New York: Warner Books, 1994.

Gosse, Van, and Richard Moser. *The World the Sixties Made: Politics and Culture in Recent America*. Philadelphia: Temple University Press, 2003.

Grant, Jaime M. "Building Community-Based Coalitions from Academe: The Union Institute and the Kitchen Table: Women of Color Press Transition Coalition." *Signs* (summer 1996): 1024–1033.

Griffin, Pat. *Strong Women, Deep Closets: Lesbians and Homophobia in Sport*. Champaign, Ill.: Human Kinetics, 1998.

Grimshaw, William J. *Bitter Fruit: Black Politics and the Chicago Machine, 1931–1991*. Chicago: University of Chicago Press, 1995.

Habermas, Jürgen. *The Structural Transformation of the Public Sphere: An Inquiry into a Category of Bourgeois Society*. Trans. Thomas Burger. Cambridge, Mass.: MIT Press, 1989.

Halberstam, Judith. *Female Masculinity*. Durham: Duke University Press, 1998.

——. *In a Queer Time and Place: Transgender Bodies, Subcultural Lives*. New York: New York University Press, 2005.

Hale, Grace Elizabeth. *Making Whiteness: The Culture of Segregation in the South, 1890–1940*. New York: Vintage, 1998.

Hall, Jacquelyn Dowd. "'The Mind that Burns in Each Body': Women, Rape, and Racial Violence." In *Powers of Desire: The Politics of Sexuality*, edited by Ann Snitow, Christine Stansell, and Sharon Thompson. New York: Monthly Review Press, 1983: 328–49.

Hammonds, Evelynn. "Black (W)holes and the Geometry of Black Female Sexuality." *differences: A Journal of Feminist Cultural Studies* 6.2 (spring 1994): 126–145.

——. "Toward a Genealogy of Black Female Sexuality: The Problematic of Silence." In *Feminist Genealogies, Colonial Legacies, Democratic Futures*, ed. M. Jacqui Alexander and Chandra Talpade Mohanty. New York: Routledge, 1997: 170–182.

Hartigan, John Jr. "Locating White Detroit." In *Displacing Whiteness: Essays in Social and Cultural Criticism*, ed. Ruth Frankenberg. New York: Routledge, 1977: 180–213.

——. *Racial Situations: Class Predicaments of Whiteness in Detroit*. Princeton, N.J.: Princeton University Press, 1999.

Hartman, Douglas. *Race, Culture, and the Revolt of the Black Athlete: The 1968 Olympics Protest and Their Aftermath*. Chicago: University of Chicago Press, 2003.

Harvey, David. *Justice, Nature and the Geography of Difference*. Cambridge: Blackwell, 1996.

Hewitt, Nancy and Susan Lebsock, eds. *Visible Women*. Chapel Hill: University of North Carolina Press, 1993.

Higginbotham, Evelyn Brooks. "African American Women's History and the Metalanguage of Race." *Signs* 17.2 (1992).

——. *Righteous Discontent: The Women's Movement in the Black Baptist Church, 1880–1920*. Cambridge, Mass.: Harvard University Press, 1993.

Hirsch, Arnold R. *Making the Second Ghetto: Race and Housing in Chicago 1940– 1960.* New York: Cambridge University Press, 1983.

hooks, bell. *Feminist Theory: From Margin to Center.* Boston: South End Press, 1984.

——. *Black Looks: Race and Representation.* Boston: South End Press, 1990.

——. "Selling Hot Pussy: Representations of Black Female Sexuality in the Cultural Marketplace." In *Black Looks: Race and Representation,* ed. bell hooks. Boston: South End Press, 1992: 61–76.

Howard, John. *Men Like That: A Southern Queer History.* Chicago: University of Chicago Press, 1999.

Hull, Gloria T., Patricia Bell Scott, and Barbara Smith, eds. *All the Women Are White, All the Blacks are Men, But Some of Us Are Brave.* New York: Feminist Press, 1982.

Hunter, Nan. "Contextualizing the Sexuality Debates: A Chronology." In *Sex Wars: Sexual Dissent and Political Culture,* ed. Lisa Duggan and Nan D. Hunter. New York: Routledge, 1995.

Ingram, Gordon Brent, Anne-Marie Bouthillette, and Yolanda Retter, eds. *Queers in Space: Communities, Public Places, Sites of Resistance.* Seattle: Bay Press, 1997.

Johnson, E. Patrick. "'Quare' Studies, or (Almost) Everything I know About Queer Studies I Learned from My Grandmother." In *Black Queer Studies: A Critical Anthology,* ed. E. Patrick Johnson and Mae Henderson. Durham: Duke University Press, 2005: 124–157.

Johnson, Marilyn S. "Gender, Race and Rumors: Re-Examining the 1943 Race Riots." *Gender and History* 10.2 (August 1998): 252–277.

Johnson, Susan. *Roaring Camp: The Social World of the California Gold Rush.* New York: W. W. Norton, 2001.

Kane, Mary Jo. "Resistance/Transformation of the Oppositional Binary: Exposing Sport as a Continuum." *Journal of Sport and Social Issues* 19 (1995): 213–240.

Kaplan, Laura. *The Story of Jane: The Legendary Underground Feminist Abortion Service.* New York: Pantheon, 1995.

Kaplan, Temma. *Crazy for Democracy: Women in Grassroots Movements.* New York: Routledge, 1997.

Karlsen, Carol. The *Devil in the Shape of a Woman: Witchcraft in Colonial New England.* New York: Norton, 1987.

Kaschak, Ellyn. *Intimate Betrayal: Domestic Violence in Lesbian Relationships.* Binghamton, N.Y.: Haworth Press, 2002.

Kaye/Kantrowitz, Melanie. "Jews in the U.S.: The Rising Costs of Whiteness." In *Names We Call Home: Autobiography on Racial Identity,* ed. Becky Thompson and Sangeeta Tyagi. New York: Routledge, 1996: 121–137.

Keating, Ann Durkin. *Building Chicago: Suburban Developers and the Creation of a Divided Metropolis.* Urbana: University of Illinois Press, 2002.

Kennedy, Elizabeth, and Madeline Davis. *Boots of Leather, Slippers of Gold: The History of a Lesbian Community.* New York: Routledge, 1993.

Kennedy, Leigh and Susan Edwards. "Lesbian Head Changes." *Lavender Woman* (September 1972): 9.

Kenyon, Amy Maria. *Dreaming Suburbia: Detroit and the Production of Postwar Space and Culture*. Detroit: Wayne State University Press, 2004.

Kerber, Linda. "Separate Spheres, Female Worlds, Women's Place: The Rhetoric Women's History." *Journal of American History* 71 (1988): 9–39.

Koedt, Anne. "The Myth of the Vaginal Orgasm." In *Voices from Women's Liberation*, ed. Leslie Tanner. New York: New American Library, 1970.

Koivisto, Mickey. "Honoring Women Who Honor Women." *Lavender Lifestyles*, September 29, 1995, 26.

Koyama, Emi. "Whose Feminism Is It Anyway? The Unspoken Racism of the Trans Inclusion Debate." In *The Transgender Studies Reader*, ed. Susan Stryker and Stephen Whittle. New York: Routledge, 2006: 698–705.

Kozol, Wendy. "Media, Nationalism, and the Question of Feminist Influence." *Signs* 20.3 (spring 1995): 646–667.

———. *Life's America: Family and Nation in Postwar Photojournalism*. Philadelphia: Temple University Press, 1994.

Kunzel, Regina. *Fallen Women, Problem Girls: Unmarried Mothers and Professionalization*. New Haven, Conn.: Yale University Press, 1993.

LaGrand, James. *Indian Metropolis: Native Americans in Chicago, 1945–1975*. Urbana: University of Illinois Press, 2002.

Landes, Joan. *Women and the Public Sphere in the Age of the French Revolution*. Ithaca, N.Y.: Cornell University Press, 1988.

Laumann, Edward, Stephen Ellingson, Jenna Mahay, Anthony Paik, and Yoosik Youm, *The Sexual Organization of the City*. Chicago: University of Chicago Press, 2004.

Lauria, Mickey, and Lawrence Knopp. "Toward an Analysis of the Role of Gay Communities in the Urban Renaissance." *Urban Geography* 6 (1995): 152–169.

Lee, Cynthia. "Feminist Target: The Ob-Gyn Man." *Detroit News*, February 5, 1978, 1C, 8–9C.

Lefebvre, Henri. *The Production of Space*. Oxford: Blackwell, 1991.

Lobel, Kerry. *Naming the Violence: Speaking Out About Lesbian Battering*. Emeryville, Calif.: Seal Press, 1986.

Lorde, Audre. *Zami: A New Spelling of My Name*. Trumansburg, N.Y.: Crossing Press, 1982.

———. *Sister Outsider*. Trumansburg, N.Y.: Crossing Press, 1984.

Low, Setha, and Neil Smith, eds. *The Politics of Public Space*. New York: Routledge, 2006.

Low, Setha, Dana Taplin, and Suzanne Scheld. *Rethinking Urban Parks: Public Space and Cultural Diversity*. Austin: University of Texas Press, 2005.

Manalansan, Martin F., IV. *Global Divas: Filipino Gay Men in the Diaspora*. Durham: Duke University Press, 2003.

Martin, Biddy. "What's Home Got to Do With It?" In *Feminist Studies/Critical Studies*, ed. Teresa de Lauretis. Bloomington: Indiana University Press, 1986: 191–212.

———. "Sexualities without Genders and Other Queer Utopias." In *Coming Out of Feminism?* ed. Mandy Merck, Naomi Segal, and Elizabeth Wright. London: Blackwell, 1998: 11–35.

Martin, Del, and Phyllis Lyon. *Lesbian/Woman*. San Francisco: Glide, 1972.

Mast, Robert H., ed. *Detroit Lives*. Philadelphia: Temple University Press, 1994.

Mason, Karen, and Carol Lacey, *Women's History Tour of the Twin Cities*. Minneapolis: Nodin, 1982.

Massey, Doreen. "Power–Geometry and a Progressive Sense of Place." In *Mapping the Futures: Local Cultures, Global Change*, ed. Jon Bird, et al. London: Routledge, 1993.

———. *Space, Place, and Gender*. Minneapolis: University of Minnesota Press, 1994.

Matthesen, Elise. "Amazon Celebrates Silver Anniversary." *Lavender Lifestyles*, September 29, 1995, 25.

Matthews, Nancy. *Confronting Rape: The Feminist Anti-Rape Movement and the State*. London: Routledge, 1994.

McBride, Dwight A. *Why I Hate Abercrombie and Fitch: Essays on Race and Sexuality*. New York: New York University, 2005.

McClennen, Joan, and John Gunther, eds. *A Professional's Guide to Understanding Gay and Lesbian Domestic Violence: Understanding Practice Interventions*. Lewiston, N.Y.: Edwin Mellen Press, 1999.

McDonald, Maureen. "Alternative Health Care." *Medical Center News* (Detroit), June 9, 1976, 4.

McDowell, Linda. *Gender, Identity, and Place: Understanding Feminist Geographies*. Minneapolis: University of Minnesota Press, 1999.

Mears, Loretta. "I'm Hurt . . . I'm Angry." *Lavender Woman*, July 1972, 4.

Medea, Andra, and Kathleen Thompson. *Against Rape*. New York: Farrar, Straus and Giroux, 1974.

Mendel-Reyes, Marta. *Reclaiming Democracy: The Sixties in Politics and Memory*. New York: Routledge, 1995.

Messner, Michael A. *Taking the Field: Women Men and Sports*. Minneapolis: University of Minnesota Press, 2002.

Messner, Michael, and Don Sabo, ed. *Sport, Men, and the Gender Order*. Champaign, Ill.: Human Kinetics, 1990.

Meyerowitz, Joanne. *How Sex Changed: A History of Transsexuality in the United States*. Cambridge, Mass.: Harvard University Press, 2004.

Meyerowitz, Joanne, ed. *Not June Cleaver: Women and Gender in Postwar America, 1945–1960*. Philadelphia: Temple University Press, 1994.

Millet, Larry. *Lost Twin Cities*. Minneapolis: Minnesota Historial Society Press, 1992.

Mitchell, Pablo. *Coyote Nation: Sexuality, Race, and Conquest in Modernizing New Mexico, 1880–1920*. Chicago: University of Chicago Press, 2005.

Modleski, Tania. "Feminism and the Power of Interpretation: Some Critical Readings." In *Feminist Studies: Critical Studies*, ed. Teresa de Lauretis. Bloomington: Indiana University Press, 1986: 121–138.

Mohanty, Chandra Talpade. "Cartographies of Struggle: Third World Women and the Politics of Feminism." In *Third World Women and the Politics of Feminism*, ed. Chandra Talpade Mohanty. Bloomington: University of Indiana Press, 1991: 1–47.

Moira, Fran. "Economic Briefs and Beefs." *Off Our Backs* 6.3 (May 31, 1976): 4.

——. "FEN: Do the Facts Speak for Themselves?" *Off Our Backs* 6.6 (September 30, 1976): 5.

Moon, Elaine Latzman. *Untold Tales, Unsung Heroes: An Oral History of Detroit's African American Community, 1918–1967*. Detroit: Wayne State University Press, 1993.

Moraga, Cherríe, and Gloria Anzaldúa. *This Bridge Called My Back: Writings by Radical Women of Color*. Watertown, Mass.: Persephone Press, 1981.

Morgan, Tracy. "Butch-Femme and the Politics of Identity." In *Sisters, Sexperts, Queers*, ed. Arlene Stein. New York: Plume, 1993.

Morgen, Sandra. *Into Our Own Hands: The Women's Health Movement in the United States, 1969–1990*. New Brunswick, N.J.: Rutgers University Press, 2002.

Morris, Bonnie J. *Eden Built by Eves: The Culture of Women's Music Festivals*. Boston: Alyson, 1999.

Morse, Susan. "Abortion Center Sues on Zoning." *Detroit Free Press*, December 14, 1976.

Mosbacher, Dee, dir. *Radical Harmonies*. San Francisco: Woman Vision, 2002.

Mumford, Kevin. *Interzones: Black/White Sex Districts in Chicago and New York in the Early Twentieth Century*. New York: Columbia University Press, 1997.

Murphy, Kevin. "Walking the Queer City." *Radical History Review* 62 (spring 1995): 195–201.

Myslik, Wayne D. "Renegotiating the Social/Sexual Identities of Places: Gay Communities as Safe Havens or Sites of Resistance?" In *Body Space: Destabilizing Geographies of Gender and Sexuality*, ed. Nancy Duncan. New York: Routledge, 1996.

Newton, Esther. *Margaret Mead Made Me Gay: Personal Essays, Public Ideas*. Durham: Duke University Press, 2000.

Omosupe, Ekua. "Black/Lesbian/Bulldagger." *Differences* 3.2 (1991): 101–111.

Parrent, Joanne. Letter to Belita Cowan and Cheryl Peck. *Her-Self* 5.3 (July 1976): 5.

Pascoe, Peggy. "Miscegenation Law, Court Cases, and Ideologies of 'Race' in Twentieth Century America." In *Sex, Love, Race: Crossing Boundaries in North American History*, ed. Martha Hodes. New York: New York University Press, 1999.

Patton, Cindy, and Benigno Sánchez-Eppler, eds. *Queer Diasporas*. Durham: Duke University Press, 2000.

Payne, Charles. *I've Got the Light of Freedom: The Organizing Tradition and the Mississippi Freedom Struggle*. Berkeley: University of California Press, 1995.

Peake, Linda. "'Race' and Sexuality: Challenging the Patriarchal Structure of Urban Social Space." *Environment and Planning D: Society and Space* 11 (1993): 415–432.

Pence, Ellen, and Melanie Shepard. "Integrating Feminist Theory and Practice: The Challenge of the Battered Women's Movement." In *Feminist Perspectives on Wife Abuse*, ed. Kersti Yllö and Michele Bograd. London: Sage, 1988: 282–298.

Perez, Gina M. *The Near Northwest Side Story: Migration, Displacement, and Puerto Rican Families*. Berkeley: University of California Press, 2004.

Portelli, Alessandro. *The Death of Luigi Trastulli and Other Stories: Form in Oral History*. Albany: State University of New York Press, 1991.

Prezzato, Jan. "Update." *Detroit Sun*, July 1976, 5, 25.

———. "War Between the Sisters." *The Sun*, May 20, 1976, 27.

Probyn, Elspeth. "Lesbians in Space: Gender, Sex, and the Structure of Missing." *Gender Place and Culture* 2.1 (1995): 77–84.

Radicalesbians. *The Woman Identified Woman*. Pittsburgh: KNOW, 1970.

Ramos-Zayas, Ana Y. *National Performances: The Politics of Class, Race, and Space in Puerto Rican Chicago*. Chicago: University of Chicago Press, 2003.

Retzloff, Tim. " 'Seer' or Queer? Postwar Fascination with Detroit's Prophet Jones." *GLQ* 8.3 (2002): 271–296.

———. "Detroit." In *GLBTQ: An Encyclopedia of Gay, Lesbian, Bisexual, Transgender, and Queer Culture*. www.glbtq.com/socialsciences/detroit.html (accessed September 20, 2005).

Riley, Denise. *"Am I that Name?" Feminism and the Category of 'Women' in History*. Minneapolis: University of Minnesota Press, 1988.

Robinson, Julie. "FEN Again: Dissension Thrives among Detroit Feminists." *Big Mama Rag* 4.5 (May 1976): 1, 14.

Rose, Gillian. *Feminism and Geography: The Limits of Geographical Knowledge*. Minneapolis: University of Minnesota Press, 1993.

Rosen, Ruth. *The Lost Sisterhood: Prostitution in America, 1900–1918*. Baltimore, Md.: Johns Hopkins University Press, 1982.

———. *The World Split Open: How the Modern Women's Movement Changed America*. New York: Viking, 2000.

Rosheim, David. *The Other Minneapolis: The Rise and Fall of the Gateway, The Old Minneapolis Skid Row*. Maquoketa, Iowa: Andromeda, 1978.

Ross, Marlon B. *Manning the Race: Reforming Black Men in the Jim Crow Era*. New York: New York University Press, 2004.

———. "Beyond the Closet as a Raceless Paradigm." In *Black Queer Studies: A Critical Anthology*, ed. E. Patrick Johnson and Mae Henderson. Durham: Duke University Press, 2005: 161–188.

Rossinow, Doug. *The Politics of Authenticity: Liberalism, Christianity, and the New Left in America*. New York: Columbia University Press, 1998.

Roth, Benita. *Separate Roads to Feminism: Black, Chicana and White Feminist Movements in America's Second Wave*. Cambridge: Cambridge University Press, 2004.

Roy, Camille. "Speaking in Tongues." In *Sisters, Sexperts, Queers,* ed. Arlene Stein. New York: Plume, 1993.

Royko, Mike. "Going to Bat for Feminism." *Chicago Daily News,* April 30, 1974.

———. "And in this Corner . . ." *Chicago Daily News,* May 3, 1974.

Rubin, Gayle. "The Traffic in Women: Notes on the 'Political Economy' of Sex." In *Toward an Anthropology of Women,* ed. Rayna Reiter. New York: Monthly Review, 1975.

———. "Thinking Sex: Notes for a Radical Theory of the Politics of Sexuality." In *Pleasure and Danger: Exploring Female Sexuality,* ed. Carol Vance. London: Routledge and Kegan Paul, 1984.

Rudy, Kathy. "Radical Feminism, Lesbian Separatism, and Queer Theory." *Feminist Studies* 27.1 (spring 2001): 191–200.

Rupp, Leila. "Sexuality and Politics in the Early Twentieth Century." *Feminist Studies* 23.3 (1997): 577–605.

———. *A Desired Past: A Short History of Same-Sex Love in America.* Chicago: University of Chicago Press, 1999.

Rupp, Leila, and Verta Taylor. *Survival in the Doldrums: The American Women's Rights Movement 1945 to the 1960s.* New York: Oxford University Press, 1987.

Ruzek, Sheryl Burt. *The Women's Health Movement: Feminist Alternatives to Medical Control.* New York: Praeger, 1978.

Ryan, Barbara, ed. *Identity Politics in the Women's Movement.* New York: New York University Press, 2001.

Ryan, Mary. *Women in Public: Between Banners and Ballots, 1825–1880.* Baltimore, Md.: Johns Hopkins University Press, 1990.

Schneider, Elizabeth M. "The Affirmative Dimensions of Douglas' Privacy." In *He Shall Not Pass This Way Again: The Legacy of Justice William O. Douglas,* ed. Stephen Wasby. Pittsburgh: University of Pittsburgh Press, 1991.

———. "The Violence of Privacy." In *The Public Nature of Private Violence: The Discovery of Domestic Abuse,* ed. Martha Fineman and Roxanne Mykitiuk. London: Routledge, 1994: 36–58.

Schulz, Debra. *Going South: Jewish Women in the Civil Rights Movement.* New York: New York University Press, 2001.

Seidman, Steven. "Identity Politics in a 'Postmodern' Gay Culture." In *Fear of a Queer Planet,* ed. Michael Warner. Minneapolis: University of Minnesota Press, 1993.

Seligman, Amanda I. *Block by Block: Neighborhoods and Public Policy on Chicago's West Side.* Chicago: University of Chicago Press, 2005.

Shokeid, Moshe. *A Gay Synagogue in New York.* New York: Columbia University Press, 1995.

Shulman, Alix Kate. "Sex and Power: Sexual Bases of Radical Feminism." *Signs* 5 (1990): 590–604.

Sklar, Kathryn Kish. *Florence Kelley and the Nation's Work: The Rise of Women's Political Culture, 1830–1900.* New Haven, Conn.: Yale University Press, 1995.

Slater, Charlotte. "Health Center Under Fire: Doctors Attack Feminist Training Program for Self-Cervical Exams." *Detroit News,* April 21, 1976, 1–3G.

——. "Conflict Clouds Feminist Club's Finances, Future." *Detroit News*, July 7, 1976, 1–2C.

Smith, Barbara, ed. *Home Girls: A Black–Feminist Anthology*. New York: Kitchen Table, 1983.

Smith, Robert. *Minneapolis-St. Paul: The Cities, Their People*. Helena, Mt.: American Geographic, 1988.

Smith, Suzanne E. *Dancing in the Streets: Motown and the Cultural Politics of Detroit*. Cambridge, Mass.: Harvard University Press, 1999.

Soja, Edward. *Postmodern Geographies: The Reassertion of Space in Critical Social Theory*. London: Verso, 1989.

Solomon, Susan G. *American Playgrounds: Revitalizing Community Space*. Lebanon, N.H.: University Press of New England, 2005.

Somerville, Siobhan. "Scientific Racism and the Invention of the Homosexual Body." In *The Gender Sexuality Reader: Culture, History, Political Economy*, ed. Roger Lancaster and Micaela di Leonardo. London: Routledge, 1997: 37–52.

Spain, Daphne. *Gendered Spaces*. Chapel Hill: University of North Carolina Press, 1992.

Spillers, Hortense. "Mama's Baby, Papa's Maybe: An American Grammar Book." *Diacritics* 17.2 (1987): 65–81.

Springer, Kimberly. *Living for the Revolution*. Durham: Duke University Press, 2004.

Stanko, Elizabeth. "Fear of Crime and the Myth of the Safe Home: A Feminist Critique of Criminology." In *Feminist Perspectives on Wife Abuse*, ed. Kersti Yllö and Michele Bograd. London: Sage, 1988.

Stansell, Christine. *City of Women: Sex and Class in New York: 1789–1860*. Champaign: University of Illinois Press, 1987.

Starr, Karen. "Fighting for a Future: Farm Women of the Nonpartisan League." *Minnesota History*, summer 1983, 255–262.

Stein, Arlene. "The Year of the Lustful Lesbian." In *Sisters, Sexperts, Beyond the Lesbian Nation*, ed. Arlene Stein. New York: Plume, Penguin, 1993.

——. *Sex and Sensibility: Stories of a Lesbian Generation*. Berkeley: University of California Press, 1997.

——. *Shameless: Sexual Dissidence in American Culture*. New York: New York University Press, 2006.

Stein, Marc. *City of Sisterly and Brotherly Loves: Lesbian and Gay Philadelphia, 1945–1972*. Chicago: University of Chicago Press, 2000.

Stoler, Ann. *Race and the Education of Desire: Foucault's History of Sexuality and the Colonial Order of Things*. Durham: Duke University Press, 1996.

Strobel, Peg. "Where Feminism Was Happening: The Chicago Womens Liberation Union of the 1970s." Unpublished manuscript in author's possession.

——. "When Sisterhood Was Blooming." Unpublished manuscript draft in author's possession.

Sugrue, Thomas. *The Origins of the Urban Crisis: Race and Inequality in Postwar Detroit*. Princeton, N.J.: Princeton University Press, 1996.

Swerdlow, Amy. *Women Strike for Peace: Traditional Motherhood and Radical Politics in the 1960s.* Chicago: University of Chicago Press, 1993.

Symanski, Richard. *The Immoral Landscape: Female Prostitution in Western Societies.* Toronto: Butterworths, 1981.

Taylor, Verta, and Leila Rupp. "Women's Culture and Lesbian Feminist Activism: A Reconsideration of Cultural Feminism." *Signs* 19 (autumn 1993): 32–61.

Thomas, Kendall. "Beyond the Privacy Principle." *Columbia Law Review* 92 (1992): 1440.

Thompson, Becky. "Multiracial Feminism: Recasting the Chronology of Second Wave Feminism," *Feminist Studies* 28.2 (summer 2002): 337–360.

Thompson, Heather Ann. *Whose Detroit? Politics, Labor, and Race in a Modern American City.* Ithaca, N.Y.: Cornell University Press, 2001.

Thorpe, Rochella. "'A house where queers go': African-American Lesbian Nightlife in Detroit, 1940–1975." In *Inventing Lesbian Cultures in America,* ed. Ellen Lewin. Boston: Beacon, 1996: 40–61.

——. "The Changing Face of Detroit's Lesbian Bars, 1940–1975." In *Creating a Place For Ourselves: Lesbian, Gay, and Bisexual Community Histories,* ed. Brett Beemyn. New York: Routledge, 1997: 72–86.

U.S. Bureau of the Census. *Census of Population and Housing, 1960.* Washington: U.S. Bureau of the Census, 1960.

——. *Census of Population and Housing, 1970.* Washington: U.S. Bureau of the Census, 1970.

——. *Census of Population and Housing, 1980.* Washington: U.S. Bureau of the Census, 1980.

U.S. Kerner Commission. *Report of the National Advisory Commission on Civil Disorders.* Washington: U.S. Government Printing Office, 1968.

Valentine, Gill. "(Re)negotiating the 'Heterosexual Street': Lesbian Production of Space." In *Body Space: Destabilizing Geographies of Gender and Sexuality,* ed. Nancy Duncan. New York: Routledge, 1996.

Valk, Anne. *Sisterhood and Separatism: Feminism and Racial Liberation in Washington, D.C.* Urbana-Champaign: University of Illinois Press, forthcoming.

Vance, John E. *Inside the Minnesota Experiment: Experimental Planning and Development in the Twin Cities Metropolitan Area.* Minneapolis: Center for Urban and Regional Affairs, 1977.

Vaughan, Sharon. "Where It All Began." *Do It NOW* (NOW National Newsletter) 9.5 (June 1976).

Vicinus, Martha. "Lesbian History: All Theory and No Facts, or All Facts and No Theory?" *Radical History Review* 60 (1994): 58.

——. *Intimate Friends: Women Who Loved Women, 1778–1928.* Chicago: University of Chicago Press, 2004.

Walker, Lisa. "'More than Just Skin–Deep: Fem(me)ininity and the Subversion of Identity." *Gender Place and Culture* 2.1 (1995): 71–76.

Walkowitz, Judith. *Prostitution and Victorian Society: Women, Class, and the State.* New York: Cambridge University Press, 1980.

———. *City of Dreadful Delight: Narratives of Sexual Danger in Victorian London.* Chicago: University of Chicago Press, 1992.

Ward, Brian. *Just My Soul Responding: Rhythm and Blues, Black Consciousness, and Race Relations.* Berkeley: University of California Press, 1998.

Warner, Michael, ed. *Fear of a Queer Planet: Queer Politics and Social Theory.* Minneapolis: University of Minnesota Press, 1993.

Warren, Donald I. "Community Dissensus: Panic in Suburbia." In *A City in Racial Crisis: The Case of Detroit Pre- and Post- the 1967 Riot,* ed. Leonard Gordon. Dubuque, Iowa: William C. Brown, 1971.

Washington, Cynthia. "We Started from Different Ends of the Spectrum." *Southern Exposure* 4.4 (winter 1977): 14–18.

Watson, Deborah, ed. *Paradise Valley Days: A Photo Album Poetry Book.* Detroit: Detroit Black Writers Guild, 1988.

Watson, Susan. "U.S. Is Auditing Feminist Credit Union." *Detroit Free Press,* April 14, 1976, 3-A.

Weightman, Barbara A. "Gay Bars as Private Places." *Landscape* 24.1 (1980): 9–16.

Welbon, Yvonne, dir. *Living with Pride: Ruth Ellis @ 100.* VHS. Our Film Works, 1999.

Weston, Kath. *Render Me, Gender Me: Lesbians Talk Sex, Class, Color, Nation, Studmuffins.* New York: Columbia University Press, 1996.

White, E. Frances. *Dark Continent of Our Bodies: Black Feminism and the Politics of Respectability.* Philadelphia: Temple University Press, 2001.

———. "Africa on My Mind: Gender, Counter Discourse, and African American Nationalism." In *Is It Nation Time? Contemporary Essays on Black Power and Black Nationalism,* ed. Eddie S. Glaude Jr. Chicago: University of Chicago Press, 2002.

Whittier, Nancy. *Feminist Generations: The Persistence of the Radical Women's Movement.* Philadelphia: Temple University Press, 1995.

Williams, Pat. "A Downtown Center Pulls It All Together." *Detroit Sun,* May 20, 1976, 5.

Wilson, Elizabeth. *The Sphinx in the City: Urban Life, the Control of Disorder and Women.* Berkeley: University of California Press, 1991.

Wingerd, Mary Lethert. *Claiming the City: Politics, Faith, and the Power of Place in St. Paul.* Ithaca, N.Y.: Cornell University Press, 2001.

Wittig, Monique. "One Is Not Born a Woman." *Feminist Issues* 1.2 (winter 1981). Reprinted in Wittig, *The Straight Mind.* Boston: Beacon Press, 1992: 9–20.

Wolcott, Victoria. *Remaking Respectability: African American Women in Interwar Detroit.* Chapel Hill: University of North Carolina Press, 2001.

Wolf, Maxine. "Invisible Women in Invisible Place: Lesbians, Lesbian Bars, and the Social Production of People/Environment Relationship." *Architecture and Behavior* 8 (1992): 137–158.

Women of All Red Nations. *Women of All Red Nations.* St. Paul: WARN, 1977.

Women's Advocates. *Women's Advocates: The Story of a Shelter.* St. Paul: Women's Advocates, 1980.

"Women's Liberation Build Strong Bodies in Many Ways." *Secret Storm*, summer 1975.

Young, Coleman and Lonnie Wheeler. *Hardstuff: The Autobiography of Coleman Young*. New York: Viking, 1994.

Zahniser, Jill. "Feminist Collectives: The Transformation of Women's Businesses in the Counterculture of the 1970s and 1980s." Ph.D. diss., University of Iowa, 1985.

Zipter, Yvonne. *Diamonds Are a Dyke's Best Friend*. Ithaca, N.Y.: Firebrand, 1988.

Index

consciousness raising, 10, 76–77, 192–93, 293–94 n. 55. *See also* men; Pride and Prejudice; Women's Advocates

Contreras, Sally, 76

cooperatives. *See* communes

Courtney, Cathy, 199, 211, 263–64

Cox, Nancy, 156

Cronin, Connie, 198

Czarnik, Cathy, 240

Dahlem, Janet, 217, 223, 233–34

Daley, Richard, 284 n. 87

Dana Gardens team, 135, 150, 152

dancing, 43, 53, 80, 221, 223; politics of embodiment and, 230–34

Daughters of Bilitis, 285 n. 95

de Certeau, Michel, 15

deindustrialization, 14, 106–7

D'Emilio, John, 275 n. 37

desegregation, 27, 106, 112; softball fields and, 121–24, 138; consciousness raising and, 192–94

Detroit, 4, 5, 12–14, 17, 21, 29, 51; riots in, 14, 33, 89, 93, 119–20; as "working class" city, 14, 95; as "black" city, 14, 115; dollar parties in, 30–38; segregation in, 33, 107, 302–3 n. 25, 303 n. 27; Poor Woman's Paradise and, 62–64, 88–99; compared to Chicago and Twin Cities, 90; women-only space and, 96–97; civic space and, 105–39; Feminist Women's Health Center and, 197–214; Feminist Women's City Club and, 218–19. *See also* white flight

Detroit Feminist Women's Health Center. *See* Feminist Women's Health Center

Devlin, Jo, 41, 48, 155–56, 158–59

D 'n' O bar, 281–82 n. 54

Dobkin, Alix, 97, 227, 260–61, 264–66

dollar parties, 28–29, 30–38; as domestic and commercial spaces, 30–31; as alternative marketplace, 35

domesticity, 6, 177; activism reaching beyond, 77; shelters and heteronormative, 182–84, 186

Dorsz, Denise, 88–92, 94, 96, 98–99

Downer, Carol, 199, 202, 318 n. 67, 330 n. 79

drag: queens, 30, 34, 188, 280 n. 39, 283–84 n. 78; women in, 43, 57. *See* passing women; transgender; transvestites

Drexel, Allen, 284 n. 88

DuBois, Jan, 152–53

Dyc, Gloria, 91–92, 100

Ebony Room bar, 51, 54

Echols, Alice, 271 n. 13, 272 n. 16, 272 n. 17

Ellis, Ruth, 279 n. 23

Erler, Monica, 182

Evans, Sara, 271 n. 13, 272 n. 16

Ezekial, Judith, 273 n. 22, 273–74 n. 23

Family of Women (rock band), 80, 97, 300 n. 117

Federal Bureau of Investigation, 69, 94, 226

Federal Credit Union Charter Agency, 202–3

Feinberg, Leslie, 275 n. 38, 277 n. 4, 278 n. 16

Female Liberation Group, 67, 290 n. 13

Female Liberation Newsletter, 67, 290 n. 13

Feminist Economic Network, 239–51, 326–27 n. 56, 328 n. 70, 328 n. 72, 329 n. 74; top-down structure of, 247

Feminist Federal Credit Union, 90, 93, 178–79, 197, 204–15, 326–27 n. 56, 328 n. 70, 329 n. 76; economic autonomy and, 202, 319–20 n. 77;

Anne Enke is an associate professor in the Women's Studies Program, the Department of History, and LGBT Studies at the University of Wisconsin, Madison.

Library of Congress Cataloging-in-Publication Data

Enke, Anne
Finding the movement : sexuality, contested space, and
feminist activism / Anne Enke.
p. cm. — (Radical perspectives)
Includes bibliographical references and index.
ISBN 978-0-8223-4062-1 (cloth : alk. paper)
ISBN 978-0-8223-4083-6 (pbk. : alk. paper)
1. Feminism—United States—History—20th century.
2. Women in politics—United States—History—20th century—Case studies.
3. Social action—United States—History—20th century—Case studies.
4. Feminist geography—United States. I. Title.
HQ1421.E65 2007
305.420973'0904—dc22 2007014126